Peripheral Labour Mobilities

Work and Everyday Life.
Ethnographic Studies on Work Cultures

Series of the Commission "Working Cultures" in the Deutsche Gesellschaft
für Volkskunde (German Society for European Ethnology and Folklore)

Edited by Irene Götz, Gertraud Koch,
Klaus Schönberger and Manfred Seifert

Volume 23

Tanja Višić, Dr. phil., is a post-doctoral researcher at the Institute of Sociology, Ludwig-Maximilian-Universität München. She holds a M.A degree in Cultural Anthropology from the University of Belgrade. She recieved her PhD from the Max Weber Institute for Advanced Cultural and Social Studies, University of Erfurt, Germany.

Tanja Višić

Peripheral Labour Mobilities

Elder Care Work between the Former Yugoslavia
and Germany

Campus Verlag
Frankfurt/New York

This book has been published with the support of the Schroubek Fonds.

This book has been honoured with the 2021 Dissertation Prize by the Fritz und Helga Exner-Foundation.

Dissertation of the Max-Weber-Kolleg at the University of Erfurt, 2021

ISBN 978-3-593-51641-7 Print
ISBN 978-3-593-45185-5 E-Book (PDF)

All rights reserved. No part of this book may be reproduced or transmitted in any form or by any means, electronic or mechanical, including photocopying, recording, or by any information storage and retrieval system, without permission in writing from the publishers.
Copyright © 2022 Campus Verlag GmbH, Frankfurt am Main
Cover design: Campus Verlag GmbH, Frankfurt am Main
Cover illustration: Vesna Nestorovic
Typesetting: Tomislav Helebrant
Printed in the United States of America

www.press.uchicago.edu

www.campus.de

Contents

Acknowledgements. 9

Introduction 11

Chapter 1
Gender, Migration, and Globalization. 25

   1.1 Gender in Theories: The Main Perspectives in Studies
       of Migration and Mobility 27

   1.2 Re-Visiting Dominant Concepts and Theories in Global
       Migration for Domestic and Care Work. 42

Chapter 2
A Critical Analytical Framework for the Ethnographic Study
of Care Labour Mobilities 57

   2.1 Peripheral Labour Mobilities 62

   2.2 Entanglements of Mobility, Immobility, and Cross-Border
       Care Work. 72

   2.3 Potential of the Concept of *Motility* 87

   2.4 Intersectional and Border Regime Approach. 99

   2.5 Commodification and Precarization of Care Work in Informal
       Care Labour Markets 102

   2.6 A Multi-Level Analysis of Care Labour Mobilities 107

6   PERIPHERAL LABOUR MOBILITIES

Chapter 3
Making a Care Labour Mobility Researchable:
Ethnography of Movement................................ 115

3.1 Ana's Case 118

3.2 Multidimensionality of Ethnographic Fieldwork 123

3.3 Doing Interviews 135

3.4 Observation with Limited Participation 142

3.5 Reflecting on an Ethnography of Care Labour Mobilities.... 146

3.6 Short Biographical Portraits 154

Chapter 4
Contextualizing Care Work Mobility from the Former
Yugoslavia to Germany 161

4.1 Snežana's Case 161

4.2 Geopolitical, Social and Economic Contextualization: Post-Yugoslav Gendered Labour Mobility to Germany.......... 166

4.3 Citizenship Policy in the Post-Yugoslav Space............. 172

4.4 Care for Germany: German Welfare, Gender and Migration Regime.. 175

Chapter 5
Routes into Care Labour Mobility 181

5.1 Portrait: Ana Wendl 184

5.2 The Construction and Contextualization of Motivations and Aspirations....................................... 193

5.3 Access to Care Labour Mobility 210

5.4 Feeling, Thinking and Doing Care Work 234

Contents

Chapter 6
"Illegalization" of Everyday Life and Work in "Elder Care Labour Mobility Industry" 261

6.1 Portrait: Isidora Bašić 266

6.2 Border Crossing Knowledge 275

6.3 Being "Illegal" 290

6.4 The "Care Labour Mobility Industry" – Business as Usual? ... 303

Chapter 7
The Private Household as Microcosm of Social Inequalities 329

7.1 Portrait: Milica Jeremić. 342

7.2 Underplaying Social Boundaries. *"Du bist mein Goldstück!"* – *"Well, I Am."* 350

7.3 Highlighting Social Boundaries. *"Don't Touch Me, Your Hands Are Dirty."* 363

Conclusions. 375

Motility for Care Labour Mobility 377

Structure/Agency Dilemma: Contesting Victim Narratives 380

Moving and Caring Across the Borders – Lessons from "the Periphery" 383

Phenomenology of Illegality 387

The Micro-Politics of Elder Care Work. 389

List of Maps 394

List of Figures 395

Literature. 397

Acknowledgements

A great many people and institutions have helped make this book possible. I remain deeply indebted to 20 women care workers, my interviewees and informants who carved out their valuable time for sharing with me their experiences, introduced me to their networks and colleagues and allowed me to be their fellow co-traveller in the world of cross-border labour mobility. I am grateful for their knowledge, worldviews, and life stories that made this book.

I have been very fortunate to have received a variety of grants that facilitated my PhD project on which this book is based. I am grateful to the Max Weber Center for Advanced Cultural and Social Studies and the University of Erfurt who generously awarded me with a three-year doctoral scholarship. My fieldwork trips wouldn't be possible without financial support of the University of Erfurt and the Research mobility grant awarded by Bayerisches Hochschulzentrum für Mittel-, Ost- und Südosteuropa. I am also very much grateful to the DAAD for awarding me a three-month scholarship that kept me going through the period of writing my dissertation during the COVID-19 pandemic in 2020.

Throughout my PhD, I was privileged and honoured to have Prof. Irene Götz, and PD Dr. Antje Linkenbach as my supervisors. I could always rely on their intellectual generosity, invaluable advice, constructive criticism, encouragement, kindness, and confidence in and patience with the finalization of my dissertation and this book. I owe them a special debt that cannot be repaid.

This book wouldn't be published without financial help. I am deeply grateful to the Schroubek Fonds Östliches Europa and Südosteuropa-Gesellschaft in collaboration with Fritz und Helga Exner-Stiftung for generous publication grants.

Introduction

This book is about female care workers from the countries of the former Yugoslavia, in particular, from the non-EU-states Serbia, Bosnia and Herzegovina, and Croatia. These women, between 40 and 60 years of age, commute to German households where they perform 24/7 work as live-in carers for elderly people in their 80s or 90s, mobile or immobile, with developed dementia or Alzheimer's disease, or suffering from cancer, stroke, or multiple sclerosis. The women who look after these people have no medical knowledge or experience in elder care work, yet they do it to the best of their ability. They make monetary use of prior experience as unpaid care workers in their own families and, with the money they earn, they and their families become better off, and they fulfil their personal dreams, even if doing so keeps them in an illegalized status working without permit or contract. They manage to save for their own old age in their hometowns, supporting their families and grown-up children; and they feel pride in having decided to travel and work independently. Despite hard, unpredictable, and culturally unfamiliar work settings, these women often highlight the pleasures and satisfactions derived from care work; they can feel a sense of achievement, fulfilment, purpose or pride. They develop emotional relationships with their clients and their families, sometimes also with the colleagues with whom they rotate in four- or three-month rotational labour mobility arrangements.

However, this ethnographic study is not simply a story of success, empowerment and emancipation. The author accompanied the care workers on their bus journeys and border crossings, sometimes even into the villages and households where they work or the homes of the workers themselves. As a result of this research, the book also dives deeply into the physical and psychological sufferings and humiliation experienced by these women as they become exposed and vulnerable to sexual harassment and abuse; as they work excessive hours for no additional payment; and as they put up with poor living conditions in the households where they perform the strenuous work of hygienic and sanitary care, lifting elderly persons up and down, and turning, repositioning, feeding, and dressing them. This ethnography reveals practices and strategies for coping with fraudulent job agencies and money-grabbing job intermediaries, for dealing with corrupt border police at the EU-border checkpoints, and for handling the bureaucrats in the government institutions who process their passports and documents as well as documenting the tactics used for dealing with competition and conflicts between care workers themselves.

Peripheral labour mobilities is, therefore, a book about elder care labour and about mobility; it is about the journeys that women undertake within the cross-border labour industry and the various actors who dictate disruptions to and continuations of movements, who shape and facilitate or hinder women's mobility. Simple as it may seem, these two topics, providing care and the movement of labour, have rarely been brought together and analysed from an anthropological or ethnographic perspective, especially not in the context of contemporary post-Yugoslavian society. Emphasis is placed on scrutinizing the specifics of a "rotational" mobility pattern in the post-Yugoslav region and on answering the central question: How is the capacity for elder care mobility constructed in the interwoven frameworks of informal care labour markets, labour laws, border regimes, manifold social relations between care workers, job intermediaries, care receivers, their families and other actors involved in the informal care labour industry? By revealing specific social and cultural labour practices alongside newly emerging forms of cross-border elder care work and new forms of relationships and bonds, in this book, I bridge the gap between mobility, immobility, and elder care work by underscoring their mutually constitutive relationship.

The analysis is centred on the journeys of elder care workers to and from their homes in the former Yugoslavian countries and Germany; the ethnographic research follows movements that range in scale from national and regional to household and bodily in nature. Such multi-scale analytic research allows me to unpack how care labour mobility induces a specific cultural interpretation of border crossings, cross-border mobility strategies, aspirations and motivations for mobility, attitudes towards performing elder care work and unique social relations, values, and cultural perceptions of care work.

The central thread that links together the manifold theoretical perspectives and concepts in this book is a feminist deconstruction of canonical approaches to structures, spaces, mobilities, scales, subjects, and spatial logics. My theoretical standpoint is largely inspired by geographer Doreen Massey (1994), who pushes us to think about the ways in which gender and other social differences (citizenship, race, class, nation, sexuality, caste, religion, disability) play a crucial role in shaping unequal "geographies of mobility". This offers a firm foundation for my ethnography as I describe, analyse, and re-conceptualize the manifold connections between mobility, space, sociality and inequality in the context of commodified care. Situated at the crossroads of European Ethnology of work and interdisciplinary approaches to mobility studies, this book focuses on practices that shape everyday work, as well as the perception of those cultural practices. Such an approach allows me to focus beyond expected behaviour in order to look at the hidden meanings of cultural practices: why do these things happen and why do they happen in that way? Why do mobile labourers behave in a certain way in their social and cultural spatio-temporal contexts, even when this often seems to go against all apparent logic or reason?

Peripheral labour mobilities is based on three years of doctoral research involving extensive and immersive ethnographic fieldwork. This inductively designed research study relies on self-collected data, narrative interviews and participant-observation, which are drawn together into case studies and thick descriptions. It builds up a unique methodological approach constructed specifically to examine this particular form of labour consisting of an "ethnography of movement", a multi-dimensional approach to the field, "expanded ethnography" (polymorphous engagements with participants, online and offline locations), and limited participant observation. This book delineates rich ethnographic evidence that articulates newly discovered interpretations of borders, cross-border mobility strategies, aspirations and motivations for mobility, attitudes towards performing elder care work and cultural perceptions of care. The material presented in the book is drawn from everyday life and tackles questions ranging from the subjectivation of work to the multiple boundaries between work, life, and im/mobility.

The in-depth ethnographic interviews were conducted, recorded, transcribed, translated and interpreted by me as a native speaker who is knowledgeable of both contexts (Germany and the former Yugoslavia). Such linguistic and cultural knowledge informed the research process and shed light on the life stories and experiences of women care workers which would otherwise have reached neither an academic audience nor the broader public. The interviews were conducted in the Serbo-Croatian language (which is my mother tongue) and then translated into English. Even though cultural translation can never be completely "authentic", I sought to translate as accurately as is possible in order to find a middle ground between the rich expressions of my interview partners (culturally and sometimes regionally specific in Serbian, Croatian and Bosnian languages) and the English language. The interview excerpts were made understandable while staying close to the original narration, meaning that the reader needs to view them as part of a spontaneous conversation. A second consideration needs to be borne in mind relating to one key term of this book – *elder care worker*. While, in the broader literature on care work across the disciplines, we can find a use of two different terms – *elderly care worker* and *elder care worker*, I have elected to use the latter. This decision is an attempt to avoid the inadvertent impression that the research subjects are themselves old (aged) care workers as the adjective "elderly" might serve to imply.

At the time I was writing this book, in 2020 and 2021, the world was facing the COVID-19 global pandemic. Health care and economic systems are currently under strain, and the pandemic has been fortifying racial, social, and political vulnerabilities. Threats caused by an ongoing pandemic are also being compounded by the challenges of climate change and environmental uncertainty, including poverty and risks to vulnerable communities. Globally, we are witnessing the gendered and racialized ways in which individuals bear the burden of fragile economic and political systems which fail to protect from escalating unemployment or to offer adequate institutional care for individuals. This calls for increasing academic research sensitivity to a moment in which global crises of health and social care are making visible the huge geopolitical differences in how these socio-economic crises can be coped with. Here, the contexts of immobility and mobility come into play: the necessity of moving or staying put in order to live a healthy and decent life is unequally distributed: care workers from the periphery commute to the households of the Global North to make their living.

The findings of this ethnographic study of care workers from South-eastern Europe in Germany serve to rethink the traditional dichotomy between mobility and immobility, which must be treated as research categories thought together as relational and co-dependent. The dialectic approach to considering how mobility defines immobility, and the other way around, underlines the importance of politics and power relations, global inequalities, and social hierarchies in a process where normalization of the movement of the privileged simultaneously enforces the immobility of others. In a time of COVID-19, researching and writing about im/mobilites, inequalities, life-making jobs (in the sectors of care, food production and distribution, health) means turning our attention to those people who can afford to be socially isolated and subjected to (in)voluntary immobility and those, at the other end of the stick, who rely on mobility for their livelihood: care workers. The life economy or global economy of care is built around maintaining, reproducing, and enhancing human life itself on a daily basis. Care requires intimacy and mobility because must be provided in-situ. Such movements create entirely new strategies and mobility patterns for elder care workers, such as the subjects of this book, who travel to Germany from surrounding countries. During the lockdown, German authorities re-instated border controls and introduced a two-week quarantine obligation after crossing into the country. This created new types of relationships, commitments, and arrangements between households and their irregularly employed care workers. Elder care workers found themselves under new pressures from border regimes and COVID-19 regulations, often being anxious about whether or not a written note from the employing family would be enough to cross the border. Access to the transportation that care workers usually use such as private buses and minivan companies is getting more complicated because the majority of these services have either stopped altogether or reduced the number of passengers and the frequency of connections whilst simultaneously increasing their ticket prices. Such conditions impose new difficulties and challenges in the process of care labour mobility. Here we are arriving at the first broad topic of this book – the process of care labour mobility. The empirical and theoretical literature on late modern society celebrates mobility as a norm and as a facilitator of freedom and equality. This celebration is reflected in Bauman's widely cited claim that "nowadays we are all on the move", even as it has amplified his sense that much of this involves us "staying put" in front of a computer screen during the time of COVID-19. The pandemic has restructured but not eliminated the distinction between two kinds of "nomadism", that of cosmopolitan, transnational, elites on the one hand, and the dispossessed migrants, "global vagabonds" in Bauman's terms, on the other, as well as a further distinction between both these categories and those that stay at home. The continued need for migrant workers in Western Europe, whether in the agricultural sector or the care sector, many of whom were both denied labour rights and placed at risk of infection, further complicated this. Therefore, this book comes at the right time in order to contribute to anthropological studies of unequal power of mobilities and stasis, focusing not only on relationships between mobility and immobility but also on "immobility in mobility" in the specific geopolitical context of the Former Yugoslavia. However, it is necessary to stress that my research was already finished when the pandemic started, so that these recent developments of fortified constraints or complications concerning the existentially necessary mobility of care workers could not have been part of the study.

The new geopolitical and historical circumstances of the Former Yugoslavian countries (Bosnia and Herzegovina, Bosnian Serb Republic, Serbia, Kosovo, Montenegro) after its dissolution, included changes to borders as well as a post-socialist political and socio-economic transition, and these in turn led to the new labour mobility dynamics. The highly gendered informal market of elder care has created specific labour mobility patterns over the last decade, in which women make journeys from their countries to Germany to perform elder care work, staying up to three months on tourist visas. This care labour mobility arrangement, operating according to a "frame of rotation" (monthly or weekly rotation system) is used by care and domestic workers from Central and Eastern Europe. The collapse of communist regimes and the re-drawing of the European map after 1989 facilitated new patterns of labour mobility, between Poland and Berlin, for instance. This situation was very well known and well researched by, mainly, German sociologists. The reader may rightly ask why I refer to the former Yugoslavia, and not to "post-socialist countries", as is usual in scholarly literature. Anthropological and ethnographic studies of post-socialism are dedicated to analysing people and places in post-socialist contexts primarily in relation to their socialist past, or as anthropologically interesting because they point to possible futures.

In this book, I have chosen to analyse post-Yugoslavian society not primarily in relation to the socialist past but to the global present. As "post-socialism" is often a political and ideological construct in cross-disciplinary research, I opt to talk about the Former Yugoslavia for two reasons. Firstly, although the legacies of post-socialist transitions in the former Yugoslavia still fundamentally shake contemporary societies (the loss of employment security, impoverishment, destruction of the public sector), this post-socialist restructuring is always part of processes embedded in global shifts of international power, as Hann, Humphrey, Verdery (2002) pointed out. Secondly, we cannot just assume that all post-socialist transitions and their outcomes are the same. We can start with the fact that the former Yugoslavia, in terms of mobility regimes, was the only country in the world under communist leadership that granted its citizens the right to travel freely. The early mobility of "Gastarbeiter" from this region was a result of this relative freedom of move-

INTRODUCTION   17

ment and by the way paved the way for the recent mobility of care workers to German households. Further, the geographical and political space once occupied by the socialist Yugoslavia was subject to fragmentation – which in turn has gradually yielded new sovereign states – in specific ways that other post-socialist countries were not. While rooted in the same political, constitutional, and economic set-up as the socialist Yugoslavia, these states have had different post-partition experiences, ranging from war to (relatively) peaceful secession, transition and European Union (EU) integration, and prolonged state transformation. These dissimilar experiences, driven largely by the interplay between national identities and statehood, have shaped the citizenship regimes of the seven new states in South-Eastern Europe, former republics of Yugoslavia. In addition, I use the Former Yugoslavia as a common denominator for countries and citizens who experienced the tectonic changes caused by the dissolution of Yugoslavia and the Yugoslavian wars. The former Yugoslavia is a state where most of the women care workers that populate the pages of this book spent decades forming families, undergoing education and imagining a better life in the future, in a context distorted by the results of the war, forced displacements, economic destruction and the re-drawing of the borders, all of which had dramatic consequences for their everyday lives and personal destinies.

Similarly, to other countries from Eastern and Central Europe that endured the period of post-socialist transition and subsequent economic, social, and political re-engineering, men and women in the Former Yugoslavia countries are equally engaged in different patterns of transnational short-term labour mobility propelled by financial insecurity and the absence of job opportunities. Gendered forms (informal sector of care and construction work) of "back and forth" labour movement, create specific work arrangements that allow them to sustain their lives in their home countries while maintaining a regular status and an irregular job in the informal elder care work sector in Germany.

The distinction and novelty that my book brings is a result of its focus on new actors in the process of responding to the new borders, and their practices of crossing the border to perform elder care work in the privacy of German households. I shift the analytical focus from structures, the state, and policies towards the actors of elder care work mobilities – how do they follow, challenge and re-create the rules of the black market of care, how do they "make their way" to find a job, "survive at that job" and when it is done, how do they find another one. Unlike studies with a "global" view on gender, migration and commodification of care and domestic work that merely underline structural economic and political conditions, this book zooms in on specific local and praxeological responses to global trends while employing a processual approach to mobility comprised of temporal and spatial dimensions. More specifically, the central concern of this book is the *potential for labour mobility* and the ways this potential is built up in relation to geopolitical constraints or to limitations created by the spatial dynamic of networks, communication and transportation, regional disparities in permeability of border crossings and border regimes.

To explain the nature of care labour mobilities in a specific geopolitical context the research questions that serve to frame the chapters through the book include: In what ways do demographics, regimes of mobility, geo-political boundaries and diverse cultural practices and values affect who provides elder care across national borders? How do care workers adapt to and/or challenge the new forms of commodified care across the borders? What new examples of care work have emerged, and under what conditions? To what extent are these labour mobilities life-shaping or life-changing? In what way are they meaningful to women care workers? How do they envision and use their potential for mobility under specific geographical, political, and socio-cultural conditions?

The aim of this is to provide deep insight into the personal experiences of elder care workers, their commuting for care work, and the multiple ways in which such gendered labour mobility transforms the lives of subjects while examining the dialectical relationship between mobility and immobility. I pay attention to the relations between different embodied experiences, events, and imaginations in the lives of women care workers from the moment prior to mobility for work, through the period of their mobility until their movement is over or a new movement starts. Moreover, the book demonstrates both how inequalities in care labour mobility are reproduced through labour markets, migration laws, and relationships with brokers, intermediaries, care receivers and their families and the ways in which socially, geographically and politically contextualised immobility and mobility play out in the reproduction of these inequalities.

The book is structured around 7 Chapters. Three of these are empirical chapters and each starts with an instructive portrait of one care worker whose specific biography and care mobility trajectory is representative and indicative of the research questions that the chapter pursues. To better reveal and represent the themes and to enable patterns of experience to emerge from the rich material I use ethnographic portraiture as an introduction to the chapters. Each portrait in this book is a result of my reflection on the participant's experiences and incorporates ethnographic observations, interview responses, impressionistic records, the interpretation of context, and my experiences and insights. Through portraiture, I demonstrate my commitment to the respondents and contextualize the depictions of individuals and events. It is my aim to (re)present the research participants through a subjective, empathetic, and critical lens, which in turn makes these portraits partial in nature. However, this partiality provides me as the portraitist, the space to acknowledge the presence of the respondent – physically, psychologically, spiritually, and emotionally – consequently dismantling the notion that the researcher is the only knower and expert on the lives and experiences of the participants.

Following the introductory chapter, Chapter 1 presents a critical review of the scholarship that has developed around the gender-migration-globalization nexus in the last decades. It has three aims. Firstly, it provides a re-examination of the cross-disciplinary body of scholarship that has developed theories and concepts linking gender, international migration, social reproduction, migration, and welfare regimes over the years. The second objective of the chapter is to show how different assumptions in analytical concepts and theories about gender and migration underpin scientific knowledge patterns. The third point is to focus on existing theories and concepts of domestic and care work in contemporary global capitalism such as the "global care chains", "care drain" transnational theories of care and inequality. While examining global market-shaping regulation of commodified care sector research agenda I identify key gaps in the research and build a platform for my own research study and analytical approach.

In Chapter 2 I present a critical analytical framework for ethnographic study of care labour mobility which foregrounds four key approaches: multi-level analysis, an intersectional approach, a border regimes approach, and a processual and critical approach to mobility studies, while also acknowledging the need to further develop the understanding of migration as not only a spatial, but also a temporal phenomenon. In the introductory part of the chapter, I introduce the analytical umbrella *peripheral labour mobilities* (Chapter 2.1) that emerged from the elaboration of theoretical perspectives in the wider field of mobility studies and studies of the commodification of care work. This sub-chapter also gives a foundation for the articulation of existing power imbalances in the dissemination and production of academic knowledge between core countries (Global North) and semi-peripheral countries (situated in the continuum of the former-communist "Global South"), regarding them as an epistemological location beyond its own geopolitical confines. Chapter 2 is divided into several thematic sub-chapters that address the process of building my own analytical standpoint by merging and questioning different, sometimes contradictory approaches in the broader literature. In the first part of the chapter, sub-chapter 2.2, I examine theoretical re-positionings in the field of mobility studies that stretch between two dominant paradigms: the nomadic "new mobilities paradigm" or "mobility turn" that has developed in urban sociology and sociology of transport and the sedentary paradigm "sociology of immobility" or "immobility turn". After assessing these extreme paradigms that reinforce either "mobility" or "immobility" as research categories while neglecting their dialectic and mutually constitutive relationship, I focus on a third solution. I opt for a "critical mobilities" approach in order to avoid scholarly discourse promoting "mobility" as an overly positively normality often attached to cultural heterogeneity and to discourses of globalization, modernization and cosmopolitanism. Decoupling paradigms of mobility and immobility, my analytical toolkit drives analysis of cross-border care labour mobility as a process through which unequal spatial conditions and differential labouring subjects are made. In sub-chapter 2.3 I critically discuss the analytical potential of the concept of "motility" (Vincent Kaufmann) in order to build the structure for empirical chapters 5, 6, and 7. In this sub-chapter, I map out the shortcomings and definitional boundaries of "motility" whilst acknowledging the usefulness of the concept as an alternative to binary theorization, by linking spatial and social mobility. I focus on the analytical benefits of the concepts for an anthropological study of elder care labour mobility.

In the rest of Chapter 2, particularly in sub-chapters 2.4, 2.5 and 2.6, I present and discuss the usefulness of additional analytical approaches to "studies of borders", transnational inequalities and informal care work. I highlight the usefulness of the "concept of transnational inequalities" for empirical investigation of the mechanisms of cross-border inequalities as "regimes of intersection" relating spatialized cross-border inequalities to other types of unequal social relations (in terms of gender, ethnicity/race, class etc.) Then, I relate this to the way the borders are thought in my study, re-thinking the logic of borders beyond their apparent role as tools of exclusion and violence. Following this, I elaborate the need for additional analytical lenses capable of exploring narratives about the peripheral "elder care labour mobilities" and I focus on the following approaches: 1) ethnographic and anthropological perspectives to work in the informal sector; 2) commodification of care work 3) precarious and vulnerable aspects of care work. I finish the Chapter by discussing macro-, meso- and micro-levels of analysis.

Chapter 3 turns its attention to methodological issues. This chapter sets out to reveal the ethnographic methods that are utilised during the research process: interviewing and observation with limited participation. In the chapter, I provide short portraits of the women care workers whose interviews are used in this book. I unfold the research process in which my positionality, my multiple roles and emotional experiences reveal specific methodological challenges and opportunities that arise from circular labour mobility. Through the sub-chapters, I describe and analyse how I entered the fieldwork and negotiated access to respondents, both as an "insider" and "outsider" and the effects that unexpected situations and the unexpected presence of certain people may have on the process of data gathering and data analysis. Along with a justification of the methodological approaches and methods used in my research, I also elaborate the "ethnography of movement" as a new methodological approach that emerged from my own research, thus re-addressing the conceptualization of "the field" and its multiple dimensions in ethnographic research.

Chapter 4 starts with the first case study of care worker Snežana Kemeneš (pseudonym) in order to illustrate a dynamic of cross-border care labour mobility and its characteristics through her personal accounts. The aim of the chapter is to provide the geographical, political, and socio-economical context for the study. It does this through discussion of two main topics. First, I identify the main structural factors that lead to the increasing incorporation of women from the former Yugoslav countries in the ever-expanding irregular care work market in Germany: restrictive migration and border regimes, social and economic backgrounds, and the specific complexities of citizenship in the former Yugoslavian countries. Secondly, I address the context of Germany. I show how contradictory policies, inconsistencies, and paradoxes between the official welfare state policy on elder care work and migration on the one hand, and the reality of demand for elder care in German households on the other, direct and shape elder care labour mobility.

The empirical chapters 5, 6 and 7 are built around the broad question of how the potential for elder care labour mobility is constructed. Structurally entrenched in the concept of "motility", these chapters probe beyond this general point of enquiry to explore what "potential for care labour mobility" consists of, what it entails and the outcomes or consequences of "being able to move for care work". Taking these three points together means investigating the perspectives of women care workers on how mobility for care work is encouraged, directed, managed, monitored and, at the same time, blocked and constrained in manifold ways where nationality, citizenship, age, marital status, ethnicity and socio-economic position intersect.

Chapter 5 scrutinises experiences of routes into elder care labour mobility. It is divided into three main sub-chapters. Sub-chapter 5.2 investigates the construction of aspirations and motivations understood not only in relation to "movement through the space", but in relation to time and within specific contexts. Sub-chapter 5.3 explores who has access to labour mobility; the ways in which access is constrained by different options and conditions, such as transportation and communication available at a given time, and how these conditions create specific patterns of mobilities for work that are marked by socio-cultural experiences and values associated with mobility. I describe how care work across the border is organized, directed and distributed, and analyse how these determine various modes of mobility and care practices, as well as attitudes, behaviours and relationships between subjects involved in elder care work mobility. I point to the importance of "social networks" in analysing women's strategies for and negotiations of organized labour mobility across three different border zones: in Northern and in Central Serbia and in Bosnia and Herzegovina.

In the final sub-chapter 5.4, I explore corporeal aspects of work and women's attitudes towards it, their performance of care tasks and the valuation of skills and knowledge. I also discuss elder caregiving and its significance for social organization, pointing to the way in which the informal market of care shapes the quality of care work and the specific care relations that are created, thereby contributing to a more nuanced understanding of how intimacy, care, money, vulnerability, and mobility across international borders are interlinked.

The next substantive focus requires a different conceptual lens – the lens of subjectivity allows us to investigate the actors involved in the subjectification of "illegalized" elder care workers. Thus, the subject of Chapter 6 is "illegality" and "illegalization" as "mode of being-in-the-world" and process that shape subjective lived experience of "illegality" of elder care workers. Through the three sub-chapters, I explore links between processes of subjectification, the labour care mobility industry, forms of agency and forms of vulnerability that come together in order to create specific forms of im/mobility. The last empirical Chapter refocuses the reader's attention on the micro-scale of mobility for care work in the domain of German households. In this chapter, I explore what kind of role elder care labour mobility plays in the development of a new form of social relations – the personal commitments and emotional attachments which are built up between women care workers and their employers (elder persons and their families). By presenting an analysis of two ethnographic cases in two sub-chapters, the focus is on the processes through which care workers, care receivers, and the families in their households conceptualize, perceive, negotiate, and manage their relationships. Re-visiting the re-politicization of the household as a segregated social space, social relations in the household and the negotiation of social boundaries, I use the concept of "boundary work" as an analytical lens to explore complex dynamics of closeness and distancing or "personalization" and "depersonalization".

The concluding chapter brings together and refines the analysis of the earlier empirical chapters, summarizing my theoretical and methodological contributions to the academic body of research on local examples of global commodification of care work and related global inequalities.

Chapter 1
Gender, Migration, and Globalization

For the last thirty years, scholars from different backgrounds and disciplines developed new gendered perspectives on racism, globalisation, economics, and welfare. The issues of migrant domestic and care work became integrated into the analysis of flourishing research on labour, ageing, and health. At the same time, while the field of research has been growing, the overlap between the questions of gender, migration and globalisation gives rise to a complex discussion. The key terms are based on many different definitions and facts are interpreted in often contrasting ways. The multiple ways in which feminist and critical (intersectional) studies affected migration studies remains sometimes unclear. Today the terms like *feminization of migration, gendered migration, gendering migration, feminization of labour, feminization of poverty, feminized labour* are used, convincingly, to show how gender perspective changes our understanding, theorizing, and analysing of links between migration and globalization and how gender-based differences and inequalities affect (and are affected) by global migrations. One reason for a dissonance among the above-mentioned terms comes from the different disciplines with different epistemologies: sociology, political economy, history, geography, anthropology. The second reason is, that they are often unarticulated assumptions and concerns about gender and gender relations that underpin scientific knowledge produced in the mentioned disciplines and their claims about female and male migration.

To show how historically the notion of "gender" made critical advances in migration studies I will use the perspective that employs the concept of *gender knowledge (Geschlechter-Wissen)*, introduced by German sociologists, Sünne Andresen and Irene Dölling (2005), which draws on the sociology of knowledge (Wetterer 2008) and focuses on the construction of gender and gender relations. Andresen/Dölling define the concept as follows:

Gender knowledge is knowledge about the difference between the sexes, the reasoning of the self-evidence and evidence of these differences, and the prevailing normative ideas about the "correct" gender relations and divisions of labour between women and men (Andresen, Dölling 2005: 175, own translation).

This concept assumes that every form of knowledge, be it everyday knowledge, expert knowledge or popular knowledge is based upon a specific perspective on gender. In other words, it is not enough to understand how women are represented as migrants, but more importantly to understand the assumptions that underpin scientific knowledge claims about female migration. The focus on gender knowledge allows us to pay more attention to the articulation of different knowledge patterns concerning, in this case, the scholarly discourses of international migration studies. I argue that critical work on gender and migration today should insist on examining the processes by which migrants are constructed as gendered rather than as universal subjects. Guided by this line of thinking, in this chapter I want to focus on produced knowledge within academia aiming to show how different approaches, theories, concepts and categorizations understand and construct the meaning of gender in migration research. I will do that by identifying when *gender* is recognized as a relational and fluid analytical category or when in more quantitative approaches is considered to speak of the binary division between men and women as based on a set of biological and physical features differently ascribed to male and female models, thus overlooking cases of transgender or intersexual people and with no distinctions based on age, sexual orientation and so forth.

It is widely accepted to understand *globalization* as a process characterized by flows and connections pertaining to people, capital, goods and time-space compression since the second half of the 20th century (Harvey 1989; Trouillot 2001; Tsing 2000). On this background, we might ask how people, men, women, children move globally crossing borders and how these movements affect their lives, their communities and whole societies. While thinking about that, I am considering the larger context in which these movements take place: the legacy of colonialism, the emerging threats of climate and environmental disasters, financial crises, and related structural adjustments, imposed austerity and generalized impoverishment, the massive displacements by warfare and military interventions, the intensification of border violence in different parts of the world. Everywhere on the globe people are crossing the borders, at different times using different means and they do that for different reasons. Also, crossing the nation-states means different things for men and women. The attitudes towards migration, the single act (or process) of migration and its outcome have different meanings and are differently experienced by men and women. Knowing this, we as researchers may ask what it means to talk about "gender" in migration in times of globalization? How far can "gender" as an analytical tool help in studying the social, political, and cultural phenomenon of mobility and migration? How do we understand gender in migration? By looking at the number of women and men that are migrating? Or asking how many men have been migrating for the last five years? How and why do these numbers change over a certain period? What caused that change? What is the position of men and women in migration flows and movements? The list of questions is endless but to answer these questions would entail that we understand, define, and theorize "gender" in a certain way. My starting premise is that the knowledge, or assumptions about what "gender" is, depends on the theory or concept that is used, the way we attain the knowledge, the historical, social and political conditions in which researchers are producing the knowledge and on the researchers themselves. Therefore, in this chapter, I problematize ambivalent dependency between gender, migration, and globalization as a theoretical opening for my ethnographic study on gender labour mobility. To that end, I will first trace the long history of scholarly efforts to show that gender is a constitutive element of spatial mobilities as well as the other way around. Re-visiting the main feminist and gender theoretical contributions in migration studies, the chapter highlight problems in the production of knowledge, which have contributed to or hindered, in a variety of ways, the understanding of female migration over the last several decades. Discussing the previous theoretical and empirical work on gender, migration and globalization the chapter positions the research presented in this book within the larger field of studies of domestic and care labour, social reproduction and globalization, identifying the relevance of distinct cases of care labour mobility and potential of its analysis in further chapters.

1.1 Gender in Theories: The Main Perspectives in Studies of Migration and Mobility

Until the 1970s and 1980s female migration was seen as irrelevant and without influence on economic conditions. Such perspective reflected how researchers and governments in emigration countries defined the status of migrant women, namely largely as dependent spouses, or relatives. Women were considered too culturally limited and traditional to be able to migrate independently, and their experience in migration was linked to family and children. Since the early 1980s strong efforts were made to fill gaps in knowledge that had been caused by the invisibility of women in migration studies. During this period researchers used demographic approaches, which treated women as variables, measured primarily concerning education and fertility. This understanding, known as *the compensatory approach* (Lutz 2008), was in comparison with research into the migratory patterns of working male migrants. Inspired by women's studies, this approach relied on a gender-role theory that perceived men and women as complementary and functional poles, each of which has a cohesive role in society. In this sense, *gender* became a static attribute rather than a product of social practice, while the space where power relations and social change take place was neglected.

A significant emphasis on gender perspectives in the study of migration in Europe during the 1980s began with a special issue of the International Migration Review-journal edited by Mirjana Morokvasic in 1984. The title of Morokvasic's introduction, "Birds of passage are also women", refers to the expression *migrants are birds of passage* used by Michael Piore (1980) in his analysis of the exploitation of the migrant workforce in market economies (Morokvasic 1984). The articles in this volume reflect the number of studies developed by the late 1970s focusing on the experience of migrant women. Most of the articles look at migrant women who arrived in Australia, Northern America or Europe over a large period (from the nineteenth century onwards) in an attempt to understand their conditions and participation in the labour market compared to migrant men and non-migrant women. It is important to note that most of the authors were social historians and labour sociologists whose scholarship was heavily influenced by the Marxist-oriented debate of the 1970s on the role of migration in the context of capitalist expansion. In this publication, Morokvasic questioned the use of men as the universal point of reference as well as drew attention to the invisibility of women and their stereotyped representation as dependent figures within the production of knowledge about migration.

In the wake of this work, it became clear that women and men participate in migration equally, but in different ways, creating different effects and migration patterns and constructing and reconstructing new migration discourses, and that the role of actors in migration processes is gender-specific. In general, feminist migration research was the first to draw academic attention to the importance of gender in migration processes and the linkage between gender and factors such as class, race and socioeconomic status, considering macro-analytical perspectives. Such research revealed the significance of gendered identity in migration processes, including the importance of gender roles, the division of labour, ideological constructions, and perceptions of women. Furthermore, feminist perspectives have shown that female migration processes differ from those of males and that women can be the initiators in the decision to migrate.

During the 1990s the statement "women are on the move" became a powerful and omnipresent mantra in the titles of articles, research projects, books and monographs on gender and migration that I will refer to in this chapter. Even today every introduction or chapter on gender, migration and globalization starts with a (more or less critical) discussion on the *feminization of migration*. The term, or the phrase, was a powerful and prominent in migration studies suggesting that women all over the world were suddenly beginning to move for work and/or a better life. Demographers and quantitative social scientists (for example, among the first female demographers were Irene Taeuber and Hope Eldridge, cited in Donato, Gabaccia 2015: 27) slowly brought the migration of women to the foreground, as women have become the majority of migrants worldwide.

Feminization of Migration?

Since the turn of the millennium, there has been a dramatic interest in *the feminization of international migration*, a trend that has usually been associated with an interest in the impact of globalization. The assumption behind labelling migration as "feminizing" is that in the past migrants were normally men. More precisely, researchers claimed that the 19th and 20th centuries were an "era of mass migration" in which men were the main actors and that the 21st century became characterised by *the feminization of migration* (Castles, Miller 1993). Castles and Miller (1993: 12) suggest that since the 1960s, women have played a major role in labour migration. Migration theory has long been informed by static and gender-biased conceptualisations of migratory models, based on the assumption that labour migration was masculinised, and that migrant woman entered the picture only as family members of the male primary migrants (Phizacklea 1998; Kofman et al. 2000). According to Eleonore Kofman (1999), Castles and Miller (1993) devoted limited attention to discussing the feminization of migration despite listing it as a key feature of new migratory patterns. She argues that their discussion of mentioned successive phases of migration holds implicit gendered meanings and thus reproduces the gendered public/private dualism. This dominant "periodisation" of international migration has been accompanied by little empirical investigation to ensure its accuracy. Feminist scholars, however, have questioned the very notion of *feminization of migration*, suggesting that it does not accurately describe the growth of women among international migrants over the past several decades (Phizacklea 1998, 2003; Kofman 1999; Oso, Catarino 2013; Catarino, Morokvasic 2005; Kofman et al. 2000; Anthias, Lazaridis 2000) and that "feminization" is not a completely new phenomenon (Phizacklea 2003). During the 1990s feminist historians, reconstructing and re-evaluating the migration processes of the 19th and early 20th centuries (Gabaccia 1996; Harzig 1997; Moch 2003), demonstrated that the assumption that the migrant actor was first and foremost a male person was seriously deceptive. Feminist historical studies indicate, for example, that half of all the Irish and Jewish immigrants to the United States between 1820 and 1928 were women. The research of historian Hsia Diner (1983) who studied female Irish migration in the nineteenth century, showed that, due to the massive economic crises coupled with an Irish system of single inheritance and single dowry, Ireland increasingly became the home for many unmarried or late married women. Claims regarding the feminisation of migration flows are contested by studies showing that the proportion of international female migrants rose by just 2.2 per cent in the period 1960–2000 (from 46.6 per cent to 48.8 per cent) (Morokvasic 2010: 30), which is doesn't give proof of international migration becoming *feminized*.

We must acknowledge that work on *the feminization of migration* during the 1980s and 1990s was a useful first step in viewing the dynamics of migration through the lens of gender, encouraging researchers to look at women as autonomous labour migrants and to rethink the causes of female migration and the composition of different types of migration. However, my suggestion is here that after three decades, one should be very careful in labelling any social phenomenon in terms of "feminization" or "masculinization". The key problem is the lack of explanatory power and descriptiveness of these terms. Moreover, there is a danger in understanding "feminization" and "masculinization" as a perpetuation of traditional dichotomous divisions based on biological characteristics. Looking at the migration through the "feminization" lens has several serious issues that affect the production of gender knowledge on female migration.

First of all, scholars in different disciplines measure feminization differently, using different statistical tools, different analytical approaches and different interpretations of quantitative data. For some scholars "feminization" in migration flows is defined by referring to rising numbers of women migrants between two years or periods, to describe recent shifts in women's roles or prominence in migrant populations, or to highlight increasing shares of women among all migrants. Scholars in different disciplines also measure "feminization" differently. While many sociologists often use sex ratios to capture granular variations, historians prefer "per cent female" as a way to describe shifts in gender composition over long periods. Spatial variation in the gender composition of contemporary global migrant populations is also significant. For instance, in 1960 the foreign-born population in the Netherlands was 61 per cent female, in 2001 in Nepal it was 70 per cent female, and more recently in South Africa, it was approximately 35 per cent. Underlying these variations are patterns and shifts in gender relations and ideologies that increasingly operate on a global scale. The distinctly female-predominant immigrant population in the Netherlands was driven both by the decolonization of Indonesia and Suriname, which motivated return migration among Dutch expatriates (many of them with Indonesian or Surinamese brides). As Katherine Donato and Donna Gabaccia (2015) showed in their historical analysis of migration demographics, some countries send men, some send women and others send both, asking why and how the gender composition of migration flows changes at different times, in different parts of the world and response to different circumstances. Answering these questions can demonstrate that variation in the gender composition of migration reflects not only the movements of women relative to men but larger shifts in immigration policies and gender relations in the changing global economy.

The second problem with the "discovery" of *the feminization of migration* is that research has focussed predominantly on the problems experienced by women migrants such as trafficking, exploitative domestic work, genital mutilation and forced marriage, and women's exposure to vulnerabilities resulting from their precarious legal status, abusive working conditions, and health risks. This work, although useful in uncovering the mentioned experiences, is failing to address the fact that these problems are the product of structures that create inequality in different ways for children, men, and women. An additional weakness is that this approach runs the risk of presenting an image of women as victims with limited capabilities to mobilize their resources, thereby denying their agency. I argue here that instead of praising the mobility of women as a revolutionary development in international/global migration, researchers should be focused on problems of social inequality and look critically at the role played by local, national, regional, and transnational socio-economic factors in creating the need for a women-centric form of human mobility.

One of the most convincing feminist contributions to migration studies is the evidence that shows how women and men migrate differently: their motivations and reasons for moving, as well as the channels they use to migrate, are never identical. Over time migration eventually became more gender-balanced because fiancées and wives followed the initial migration of the men. Such increases in female migration, an aspect of the so-called *feminization of migration*, are the consequence of marriage migration and family unification (Donato, Gabaccia 2015: 47). From the 1970s onwards, many European states (for example, Germany, Denmark and Netherlands) moved from implementing programmes to recruit migrant workers to more restrictive policies as the demand for labour declined and unemployment in male industrial jobs increased. However, alongside these "stoppage policies", immigration legislation in many European countries allowed for family reunions, and the number of women migrating to Europe increased (Thranhardt 1992). Feminist studies of migration also invite us to reconsider the stereotype of family reunion migration as exclusively feminine. From the 1980s onwards, a process of *masculinization* of family reunion and of family formation (through which migrants seek a spouse in the home country and reunite with him/her in the host society) was already observable in different European countries (Kofman et al. 2000; Bhaba 1996). Here is important to stress, as Gallo and Scrinzi highlighted – that labour market dynamics interplay with the gendered nature of immigration policies, and this interplay contributes to establishing a gendered and racialised division of work in the migratory context (Gallo, Scrinzi 2016: 43). They draw on the work of authors whose research proved that the immigration law, informed by a "breadwinner ideology", constructs migrant men as breadwinners and migrant women as economic and juridical dependants. This was the case, especially in those countries where labour migrants arrived through the family reunion and most of them were women. As they didn't have immediate access to the formal labour market, they were forced to work in the informal economy, especially those oriented towards "privatized spheres of work" such as domestic, care and sex work, or jobs in the informal service economy and textile industries (Phizaklea 1998: 29; Van Walsum, Spijkerboer 2007, in Gallo, Scrinzi 2016: 43). For instance, in the 1960s and 1970s, British immigration law prevented Asian women from bringing their husbands into the UK but did not prevent migrant men from bringing their wives (Bhabha 1996, in Gallo, Scrinzi 2016: 44). The public discourses in Britain at the time had seen husbands who came through family reunions as a potential threat to the national labour market. This led to an assumption that female newcomers will have a much more passive role in British society and thus are not considered competition in the labour market.

The fact that labour migration was viewed as a relevant subject of research whilst women's migration as dependents was not to the same degree, does not prove that men were more active, but just that they were more visible. The moment when we overcame the dominant idea of male guest-worker migration as the only or the most important one, female movements received well-deserved attention. These arguments are convincing enough to inspire researchers to use the term *gender transition* (Morokvasic 2010: 45), which seems more correct. Or, more precisely, as Gabaccia and Zanoni (2012) have suggested, more research is needed to examine the timing and causes of transitions – from male-dominated to gender-balanced flows – in international migrant gender ratios. The bright career of *the feminization of migration* took place due to several factors including gaps in the empirical evidence, the popularity of positivist quantitative approaches which often failed to contextualize the data and how "migrant" is defined in terms of creating complex categories of migrants regarding their different motivations and intentions.

The main reason for the increasing academic interest in gendered aspects of migration which has contributed to the perception that there is an increasing *feminization of migration* relate, primarily, to changes in the politics and research agendas of research institutions, universities, and international organizations. These collectively encouraged a movement to the *feminization of the migratory discourse* (Oso, Garson 2005). Feminist researchers have additionally suggested that the earlier gender bias was a product of the absence of female researchers in the field, arguing that theory building is never dissociated from the persons collecting data and evidence. In other words, knowledge production should never be separated from social structures, relations, and processes of scholarly inquiry. The way scholars understand relations between sex, gender and migration greatly affects scholarly work and its results. To illustrate this, I will show in the next sub-chapter how gender adds value to migration theories and changed the lens through which scholars tend to look at the migration processes.

Neoclassical Theory, Network Theory and Transnational Paradigm

The *neoclassical macro theory* of migration is the oldest and best-known theory of international migration which has been developed originally to explain labour migration concerning economic development (Lewis 1954; Ranis, Fei 1961). According to this theory, migration is triggered by geographic differences in economic opportunities, more precisely differences in the supply of and demand for labour. Corresponding to the neoclassical macro theory is the neoclassical micro model/theory, which explains mentioned behaviour. The most extreme version of this perspective positions the migrant as a calculating economic actor driven exclusively by his interests, comparing his current income to potential earnings in other locations or countries.

This theoretical approach to migration is not difficult to criticize today. However, one should have in mind that neoclassical economic theories are responsible for the use of formal, idealized models and econometric techniques in studies which are the empirical basis for reports about flows, costs and benefits of migration in institutions such as the World Bank, the OECD or IOM and consequently, create recommendations for migration policies (for an in-depth critique see Schwenken 2008). Patricia Pessar (1999) an American anthropologist, argued that in the 1950s and 60s the neoclassical debate about mobility was influenced by the role model of the "Western man" or *Homo Oeconomicus*. Despite many empirical studies, which showed that this hegemonic figure is far from the reality where immigrant men are marked as cheap labour and deskilled as a result of discrimination based on race, ethnicity or age, the neoclassical models had a brilliant career within economic migration research. However, the post-structuralist perspective takes economics as a discourse that produces certain subjects of knowledge. In this sense, critical migration work insists on examining the economy and its gendered power relations as fluid social processes and the migrant worker as a gendered subject rather than an anonymous workforce.

The neoclassical analysis provides a one-dimensional view of human activity, amalgamating together a complex range of individual calculations arising within a complex range of social processes. The assumptions of this paradigm tend to ignore unexpected social structures that shape migration and non-monetary factors (such as love, sex, academic opportunities, desire for adventure, etc.) so that individual calculations seem to be occurring in a historical, political and economic vacuum. Circumstances that stimulate "push-pull" factors were not explored but assumed to emerge from the universal conditions that prevail in all societies. Theories based on macro-structural transformations, or "push-pull" analysis were not able to explain the unpredictable variations between socially distinct migratory routes. Agency is generally neglected, and the analysis of diverse power issues at play (apart from financial and economic aspects) is not an integral part of this way of understanding migration movements. Differences due to gender, ethnicity, race and class are usually overlooked. When these aspects are considered, it is only in very restricted and single-sided ways: women are for instance usually not seen as agents of migration but as mere dependants.

If we examine, for example, family patterns in which husbands migrate earlier than their wives we can ask why this pattern has been so persistent even in situations with statistical evidence of a growing need for the work of migrant women? To answer this question, we have to take into account the immediate social, cultural and historical context in which migration is taking place. Parallel to these broader concerns, feminist migration research in geography during the 1990s began to explore specifically the role that migration plays in shaping social orders, geographies of inequality, spatialized subjectivities – that is spatial mobility a social and political process (for an overview of the literature that tackles these themes see Silvey Rachel 2004). One of the main contributions of feminist geographers to migration studies is their critique of the neoclassical approach, arguing that it does not address the political or gendered specificity of migration processes. Feminist geographers are interested in the gender and diversity policies that provide a framework for the production of knowledge about the dynamics and meanings of spatial categories such as households, regions, nations and or supranational entities such as the European Union. The best example is – the nation. For neoclassical theorists, the nation is an objective spatial category whose economic conditions are a key force that encourages or inhibits inter-ethnic migrations (Massey D. 1993). However, numerous feminist studies treat the nation as something produced through social and political processes that privilege some identities and exclude others.

An emphasis on the need to consider gender in the theory of international migration has also influenced *network theory*. Network theory is a dynamic theory of international migration which dates back to the 1980s and 1990s (Massey 1993; Gurak, Cace 1992). The theory sees international migration as a cumulative social process – networks are composed of interpersonal links between migrants, ex-migrants and non-migrants both in the country of origin and in the destination country. Social networks increase mobility because they reduce the costs and risks of the migration process. The acquisition of a network of relationships represents a kind of social capital that people use to gain access to employment in the country of migration. Early research on networks was driven by two principles. The first was an emphasis on the importance of networks (although largely male networks) in encouraging or preventing migration from one area to another. The second was the insight that social networks were based on solidarity in which gender was completely neglected. Revisionist research has shown that social networks can be very controversial resources, which are not always shared equally within the family or between spouses (Pessar, Mahler 2006: 33). The point is that families and migrant networks are gender-based institutions. The feminist critique was grounded, in fact, on the criticism of family structures, aiming to demonstrate that households and families are neither unifying nor united, neither generational nor gender-based entities in which there are no hierarchies of authority, power and resources. Since the 1990s, research has shown that women have their own networks including other women and they use these networks to migrate and settle in other countries. Hondagneu-Sotelo, in her 1994 monograph, *Gender Transitions: Mexican Experiences of Migration* has shown that social networks that mediate between migrants are deeply embedded in gender-specific ideologies and the redistribution of power and that men and women have different networks even when they belong to the same families. Family and community relationships help us to determine how the possibilities and constraints of political and economic forces are translated into different migration patterns. In this study, Hondagneu-Sotelo starts from the assumption that we must question and explore the gender-based character of migrant social networks to understand migration patterns. We cannot assume, for example, that women automatically have access to male-dominant migrant networks, or that women necessarily migrate with the help of other women. Mid-level concepts introduced by Goss and Lindquist (1995) help to overcome the dualism between agency and structure focusing on how the routes of migration are negotiated by migrants. The presumption that women automatically migrate with the help of other women seems didn't find empirical evidence. The more fruitful approach, that dominates in my research presented in this book is to look at how women access and mobilize social networks during the process of mobility.

Feminist migration researchers focused their criticism on those analyses that represented the household as a unilateral, monolithic, and universally homogeneous community based on altruism and mutual solidarity in which there were hierarchies of power, authority, and resources based on gender or age. They highlighted how existing work often ignored the divergent and conflicting interests that made gender and generational relations invisible within different phases of the migration process (Grassmuck, Pessar 1991; Hondagneu-Sotelo 1994). This "critical household lens" has uncovered the conflict and tension within migrant households emerging from gendered power relations and thus allowed to unveil how the migration process (from the decision to migrate through the period of settlement in and adaptation to the host society) is intricately tied to gender relations (Anthias 2000; Hondagneu-Sotelo 1992, 1994; Kofman 2000). The impetus for redirecting research attention from macro-structural transformations to meso-levels of analysis such as the households or social networks came from anthropologists who argued that migration is not a process that can be understood exclusively in economic and political terms, but that migration is a socio-cultural process that is entwined with institutions, practices and ideologies of gender and kinship (Pessar, Mahler 2006: 33). Needless to say, this approach also carries potential disadvantages such as an overly narrow focus on the domain of family and household, ignoring the gendered aspects of other areas of life such as migrant jobs, immigration offices, employment agencies and border controls – topics that will be addressed later in this chapter.

The emergence of *transnationalism* as a paradigm marked a new era in the study of migrations at the end of the 1980s and through into the 1990s. With its focus on the international dimension of migration. This perspective has shifted the attention from the dominant topic of migrants' inclusion and settlement within new societies to the relationships that migrants attain and maintain with their country of origin. Migration has thus started to be seen as a multi-level process, with new perspectives challenging purely economic and macro-level approaches by examining how these processes are activated and lived on the micro-level of the communities and the level of individuals. Moving away from economic perspectives towards migrant practices and strategies the transnational approach introduces the importance of social and symbolic capital in migration processes (Levitt 2001: 54) and focuses on the benefits that migrants have from modern means of communication (Vertovec 2004) and transportation, the resources and opportunities provided by the global market, and on the new social forms, political challenges and cultural resources arising from linkages formed between multiple geographic locations. The most celebrated contribution of transnationalism to migration studies was the questioning of the equivalence between the national state and society known as "methodological nationalism", an approach that rejects the national state as the only starting point for empirical analysis and calls for the denaturalization of categories such as nation and space (Basch, Glick Schiller, Szanton Blanc 1994; Vertovec 2007; Wimmer, Glick Schiller 2003; Pries 2001). The most important object of criticism, at least from my perspective, is the unwarranted generalization of models of behaviour based on only a small proportion of migratory populations, so-called "transnational elites" (Portes 2003). The problem of transnationalism is that it does not adequately differentiate between migrant groups according to gender, class, race, ethnicity, nationality, and age-specificity. Gender-focussed approaches in research reveal that migrant women are not involved in national political communities as can be seen in the example of Filipinos and women from the Caribbean described by Basch, Glick-Schiller and Szanton-Blanc (1994). Phizahklea (2003) argued that "transnationalism from below as a method of countering and subverting the logic of transnational capital" – may not be a strategy open to all. As she pointed out rightly, it is not possible to compare "the fortnightly phone call" and "desperately small amounts of money" remitted by Sri Lankan migrant domestic workers in the Gulf States to the transnational business deals of cosmopolitan entrepreneurs, without recourse to class analysis. Simply put, beyond saying that all these transactions are transnational, it is to acknowledge that the actors involved have very different points of departure or degrees of autonomy over the nature of transnational transactions. In addition, one might argue that access to transnational activities is highly gendered. The focus on migrant women highlights a different experience of transnationalism from their male counterparts. Anthropologist Ruba Salih in her research among Moroccan migrant women in Italy shows how tensions between structures, gender and agency are vital in explaining movements and transnational activities that take place within, and not despite, national normative and cultural constraints. As she argued, these movements and activities are conditioned by a set of legal and cultural provisions based on the governing interpretations of gender roles both in Italy and Morocco. These rules determine women's activities, their identities as well as their mobility across borders or residence in Italy, and at the same time, women develop a dialectical relationship with these rules producing counter-hegemonic discourses and challenging behaviour (Salih 2013: 10). In her ethnography about Dominican sex workers, Denise Brennan shows connections between large structural forces in the globalized economy and their effects on individuals by examining two transnational processes: sex tourism and migration (Brennan 2004). These transnational processes and the linkages affect individuals' lives unequally – depending on hierarchies of race, class, citizenship, mobility, gender and sexuality. Her work is illuminating because it explores how transnational flows are not equally liberating for everyone but instead offer some subjects opportunities to enhance their possibilities while contributing to the subordination of other, less privileged subjects. She suggests that the task on the part of the researcher should be to explore the ways transnationalism remakes inequalities. The conditions for transnational mobility are not always favourable to women and often limit them to normative cultural gender rules.

As the transnational perspective is tightly connected to issues of citizenship and states, another illuminating perspective mobilizes somewhat different analytic lenses of *human rights and feminism*. Benhabib and Resnik (2009) – in their edited volume on gender and citizenship – opened the doors to merging gender theory, citizenship, and migration studies. They argue that when one brings into mutual relation citizenship, sovereignty, and migration theories with gender analysis, new questions emerge both about feminist conceptions of women and men and political theories of the state (2009: 5). The answers to these questions shed new light on disagreements about the normative desirability of the categories of citizenship and state and their implications for women and men in different parts of the world. The authors pointed out that citizens, migrants, refugees, and members of host communities are not disembodied individuals but are adults or children travelling with or leaving family members. They argue that laws, policies, theories of citizenship, jurisdiction, family life and migration must be seen as a product of discrimination and subordination based on gender that affects the conceptualization and implementations of rights, opportunities and nation-state powers.

To illustrate this, I provide an example. A Colombian mother Joyce is a single parent who travelled to the Netherlands to visit her sister and explore life there while leaving her six-year-old daughter Emily in the care of other family members as Sarah van Walsum (in Benhabib, Resnik 2009: 13) explains, after the expiration of a tourist visa, Joyce remained in the Netherlands illegally until she obtained a residence permit based on her relationship with a Dutchman, with whom she subsequently became the parent of another child. The Dutch authorities rejected Joyce's application for her daughter to join the family because, under Dutch law, Joyce had failed to demonstrate that during the period of separation she had maintained an "effective family bond", which is to say that, despite the geographic separation, she had been effectively involved in the financial support and upbringing of the child. By the time Joyce lost her appeal, she was a Dutch citizen who had given up her Colombian nationality. Van Walsum makes clear that when making evaluations about the provision of "effective care", officials had preconceived views about "good mothers" or "good fathers" that were predicated on cultural assumptions shaped by the customs in both host countries and countries of origin. Further, as she artfully illuminates, feminist efforts to obtain recognition in the domestic law of the rights of those providing "substantive" care (in contrast to a focus on the status of a person as legally the parent) had influenced some decision-makers to undervalue the legal status of migrants as parents and their needs to have other persons give care to their children when those parents travelled abroad. The challenge is to shape laws and practices that recognize a range of life choices and are respectful of the variation in family care patterns and the perspective of migrant mothers.

This short story teaches us that the mobility of some has consequences for or corresponds to the immobility of others. All these persons are engendered in their relationships with others, with the politics from which they came and those they seek to enter. As van Walsum explicates, women's mobility is rarely a simple matter of the movement across state boundaries of a single, isolated individual. Women's mobility is a nodal point in a network of relationships that almost always involves dependent children, dependent elderly, the men with whom women are affiliated and other family members or the women who are parts of networks in which women, both givers and recipients of care, are reliant on others.

Another criticism of the transnational approach comes from the debate on specific forms of mobility. Criticizing the shortcomings of transnationalism, such as an emphasis on sustainability and the duration of transnational connections over time, Mirjana Morokvasic has called for the inclusion of short-term migrations such as those from Central and Eastern Europe (Morokvasic 2004). She noted the poor recognition of transnationalism as an entrepreneurial asset, which throughout history has catalysed changes to immigration rules and economic structures. Morokvasic emphasizes that the identification of the conditions under which transnational practices can take place can reveal a wide range of migration types (from migration by choice to forced migration), as well as highlighting the power differentials between participants in different forms of labour in transnational space. Her field research among Poles in Berlin between 1991 and 1992 demonstrated, for example, that circular journeys (which can include the smuggling of goods, domestic and care work etc.) are a way of life that is "settled in mobility" – moved far away from the expected classical pattern of migration to and settlement in another country (Morokvasic 2004; Cyrus 2008). She stressed that although transnational perspectives have challenged the classical approach to migration and its overwhelming focus on the durability and sustainability of transnational links over time, it nevertheless leaves little space for the exploration of short-term transnational mobility as a social and cultural phenomenon. It excludes phenomena that can be transnational but somewhat ephemeral such as migration from and within South-Eastern Europe.

Despite its merits, the transnational perspective has been criticized by scholars such as Hondagneu-Sotelo and Avila, who argue that this perspective fails to adequately incorporate gender into its consideration of transnational migrants (Hondagneu-Sotelo, Avila 1997). Based on ethnographic materials gathered among immigrant Latina domestic workers in Los Angeles, Pierrette Hondagneu-Sotelo and Ernestine Avila (1997) have shown how domestic workers transform the meaning of motherhood to accommodate spatial and temporal separation from their children. Generally, the period that marked the transnational perspective was also the time when the gender approach to migration studies brought to the fore other forms of movement of human beings beyond international migration (immigration) as a global phenomenon. The focus was re-directed to varieties of migration patterns that are caused by different migration and legal regimes governing access to the residence, social and economic resources, political and social rights and as showed previously, are highly gendered or better say, with an underlying gender knowledge. The relevance of place, mobility and gender combined with the relevance of citizenship, labour migration, health, education made questions of the role of globalization, nation-state, international economic and political forces both pressing and contested.

The attractive side of transnationalism, globalization and a "borderless world of networks" is in its power to blind us with alternative definitions of social entities as "de-territorialized and territorialized at the same time" (Faist

2012: 57). Yet, such enthusiastic views of "world without borders" (Levitt, Khagam 2007) carries the risk of neglecting national borders. These, as Bridget Anderson (2019) argues whilst proposing methodological de-nationalism, are politically constituted and historically and economically embedded. She reminds us that nationalised subjectivities matter to how we imagine ourselves and to where do we belong. Ideas about our place in the "national order of things" give rise to many different forms of socialites so that border crossings are material realities of the national order of things. For those people in migration processes that we are doing research on, nation and borders matter both normatively and empirically. On the other hand, we cannot dispute that "globalization" is not useful in challenging the state-centric (or territorial) model in social science highlighting the importance of mobilities in contemporary societies (Bauman 1998 among others). And indeed, globalization is a general context in which we can think and theorize about international migration and mobilities. However, there is no clear cut between global and national. The dynamics of nation-global overlap, Sassen (2000) explained by arguing that modern nation-states themselves never achieved to be a spatio-temporal unity because of the global economic restructurings that threaten them. In other words, nation-states adapt and redefine their strategies and practices to deal with the consequences of global economic restructuring (Ong 1999). When it comes to migration, nation-states are still in power over decisions, controlling migration flows and crating transnational and political fields and this fact shouldn't be overlooked.

1.2 Re-Visiting Dominant Concepts and Theories in Global Migration for Domestic and Care Work

Starting in the late 1990s feminist theory has experienced a proliferation of perspectives and topics for research. The central issue within this phase, as Hondagneu-Sotelo describes it, is to what extent gender permeates various practices, identities and institutions. In this period, forms of engagement, entrepreneurship in ethnic communities, citizenship, sexuality and ethnic identity have been examined in a way that reveals how gender is incorporated into everyday life and institutional, political and economic structures (Hondegnau-Sotelo 2000: 117). Studies focus on the lives of recent female migrants with an emphasis on the labour market, housework, work in the care sector and prostitution using biographic analysis (in Germany notably Karakayali 2009; Inowlocki, Lutz 2000; Hess 2005; Hess, Puckhaber 2004). Research has shown that there is a link between the ambitions and motivations of migrants, their needs and expectations on the one hand, and the needs of the labour markets of the countries of the European Union on the other, despite such issues being framed through the obvious paradoxes of restrictive migration policies and discourse on integration and legal measures. This work has provided the basis for more serious analyses of how gender hierarchies are related to other social relationships of power, revealing contradictory assumptions regarding integration where normative concepts were highly problematic (Anthias, Morokvasic-Müller, Kontos 2012). Also, issues such as local examples of global inequalities, queer-feminist decolonial epistemology and critical approaches to intersectionality in migration studies came into sight. Issues that become relevant are those related to the relationship between colonial studies, the "feminization of labour" and "masculinization of labour" and migration policies and work in the care and domestic sector. Gender-related analyses have helped to understand the centrality of sexual heteronormativity in connection to the relationships between migration, power, and the establishment of social order. Queer theory has altered the framing of questions about subjectivity and identity through essentialist gender formulations by examining the equivalences between women/femininity and men/masculinity. New endeavours within migration research, inspired by gay and lesbian studies, we're beginning to address the construction of heterosexual norms, the transformation of sexual practices and norms, and our understanding of both how sexuality intervenes and shapes migrations and how migrations affect sexual practices and identities (for example, Petzen 2005). The new perspective questioned the validity of Western/European ascriptive labels such as "homosexual", "heterosexual" or "queer": what does this mean for migrants' concepts of self? Further, it challenged the idea of "queer migration" as being a migration from "oppression" to "freedom". Rather, it suggests a focus on the construction, regulation and governance of those sexual and gendered identities beyond the heteronormative paradigm in the context of migration processes and migration regimes. This transformation applies particularly to research related to the commodification of privacy, prostitution, sexual exploitation, and trafficking (Pajnik 2008; Andrijasevic 2010). But just as important, when we think about sexuality, we also must consider moral norms, taken-for-granted naturalizations and laws that regulate sexual behaviour and identifications, and we need to, maybe most surprisingly, also think about forms of intimacy, love, kinship and care responsibilities – topics that will be discussed further in this chapter.

Over the past 20 years, there has been a significant increase in studies focusing on domestic and care work in the production of knowledge within the field of migration and gender. A significant number of studies on the intersection of feminist theory of domestic work, elderly and child care, migration, globalization and social policies have drawn attention to the processes through which migrants from the "periphery of capitalism" fill the deficit of care in the middle class in developed capitalist countries. Partly, the increase in research was due to the collapse of the Soviet Union and the consequent large-scale migration of women from East to West Europe, very often employed in domestic, care, and sex work (Ferreira 1998; Vianello 2014). Other studies have focused on labour migration in the domestic labour sector from Latin America, the Caribbean, Southeast Asia (in particular the Philippines and Sri Lanka) and some African countries. As an outcome of this new research trend, the years 1999–2001 were marked by the publications such as a ground-breaking monograph by Jaqueline Andall (2000), Rhacel Parreñas (2001), Bridget Anderson (2000) and Pierrette Hondagneu-Sotelo (2001), as well as the edited volume by Janet Momsen (1999). They are followed, in 2002, by the volume Global Woman: Nannies, Maids and Sex Workers in the New Economy edited by Barbara Ehrenreich and Arlie R. Hochschild, which collects the works of new emerging authors in this field. These volumes inaugurated a period of emphasis on migrant domestic and care work. Also, within the same period, important journals in Sociology, Geography and Women's Studies devoted special issues to migrant women, establishing the cross-fertilisation between the disciplinary fields of studies (for example articles in the special issue of the American Behavioral Scientist, edited by Pierrette Hondagneu-Sotelo in 1999; Identities: Global Studies in Culture and Power, edited by Sarah J. Mahler and Patricia Pessar in 2001; and, finally, Signs: Journal of Women in Culture and Society (edited by Amrita Basu et al. in 2001).

The next decade sees an incredible increase in the number of international scholars focusing on the issues of migrant domestic and care workers who share a solid corpus of methodological and theoretical tools, highly interdisciplinary, which they can adapt to the analysis of migrant women's experiences in different parts of the world, and at different times. The important scholarship is represented by Helma Lutz (2011), Rosie Cox (2015), Raffaella Sarti (2002), Sarah van Walsum (2011) and Fiona Williams (2012), Sabine

Hess (2005) for the European context. Among those from outside Europe it is important to mention Pei-Chia Lan (2006) for Southeast Asia; Raka Ray and Seeming Qayum (2009) for India; Gioconda Herrera (2013) for Latin America, as well as Marina de Regt (2009) on Yemen and Gül Özyeğin (2010) on Turkey. Also, migration for sex work becomes an important topic, although quite separate from the one of migration in domestic and care work (see Andrijasevic 2010; Mai 2013). All these studies that represent only part of the work recently produced, reflect on political and economic realities on a global level.

One of the most striking features of contemporary global capitalism is the heightened *commodification of intimacy* that pervades social life. We all depend on services to fulfil our obligations or display closeness to others. One could argue: "So, did 19th century Victorian upper class in Britain." Yes, but our time is distinguished by both the intensification of commodification and monetization of daily life and neoliberal economic restructuring that have displaced workers in many countries, creating greater mobility for intimate labour. Intimate labour serves as a springboard not only for understanding women's labour market activities but also as a key lens for examining the impact of macrostructural forces of economic globalization and the neoliberal state. The services or, to say, tasks we need to complete are functional to people's prosperous living – day after day, and across generations, at the material and symbolic levels – like preparing food, mending clothing, cleaning homes, giving birth and raising children, assisting elderly and sick people. Feminist scholars define these tasks (whether paid or unpaid) as social reproduction; that is, simply put, the labour that is necessary for the reproduction of the labour force. Increasing segments of these activities are commodified: meals prepared by professional cooks can be bought in restaurants; elderly people are assisted by paid cacaregivers in nursing homes. This is a growing and seemingly unstoppable process, with always new intimate and private tasks, especially those related to different types of *body work* as *body labour* being incorporated into the market called *intimate labour* as a comprehensive category of an investigation into gender, race, class, and other power relations in the context of global economic transformations (Parreñas, Boris 2010; Wolkowitz 2006). Intimacy and intimate relations have become more explicitly commodified, linked to commodities and to commodified global processes which make scholars talk of a *care economy* (Folbre 2001; Zelizer 2009) characterised by the (often informal) employment of a precarious workforce with strong gender, race, class-based connotations (Sassen

2002). If we look at it from a gender perspective, we can see that women take up a bigger share of the care economy than their male counterparts; but it is also true that amongst women, reproductive work is more often done by black or migrant women, and in general, women who are from a minority and racialised groups (Rollins 1985; Glenn-Nakano 2002; Palmer 1989).

In most industrialised countries, it has been especially noted how *citizenship* is crucial for understanding the large numbers of undocumented migrants (mostly women, but also men) who work in house cleaning, elderly care, catering and restaurants. Private employment of domestic and care workers, in particular, is negatively impacted by existing migration policies that make the regular employment of migrants difficult (Triandafyllidou 2016; Ong 1999). The social stratification between the subjects involved in reproductive work contributes to the under-valuation of these jobs as far as these are considered "naturally" assigned to the most vulnerable and stigmatised subjects (Gutiérrez-Rodríguez 2010; Lan 2006).

Care and domestic labour migration have added an important dimension to our understanding how care is commodified in the context of globalization. Reproductive labour is increasingly commodified across nation-state borders, as the growing research literature on the subject has demonstrated (e.g. Anderson 2000; Ehrenreich, Hochschild 2002; Hochschild 2000; Hondagneu-Sotelo, Avila 1997; Hondagneu-Sotelo 2000; Isaksen 2010; Lutz 2002, 2008a; Parreñas 2001; Yeates 2009). The globalization of the capitalist economy impacts not only production but also reproduction (Sassen 2000, 2003). However, unlike manufactured goods, where production can be relocated to parts of the world with lower labour costs, care and domestic work are non-transferable, labour-intensive forms of (re)production that requires the availability of cheap labour in situ (Yeates 2004: 93). In this strand of the literature, the globalization of care has been defined in different ways: as a *global commodification of reproductive labour* (Anderson 2000); *globalizing mothering* (Parreñas 2001); *transnational motherhood* (Hondagneu-Sotelo, Avila 1997; Lutz 2002), the *new international division of reproductive labour* (Parreñas, 2001) and *global care chains* and *care drain* (Hochschild 2000).

Rhacel Parreñas introduced *the international division of reproductive labour* formula to expand the view from its "racial" division (Glenn-Nakano 2002) to the global level. Parreñas emphasises how this work is generally unequally distributed along with a "three-tier" transfer of reproductive labour in globalization between the following groups of women: (1) middle-class women in receiving nations, (2) migrant domestic workers, and (3) Third

World women who are too poor to migrate (Parreñas 2000: 560). In her study on the Filipino diaspora, she found that the same Filipino women employed in Western households to care for children and elders are delegating their family commitments to other women: to female family members but also other women, from poorer backgrounds, whom they pay a salary of about USD 40 per month out of the USD 1000 they earn abroad – for doing the same job (Parreñas 2009). In this view, globalization is the scenario against which reproductive work is divided and passed on from one woman to another, who is in a less privileged position.

Global Care Chains

The above-mentioned idea has taken up by Arlie Russell Hochschild whose concept of *the global care chain* (a special issue dedicated to the concept is published in *Gender and Society*, 2002) has found the most resonance within the research community. *Global care chain* (further in the text as abbreviation GCC), Arlie Hochschild's concept is valuable because it can be easily adapted to different forms of globalized care, although in her original definition the emphasis is on motherly care. Hochschild (2000: 131) defines *global care chains* as a "series of personal links between people across the globe based on the paid or unpaid work of caring". To illustrate the nature of these chains, she gives the example of "an older daughter from a poor family who cares for her siblings while her mother works as a nanny caring for the children of a migrating nanny who, in turn, cares for the child of a family in a rich country" (ibid).

Taking up a critical position on this concept I want to show how the "feminization of scholarship" or "feminization of scholarly discourse on women's migration for care and domestic work" produces knowledge that has two results. The first is the potential devaluation of women's care work and the construction of an image of the female migrant as a feminine, caring subject that is premised on white, Western, middle-class gender norms and which contributes to the construction of a premodern non-Western subject. Secondly, this knowledge created in the "core" appears to be universal and cannot be applied in semi-peripheral countries without addressing geographical, cultural, political and economic contexts.

In her original work on GCC, Hochschild centres on care work particularly in the form of nannies and live-in caregivers. Although the concept has been criticised and expanded since its introduction (Yeates 2004, 2009; Parreñas 2001; Manalasan 2008; Kilkey 2010), here we focus on the original idea of commodified care as *a surplus-value* that is taken from the migrant workers and their home countries (periphery countries) in migration to richer nations (core countries). Hochschild and her followers introduced the economic notions of *care surplus* and *care drain* which are grounded in neo-Marxist dependency theories used to explain the mechanisms supporting economic inequalities between the global North and the global South. According to this perspective, GCC is created by importing care from poor to rich countries, leading to new care deficits or "care drains" by which migrants as mothers and their children become most affected. In contrast to this, parent-employers and their children enjoy the benefits of outsourcing the care work, conceptualized in terms of *surplus love*. This perspective expands the notion of economic inequalities to inequalities of emotion (Yeates 2009). Hochschild compares the care and love provided by third world women with "the nineteenth-century extraction of gold, ivory and rubber from the Third world" (Hochschild 2000). The "new gold" which is extracted at a low cost from the poorer countries by richer ones gives us an image of a third world woman as a person without any agency and who is necessarily on the losing side. Portrayals of the miserable woman who must migrate to ensure the economic survival of her family are one-dimensional because women involved in the GCC come from a variety of backgrounds and levels of privilege. Viewing migrants from one perspective only creates invisible groups who do not fall into this category including, for example, women who have advanced education involving medical and nursing degrees and thus comparatively better skills. This perspective, therefore, gives an overly straightforward description of the globalization of care processes. It connotes a simplistic and unilateral dependency between households in developing and developed countries. The second problem with this perspective is that "care chains" do not exist everywhere, and there is a danger of generalization. Care chains involve different countries and cultures with different, culturally specific logics of exchange (Williams, Gavanas 2008). In the context of intra-European migration in which the sending country is geographically close to the country of work, travel costs are affordable and migration laws make it possible to cross borders. It is more likely to encounter "interrupted care chains", a typical form of chain in former socialist countries such as Poland and Ukraine. Moreover, this perspective overlooks how migrant care workers manage to combine their reproductive labour and continuing transnational care. In addition to this, the literature on transnational care and transnational families has demonstrated that migrant care workers continue providing care transnationally in their home countries (Baldassar, Baldock, Wilding 2007; Bryceson, Vuorela 2002). Finally, the original formulation of GCC portrays them as feminine, overlooking care work done by men, both paid as well as unpaid (see e. g. Manalansan 2006 for critique). In my view, the GCC framework should analyse how the globalization of care is gendered in multiple ways. GCC should be contextualized both historically and geographically. More to the point, criticism in this book is directed to the question of the generalisability of research that uncritically applies the concept of care chains, especially in the countries of Central Eastern Europe and the former Soviet Union (for example, Palenga-Möllenbeck 2013; Lutz, Möllenbeck 2012; Redlova 2013).

Another concept developed by the same author is that of *care drain* – a metaphor aiming to characterize women's labour migration as a loss. The concept operates as a female counterpart to *brain drain*. Hochschild points out that care and domestic labour migration has added an important dimension to how care is commodified. In this way, care work has become associated with women who, as a result, are exclusively studied as caregivers without any interest in their professional ambitions or how migration provides or reduces opportunities. The legal statuses of these women, their negotiations with employers and their responses to exploitation have not been part of the picture. "Care" has been understood as a commodified extension of "motherly love" neglecting the consideration of, firstly, the involvement of men in reproductive labour; secondly, other forms of caregiving, such as care for elderly or disabled persons; thirdly, *care gain* (Dumitru 2014: 209) – or the positive outcomes of care work abroad such as a change of attitudes towards the family of migrant workers and the development of care skills which can show us how care can be learned and improved within migration contexts. As Dumitru (ibid) has rightly argued, constructing female migration as a "care drain" is dangerous in two respects. "Care drain" describes care as an attribute necessarily attached to specific categories of people such as women and mothers. The other problem is the representation of care migrants based on their social remit rather than as bearers of knowledge. The "feminization of migration" is here based on the assumption that women migrate in increasing numbers as potential caregivers in receiving countries. While this may be true in terms of global structural inequalities, gender inequalities, and the crisis of the welfare state, we cannot assume that all female migrants are mothers and that care, nurture, and love are qualities tied to the biological female body, nor that struggles regarding care are new or evident only in global relations. An exclusive focus on the feminine caring subject according to gender can easily fall into the trap of accepting the gender-role theory, which in turn carries the possibility of leading us into methodological sexism, as Speranta Dumitru concluded.

As the ethnographic study presented in this book demonstrates, questioning the globalization of care work and the outsourcing of domestic and care work to "migrant women from the "Global South" reveals how boundaries between realms where care is taking place – such as families as the main caregivers, the market where care services are organized, third sector and the state – are blurred, resulting in overlaps and mixed forms. Also, care markets are globalized, and care is commodified not only in the countries of the "centre" but also in the "periphery", as several historical and contemporary analyses from different parts of the world have shown (e. g. Constable 1997; Hansen 1986; Moya 2007; Sanjek, Colen 1990; Sarti 2008). Another problem is that the majority of studies on globalization, feminization and commodification of care and domestic work trends are termed "Global South to Global North movements". This description, however, falls short when it comes to the care migration between Asian countries (Michel, Peng 2012) and from Asia to the Middle East (Gamburd 2000; Samarasinghe 1998). It also fails to describe the situation in Europe: the vast majority of Europe's care migrants come from Eastern Europe. This results not only in East-to-West but also involves East-to-East migration where Moldavian, Georgian, and especially Ukrainian and Belarusian, women work in wealthy upper- and middle-class homes in the booming cities of Poland and the Czech Republic, while Slovakian, Polish, Ukrainian, Romanian, Bulgarian and Latvian women from rural areas are employed in Germany, the Netherlands, Italy, Spain, the UK and Austria (Cox 2015; Krzyżowski 2013; Leon 2014; Näre 2011; Lutz 2010, 2011; Österle, Bauer 2016).

Summing this all up, the geopolitical framing of "Global South to Global North" needs to be amended by analysing the wide-ranging and multiple scaling of care migrations, understood as complex relations, where in each case the respective gendered, ethnic and class dimensions of the phenomenon are taken into account (Lutz, 2017; Lutz, Palanga-Möllenbeck 2014). Care migrations are multifaceted, so empirical research on them presents a constant challenge to theory building and existing concepts as the following sub-chapter will demonstrate.

Theories of Transnational Care Inequalities

Theorizing and conceptualizing problems regarding global migration for care work and outsourcing of care work to migrants developed over the years since Arlie Hochschild made a breakthrough with the GCC theory. The amendments were made with a new and growing interest in investigations of the gendered dimensions of globalization and international migration while avoiding the essentialist association of "gender" with "women". By focusing on men, studies that cover a wide range of disciplines (sociology, anthropology, and history) and methodologies (both qualitative and quantitative) contributed by filling the gap and showing how domestic service as a site where "hegemonic" and "subaltern" masculinities are produced and negotiated at the interplay of multiple social relations (Scrinzi, Sarti 2010; Näre 2010; Gallo, Scrinzi 2016). In the last decade, we can observe the emerging research agenda on fatherhood in transnational care migration (Kilkey, Perons, Plomien 2013).

The problem of the "deficit model" of GCC, where migrant mothers are supposed to be caregivers and their children/families are said to stay behind and suffer from a lack of care, ignored virtual communication and various technological advances in telecommunication tools (although many of them were not existent twenty years ago when Hochschild developed the theory) that enable emotional exchange and maintain social relations and intimacy. Further amendments to the theory are made by new concepts.

The concept of care circulation contributes to an analysis of the mobilities of care from the perspective of intra-familial duties and solidarities (Baldassar, Merla 2014). Laura Merla and Loretta Baldassar created the concept to understand how people are "doing family" and maintain a sense of familyhood across distance and time, through the lens of their care practices. They offered a framework that enables researchers to analyse the whole spectrum of transnational families – not only formal and informal migrant care workers, but also refugees, economic migrants, middle class and professional expatriates – regardless of their sector of activity. Their notion of "care circulation" is both a conceptual framework and a methodological lens allowing for "follow the thing" – care – in all its formulations, across distance and over time. Tracing the exchange of informal care in families in this way reveals it to be inherently reciprocal and asymmetrical, governed by cultural understandings and histories. A *care circulation* framework helps to capture all the actors involved in family life as well as the full extent of their care activity, including practical, emotional, and symbolic, that defines their membership in a family. Central to the concept is the importance of distance in transnational families that is mediated by information and communication technologies. *The care circulation concept* highlighted the way new media has impacted the capacity of family members to care across distances by tracing how that care is enacted, performed, and exchanged. As technology has its limits, the concept opened a new room for discussions about care as dis/embodied practice and invites us to re-think the debate about the merits of physical as opposed to virtual communication, focusing on examining their interconnection and how they impact each other.

The care-related transnational social inequality concept through its three dimensions: 1. emotional and care inequality; 2. the absence of adequate social protection; 3. the racialization and gendered naturalization of care work – illuminates the emergence and co-production of social inequalities in and through transnational space. Anna Amelina (2017: 173) identifies cross-border inequalities as the "doing" of spatialized inequalities, but this "doing" is subject to structural restrictions: the availability of care as a desirable commodity at both ends of the caregiving – care receiving nexus becomes a decisive factor in the quality of life and life chances. Its presence on one side implies its (corporal) absence on the other. Therefore, emotional and care inequality is an implicit aspect of transnational caregiving, where the provision of physical care is restricted to the care recipient in the receiving country, while contacts with stay-behind family members are reduced to digital connectivity and temporary visits.

Both the *Care Circulation Concept* and *Theory of Transnational Social Inequality*, as Helma Lutz (2018) concluded by comparing them with GCC theory, are equally important in studying specific cases of care migration within the scope of the global care economy. While these are useful in explaining global flows of domestic and care work, distribution of work and national and international policies, gender, migration and care regimes, they are mostly focused on market economy-based theories and categorizations. Sociological fixed categories of family, parenthood, care and overly focus on them as a start of every study might not be fruitful for anthropological (ethnographic) exploration where gender is, first of all, understood as a relational and fluid concept. This perspective is reflected in an abundance of new publications on migration reviewed so far. Unfortunately, it still needs to be pointed out across different academic disciplines that there is no single, universal model of sexual identities, and no universal model of how people form and think about families, intimate relations and so on. Across different academic disciplines but also in contexts of queer activism and international human rights, we can recognize particular hegemonic models of gender relations, kinship and family (Collier, Fishbourn, Yanagisako 1987; Schneider 1984; Strathern 1992).

Within the vast area of research, domestic and care work, especially in informal markets, is mostly presented and studied as a homogenous category that is rarely differentiated between care for children, care for elderly, disabled people or domestic work (cleaning and cooking), or au-pair arrangements. The main reason for this is that all these jobs fall in the category of work where job tasks are performed by employment terms and conditions, in a living-in arrangement . Migrants who work 24h are more likely to be perceived as "flexible" both in terms of tasks performed that include caring, cleaning and cooking. The second reason is a result of public debate on the professionalization of care work where, as it is in the German case, domestic work or work in a domestic setting is divided between *object-related tasks* (washing, cleaning, ironing, cooking) and *person-related tasks* (care and support services for elderly and children) (Lutz 2011: 7). While this clear-cut differentiation might be useful for institutionalized care work, in the research on the irregular sector of care work I find it futile. As Duga Mavrinac argued, aspects of elderly care, which are both material and emotional, are "underlined by strict everyday regime and rules, imbalance of emotional and the lack of capacity to relate to the elder, as well as challenges which arise from a different definition of care between care workers themselves as well as family members" (Mavrinac 2015: 90). And, if we add to this the diverse channels of recruitment for live-in care work, unsuitable preparation for that work for those who have no experience in elderly care at all, the absence of regulation and organization of work, it is clear that such specific work and those who perform this work deserve our special attention.

Another problem deriving from a research agenda focused on global market-shaping regulation of commodified care sector is (over)emphasising the broad range of vulnerabilities, and varied forms of subordination, exploitation and abuse, associated with live-in paid care and domestic work in households across the globe (Pratt 2012 in Canada; Yeoh, Huang 2010 in Singapore; Constable 2002 in Hong Kong; Lutz 2011 in Germany; Mantouvalou 2015 in the UK, the Gulf states and North Africa; Silvey 2004a, on Saudi Arabia). Many countries exempt domestic and care work in the household from employment protection (Cox 2012; England 2017). Under the pretence of the worker being "one of the family", employers legitimise overlong working hours and constant surveillance (Bakan, Stasiulis 1997; Hess 2004). For many domestic and care workers, the home becomes a place of psychological and physical abuse, where they are forced into servitude, hit and even raped (Yeoh, Huang 2007). While acknowledging the systemic subordination and widespread abuse, scholars nevertheless caution against oversimplified narratives of victimhood (Pratt 2012). However, there is a body of literature on migrant care workers across a range of contexts exercising individual and collective agency, supported not only by labour unions but also by women's, migrant, religious and other non-governmental organisations (for an overview, see Ally 2005; see also England 2017; Lim 2016; Piper 2006; Pratt 2012; Schilliger 2015; Schwenken 2016). Furthermore, live-in workers employ diverse strategies to improve their situations. There are ethnographic examples that problematize established binaries of victimhood, exploitation, and protection by focusing on the multiple ways in which women cope and wrest autonomy within a patriarchal system of both, the sending and receiving countries, thus facilitating a layered and heterogeneous approach to the experience of women's migration (for example, Ally 2009 on South Africa).

Looking at the migrant care workers exclusively from the economic perspective we are at risk to end up with a scholarship that is divided into those who look positively at migration as an opportunity to escape oppressive marriages, gain economic independence by becoming a self-sufficient earner and improve one's social position vis-à-vis the context of origin, and those who apply a negative lens and emphasize aspects like "status paradox" (Nieswand 2011) or "contradictory social mobility" (Parreñas 2001), with that highlighting processes of downgrading by taking low-skilled and stigmatised jobs.

As my research approach suggests, there is the third perspective – to study processes and situations in which women are becoming empowered or disempowered and how the interaction between citizenship, gender, and age permeates the process of labour mobility and the way it creates social injustice. This perspective shifts our attention away from (without denying the importance of it) the emotional experiences of migrants and the often-predictable forms of injustice they face in destination countries, to the brokerage systems and social networks that move them from one place to another. As empirical results from my study show in this book, circular migration and its temporalities are not only dictated by macro-structural factors but also by relations between care labour recruitments and agencies on the one side, and care workers and their mutual relationships on the other. As Helma Lutz rightfully pointed out: "migrant women are not "cultural dopes", acting on the demand of employers and migration regimes. They have their agendas, and their subjectivity needs to be emphasised" (Lutz 2008: 6).

Chapter 2
A Critical Analytical Framework
for the Ethnographic Study of Care Labour
Mobilities

While in the previous chapter I highlighted ambivalences between studies of globalization, migration and gender and global trends in migration linked to social reproduction in this chapter I want to present my analytical framework for a more geographically contextualized study that focuses on a particular pattern of gender labour mobility. To refresh and contribute to existing conceptualizations and understanding of new patterns of gendered labour mobility, I wish to join the cohort of researchers who decentre away from the epicentre of Western understandings of "global care migration" and insist on a fuller understanding of the heterogeneity of labour mobility experiences of both Global North and the Global South. For the last twenty years in the scholarship on gender, labour and migration the binaries such as North/South, internal/international, labour/family, urban/rural divided not only researchers but also a hidden multiplicity of migration flow and patterns, the significance of, for example, South-South flows or, specific cross-border labour mobility in Europe which this book is dedicated to.

As Vered Amit and Nigel Rapport (Amit 2002: 34, 35) pointed out, economic globalization has changed the nature of human mobility and blurred the conventional distinctions between various moving subjects. Increasing homogenization of people on the move and their experiences blur the line between emerging types of researchable entities that arise from global economic and political transformations. This poses a challenge to the widely shared academic consensus for drawing clear analytical and conceptual boundaries between mobile subjects. This book takes up this challenge by showing how labour mobility for care work with a distinctive characteristic creates a specific pattern of gendered mobility for labour, working and living arrangements and specific experiences that transform the lives of live-in elder care workers who commute between the former Yugoslavia countries and German households.

Disciplinary situated in the field of study of labour within European Ethnology and Cultural Anthropology, interdisciplinary approach to mobility studies this book aims to reveal how global neoliberal economies of care have fundamental impacts upon informal care markets between countries. I shift the analytical focus from structures, the state and policies towards the actors of elder care work mobilities – how do they follow, challenge and re-create the rules of the black market of care, "make their way" to find the job, "survive at that job" and when it is done to find another one. More specifically, the central concern of this book is the processual character of spatial multilocal labour mobilities – capacity for mobility. The focus is thus on the potential for labour mobility and the ways this potential is built taking into account a variety of geographical, political, social, and cultural contexts in the former Yugoslavia countries. To explain the nature of care labour mobilities in a specific geopolitical context the research questions that will lead chapters through the book are: In what ways changing demographics, regimes of mobility, geopolitical boundaries and diverse cultural practices and values affect those who provide elder care across national borders? How do care workers adapt to or/and challenge the new forms of commodified care across the borders? What are new examples of care work that have emerged, and under what conditions? To what extent these mobilities are life-shaping, life-changing for my respondents? In what way they are meaningful to them? How do women care workers from my study envision and use their potential for mobility under specific geographical, political, and socio-cultural conditions? By analysing narratives and ethnographic case studies, I provide deep insight into the personal experiences of elder care workers, their commuting for care work, which presents a specific pattern of mobilities that induces specific cultural practices and social relations. My wish is to present multiple ways in which such gendered labour mobility transforms the life of subjects while examining the dialectical relationship between mobility and immobility. Ethnography of gendered mobility for care in this book pays attention to the relations between different experiences, events, imaginations in the lives of women care workers in the continuum from the moment before mobility for work, through a period of mobility until movement is over, and when the new movement starts. It provides an analysis of how the inequalities in the care labour mobility are reproduced through labour markets, migration laws, and relationships with brokers, intermediaries, care receivers and their families – and the ways socially, geographically and politically contextualised immobility and mobility play out in reproduction of these inequalities. In addition, the book introduces a new analytical framework that will support above listed research questions and allow for a deeper understanding of interrelations between the social and cultural organization of elder care work and cross-border labour mobility within mobility regimes.

Whilst, as we could have seen in the previous chapter, the "global" view on gender, migration and commodification of care and domestic work underly structural economic and political conditions, the task of this book is to zoom into specific local responses to global trends of gendered labour mobilities. Most of the work on transnational and global spaces of care draws on national policy analysis whereas prevails international overseas patterns of migration as research starting point. There has been a huge step forward from rational choice theories and structuralist approaches towards more integrative explanations of migration, focusing on the mediation between the individual migrant and the global economy through social networks, households (Boyd 1989), migrant institutions (Goss, Lindquist 1995) thus opening a space for taking into account social and cultural context and social forces along with the economic ones. Yet, there is not enough ethnographic research in the gendered realm of informal (undeclared) paid care work which shifts the focus from the structural context of migration to the practices of the social agents, asking how structures are negotiated and altered by care workers, hence giving recognition to the transformative power of care work in the global political economy. One of the challenges of researching care work and mobility and migration is exploring both global and local im/ mobilities and how they are interlinked.

Both, Robertson's notion of "glocalization" (1995) and Burawoy's notion of "global ethnography" (2000) invited us to think and perceive globalization not only as a large-scale macro-sociological process but as something which itself is always localized while the local is constantly shaped and reshaped by global. This fundamental methodological challenge in research on gender and migration for domestic and care work was taken up by numerous studies in European scholarship, focused on migrant domestic and care workers in an unregulated, "black" labour market in German "global cities" like Munich, Berlin and Hamburg (for example, see Lutz 2011). The results of most of the similar studies to the one presented in this book show that women, migrant domestic workers share almost the same characteristics: they are live-out or live-in domestic and care workers in an informal sector; within their country of origin they belong to the middle class and, they come from financially weaker countries, some of them are educated to the same level as their employers and that most of them are mothers who had to leave their children behind to earn money for their well-being and education. While one could recognize similarities with the characteristics of ethnographic case studies presented in this book, some complexities arise from different geographical spaces, possibilities and nodes of gendered labour subjectivities in contemporary societies where increasingly changing mobility patterns significantly affects and challenges lifeworlds, discourses, norms and behaviours.

It can be observed that in the growing corpus of academic research on the transnational migration for care and domestic work, most of the attention has been paid to the plight of women in destination countries, as well as their relationships with family members, particularly children who remain behind. The majority of mentioned literature focuses on "women from poorer countries" who provide paid long-term care in wealthier countries, while their care obligations at home are redirected to another (migrant) paid woman. Surely, we cannot automatically assume, for instance, that all care workers are mothers or that they are bounded by care responsibilities in their families, that they don't have education in care or professional skills, or that predominantly move for the care labour abroad out of hardship or poverty, or that they are young or middle-aged. As results of my intensive ethnographic research show in the case of the former-Yugoslavia countries, this scenario cannot be found. My research respondents are women in their fifties or sixties years of age, mostly divorced or separated, with children who are grown-up and do not need parental care, women who have different working biographies from those who have never been employed, who want to commute between two countries and have no wish to migrate and settle in Germany. In addition to this, my material shows the other specificities of this new pattern of mobility for care work and its actors:

a) care workers are commuting between Germany and their homes in the frame of the rotational system on the three months tourist visa;
b) rotational system means that there are two (or more) care workers replacing each other on a four-weekly, five-weekly or monthly basis;
c) the length of weekly or monthly shifts and transport is mainly regulated by brokers or agencies who operate in the informal market of care between ex-Yugoslavia countries and Germany;
d) women are most likely to be employed in rural areas (small towns, villages) or on the outskirts of big cities;
e) most of them are fifty years of age or older and come from rural areas;

A CRITICAL ANALYTICAL FRAMEWORK

f) they work in a live-in arrangement, seven days inraa week, twenty-four-hour care for elderly people in private households;
g) majority of women do not have (or do have very limited) knowledge of the German language before taking a job.

The problem with most of the studies is the homogenization of actors, caused by a rigid methodological and analytical framework that does not allow researchers to look at how the care work environment is built, how it enables care workers to develop and to expand their capabilities as individuals and professionals. As my interviews show in this book, care work does not necessarily mean "draining of emotions, energy, health or love" (which are, to a certain extent, consequences of performing care work as a very demanding occupation), but it also brings the gains in terms of income, self-trust and confidence, social and cultural capital and sometimes freedom from restrictive gender norms. It is not always a matter of subordination, inequalities, freedom limitations or precarious position. On the contrary, it may create new forms of interaction, liberty and solidarity and new forms of aggregation and mobilization. New spaces and avenues for agency evolve, channels for autonomy, mutual trust (or distrust) and networking; innovative ways of interacting with people in Germany, with other women, colleagues who do the same work, institutions and informal structures. Therefore, we encounter a "status enrichment" (rather than "status paradox") of actors involved in the care and domestic labour migration; different patterns of mobility (long term migration, circular migration or commuting between home and work on a weekly basis); different level of education; with a plurality of motives for taking a job in care work sector in specific geopolitical context and under different conditions.

To bring to the light highly diversified responses to the structural conditions that create demand for care jobs with distinctive characteristics listed above, requires multiple analytic frameworks, adjusted methodological approaches and theoretical concepts. Therefore, in the sub-chapters that follow I provide an analytical framework that is foregrounded by four key approaches: multi-level analysis, intersectional approach, border regime approach and more processual approach to mobility studies while acknowledging the need to further develop the understanding of cross border elder care mobility as a distinctive form of care labour mobility in terms of its complexities, inequalities, temporalities, and power relations. This approach will contribute to questioning and reshaping some of the "debates at the core" on migration, gender and care scholarship.

2.1 Peripheral Labour Mobilities

What exactly are "peripheral labour mobilities"? What does "peripheral" refer to? These are the first questions that come to readers' minds when they see the book title. Rather than a theoretical or analytical concept, *peripheral labour mobilities* are constructed as a heuristic tool or more precisely as an analytical prism, that enables comparative research on particularities of different cases and structural inequalities among different mobile subjects and their responses in politically, economically and socially globalized world regardless of the geography frame. It also speaks for the knowledge that is often "peripheral" because it is based on research on those mobile subjects who blur the lines between mobility and migration induced by the policy frameworks or state regimes of mobility control and citizenship. "Peripheral" refers to the geopolitical position of the countries in the Global South and at the periphery where the knowledge is produced. Also, it suggests multiple local settings that lie outside the global "core" that is socially, culturally, and economically marginalized areas. Secondly, it refers to epistemological localities and inequality in the production and dissemination of knowledge in the global South and Global north. Thus, we have two distinctive criteria for "peripherality". One is the relevance of epistemological South or epistemology from the "periphery" in the global knowledge market that invites the problematization of "power-knowledge" privileged by the epistemologies of the North. The second is terminological rigidness that mirrors concepts and theories that do not adapt to increasingly complex changes due to the intensification of global connectedness, a proliferation of global media, improved transport systems and the internationalization of business and labour markets. Now, let's see how the lens of peripheral labour mobilities works in the context of the production of knowledge on contemporary elder care labour mobilities between former Yugoslavian societies and Germany.

For the start, I prefer to use the term "semiperiphery" for former Yugoslavia because of its geopolitical distinctiveness as "transitional countries at the semiperiphery of Europe, former communist countries which are in different stages of the process of the European Union enlargement, although in many ways different between themselves, are also very deeply embedded in their semiperipheral position of the global market and global knowledge production" (Blagojević 2009: 67). As this ethnographic study of care cross-border labour mobilities from the former Yugoslavia countries to Germany is the first study, undertaken by the person from "the semiperiphery" and produced in the North, it would be useful to interrogate the reasons why the production of knowledge on gender and migration is, practically, non-existent in the semiperiphery and what are the consequences of that. One of the consequences is that often in the literature on gender, care and migration/mobility, we can find theories and concepts created in the Global North that are often imported and in an unproblematized and uncritical way applied to the local examples reducing the world to a unidimensional place. Moreover, such applications overlook the plurality of migration and other kinds of human movements, diverse cultural understandings, and the conceptualizations that these movements produce in wide political, social, and economic contexts. In this book I am concerned with how the semiperiphery works by itself, its autonomy, agency, and capacity to change. As argued in the previous chapter even the theory of gender and migration focus on the commodification of care labour through migration can be analytically poor and reduces actors of migration to losers, without any agency. This book joins those who think that there is no global justice without cognitive justice. The profound inequalities and discrimination that characterised contemporary societies, in general, cannot be fought without epistemic, political, and methodological tools, and ecologies of knowledge.

Over the past 15 years a considerable amount of literature (which is not possible to list here without doing injustice to many authors) has been published on domestic work and care work in Germany: Hess, Lenz 2001; Hess 2005; Rerrich 2002; Geissler 2006; Lutz 2008, 2010, 2011, 2017; Kyoko Shinozaki 2003, 2015; Metz-Göckel 2008, 2010; Karakayali 2010; Kontos 2013; Gutierrez Rodriguez 2007, 2010; Roig 2014; Karina Becker 2016; Ewa Palenga Möllenbeck 2011, 2013, 2014; Helen Schwenken 2011a, 2011b, 2016; Ursula Aptiscz 2010; Tine Haubner 2014; Gabriele Winker 2015 and many others. Little is yet known about the way experiences of domestic and care workers from the former Yugoslavian countries in Germany. Research into the dynamics and structuring effects of gender as well as other dimensions of diversity (e. g. ethnicity, citizenship, religion) in the context of post-Yugoslavian migration, that is after 2000. for domestic and care work is generally lacking – with only a few exceptions from Croatia and Slovenia (for instance, see Loncar 2013; Hrzenjak 2014). There is still a significant gap in the literature on gendered migration and a lack of empirical descriptive work on the gender composition of historical migration flows, leaving this aspect of migration as under-researched. How can we explain this discrepancy in intensity and volume of production of knowledge between former Yugoslavian and German scientific research?

Numerous studies coming from former-Yugoslavian scholars have attempted to explain the process of acculturation in Germany, analysing the life stories of guest-workers *(Gastarbeiter)* from the former Yugoslavia with a focus on the reasons why workers decided to return to their home country, or on historical studies of labour migration in the (post-)Yugoslav region. The gendered aspect of women in migration processes (still) remains almost unaddressed in these studies. Rather, women are usually treated as secondary migrants who migrate as part of a family-level strategy for survival and not as individual and independent agents.

Notwithstanding very vivid and inspiring discussions among scholars of gender, migration, and globalization "at the core", scholarship in the same field in the former Yugoslavia can be criticized as "gender-blind" for failing to acknowledge the gender selectiveness of migration processes, neglecting gender-specific types of mobilities, a lack of empirical descriptive work on the gender composition of historical migration flows, leaving this aspect of migration significantly under-researched. Despite the developed feminist-oriented scholarship in the former Yugoslavia academic landscape, women were not recognized as autonomous actors of migration. This situation is attributed to unfavourable material conditions for performing a scientific activity, as well as the general weakness of the feminist community in the social sciences, slow development of migration studies and insufficient academic institutionalization.

Generally, the scientific production of knowledge on migrations in the former Yugoslavia countries is characterised by the slow development of the systematic study of this phenomenon, which is a consequence of its semi-peripheral position in the global (academic) system. The academic situation in the home country of migrants, the lack of resources, and the conservatism of the scientific community are very important determinants for the acceptance and usage of new findings, mainly coming from the "developed" countries. On the other hand, as Marina Blagojević (2009: 39) pointed out, the semi-periphery cannot simply rely on theoretical frameworks created in "the core countries" and just "add-in" local examples: it would be unreasonable to claim that knowledge created in "the core" would "cover" the realities of the semi-periphery. Similarly, the semi-periphery's rejection of new knowledge produced in the core, nor its implementation without critical review itself, cannot be considered heuristically fruitful. With this being said, we can differentiate a twofold academic field of migration studies: the core, with its theoretical, methodological, epistemological and empirical discoveries, and the semi-periphery, lagging behind, being forced to copy and apply the paradigms built in the countries of the core. However, the situation is slightly more complicated than this.

In their analysis of contemporary studies on migration in Serbia (one of the former Yugoslavia countries) Tanja Višić and Dunja Poleti (2018) concluded that the political and social context dictated migration mainstream research. In the former Yugoslavia, trends in international migration followed the typical pattern of European labour force movements at the time because of the bilateral agreement between Yugoslavia and Germany on the "*Gastarbeiter* labour migration scheme". During the 1970s and 1980s men were seen as the central actors of migration – they were the ones who had moved to Western Europe to be followed by wives and families. In the 1990s patterns and forms of migration transformed, due to the Yugoslavian wars into mainly refugee and asylum patterns. In the period after 2000, and especially after the visa liberalisation regime which began in 2009, migrant flows become more diversified by their temporalities (business, studying, skilled migration and family reunion), as well as by heterogeneous gender patterns. Some of the studies about these movements were focused on measuring the economic effects, whereas others have attempted to explain the process of acculturation in Western European countries from an anthropological perspective. Studies focused on migration from 1990 onwards have shown a growing interest in female migrants but without recognition of their agency and independence in migration flows. Gender approaches to migrations in Serbia remain rather scarce. Except for occasional publications the female experience, the contribution is given by women in the migration processes, as well as their influence on these processes, are completely left out. In almost all research, gender is defined through binary categories in which women are defined versus men.

The other problems that Višić and Poleti identified are methodological approaches and disciplinary orientations. According to them, a significant number of studies in Serbia showed overwhelmingly positivistic quantitative approaches within economics, demographic, geographic or sociological fields of research (Višić, Poleti 2018: 268). Moreover, the dominant, quantitative methodological approaches cannot adequately grasp all forms of female mobilities. Namely, the unavailability of comprehensive statistics that would give correct data on the number of women has partially been caused by the impossibility of recording labour migrations in the informal undeclared labour market (ibid.). Empirical research forms the basis for offering insights into the paths and mechanisms that lead to migration, its ways of realization and the effects of migration on women, their families and the community. In the academic centres in the Former Yugoslavia countries, very little has been done to deepen the understanding of women's migration, especially to explain undocumented and circular forms of mobility.

One of the biggest problems with quantitative approaches is that most surveys underestimate the undocumented population as well as those entering countries in an irregular manner, without work permits. To improve our understanding of gender and migration, qualitative research in mobility and migration studies over multiple locations (so-called "multi-sited research") must be a salient methodological approach. Only this, can bring together the core and the semiperiphery and creates *contextualized knowledge* (Blagojević 2009: 193) that is not based on generalizations but moves beyond one paradigm while theorizing upon the context, and it does not simply contextualize the theory (ibid). Yet, to carry out such research projects applying mixed qualitative and quantitative methods could prove financially and time demanding and weaken the willingness of those who fund such projects. In the former Yugoslavia and, especially after the dissolution of Yugoslavia followed by the wars, academia faced serious financial limitations at universities and research institutions. The new financiers become international institutions, non-governmental organizations, or certain states interested in the region. An outcome of this is studies and research projects written at the request of these funding bodies which usually match their political and ideological agendas.

Mobility for care work between the former Yugoslavia and Germany challenges the widely shared consensus for drawing clear analytical and conceptual boundaries between the mobile subjects from the Global North and Global South. The problem of overlooking gendered labour mobility either on the periphery or in the core, lays in different understandings and theorizations of who migrants are and the different ways in which policymakers, state, non-governmental sectors define and classify migration and mobility – the topic crucial for defining peripheral labour mobilities in this book. The obstacle I come across that hinders delving deeper into the cultural logics of contemporary mobile work-lives is a contemporary analytical language of migration and mobility studies that lacks an appropriate analytic term for labour mobilities like cross-border mobility for care work.

Justification for preferring to use the term "mobility" or "labour mobility" over the term "migration", "migrants" or "labour migration" calls for answering the question: what does the concept of "mobility" mean in relation to the definition of the term "migrant"? As Bridget Anderson points out: "(…) the figure of the migrant is first and foremost constructed by the state, and while this does not mean that the desire to move is simply the result of the state or capitalism, how much movement is shaped and controlled – its channelling and endless categorisation, is in part a manifestation of state relations to both capital and labour" (Anderson, 2009: 408). The category of "migrant" is a direct result of sovereign nation-states and the legal frameworks that emerge within them. Moreover, who counts as a migrant is produced by the legal mechanisms of the regime of mobility control and citizenship legislation. However, "the migrant" is not simply shaped through legal mechanisms and the state, but also through the practices and discourses of an array of other bodies and agents – from NGOs, the media, trade unions and academics, as well as individuals (both citizens and non-citizens). Thus, the term is loaded with a political connotation that does not allow me to capture the processual character of human mobility which is defining facet of what I define as "mobility" for the analysis of elder care labour mobility. In highlighting the term "mobility" and its processual character, I aim at two goals. The first is to affirm the importance of practices and strategies through which mobility is maintained. Secondly, I foreground the crucial role that controls over mobility play in creating the living and working conditions that individuals subject to them must negotiate to sustain their mobile trajectories. Referring to "mobility", "being mobile", "being on the move for work", "labour mobility", I refer to mobile populations, people on the move who are subject to the mechanisms of mobility control and who do not receive any lessened restrictions on their mobility due to, for instance, material wealth, or citizenship status. Also, they are not forced to move, but they are not free to stay put. The people I am concerned with within this book are those whose mobility is very much entangled with labour and who fall within a broad "global working class". Characteristics of labour mobilities in my study are the movements are unstable; they occur along loosely defined trajectories; there is a dynamic between stillness and movement; the subjects are in a constant process of negotiation with the state bureaucracies, border regimes and networks they move within in; mobility for labour is not entirely voluntary nor entirely forced; social worlds are marked by life and work between two (or more places) and liminality. Ethnographic and anthropological research on such mobilities in comparison to the mobility of the independently wealthy, or the broader capitalist class has been heavily neglected. This is not to say that such "elite" forms of mobility are not in themselves important or worthy of scholarly attention, but rather the vast majority of the short-term labour migration experiences continue to be those of relatively privileged population.

In the national, supranational and international regimes of mobility and scenarios of development, certain forms of mobilities are characterized by being legal, privileged, and even desired – such as tourism and leisure mobilities (Rickly, Hannam, Mostafanezhad 2017), academic mobility of scientists (Scheibelhofer 2010), retirement migration, for example of German retirees in Hungary (Szöke 2006), and in Turkey (Karacan 2020), the movement of skilled professionals (Kesselring 2006), "lifestyle migration" (Benson, O'Reilly 2009), etc. On the other hand, forms of human mobilities such as smuggling, nomadism, short labour migration in the construction sector, sector of sex work and service sectors haven't gotten such prominent attention. As being marginalised, they simply remain hardly visible in schemes of affluent mobile population and are perceived as "illegal" or "irregular". Each of the selected ethnographic cases in this book overlaps significantly with recognised forms of mobilities such as circular migration, lifestyle migration, shuttle mobility, etc. However, I argue that numerous criteria allow me to speak about them as representatives of distinctive types of contemporary mobilities, which are characterized by peripatetic economic strategy, marginality, and inventiveness. The challenge in my dissertation is to show the ethnographic diversity of experiences of elder care labour mobility.

Transnational studies, thoroughly discussed in Chapter 1, are focused on various forms of interactions and communication that link both people and institutions across the borders of nation-states in increasingly globalized ways (Basch, Glick Schiller, Szanton Blanc 1992; Portes, Guarnizo, Landolt 1999; Smith, Guarnizo 1998). A focus on transnational processes and phenomena has enabled anthropologists to understand complex social and cultural processes that reach beyond spatially bounded communities and strictly spatialized referents of social identification. While transnational ethnography has profoundly contributed to the understanding of how mobility shapes people's lives, the careful cross-cultural analysis of the contemporary forms of highly mobile lives in short-term movements is less common in anthropology. Very often migration for domestic and care work, especially in the long-term migration flows are labelled as transnational. Such accounts do not challenge the paradigm of distinguishing between mobilities from the Global North and South, which fixes the identities of contemporary mobile subjects into unchangeable, static, culturally bounded and petrified figures. While there is a large body of migration and transnationalism studies that explore such cases, they hardly ever deal with the process of mobility itself.

The first studies on gendered mobilities in Europe and focus on women and men as "social innovators" began with the research of Mirjana Morokvasic (2006) on post-wall European mobilities. Thus, the research focus was redirected to a short-term migration (or a transborder migration) as a "social innovation" and potential for the social impact of mobility that brought new chances and life opportunities (Morokvasic 2006: 2). The redrawing of the European map in the aftermath of the events of 1989 and the collapse of the communist regimes triggered unprecedented mobility of persons and heralded a new phase in European migrations. It is not only that a new pattern of movements become a new opportunity and "social capital" but it also changed the directions of migratory flows – circulation of East Europeans, citizens of Rumania, Poland, Moldova, Ukraine to Southern Europe – which in turn challenged old perceptions of migration as East-to-West and South-to-North. As Morokvasic showed, the opening of borders introduced new highly diversified patterns of mobility: refugees, "repatriates", shuttle/commuter migrants, and undocumented and trafficked migrants as some the categories. She opened the space for further research that can illuminate how crossing borders after 1989 not only represents a realized dream but can also yield an opportunity for a better life at home, that is, no longer necessarily on the other side of the border. This was very important for perceiving human movements not solely as a physical move through space, but also an emotional and cognitive one. As stated by Papastergiadis (2000: 11), "movement is not just the experience of shifting from place to place; it is also linked to our ability to imagine an alternative".

Another dimension that became visible in research in East and Central European countries in the post-wall period are dual and multiple citizenships as facilitators as well as outcomes of transnational movements and transnational belonging. This trait of short-term movements very much reminds us of the contemporary dynamic of citizenship in former Yugoslavia countries which largely facilitate care work mobility to Germany. Being, for instance, German in the Schengen space while remaining Russian in Russia, is the same as being today Serbian with Hungarian citizenship living in Serbia and going to Germany to perform care work with no tourist-visa limitations.

Also, we can observe a similar pattern as the contemporary one that is my research focus in this book – the "self-managed" rotation system set up by migrant women domestic and care workers in Germany. Performing domestic and care work in these sectors, women from Eastern Europe nevertheless, as Morokvasic argued, innovated the organization of their work and private life transnationally, as the rotation system enabled women a transnational double presence that combines life here and there.

Change of the borders and post-socialist transition created new connections, circulation of ideas, people, goods and services between EU and non-EU countries. Although the pattern of mobility for care work and especially its "rotational" feature shares a lot with the one in former Yugoslavian republics, it is worth looking after three decades how new actors respond to the opening of borders, their aspirations, their cultural interpretations of border crossings, and their mobility strategies. My field observations suggest that new technologies and increasing communications affordances enable faster connections across geographical distances – women engaged in labour mobilities for care work today easier connect with their homes but also with other women, their colleagues – and that their connectivity induces, maintaining face-to-face interaction and make labour mobility possible.

The particular live-in care work arrangements allow a biweekly or monthly alteration between care work in Germany and staying in the country. Together with the earnings perspective (attractive salary), a combination of working abroad and living in the home country cut down extra expenses for a second household. This cost-saving constellation works as one of the main motives for women care workers to take on such a care job in Germany. But not the only one. The cultural and social dimensions of their decisions to put themselves on the move for elder care work in Germany is result of the impossibility to relocate the centre of life to Germany which enhances the circularity as they keep their personal lives in their home countries. Either they "muddle through" periods of unemployment until they obtain their pensions or they work and use several income making strategies while on the move, these women are building a *life in-between*. An umbrella term that the case of mobile labourers from my study should fit in is – *circular migration.* The term stems from the EU policymakers concerned with a labour market shortage in the EU who fabricated the idea of *circular labour mobility* in 2007 as a solution to the problem of integration challenges. This political idea of circular migration schemas could not have lasted long due to the global recession that started in 2008. Since than circular migration as a scholarly term has been a topic in academic literature mainly focused on critical assessment of the assumptions of policy makers, the development and benefits of circular migration (Wickramasekara 2011) and its realities presented by empirically driven scholars (Triandafyllidou 2013). Although some researchers label care migration as a "circular migration" (Vianello 2008) I find it problematic because limits possibilities of research sensitiveness to inequality, deeper ethnographic understanding of short mobility practices and strong orientation toward quantitative methodologies.

I argue that the phenomenon of elder care labour mobility across transnational state unregulated care markets demands a new theoretical and analytical reflection from migration and mobility studies – conceptualized as peripheral labour mobility. However, I do not suggest a strict and all-encompassing definition that refers to a "periphery" as a structuralist understanding of global dependencies or simply as a geopolitical term. I conceptualize it rather as an analytical umbrella that opens new possibilities for understanding contemporary mobilities that remain largely unaddressed in the academic discourses. Labelling the phenomenon as *peripheral labour mobilities*, I hope to provide a new lens, not only for the labour mobility as the subject of this book but for wider spectrum of labour mobilities freed from policymakers' established frameworks, with a strong ethnographic methodological approach that can reveal external forces and respond to these forces from, as this book demonstrates, legally and politically marginalized mobile labourers whose movements are often vulnerable and unpredictable. In addition, I propose *peripheral labour mobilities* as an impetus for innovative ethnographic approaches to labour and mobility, sensitive to ideologies of mobilities, processes and conditions of inclusion and exclusion. Such an approach allows for exploring how labour mobility helps to create and perpetuate conditions of discrimination and differentiation in regards not only to gender but also citizenship, nationality, race, religion, ethnicity, ability, etc. I develop a framework for studying *care labour mobilities* that insist on the meaning of interpretation of movements not only as *de facto* changes of geographical space movement but also as those who produce, mediate knowledge and push the limits of cultural norms across the borders which inevitably calls for further closer examination of "potential" or ability for labour mobility – the central analytical tool in my dissertation that will be discussed in-depth in the next sub-chapters.

2.2 Entanglements of Mobility, Immobility, and Cross-Border Care Work

As I do research and write about the mobile lives of elder care worker commuters between two countries in this book, that inevitably requires situating my analytical framework within this broad field of mobility studies. Reflecting on almost more than two decades of theoretical re-positioning and empirical research in the wide field of studying human mobilities and theoretical program *new mobilities paradigm* and *critical mobilities research*, I want to present my choice of analytical glasses I chose from the field. Given the rise of contemporary "mobilities studies" that regarded mobility as an "all-inclusive" analytical category, and then followed by a critique of this perspective, it seems necessary to re-visit and assess the theoretical and analytical standpoints that guided me to create my analytical framework to provide a more nuanced understanding of the world of cross-border mobile care workers. In doing so, I start with the focus on several important questions that arose from various authors and perspectives merged in several lines of analytical inquiries: 1. How do certain dominant social theories influence analytical dynamics and tension between stasis and movement, sedentarism and nomadism? 2. Why despite its "all-inclusive" architecture in mobility studies, certain forms of human mobility are side-lined? 3. What are the solutions for overcoming divided academic discourses on the value of mobility?

Scientific discourse in social theory on how people move, why do they move, how fast, how long and what meaning of that movement is produced, has been for a long time considered as two opposite poles of two meta-narratives: human stasis and human movement.

"Sedentary metanarratives" presume the "rootedness of people" as the natural and desirable state (Malkki 1992: 31). Many strands of social theory, particularly functionalist and neoclassical perspectives, present equilibrium and stasis as the default state of people and social systems (Massey 1993; Sheller, Urry 2006; De Haas 2010). From this perspective, immobility is normal, and migration is the "aberration" requiring explanation and investigation. As a result, migration researchers often assign stayers/not movers to the margins of social analysis and take their settled lives for granted.

To counter sedentary perspectives in the social sciences, a novel strand of theory and research, called the "mobility turn" in the social sciences, introduced a way of seeing the world that put mobility and flux at the centre (Urry 2000; Sheller, Urry 2006). Although this perspective recognized that

A CRITICAL ANALYTICAL FRAMEWORK 73

mobility requires "moorings" (Urry 2003; Adey 2006), the research agenda became focused on developing a "nomadic metaphysics" and "mobile methods" that tended to replace *one positively loaded pole, sedentarism … by its opposite, nomadism"* (Faist 2013: 1644). The "new mobility paradigm" incorporates new ways of theorizing how people, objects, and ideas move around, particularly by examining social phenomena through the lens of movement (Hannam, Sheller, Urry 2006). This transdisciplinary field of mobilities research encompasses research on the spatial mobility of humans, nonhumans and objects; the circulation of information, images and capital, as well as the study of the physical means for movement such as infrastructures, vehicles and software systems that enable travel and communication to take place. It focused on a wide range of individuals who circled the globe whether they were seeking refuge or were students, consultants, volunteers, tourists, labour or return migrants – they all came to be studied through the same analytical lens (Frändberg 2008; Lindquist 2009; Salazar 2011a; Urry 2000). As research on tourism, exchange students, retirement, labour contracting and forms of professional work-related travel developed, scholars questioned the division between categories such as international migrants and temporary travellers (Bell, Ward 2000; Hall, Williams 2002; Kesselring 2006; King, Ruiz-Gelices 2003; Nowicka 2007; Nyıri 2010). Some writers began to insist that all forms of movement, from walking across the room to the flowing of water downstream, be addressed within the same "new mobilities" research paradigm (Hannam et al. 2006; Sheller, Urry 2006; Urry 2007). Researchers' focus on practices like walking, running, dancing, driving and flying; spaces like roads and airports; and subjects like commuters, tourists and refugees, marked "mothe bilitycus turn" as a shift of the social sciences in response to the increasing importance of various forms of movement (Urry 2000, 2007). Mobilities research thus encompasses not only corporeal travel of people and the physical movement of objects, but also imaginative travel, virtual travel and communicative travel (Urry 2007), enabling and coercing (some) people to live more "mobile lives" (Elliott, Urry 2010).

Imperative of Mobility

Influential theorists such as Anthony Giddens, Arjun Appadurai, Ulrich Beck, Manuel Castells, Bruno Latour, David Harvey, Zygmunt Bauman, and John Urry all conceive contemporary capitalism and globalization in terms of increasing volumes and varieties of mobility: the fluid, continuous (and often seamless) movement of people, ideas, and goods through and across space. Academic discourses of mobility explicitly privileged the notion of movement and process rather than stability and fixity pointing out that identities and socio-cultural relations are not produced from their fixed relationships to the territory. Thus, the grand narratives of hypermobility, flux, and fluidity associated with modernity and progress imagined movement and mobility flows as a novelty, an exception. The result was a divorce of a new theoretical and analytical perspective from classical social theories that perceived social relationships as territorially based and the human population as a fixed territorialised social fact (for example, Emil Durkheim 1982). Beck (2002) puts aside "methodological nationalism" and argues for a "cosmopolitan sociology" adequate to phenomena like networks, "scapes" and flows beyond the nation-state and its structurations. A new terminology with notions like "(socio)spheres", "scapes" (Appadurai 1996; Urry 2000), transnational social spaces (Pries 1998), connectivity (Tomlinson 1999), interconnectedness, liquidity (Bauman 2000), fluids (Mol, Law 1994) and mobility (Urry 2000) indicate another perception of society and its structures as mobile, transitory, transformative, and liquid.

The interconnection between mobility and modernity arises from the idea that late modernity is closely connected to and dependent on mobility in that they encourage each other in a reciprocal process (Harvey 1989; Giddens 1994; Urry 2000; Beckmann 2000; Kaufman 2002; Kesselring, Vogel 2004) because modernity both demands and facilitates mobility. Mobility is an essential part of nearly all lifestyles (Giddens 1991; Thrift 1996; Baumann 2000; Urry 2000). Bauman (1998), for example, argued that the ability to migrate has become a coveted and powerful stratifying factor in contemporary society. Mobility is a requirement – the more mobile the individual is, the more possibilities are available. Important in this context is that mobility is becoming the vital link between these elements of a lifestyle, making it impossible to exclude some and include others, and to bridge the distance between different lifestyles (Urry 2000). Choosing a lifestyle gives the individual a continuing sense of ontological security while containing a certain unity that connects the large number of options that appear in our everyday life (Giddens 1991). In this modernistic project, the individual was seen as no longer restrained by tradition, place, social relationships, and activities; the modern individual has developed a need to seek out new and different social interactions. Late modern life is thereby marked by provisionality (Bauman

2000), to be mobile becomes important. Led by mentioned ideas, the researchers were striving for a deeper understanding of the social dynamics of an era described as *reflexive modernity* where security and reliance increasingly dissolve (Beck, Bonß 2003; also Bauman 2007).

The ideas of the school of theories of mobilities, theories of reflexive modernity and liquid modernity aspired numerous research projects on "mobility pioneers", highly mobile members of European Western societies and their strategies used to navigate and manage their lives under conditions of uncertainty and condensation of time and space in the time of globalization. Connecting mobility with freedom, researchers were on the task to show how "modern actors" adapt themselves to the imperative of mobility by developing new forms of mobility management facilitated by technological change, especially in the realm of media and communication. A very good example is Kesselring's (Kesselring 2006) empirical research within the project "Pioneers of mobility". The paradigmatic case of Kesselrings' mobility pioneer is Wolfgang, a German freelance journalist, unmarried, with no children who was a successful editor and department manager in the business-news section of a major radio and television station before becoming a freelance journalist.

"He established residence on one of the Balearic Islands but retained his small flat in Germany as a 'base camp'. Today it is his starting point for expeditions into his new life as a self-employed person. Wolfgang spends his time moving between the Balearic Islands, Germany, Italy, and, more and more, the United States and Russia. From his base in a middle-sized German city, he manages his seminars and makes journalistic investigations; an Italian enclave is his favourite location for recreation and Buddhist exercises. During the last few years, he has become acquainted with places and people all over the world. Wolfgang's experience represents a multiplex network of places, people, ideas, and cultures. He is a frequent flyer and does not possess a car. (…) Virtual networks are part of his motility and enable him to spend much of his time on the Balearic Islands. These networks function as a resource for his worldwide presence without being physically present. Technologies such as the Internet, e-mail, and mobile telephones permit him to be away and still be accessible." (Kesselring 2006: 272–273)

According to Kesselring, the Wolfgang case exemplifies a decentred pattern of "mobility management". Mobility management according to Kesselring is the way an individual overcomes mobility constraints. Whilst Kesselring defines mobility as "an actor's competence to realize specific projects and plans while on the move "(Bonss, Kesselring 2001), he leaves the space for the critical re-examination of the "autonomy of modern subjects and their capacity to use physical movement as a tool for creativity and self-fulfilment" through empirical research (Kesselring 2006: 270). In addition, author asserts that "mobility pioneers" dictate their own movements and activate their potential for mobility in their own best interest. Kesselring here evokes the figure of the modern and skilled worker that German industrial sociologists have conceived as the "entrepreneur of his labour" (Voss, Pongratz 1998). According to this perspective, people of this type view themselves as actors who manage their situations to exploit economic and social opportunities and avoid risks. In the same vein, Wolfgang manages to find a new way how to be mobile and to realize social belonging without being bound to a place, thus resisting the modern pressure to travel and to be physically present. What is important for the further discussion on mobility and its counter-strategies is that Wolfgang's case illustrates a possibility of decoupling spatial and social mobility – being able to interact beyond time and space and discover ways to be connected without meeting. Mobility pioneers such as Wolfgang need to be continuously in contact with others. They reinvent themselves in complex social, material, and technological environments and networks using connectivity spaces, global transfer spots (such as airports, major railway stations and global cities) as resources of creativity and power. This cosmopolitan figure central to the cosmopolitan theory of modern societies (Beck 2000; Vertovec, Cohen 2002) uses the social and technological competencies and skills needed to manage complex networks with numerous opportunities and risks and to be worldwide present and at the same time reduce physical movement. Kesselring's analysis of this type has one important insight for the analysis of "cosmopolitan mobilities" – challenging the "mobility bias" of the modernistic imperative to be mobile by – having the freedom to refuse to be on the move.

In contrast to Kesselring's well paid and hypermobile freelance journalist supported by institutional settings that provide infrastructure for professional spatial mobility with knowledge and skills for using technological systems of communications and networks, there is another type of "mobility pioneer" – Polish domestic worker illegally employed in Berlin households. As a part of the same project "Pioneers of mobility", Norbert Cyrus (2008) carried out research among Polish domestic workers who commute between Berlin and their Polish towns with a frequency ranging from every weekend to every three months. Cyrus attempted to find out how these women place themselves in an ambiguous relationship with Berlin and Polish towns of origin and how such a multi-local lifestyle helps them to establish and maintain security and predictability in their lives. His findings are framed in the functional categorization of the places where, for example, Berlin is the place of economic activity, and the relationship to the city remains distant and instrumental. More importantly, he found out that multi-local lifestyles initially aimed to maintain and stabilize a conventional family life in the hometown and a strategy to keep their standards of living. According to Cyrus, this income-seeking mobility has produced a spatial separation of the areas with economic and lifeworld functions. As consequence, mobile Polish housekeepers are absent from their homes for a considerable time. This absence urges *"them to 'socially neutralize' their absence and ensure that daily household tasks are continued"* (Cyrus 2008: 190). To cope with these challenges of mobility lifestyle, women from Cyrus's study depend on the support and cooperation of third parties. This suggests that managing mobility, in this case, means maintaining a household in Poland from Berlin by transferring their household domestic obligations to their mothers or other supporting people who play an active part in their labour migration projects (Cyrus 2008: 192).

Cyrus's central analytical focus on the household (and family) gives impression that "gender" is enclosed exclusively within the domestic domain. This perspective was the dominant approach until feminist migration geographers didn't start to rework canonical approaches to structures, scales, subjects and spatial logics proving that the roles that gender and other social differences (citizenship, race, class, nation, sexuality, caste, religion, disability) play a crucial role in shaping unequal "geographies of mobility" (Massey 1993; Silvey 2006). Unpacking household challenged gender-neutral theorizations of the household viewed it as the migration decision-making unit and ask important questions: how gender and age hierarchies within household shape migration patterns and more importantly, what are the differences in the ways that costs and benefits of migration might accrue to women and men within households. It is of huge analytical importance for researchers to understand that "there is nothing ontologically given about the traditional division between home and locality, urban and regional, national and global scales." (Neil Smith 1992–73, as cited in Silvey 2006: 68).

In the analysis of women's self-description and evaluation of their mobile lifestyle Cyrus concludes that although women's labour mobility is never taken on voluntarily and was always the result of a difficult material situation, the attitudes towards it are positive. They are expressions of positive changes such as "widening their horizons", gaining self-esteem and self-confidence, personal growth and so on (Cyrus 2008: 194–195). The accent here is on the positive value of such a mobility lifestyle even though domestic and care workers, on balance, are the most vulnerable and exploited "global workforce".

Both cases presented here are raising scepticism about an obvious tendency to the celebratory tone of mobilities as being on the move is connected to the value of freedom, economic growth, capacity to make choices, etc. What is evident from both of the cases I used as an illustration for further discussion on unequal power over mobilities is analytical weakness in recognizing the flip side of the hyper-mobile pioneers either there are Wolfgang, an affluent cosmopolitan hyper-mobile member of the international elite or Magda, Polish irregular domestic worker who is under conditions of scarce material resources, legal exclusion and economic and social marginalization. It seems that both figures one privileged and one not, have one thing in common – their freedom of mobility and the capacity to travel. They were thus linked, and their mobility is positively valued. However, what we might overlook is "involuntary mobility" in both cases.

Among sociologists of disparity, Bauman was most successful in clarifying the idea that geographic mobility of people in time of globalization is a crucial factor of social stratifications which divides people between the elite who travel frequently and has the freedom to choose where to settle and those who remain trapped in their locations. This definition of mobiity falls short in our attempt to explain the lives of those who are "settled in mobility" like Polish domestic workers from Cyrus' study or elder care workers in this dissertation. Nevertheless, Bauman sends a very important message:

"(…) What appears as globalization for some, means localization for others; signalling new freedom for some, upon many others it descends as an uninvited and cruel fate" (Bauman 1998: 1).

What Bauman anticipates here is not only uniformity but also disparities. Though, within the same group. Thus, the risk is in homogenizing the figure of the "cosmopolitan global elite" by not questioning their attitudes towards the "imperative of labour mobility" imposed on them and the meanings attached to it. Laura Gherardi rightly pointed out that the image of elite "which financial capitalism has liberated from all spatial constraints and which, therefore, produces the only social group able to choose freely between mobility and immobility" illustrates "the problematic nature of romantic mobility in advanced capitalism" (Gherardi 2011: 108) To challenge this image, Laura Gherardi in her empirical study on mobile life of top international managers showed that her interviewees express the pressure of "imperative of constant mobility around globe" as a necessary recourse in career acceleration. This specific gender labour mobility (because of it dominantly male composition) comes with a personal cost – problems of identity, psychological and physical consequences like stress, obesity, insecurity, feelings of isolation and loneliness, etc. (Gherardi 2011: 111). The research of Gherardi challenges the "freedom" of hyper-mobility where the voluntary aspect of mobility and its aspect of power and privilege does not seem to be unquestionable anymore.

Attributing the quality of cosmopolitans and global nomads to the poor and disadvantaged such Polish domestic workers and making them equal to privileged elite makes us analytically insensible for multifaceted experiences of human movement in terms of class and power relationships. The positive bias of "frequent travellers" hides those experiences of people who are managing a mobile life under conditions of scarce material resources, legal exclusion and social marginalization. The case of Snežana I present in Chapter 4 best illustrates this: although she travels across the borders frequently her movement is very often unwanted, sometimes dangerous, and sometimes impossible creating thus confinement and involuntary immobility. The relationship between movements of those who are poor, powerless, and exploited on the one side, and those who are relatively privileged on the other, calls for a different analytical approach that allows for exploration the ongoing dynamics between stasis and movement. This task is taken by Noel Salazar and Ninna Glick Shiller (2013) who coined the term *regimes of mobility* – an approach that goes beyond equation of mobility with freedom by examining not only movement as a connection but also as an aspect of new confinements and modes of exploitation. To allow for a critical interrogation of binary "mobility vs stasis" Salazar and Schiller build on the work of social theorists working with connectivity and relationality (Latour, Deleuze, Guatari) moving a step further – creating the framework for addressing multiple and differential forms of power (Schiller, Salazar 2013: 5). Thus, a new task for researchers would be to interrogate the situations in which certain kinds of mobility of certain types of mobile individuals are facilitated and those where barriers are imposed on them. In other words, by acknowledging unequal globe-spanning relationships of power where unequal relationalities are shaped by the social, political, cultural contexts (but not neglecting the role of the state actors among many others) researchers should study how mobility and immobility define each other. More precisely, as Schiller and Salazar put it "mobility studies to explore the relationships between the privileged movements of some and the co-dependent but stigmatised and forbidden movement". Such perspective highlights the agency of the "regimes of mobility" and opens up the ways for researchers to look more closely at the processes where normalization of the movement of the privileged, simultaneously enforce the immobility of others or even criminalize them.

Schiller and Salazar join other researchers like Shamir and Turner who argued against the glorification of globalization warning that it can be "processes of closure, entrapment, and containment" (Shamir 2005) and paradoxically, produce significant forms of immobility for political regulation of persons alongside the mobility of goods and services (Turner 2007). The rhetoric of mobility in early mobility studies and urban sociology and sociology of transport promoted mobility as normality by celebrating cultural heterogeneity, discourses of globalization, and cosmopolitanism. Mobility became a norm that enables equality and freedom. This tendency to ignore flourishing and ever-growing creative practices of border-crossings assisted researchers in losing sight of the global political system of nation-states, geopolitical reframing of borders that direct and manage transnational movements creating an immobilized population that equally needs our attention to make us be able to explain the movement itself.

The Thrill of the Still: Immobility as a Valuable Research Category

Contrary to the modernity seen as firmly linked to rapid movement in all forms and shapes, some researchers put effort to look closely into the slow modes proposing the idea of a counterpart to movement but not simply as a not-movement. In contemporary sociology and geography, there has been significant interest in the idea of mobility, the decline of the nation-state, the rise of flexible citizenship, and the porous quality of political boundaries.

When Giddens famously suggested that "even the most seemingly powerless individuals can mobilize resources, whereby they carve out 'spaces of control'" (Giddens 1982), certainly, he couldn't have anticipated the current scope and scale of infrastructures and policies aimed at monitoring, immobilising, and controlling migration such as the proliferation of securitization of migration, technologized management of borders, surveillance technologies, biometric identification, including investments in the building and militarization of border walls, systems, and business of bordering such as an extreme case of illegal migration industry along African-European borders (Andersson 2014).

At the moment when this book was in making (in 2020 and 2021), there was no better example of immobility and confinement than the worldwide COVID-19 pandemic, quarantine and self-isolation which have become the dominant forms of social life in numerous countries and prevented mobility in the unprecedented way that was unimaginable in the light of modernistic fantasy about an unstoppable process of globalization, transnationalization, liquidity, fluidity and flows, global networks and spatial transgression. A decade before this moment, scholars like Turner (2007) suggested that move forward is "sociology of immobility" while others like Schewel Kerilyn (2019) calls for "immobility turn" as a new pair of lenses that challenge the dominant narrative of mobility. She asserts that migration studies suffer from "migration bias" which as a consequence led researchers to look only at "migration drivers and to overlook the countervailing forces".

This perspective in migration studies opened a new analytical perspective where immobility is relative to a range of boundaries – administrative, political, social, cultural, religious, economic. It showed that immobility is not only the other side of continuum "mobility – immobility" but it occurs and is experienced across the spectrum of "forced" to "voluntary" immobility. This means, that questions of "who doesn't move and why" challenge the idea of mobility as a motif of modernity but answering them reveals inequalities in access to mobility and control over mobility as a key feature of globalization. The discussion on immobility in migration studies opened the questions of aspirations, abilities, wishes, desires, or lack of these as well as complexity of decision-making process in migration. An analytical benefit from this, for example, is the conceptual framework called *aspiration/ability model* developed by Carling (2002) and revised by Carling and Schewel (2018). This model centres on the break-up of migration into two steps: the evaluation of migration as a potential course of action and the realisation of actual mobility or immobility at a given moment. Such perspective stimulated researchers to look closer to the ways that thoughts and feelings about migration precede actions that might lead to actual movements. Their model also raises important issuesthat are key to understanding migration aspirations. There are aspirations to stay evident in the orientation of culture and life towards remaining in place and this is often more prevalent than aspirations to migrate. Carling and Schewel (2018) highlight structural constraints, particularly in relation to the notion of "involuntary immobility" and immobile subjects. Migration, Carling suggested, requires both, while immobility results from the lack of either one. The resultant *aspiration/ability model* proposed three mobility categories: mobility (i. e., having both the aspiration and ability to migrate), involuntary immobility (i. e., having the aspiration but not the ability to migrate), and voluntary immobility (i. e., having the ability but not the aspiration to migrate).

Finally, "standing still" caught the researcher's deserving attention. The gaze of researchers is shifted to topics of immobility and temporality (waiting) as central analytical focus. For example, Lubkemann (2008) goes beyond the research of refuges who flee to escape the war and look at those who are stuck because of the war. He explores "displacement in place" experienced by people with a local mobility-based survival is interrupted by violence in conflict zones. In the similar vein, geographers Black and Collyer (2014) focused on research on humanitarian crises, use the metaphor of being "trapped" to describe populations who are in need of escaping danger but are unable to do so. From this perspective, "immobility" is predominantly cast as involuntary, a result of constraints on the freedom and desire to move. Yet just as mobility "is a highly differentiated activity where many different people move in many different ways" (Adey 2006: 83), we could say, so too is immobility. Here, as well, immobility can be fuelled with a positive value, as a norm. However, to answer the question why people do not put themselves on the move, constraints alone tell us little about the categories of voluntary immobility and cannot provide us with understanding of why some individuals or households prefer to stay where they are. Migration scholars usually frame "repelling factors" in decision-making suggesting that they can range from social, economic; political, and cultural dimensions – ranging from the prospect of unemployment to the perceived moral deprivation of Western countries to the physical dangers and risks of the migration journey itself. On the other hand, if we look at the factors that keep people in one place over the life cycle or for a long time period, we could get insight into richness of "sedentary life" induced by certain values and norms – a dynamic social life, community engagement, place commitment, family commitment – all these can be "location-specific" values. These would be lost by migrating. I would add here another important point. In some cases, as for example, my research shows, reasons for staying, paradoxically, can lead to short term (circular) labour mobility for care work. While I was examining the aspiration to move for elder care work, my interviewees expressed preferences to not migrate, or not to settle more permanently in Germany even if they have opportunity to do so (see Chapter 7). These preferences to stay help us to see the positive value of immobility. The retain factors that my interviews underlined tend to strengthen over their life cycle. When the value of immobility is assessed in relation to imagined alternatives, negative perceptions of "German culture" and "way of life" further strengthen immobility preferences.

Immobility is deeply gendered as well as mobility. In some contexts, gendered norms may be characterized as internal constraints – for example, the expectation that women fulfil social roles at home, such as caring for children or the elderly. Yet explaining gendered differences in the motivation to stay in terms of internal constraints can slip into minimizing importance of non-economic motivations or devaluing those economic motivations that are deeply rooted in the specific cultures in non-Western societies. As I pointed out in the previous chapter, scholars in gender and migration studies argue about omission of women's experiences in migration flows where men were "male migrants in search of wage labour figure" has long been the model-actor for demographic, economic, and sociological theories of migration. While this fact remains indisputable, as an opposite trend, increasing interest in "feminization of migration" where women migrants are presented as empowered and agentive resulted in the lack of research focus on women stayers – "left-behind wives" or "passive followers". A new strand of literature on gender differentiation in immobility generated a great interest in interactions between mobility and immobility explaining the "immobility paradox" where mobility of some requires immobility of others. More than that, experiences of immobility of women as stayers-on are thus explained by looking at the reasons for staying and the consequence of not moving. For instance, the negative consequences of immobility are discussed in Sarah Ahmed's study (2020) among Pakistani women whose immobility results from the local rural-to-urban male mobility of their husbands. Ahmed showed that the mobility of husbands makes women subject to patriarchal norms and surveillance by the remaining in-laws, including other women that confine and monitor their movement. Hence, patriarchal customs, religion, family structure and gender dynamics are interwoven to confine women's mobility and agency.

In quite opposite direction goes research Caroline Archambault (2010). Her work challenges the label of "left behind" showing multiplicity of ways in which women in Ugweno, Tanzania are part of migration projects and migration decisions of their husbands. Based on ethnographic explorations

84   PERIPHERAL LABOUR MOBILITIES

of the migration histories and lives of women, Archambault findings suggest that for women, unlike in previous example, remaining on the rural farm is part of an empowering strategy, offering women a degree of economic autonomy and social well-being that they would not necessarily have found as migrants.

Another relevant body of work on immobility emerged from the field of gender, migration, and care. In the numerous studies on temporary migrant care workers who cross international borders to perform live-in care work either they documented or undocumented, paid, or unpaid, experience some forms of confinement and involuntary immobility. The involuntary immobility of care workers is obvious and widespread phenomenon in the world of global domestic and care labour. Every now and then we can come across the news or media reports on documented cruel treatment of live-in domestic and care workers that includes passport and mobile phone confiscation and physical confinement. The *International Labour Organisation* and *Human rights watch* have been reporting on numerous cases of employers who forbid domestic workers from leaving the house, locking them inside alone in extended periods, and subjecting them to psychological, physical, and sexual abuse. The extreme variant of forced labour coupled with forced immobility can be found in the countries of Arab Middle East where migrant domestic work is organized under exploitative Kafala system[1] often described as a modern slavery.

Generally, degrees and forms of immobility of domestic and care workers vary depending on employers who, despite national regulations and norms, enforce various levels of control, confinement and regulation within their own household or workplace. Nevertheless, care migrants provide vivid illustration of human agency and creative responses to the limits they confront and to subvert the involuntary immobility to which they are subjected as the case studies in this book will reveal.

---

1 *Kafala system* is a form of visa sponsorship aimed to accommodate foreign domestic workers, mostly from South Asian countries like Pakistan, Sri Lanka and Bangladesh. Originally, the system evolved from helping protect migrants to severely limiting domestic workers' rights. Under today's Kafala, migrants are not allowed to leave her employer without the employer's consent. They are also forbidden from changing employers or traveling out of the country. Escaping is a crime, punishable by arrest and deportation. Human Rights Watch has long argued that no secondary regulation can guarantee the safety of domestic workers as long as the Kafala keeps them legally handcuffed to their employers.

Conceptual Decoupling of Immobility and Mobility

Equally important, nomadism leaves little room for immobility, since, as Cresswell notes, *"when seen through the lens of a nomadic metaphysics, everything is in motion, and stability is illusory"* (2006: 55). Thus, the extremes of both paradigms, the sedentary and the nomadic, reinforce either "mobility" or "immobility" bias by neglecting their dialectic and mutual constitutive relationship as a valid research category.

While mobility pioneers from Kesselring study can make a choice to not to move as a reaction to an increasing dictate of "mobility imperative", others like, Snežana from Chapter 4, are forced to move across the borders whilst experiencing both involuntary mobility and unvoluntary immobility (at the workplace), and under extremely difficult conditions. Thus, it seems that we live in the world of extreme inequalities in opportunities for mobility. However, we might not forget that access and potential of mobility is highly uneven for different people in different places. Also, we must not forget that there are people who do have potential for movement but do not realize this potential due to various macro-structural constraints or individual reasons. Then, we have people who are on the move but experience different forms of blocked movement. That can be temporary involuntary immobility like in the mentioned case of domestic and care workers. Alternatively, it can be temporary voluntary immobility of a growing cohort of the global workforce, for instance, computer technicians, international managers, engineers, academics with fixed work contracts that confine them to a specific employer and perhaps residence as a condition of their mobility. These realities invite the thought that the conceptual analytical dichotomy *being able to move* vs *not being able to move* is no longer viable.

To analyse the dynamics between movement and staying in place, further in the text I will use the term, "im/mobility", with the slash to connect mobility and immobility and emphasise importance of the mutually constitutive relationship between particular forms of movement and the regulations and disciplinary pressures that delimit that movement. In the field of gender, care and migration the term that depict the highly constrained nature of everyday mobility among care workers when they are abroad is "immobility in mobility" and present a core feature of the care work. The term is introduced the recent special issue of *Journal of Ethnic and Migration Studies* edited by Daniele Bélanger and Rachel Silvey. The editors of this volume through the various contributions demonstrated how the inequalities in the global care economy are reproduced, through immigration policies, labour markets, marriage and citizenship laws, family relationships, and the dynamics of virtual intimacy and family separation (Bélanger, Silvey 2019). The example of care workers is paradigmatic example of unequal power relations and signal for researchers to look at the mobility and migration are highly political phenomena. As Schiller and Salazar (2012) pointed out, control over power people's potential of mobility and mobility itself became important part of global and national governance. If we decide to see mobilites and movements related to our personal rights, our capabilities, and capacities to put ourselves on the move, abilities, disabilities, fear, schedules, time constraints – all of the elements that characterized labour mobility of case studies presented in this book – we might reduce mobility to be a consequence of free choice and individual rights. However, as critical mobilities research suggests, mobility is indeed related to sovereignty and state power. Mobility injustices are as Mimi Sheller put it *processes through which unequal spatial conditions and differential subjects are made* (Sheller 2018: 21). She also asserts that the theoretical approach to mobility injustice, must go beyond an egalitarian frame of many other theories of justice (fairness, equity, and inclusion) and must be supplemented with: 1. feminist, critical race perspectives, disability and queer theory perspectives on corporeality, relationality, materiality and accessibility; 2. its historical dimension by interrogating indigenous, non-Western and postcolonial perspectives (Sheller 2018). This means that question of politics and power relations are at the heart of a relational analytical perspective that regards immobility and mobility as always connected, relational and co-dependent and that we always should think of them together.

The fundamental interaction between mobility and immobility is usually framed in the concept of "im/mobility", as argued before in the text, capture interplay whereby the mobility of some requires the immobility of others. Following this impeccable logic, the group of early career researchers, gathered around the book project *"Ethnographic perspectives on Social Hierarchies and Global inequalities"*, (Gutekunst, Hackl, Leoncini, Schwarz, Götz 2016) extended the term "im/mobilites" to "bounded mobilites" wanting to emphasise "centrality of limitations and entrapment within rather than outside these mobilities". Authors underline obvious yet often overlooked dynamic of processes of enabling movement and process of restricting movement that are not separable: *Consequently, constraints always exist within movements and movement often occurs within constraints* (Gill, Caletrío, Mason 2011: 302, cited in Gutekunst, Hackl, Leoncini, Schwarz, Götz, 2016: 23). They take up a crucial point in study of mobilities: inequalities and social hierarchies are the core of mentioned dynamic. More to the point, this dynamic is always contextualized and determined by political, economic, social and cultural factors as my empirical chapters show. Another important contribution that came from authors is a strong anthropological approach to im/mobilities as socio-cultural constructs – how they are experienced, imagined, and what kind of meanings, values and ideas are attached to them. People who experience im/mobility are not empty vessels. They create meanings and values that result often in ideologies that create inequalities – otherness, prejudice, exclusion or simply privileging certain mobilities over others. Paying a closer look to mentioned dynamics and processes requires, as authors showed, specific methodological approach – ethnographic approach. The ethnographic sensibility of fieldworkers who delve deep into process and issues while learning about im/moblities in the multiple contexts where they occur is indispensable.

2.3 Potential of the Concept of *Motility*

In the last decade, in social sciences across the disciplines there has been a growing interest in potential for mobility as the other side of the coin – realized or practiced mobility. Examination of potential for mobility as preparatory phase, capability, or ability to become move that eventually can enact mobility has become the central issue in mobility studies. Because of the analytical developments in study of im/mobilites discussed previously, the need for the concept that will help empirical researchers to overcome gap between immobility and mobility was required. To achieve this, Vincent Kaufmann, Swiss urban sociologist, developed the analytical concept of heuristic device *motility*. He created the concept as an alternative to binary theorization: the classical structuralist accounts of society on the one hand, and postmodern accounts on the other – by linking spatial and social mobility. Kaufmann asserts that fluidification of society is much more complex and goes beyond social mobility and it forces us to rethink the dimensionality of space and its relation to social phenomena and social structures. To justify his concept of *motility*, Kaufmann re-evaluates concept of mobility used in sociology, geography and economy and diagnoses several shortcomings (Kaufmann 2004):

- Under the umbrella "the mobility turn", mobility broadly defined losing its ability to describe and grasp contemporary social and societal changes.
- Studies of spatial mobility tend to focus on movement in space-time rather than on the interaction between actors, structures and context.
- Many spatial and social mobility studies tend to limit their scope by merely describing actual and past fluidity. It focuses on actual travel and rarely looks at the mobility potential of actors.
- It measures in a functional manner, using indicators relative to movement in space and time (spatial scope, travel time budget, speed, motive, etc.), and does not consider the experience of mobility and its imaginaries.

Based on these pitfalls, Kaufmann proposes "study of the potential of movement that will reveal new aspects of the mobility of people with regard to possibilities and constraints of their manoeuvres, as well as the wider societal consequences of social and spatial mobility. For example, knowledge about the territorial constraints for the movement of goods or people, or the conditions of social mobility within a particular regional context, may shed light on a field that has largely neglected contextual qualification" (Kaufmann, Bergmann, Joye 2004: 749).

Kaufmann criticizes the tendency in mobility studies to measure mobility based on how fast we move and how far we go and idea that people who move fast and travel great distances are somehow more mobile than those who move slowly and locally. This is essential for questioning overall focus on highly mobile people those who commute long-distance on a daily basis, who might have several hundred kilometres between their home and their place of work. They are classed as "hyper-mobile" because they travel further and faster than most people do daily. Kaufmann himself goes further considering mobility as the intention and act of moving in the space which implies social change. His definition of mobility incorporates both aim and action, potential and fulfilment and social and spatial aspects. Based on definition above, Kaufmann argues that mobility incorporates factors including experiences and values associated with mobility. Re-directing our focus on *"potential of mobility"* or *"motility"*, we become able to reveal structural and cultural dimensions of movement – that potential capacity for spatio-social mobility may be realized differently or have different consequences across varying socio-cultural contexts. He sees actors in mobility as socio-structurally embedded in the specific contexts that delimit or make possible movement.

The first time that Kaufmann introduced the concept of motility was in his book *Re-thinking mobility* (Kaufmann 2002), in which he initially defined it as the "capacity of a person to be mobile," or "the way in which an individual appropriates what is possible in the domain of mobility and puts this potential to use for his or her activities" (Kaufmann 2002: 37).

However, when it comes to clarity of definition of "motility", most of the researchers face fogginess as Kaufmann and his partners (Kaufmann et al. 2004; Flamm, Kaufmann 2006) offer multiple definitions of the term in different texts and articles where they attempt to develop the notion of motility and to expand on it. Though this notion was discussed in various mobility texts published in the last two decades (Kellerman 2006; Adey 2006), and it was further incorporated into the mobilities paradigm (Urry 2007), surprisingly it was applied only partially in an empirical study (Kesselring 2006), other than Kaufmann's (2002) own. Altogether six definitions for motility were found:

a) The way in which an actor appropriates the field of possible action in the area of mobility, and uses it to develop personal projects (Kaufmann 2002: 3).
b) Motility can be defined as the operation of transforming speed potentials into mobility potentials (Kaufmann 2002: 99).
c) Motility can be defined as the capacity of entities (e. g. goods, information or persons) to be mobile in social and geographic space, or as the way in which entities access and appropriate the capacity for socio-spatial mobility according to their circumstances (Kaufmann et al. 2004: 750).
d) Motility can be defined as how an individual or group takes possession of the realm of possibilities for mobility and builds on it to develop personal projects (Flamm, Kaufmann 2006: 168).
e) Motility may be defined as the manner in which an individual or a group appropriates the field of possibilities relative to movement and uses them (Kaufmann, Montulet 2008: 45).

The variations in the definition of the concept can be explained by evolution of thought and operationalization of the concept based of qualitative explorations that Kaufmann with his research partners undertook in two big research projects. The first one concerns of research on urban transportation based on qualitative survey of the travel habits and histories of people living in Switzerland, basically focused on private car ownership and daily transport routines (Flamm, Kaufmann 2006). The other project was aimed at analysing relation between job mobilities and family lives in Europe, particularly focusing on the links between travel practices and the spatialization of social networks. So, even though Kaufmann's model of motility has great potential as an innovative analytic tool, its application and empirical testing have been largely confined to the field of urban transport. According to Kaufmann, social and economic aspects of life are affected by increased mobility of people, goods and information induced by economic concerns and diffusion of technical innovations. Kaufmann refers to *motility* as an instrument for examination of Western societies trough the modern transport and telecommunications whereas the ability to move is crucial for social and economic inclusion. Similarly to modernistic visions, Kaufmann speaks of the change as tightly connected to growing demand to flexibility, whereas the imperative is not anymore just "'climbing the ladder' within the hierarchical structure, but of being able to 'rebound,' glide from one project to the next and 'surf' from one enviable position to another in a changing environment" (Kaufmann, 2014: 10). In other words, flexibility has become a job requirement, and flexibility often implies mobility. "A growing number of fixed-term contracts, flexi-time (in certain fields, even work on demand has made a comeback), working abroad, and general job-related travel make the ability to be mobile indispensable, with those not fulfilling the requirement excluded from the workforce" (Flamm, Kaufmann 2004: 2). In addition to this, technological and social innovations in the realm of transportation and telecommunication lead individuals to adapt and develops capacity to appropriate technological systems by acquiring the skills needed to build this capacity.

Finally, the latest definition based on understanding of society and mobility entrenched in urban sociology of transportation offered by Kaufmann would be:

"(…) all of the characteristics of a given actor that allow him/her/it to be mobile (i. e. physical skills, income, aspirations (to move or be sedentary), the social conditions of access to existing transportation and telecommunication systems, and acquired skills (job training, a driver's license, international English for travel, etc.) Motility therefore refers to the social conditions of access (the conditions required to use the offer in the broadest sense of the term), the knowledge and skills (those required to make use of the offer), and mobility projects (the actual use of the offer that makes it possible to realize them. What is new is the opportunity for individual or collective actors to locate or relocate based on the many possibilities offered by both transportation and telecommunication systems, and urban spaces' receptiveness to different projects." (Kaufmann 2014)

Kaufmann and his colleagues Michael Flamm, Manfred Bergman and Dominique Joye operationalize *concept of motility* by defining essential components or factors which determinate a person's motility: *Access, Competence* (skills and knowledge) and *Cognitive appropriation*. All three elements of motility interdependent with each other and are fundamentally linked to social, cultural, economic, and political processes and structures within which mobility is embedded and enacted. I will explain each of the factors as authors framed them in two different publications (Kaufmann, Flamm 2004; Kaufman, Bergman, Joye 2004: 750).

1. Access is constrained by options and conditions. These options refer to the entire range of means of transportation and communication available at a given time. Access depends on the spatial distribution of the population and infrastructure (e.g. towns and cities provide different job opportunities and services), accessibility of social networks, and one's socio-economic position within them (e.g. purchasing power, position in a hierarchy or social network). This factor is influenced by networks and their dynamics between territories.

2. *Competence* includes skills and abilities that may directly or indirectly relate to access and appropriation. Three aspects are central to the competence component of motility: physical ability, e.g. the ability to transfer an entity from one place to another within given constraints; acquired skills relating to rules and regulations of movement, e.g. licenses, permits, specific knowledge of the terrain or codes; and organizational skills, e.g. planning and synchronizing activities including the acquisition of information, abilities and skills. Competence is multifaceted and interdependent with access and appropriation.

3. *Appropriation* is shaped by aspirations and plans, and is intrinsically linked to an individual's internalization of values, perceptions, and habits. Indeed, this is the most important aspect of the motility model. It refers to how individuals interpret and act upon perceived or real access and skills. Appropriation is shaped by the needs, plans, aspirations, and understandings of individuals, and relates to strategies, motives, values, and habits. Appropriation describes how individuals consider, appropriate, and select specific options. It is also the means which skills and decisions are evaluated. This can include the question of plans – in this sense, motility relates to what we want to do. Moreover, it can also refer to an attitude towards mobility – how different people approach the activity of travelling back and forth – and whether they do it out of enthusiasm

or necessity. In other words, some people are motivated by curiosity or a sense of adventure; whilst others are spurred on by financial deprivation.

Taking all these factors together, Kaufmann conceptualize them as an expression of "movement capital" as the result (Kaufmann et al. 2004) of the uneven distribution of capacities and competencies, linked to the physical surrounding and social and political affordances for movement. Elliott and Urry (2010: 10–11) similarly describe "network capital" as a combination of capacities to be mobile, including appropriate documents, money and qualifications. Urry himself asserts that networking and social relations depend more and more on communications so that access to communications, transport and social and technical skills of networking is thus crucial for sustaining social wellbeing (Urry 2007: 52). Kaufmann builds up on work of Bourdieu, more recently Sen and Putnam, arguing that individuals' ability to move constitutes a resource, a form of capital that is not simply a question of their income, education, and social networks. In addition to this, Kaufmann claims that motility viewed as a capital is linked to and can be exchanged for other types of capital.

In the following two sections I will critically explore the concept of motility identifying its shortcomings and limitations, but also the reasons why the concept is analytically useful in ethnographic approach to care labour mobilities.

Critical Engagements with the Concept and Its Limitations

The first weakness of the concept I find in the complicated question of the relationship between freedom and mobility, and the structures that constrain us in making our choices. Kaufmann's understanding of actors as free individuals who are making free choices is slightly problematic. It is questionable whether the autonomy of individuals is universal, and whether individuals are always capable of making free choices.

"Considering the importance of the techniques used to travel, analysing individuals' mobility potential means in effect looking at the way in which actors organise their travel using technological networks, and therefore focusing on the individual and group choices, constraints and appropriations on which the use of these technological systems is based." (Flamm, Kaufman 2004: 2)

Here we are facing a fuzziness in Kaufmann's idea of freedom related to mobility: on the one hand he argues that people are not free from the structures and constraints imposed on them, but on the other hand they are autonomous individual actors that make choices *"from the range of possibilities that are offered to them"*. Apparent Kaufmann's occupation with a problem of "free agent" and "rational actor theory" and difficulty to firmly position himself within, basically more complex sociological theoretical problem has its roots in his methodological choice – *methodological individualism*. This doctrine, that has been particularly appealing in economics and political science, is based on the principle that we can explain social outcomes as an aggregate result of the actions, choices, and mentalities of individuals. Individuals' behaviour and choice constitute the causal dynamics of social outcomes. Thus, the subjective individual motivation explains social phenomena, rather than class or group dynamics. The application of methodological individualism in the studies of im/mobility doesn't do any favours to researchers of mobilities in contemporary world, at least, in two respects.

For one, "agent-centered" rational-choice approaches frame people's decision-making in terms of an individual cost/benefit analysis but when costs and benefits are framed in strictly economic terms (e. g., income-maximization), rational-choice models fail to predict real-world mobility trends, patterns and outcomes. People neither universally move to areas where the highest income can be obtained nor put themselves on the move when it would be economically beneficial to do so. As I show in Chapter 5 and Chapter 6, the same phenomena that rational-choice frameworks struggle most to explain – behaviours related to family, religion, or gender or socio-cultural conceptualizations of economic exchange – come to the fore in explanations of im/mobility. Interrogating the reasons, motivations and aspirations for movement is crucial to understanding decision-making: when the preference to move overrides compelling economic reasons to stay, non-economic values and economic "irrationality" cannot be overlooked.

Secondly, neglecting the issue of power structures, global power relations and social hierarchies that structure and stabilize the mobility of certain groups of people, Kaufmann does not leave the room for what was discussed in previous sections – analysis of problem linkages of mobilities and inequalities in various socio-cultural contexts. What he fails to see is that motility is not only potential of people to choose a mean of transportation in their cities, but that "transportation" is inflected by racial and classed processes, gendered practices and discourses and social shaping of for instance, disabilities and sexualities (Sheller 2018). Kaufman stresses: "not focusing on the poorer sector of the population and describing difficulties these people encounter in acquiring their motility and transforming it into mobility but instead, implies highlighting the obstacles encountered by the entire population in its quest to carry out projects of mobility" (Kaufmann 2002). But he does show awareness of exclusion of class dimension in his work but making a footnote within the analysis where he demarcates their research from those whose research is centred on precarious daily movements like Le Breton's article *La mobilité quotidienne dans la vie précaire.*

"Let us first of all say here that we take it for granted that the individual possesses general knowledge skills that comprise an essential foundation for his or her capacity for movement (good knowledge of the local language or otherwise of a "universal" language such as English, knowledge of the customs of the country in question, etc.). Nonetheless, even if we restrict our analysis to travel that can be qualified as daily and we disregard exceptional mobility (business trips or leisure trips abroad), this hypothesis does not prove valid in all cases: for example, Eric Le Breton (2002) showed that this aspect can contribute to the immobility of poor and immigrant populations." (footnote, Flamm, Kaufmann 2004: 10)

The latter statement in form of the footnote from his article clearly shows distancing from disadvantaged population in terms of their motility. More explicitly, further on, Kaufman confirms this:

"Motility invites us to adjust our perspective to new dynamics of highly mobile, modern societies, and to develop pertinent conceptual and methodological tools without abandoning invaluable insights from studies on spatial and social mobility." (Kaufman, Bergman, Joye 2004: 754)

Forming an analytical concept based on the statement that *concept of motility* is confined to highly mobile populations disregarding unequally positioned people implies that process of im/mobility, such as involuntary temporary mobility or involuntary mobility (for example, mobility of care workers in my study) and actors of these processes completely fall outside of conceptualization of motility.

In connection to previous concerns about the concept, we could argue that general problem lays in the hegemonic nature of the concept. Although we must admit that Kaufman's *concept of motility* arose from the field of urban sociology and was operationalized in the field of research on the European transportation systems and their users, still it is heavily preoccupied with the questions of travelling, transit and mobility and idea that intensity and forms of mobility are linked to the broadness of the degree of freedom in people's lives. While that might hold the truth for the targeted research participants, train commuters in Swiss cities of Basel, Bern, Geneva and Lausanne, the concept of motility as such, allow for no reflection upon the question of how far such culturally specific expressions of class and residential behaviour can be taken to be universal. Thus, the concept suffers from Eurocentric bias. Despite the fact that Kaufmann's *concept of motility* is conceptualized within the highly advanced infrastructure of Western Europe and has been empirically tested mainly in the setting of European urban and daily commuting, it leaves very little space for other experiences, such as that of "the actors" interviewed in my research. Although elder care workers in my study have the freedom to commute, they build their "motility" in unimaginable number of alternative creative ways to "know-how" to move across the border.

Finally, an additional problem with motility, apart from Eurocentricity, is the tendency to understand the concept in more economic terms given the market-based vocabulary choices that Kaufmann uses such as: access, options, offers, conditions, agents, management, project, action or:

"In a world where flexibility is an economic imperative and where the future is therefore uncertain, individual actors tend to broaden their mobility potential to the greatest extent possible in order to compensate for all of the undesired changes in their socio-economic conditions." (Kaufmann 2014: 12).

Thus, this tendency toward economic and market principle organized analysis of human movement and potential for that movement conceals a wide spectrum of historical, social, political, and cultural processes that contribute to the interplay between immobility and mobility. While Kaufmann's concept might be a perfect tool for researching privileged citizens in one of the most richest European countries, highly mobile individuals with the possibility of making choices, equally or even more would be insightful to take a closer look to those countries with significantly lower GDP, where using personal means of mobility is not a norm and where individuals, like the women care workers in this book have a different challenges in making their choices.

"Motility" in the Ethnographic Study of Mobility for Elder Care Work

Ever since I encountered the concept of motility, I have noticed that Kaufmann's approach coincides with my own, which is to focus on individual decisions and strategies, embedded within the background taking into consideration the conditions and influences that shape women's capacities and opportunities to move, given that these constitute an important basis for understanding their experiences and practices. However, considering the critical limitations of the analytical potential of motility previously identified, one could pointedly ask: What is then the analytical purchase of concept of motility in my study of mobility for elder care work? In what follows, I will answer this question by pointing down numerous analytically useful aspects of motility as, despite the abovementioned critics, I would argue, is an original analytical approach.

Firstly, we cannot ignore the fact that theoretical and analytical questions articulated around the "the space-time-identity triad" and "spatial-social mobility diad" are not uncommon in antropology. Eliot, Norum and Salazar underlined importance of conceptual links between geographical movement and social meaning. In his "anthropology of movement", Alain Tarrius (Tarrius 2000: 124, cited in Eliot, Norum, Salazar 2017: 6) proposes, "methodological indicating the circulatory process of migratory movements whereby spatial mobility is linked to other types of mobility (informational, cognitive, technological, and economic)". What he describes as "circulatory territories" are new spaces of movement that "encompass the networks defined by the mobility of populations whose status derives from their circulation know-how". More to the point, anthropological approach to movement is build around investigating intrinsic mutually constitutive relationship between spaces of movements and those who move across them. Similarly, I find that *concept of motility* can be anthropologically useful because it goes beyond a simplistic separation between social mobility and geographic space by integrating these on the levels of actors, culture, networks, institutions, and society.

Kaufmann's contribution with idea that "motility" can be capital appears to be novelty in terms of linkages of "motility capital" to other types of capital. Just as economic capital is related to knowledge, cultural wealth, and social position, so motility represents a form of capital that may form linkages to other forms of capital or be exchanged for. An anthropological perspective can enrich the concept by looking at socio-cultural factors as features of this exchange, which in turn can direct us to processes whereas inequality can be created or reinforced by motility. In the case of mobility for care work, motility understood as capital can reveal how care workers commuters valorise their movements, what significance and meanings they give to it and more specifically, what are the resources, knowledge or skills that are gained by being mobile and eventually turned into "motility capital".

Multi-local mobile lives or "lives-in-between" as distinguished characteristic of care labour mobility invites us to look more carefully at social networks that play a crucial role in process of building potential for mobility. Throughout the experience of labour mobility care workers' increasing ability to strategize may depend on many individual factors such as language skills, citizenship, care work skills, but above all it depends on collective recourses. *The concept of motility* makes it possible to account for the strategies and constraints in the negotiation of social and geographic space in relation to territories and networks. In addition to this, it directs our attention to the way care workers create new or alternative networks at the point of not only departure or when they arrive at the destination, but also during commuting. Important socio-professional relations formed in this way can be regarded as the result of the motility of the actors.

One of the most significant and original contributions of Kaufmann's concept certainly is capacity to reveal "ambiguity of mobility". As motility underlines the potential for mobility, it means that the analytical gaze is directed towards intentions relative to mobility and the actual act of moving, more than the movement itself. As Leivestad argued (Leivestad 2016: 147) analytical strength of motility concept is its potential "to direct us towards those situations and positions of the temporality of everyday life and work in which mobility is 'not-yet-realized or yet-to-be-completed'". Thus, it allows for an interrogation of the circumstances and conditions under which this potential mobility is enacted, and whether it is denied or constrained. As my interviews demonstrate, sometimes it is possible to choose to move, yet lack the effective capacity to do so. In other words, mobility conceptualized as potential compounded by temporal dimensions can drive researchers to explore the interplay between time, (im)mobility and vulnerability, for example. Moreover, it certainly induces my analytical curiosity about how the experience and practice of time affect or are affected, by a person's (in)capacity and potentiality to move. Why some women fail to complete their trips for care work to Germany is an important research question. In addition, it helps how to understand and explain those situations where women become "stuck" at home, between two jobs, immobilized until the next job opportunity comes? Equally important is to investigate why some women stop commuting for the job while others continue.

An ethnographic approach to motility in my study addresses Kaufmann's central factor of motility – *appropriation* which he conceptualizes as an element of motility that is shaped by needs, plans, aspirations. The process of appropriation is the most complex and thus requires an attentive exploration of precisely how people envision their potential mobility, and how they are aspired. Aspiration in my understanding is subjective constructions of the future. The reasons for moving or staying put are closely attached to aspirations for mobility: how do we imagine our future to be? I argue that aspiration is the key element in studying elder care mobility because it shapes the life of women in my study and it is the main detector and indicator of how women understand themselves, other people they interact and places they visit and reside. Aspirations and desire for labour mobility remain relatively understudied unless they are reduced to economic dimensions. Aspirations are closely linked to "choices". The analysis of narratives of aspirations and motives serve as a nuanced reading of "choices" that women make about the best present action to achieve their future goals. Aspirations are also placed within constraints and complex power relations which requires our research attention.

Despite women's rising participation in cross-border care work, their mobility is directed, managed, monitored, and, at the same time blocked, constrained in gender-specific ways that intersect with nationality, citizenship, age, marital status, ethnicity, and socio-economic class. The analysis of how their motility is built reveals experiences that are organized around several moments of labour mobility cycles: before they put themselves on the move (which includes motivation, aspiration, preparation and imagination), during the travel to their job destination, at the job destination and when they leave the destination and move to another one. In other words, my research is centred on the journey of elder care workers to and from fixed sites in the former Yugoslavia countries (their homes) and Germany (households they perform care work) but it is important to note that their movement ranges across scales from national and regional to the body (household) scale. I argue the journeys they take to and from fixed sites require skills and knowledge (such as the ability to navigate the travel routes, language, care work skills) and accumulated together are considered as a motility or "capacity to move for care labour". If we add to this the fact that much of the literature centres on the global hypermobile elite mobility experiences, the research focus of cross-border care worker's "motilities" and power relations associated the unequal distribution of choice around mobility might be a good start for extended understanding of the concept of motility and its utility.

2.4 Intersectional and Border Regime Approach

Discussing experiences of care workers on the move, just as a "mobile experience" or just as "experiences of performing care work" in the "feminized labour sector" shadows the range and nuances of labour mobility for care work. For instance, the way mobile labourers practice border- crossing heavily depends on their social, cultural and political context. As I am going to show later, to cross the border one needs to pose a social knowledge about border crossing. This knowledge is not a common knowledge, and it is not evenly distributed. An opportunity to cross the border and become mobile certainly is not the same for women and men. If we only look at the biographies of women care workers from my study, it becomes clear that on the one hand, restrictions and obstacles to women's mobility persist due to the various reasons linked to the border crossing regulations, labour laws, lack of the access to networks and information, etc. On the other hand, their mobility is encouraged by the fact that irregular (undeclared) care work is in reproductive private sphere of German households where their presence can be concealed and where they can earn a significant amount of money for a short time. This obvious contradiction between spatial and social constraints and an attractiveness of seemingly good earning opportunity is more complex than it seems. The cross-border relations and cross-border practices are socially generated and an inherent element of contemporary social inequalities. Anna Amelina's concept of *transnational inequalities* urges us to take an analytical look at the mechanisms of cross-border inequalities as "regimes of intersection" relating spatialized cross-border inequalities to other types of unequal social relations (in terms of gender, ethnicity/race, class etc.) (Amelina 2017). As the focus of my research is on process of acquiring labour mobility, preparedness and building potential for it, it is vital to analyse life chances and life opportunities, as they appear to be unequal in geographical and social space. This inequality emerges in the realm of cross-border where different actors and forms of social interaction in the process of mobility take place. More precisely, my analysis of ethnographic material centres on the interplay of different dimensions of social inequality (gender, ethnicity/race, class, etc.) and transnationalized relations to uncover care workers' multilocally organized work and lifeworlds. To stress the multidimensional quality of the production of social inequality, intersectional research abandons the conventional distinction between class-specific inequalities and gender and ethnicity -related inequalities. The "grid", the metaphor that Floya Anthias uses (2001), illustrates processes of building social hierarchies showing that patterns involved in the unequal distribution of life chances should be studied from a multidimensional and relational perspective. I use this approach because it considers the complex interplay of hierarchizing attributions not only within a given dimension of inequality (e. g. dimension of gender relations) but also among the different dimensions – class, ethnicity, race, gender, age and nationality and citizenship. The question of who will be denied the opportunity to move, who works and where; whose work is acknowledged as work; whose is invisible and unrecognized; how gendered ways of life are destabilized and reshaped in the process of mobility and how other "axes of difference" intersect with gendered ones. In these processes borders and border-crossing are essential for exploration of different movement barriers, the relationship between privileged and stigmatised im/mobility and to define movement within social and economic relationships rather than simply across borders. I focus on examining the meaning of borders – the spaces where migration policies and restrictions are materially condensed – in the lives of care workers. The role of the borders is crucial in creating living and working conditions for care workers within the European border regime. The regime both restricts and enables a structural background for mobility for care work. For this reason, I pay closer attention to the heterogeneity of different citizenship statuses and their effect on the movements across the borders, working conditions and social relations. In this light, borders are viewed as institutions that produce a whole range of different social relations.

Thinking borders through this book means to re-think the logic of borders beyond their apparent role as tools of exclusion and violence, thus allowing for the more open and complex ways in which borders react to diversity of migrant subjectivities and thereby operate to produce differentiated forms of access and "rights." Re-directing my attention from the negative power of borders was necessary for developing a more nuanced understanding of cultural logic of bordering. Looking at the borders as heterogeneous and multifaced whose changing dynamics in different geo-political settings, different historical periods hinder or encourage its crossing with different actors and their creative responses to how to cross the border when the border is closed for them – it is crucial for analysis of ethnographic cases in my study. This theoretical and paradigmatic shift in migration and mobility studies is a result of efforts of the new epistemic community that emerged in the last decade all over the world. Activists and scholars have become increasingly engaged in attempting to go beyond the established paradigms of both traditional and critical migration studies to create different relationships with migrants and migrants' struggles as well as a more open reading of the border. The critical studies of migration governance (Karakayalı, Tsianos 2010; Walters 2002), the autonomy-of migration approach (Hess 2017; Bojadžijev, Karakayalı 2010; Scheel 2013) and a number of recent writings in the political sciences have identified several lacunas in the vocabulary of migration research calling into question the naturalization of borders, the epistemological privilege of structure over agency and of sedentarism over mobility. According to some scholars (among others, Nieswand, Drotbohm 2014), this wave of epistemological and conceptual reflections has contributed to an epistemological, conceptual and methodological shift in the way we think about, how we envision, and how we research borders. The call to "denaturalize" border (Walters 2002) means to take a radically constructivist approach that involves not only governmental logic but also the production of borders from and with a perspective of migration.

It is certainly a common place in the interdisciplinary field of "border studies" that the border can only be conceptualized as being shaped and produced by a multiplicity of actors, movements, and discourses. Nevertheless, most of these studies still perceive the practices of doing "borderwork" and making borders as acts and techniques of state and para-state institutions. In contrast, recent work on borders aims to reach beyond the underlying basic binary logic of structure/agency in order to demonstrate how at the border there is no single, uniform organizing logic at work. Instead, the border constitutes a site of constant encounter, tension, conflict, and contestation. In this view, migration is a co constituent of the border as a site of conflict and as a political space. It is the excess of forces and movements of migration that challenge and reshape borders, and in the same time these forces are stabilized, controlled, and managed by various state agencies and policy schemes as they seek to invoke the border as a stable, controllable, and manageable tool of selective or differential inclusion.

Taking into account border-crossings as a defining force in producing what the border is, and reconceptualising the border, requires the "reflexive turn" that allows for a more critical examination of the analytical potential of terms, definitions and categorizations of human movements in migration and mobility studies. Peripheral labour mobilities previously introduced, are reaction to economic constraints, the marginalization in the labour market but also a reaction to migration and border regimes. While it certainly does not hold true for every border, still borders today are a predominant technology of governing mobile populations. As the border constitutes a site of contestation and struggle, a perspective informed by regime analysis allows us to understand the social, economic, political, and even cultural conditions of today's borders. The foci of the analysis in this book is not border regime itself. Rather, a careful examination of what border regimes between the EU and non-EU means in women's care workers experience – their agency to resist the borders, their conflicts and negotiations and inventiveness and resourcefulness in trying to circumvent them and even use them as a resource – are the main features in analysis in elder care work mobilities.

2.5 Commodification and Precarization of Care Work in Informal Care Labour Markets

In addition to perspectives related to the "peripheral" phenomenon of care mobilities and its motility, in this sub-chapter, I want to outline the several theoretical perspectives that lead my analysis of care work within transnational informal care markets. To avoid broader theorization already mentioned in the literature chapter I rather focus here on three pillars in exploration of experiences in performing elder care work: 1) ethnographic and anthropological perspectives to work in the informal sector; 2) commodification of care work 3) precarious and vulnerable aspects of care work.

1) Anthropological approach to studying work has a several distinctive characteristics. Comparing to other disciplines, the perspective allows for a less dichotomizing way of thinking about economies and labour, questioning the suitability and usefulness of analytical distinctions such as modern-traditional, formal-informal or work-leisure. An anthropological lens is suitable for examining economic processes as social processes and phenomena that reach beyond national borders – it is a study of the meanings, manifestations, institutional settings and representations of labour in its diversity and societal interconnectedness. Moreover, notions of work related to personhood, iden-

tity-building, and daily processes, skills and motivations are subjects worth studying.

As discussed in Chapter 1, the fact is that every migration decision is socially and culturally embedded, and it is not purely the result of individual decision-making as assumed by neoclassical theory, nor does migration bring national wages into line. Push- and pull factors (defined as global wealth disparities and the demand for cheap labour in the receiving countries) are still relevant to understand the causes of migration. Also, we cannot deny that people are calculating economic actors driven by the opportunity to increase the income, by comparing income in their country to potential earnings in other locations or countries. However, this view must be amended and evaluated by considering the impact and role of social relationships, cultural practices, and values in labour migration as well as unequal access to information, knowledge and capital.

For the subject of this book, it is particularly relevant to consider "work" itself, the ways how people work, how they connect with others at work, and how relations of inequality and solidarity, or notions of difference and commonality are produced, contested and rejected there. Influential in this regard has been the distinction Michael Burawoy (1979) made between "relations of production", i. e. the larger structural relations between capital and labour, and "relations in production", i. e. the social relations that develop between and among workers and managers on specific factory floors. In this book, I am committed to an ethnographic approach to the ways people go about working and how they engage with different norms, categories, structures that regulate their working lives. As Irene Götz argued in her article on the interdisciplinary exchange of sociologists and European ethnologist in studying working worlds, "the perspective on social transformation processes in radically economising lifeworld, must include the observation of the capitalization of labour in a resounding way that involves the person, their feelings and non-professional aspects, so that work and non-work are no longer separable (Götz 2016). In the same place, Götz specifies that compared to sociologists, European anthropologists are using methodologically more open procedures in inductively designed research that involves "a principle of "nosing around", researcher's self-reflection as part of the cognitive process and an often very experiential writing style that remains close to the actors and testifies to the actual "having been there" as an authentication strategy (Götz 2016: 102). Through work, people produce specific social relationships, not only goods and services. But how relationships are produced depends on the ways political, economic and social regulatory frames are interlocked in specific workplaces at specific historical, political, social and cultural junctures.

The analysis of the commodified elder care work performed by women commuters encompasses important aspects of the informality of the sector where the work is organized. Understanding of what the informal sector is and how it is theorized in social sciences have largely shifted from being considered a drain on the formal wage-earning sector of the economy or as "resistant" to capitalist production, to being seen as part of an integral co-existence, and a realm of self-made income in the face of high unemployment and limited wage-earning alternatives. Portes and Walton's (1981) discussion of the relationships between formal and informal sectors and their simultaneous relationship to patterns of labour migration sets the stage for my point that – these are not just integral structural links, but also an increasing part of individual experience.

For many decades, the formal and informal economies were represented as separate realms. Rather than depict all formal work as possessing positive qualities and informal economic activities as always possessing negative qualities, it has been widely shown that not all formal work is progressive (e. g. zero-hours contracts, false self-employment) and neither are informal economic activities necessarily always regressive. Informal work is a specific type of activity within the grey economy. In this book, special attention will be paid to how informal or irregular work in the care sector informs women's mobility trajectories, their working identities,shifting their life strategies and life biographies and above all shape their motility for care labour mobility.

A large stream of research on informality (also known as informal sector, "grey" or "shadow" economy) claim that people often recur to informality to deal with the shortcomings of ineffective and inadequate economic reforms, or lack of the same (De Soto 1989). These findings were elaborated , for example, by Gibson-Graham (1996), in her seminal feminist critique of capitalism who demonstrated that, in contrast to most neoliberal assumptions, individuals play a major role in perpetuating local informal economies. Other studies, instead, looked at informality as a coping mechanism for the implementation of neoliberal reforms (Kaneff 2002; Smith, Stenning 2006). I refer to the informality of care work in my study to explain how the systemic informal labour practices are built, what kind of social relations this informality generates, and thus redirecting analytic focus to the aspirations, motivations, needs, plans, strategies, motives, and values in the working lives of women who move between German cities/villages and their home communities.

2) My research deals with a care labour mobility where the value of informal paid care for elderly people in German households is replaced by ethicized labour by monetary reward and arranged through several persons involved in recruitment strategies, organization and realization of care work. This directs my ethnographic attention to diverse situations, actors and personal and intimate connections that are part of the process of commodification, production, consumption, and distribution. Most of the researchers on care work, either that be care for the elderly or children easily fall into the trap of two perspectives. The *prisoner of love framework* (Folbre 2001) focuses on the genuine care that motivates some care workers, pointing out the cruel irony that these intrinsic motives may make it easier for employers to get away with paying care workers less. In this view emotional bonds that care workers develop with care recipients are putting them in a vulnerable position, discouraging them from demanding higher wages or changes in working conditions.

The second perspective, in opposition to former, holds the idea that someone is always harmed when care is sold. Hochschild's (1983) view of the perils of commodification seems to draw from this oppositional imagery to conclude that workers are harmed when they must sell a part of themselves and that this is worse the more intimate the part of the self-involved. Whereas the *prisoner of love perspective* focuses on how care work is emotionally satisfying – so much so that workers will take a lower wage, Hochschild is worried about psychological distress from "deep acting", showing emotions that flying attendants (subjects in her research) do not really feel.

As I found both perspectives extreme without resonance with my empirical evidence, I would rather opt for an analytically more useful perspective created by Viviana Zelizer (2009) who made clear that personal and intimate connections enter transfer of economic value without being corrupted. Making the distinction between spheres of sentimental, emotional, intimate, and rational prevent us from understanding affection and emotion as elements of social relations. The question of the analytical distinction between "love and money" Zelizer resolves showing the never-ending interplay of human interests, emotions, and relations, andconsidersr the finest nuances in people's motives and actions. Zelizer suggests that the claim that only profits and self-interest rule in the market, while more caring values rule in families, nonprofits, or governments, are often unquestionable. She contests this claim by arguing that culture often rules in such matters so that norms specify the way that money and sentiment can be combined for particular kinds of ties. And here, Zelizer thinks as anthropologists do – avoiding the "hostile-worlds" approach that simply assumes that personal relations and money are radically incommensurable and should not be allowed to mix, Zelizer rather argues that empirically, life is both more complex and less clear-cut than that: people contest these boundaries all the time in their everyday lives and that money does not dry up social relations and ties, rather, it organizes them and reveals their nature (Zelizer 2013).

3) The concepts of precarity, precariousness, and precarization have become popular in current public and academic discussions around the ongoing changes in the capitalist mode of production, working conditions, and modes of life in general. Many theorists and empirical researchers refer to these changes by tracing the shift from a Fordist to a post-Fordist organization of production and labour force understanding precarity as a condition tend to divide between those who see it as something specific to work under neoliberal labour market conditions (e. g. Bourdieu 1998; Standing 2011, in German academic context contributions by Klaus Dörre 2006; Götz, Lemberger 2009) These concepts refer to the same ongoing social processes and their effects in contemporary Western societies, but carry slightly different meanings: as adjectives, precarious and precarity can refer to the shared ontological vulnerability of life, or to socially produced conditions of precarity. Precarization, on the other hand, refers more precisely to the social processes that expose people to precarity and produce precarious conditions. Researchers have mainly applied precarization to the sphere of employment, where it is understood as a consenquence of atypical or irregular jobs. I argue, that along with a broader definition of precarity, basically a lack of individual and collective control over wages and conditions as a consequence of the flexibility of the labour market, precarization also holds a deeper and more comprehensive meaning, – the crises of mechanisms that sustain modern social life, as well as the institutions that bring stability and continuity to life: the welfare state, education system, and wage labour. Precarization means a process which produces a lack of protection, insecurity, instability, and social or economic vulnerability. Engaging with the concept of precarization as "something more" than a position in the labour market, imposes on researcher task to capture how employment effects and is intertwined with other areas of

life, such as household dynamic, personal biographies, welfare system and socio-cultural context. In the context of my empirical focus on care labour, precarity is the feature within all micro-spaces of everyday life. This means that the concept of precarity is far more illuminating when we acknowledge the profoundly destabilizing effects of precarious work for broader life words. Then, precarity is seen also as a subjective process and ask questions: who consider him/herself to be precarious? Under what conditions? As Götz rightly argued: "(…) precarious refers to not only on the objective material situation but also to the subjectively perceived vulnerability or the anticipation, that the everyday framework that has been built up can collapse at any time" (Götz 2019: 24, my translation from German into English).

As my empirical evidence demonstrates, the precarious lives of women care workers in Germany is generated by combination of border regulations between the EU and non-EU countries and care regimes in Germany in a deregulated care labour market. "Precariousness" thus captures the way how gendered care labour mobility, German welfare regimes combine to create the "demand and supply" of informal elder care workers who are undoubtedly subject to multidimensional insecurity (physical, emotional, financial, mental) and exploitation. Apart from these "bad" aspects of precarity, I argue that precarization has a manifold characteristic. Precarization understood as, for instance, the accumulation of multiple skills and knowledge, or flexibility, is potentially creative, and not necessarily always a forced condition. This perspective enables me to detect the controversial and problematic nature of elder care work and im/mobility, as both forms of agency and life strategies, and at the same time processes that are subjected to various forms of control and management.

2.6 A Multi-Level Analysis of Care Labour Mobilities

Given the complexity and richness of analytic concepts and theoretical perspectives previously outlined, this study employs all levels of the analysis – macro, meso and micro levels in order to make deeper insight into culturally specific and geographically situated conditions and the experiences of women in the course of care work mobility. These levels, however, I do not treat separately but as elements of one complex story.

1. The macro-level of the study concerns the structural conditions of contemporary societies in German and ex-Yugoslavian countries – the global economy and its implications for gender in the context of geopolitical transformations such as post-socialist transformation and neoliberal forms of economic transition in post-Yugoslav societies. The structural factors that contribute to increased mobility of women for elder care work in the informal sector in Germany are located at the intersection of three different national policies or regimes – the gender, care and migration regimes. This intersection is a phenomenon of the European experience, and it is closely connected to the European Union and its changeable nature and dynamics that exist between flexible borders between EU and non-EU countries. This is the main spot in analyses of the changing socioeconomic structures, welfare regimes and political institutions. It is important to stress that structural factors in my study do not derive from social and policy analysis, but from the narratives of the women interviewed in the study. Women's narratives reveal that specific pattern of mobility for informal care work is shaped by a cross-section of citizenship, migration policies, legal and bureaucratic loopholes in their countries which in turn produces different experiences and variance in terms of social positions, power relations, and livelihoods.

2. At the meso-level I look at the institutions which mediate and shape labour mobility such as labour recruiters, semi-legal recruitment agencies and social networks where gendered identities of women are constructed and negotiated. Moving away from before mentioned macro-structural condition, now I want to reappraise the importance of self-organised networks of women care workers. I am concerned not only with *who moves* for work but also *what* or *who does move* women from one place to another. I argue that the way how women build social networks to get a job is a crucial element of their biographies and mobility potentialities and trajectories. I explore what kind of role social networks – both virtual and real – play in facilitating care labour mobilities. The narratives of women I interviewed, show that being part of networks can build one's capacity for mobility as well as obstruct such mobility. The exploration of how women perceive their position in these networks gives insight into hierarchies built into the mobility and care labour market intersected with ethnic, national and other dimensions.

While much is known from the literature on care and domestic work migration about women and their reasons for migration, their working conditions, consequences of such migration, particularly for children and families left behind, there is not much, especially not ethnographic, knowledge on the actual process of labour recruitment for jobs, foray into labour migration and focus on "migrant institutions" (Goss, Lindquist 1995). Twenty years ago, to explain changes in recruitment practices in managing employment in international migration, Goss and Lindquist proposed mid-level concepts such as "migration institutions" business" of migration or as "migration industry". In his study on gendered migration from Indonesia to Malaysia and Saudi Arabia, Lindquist (2010a, 2010b) argues that a critical empirical vantage point that still missing in ethnographic literature is brokerage or infrastructure that allows more deeper insights into how different intermediaries, labour recruitment agencies and individuals facilitate the process of labour mobility. In this book I use the benefit of these concept and direct my attention to recruitment strategies of care workers that reveal mobility processes, disruptions, continuations. As it is evident from my material the process of recruitment is characterised by both, agencies who legally recruit labour force from different sectors, and those who operates in an "illegal" mode – the process which is in effect highly gendered and ethicised. On the other hand, the "migration industry" produces cases of immobility, wherein some women are "stopped before they start". Most of my interviewees recount and describe complex and costly processes before they engage into labour mobility in Germany. The process involves paying commission for intermediaries, sometimes mandatory pre-departure language course organized by recruiters and waiting to be called for the job. Sometimes waiting is too long that women decide to undertake tedious, costly, and legally controversial procedures to put themselves on the move as I demonstrated in Chapter 6.

3. Micro-level analysis brings into focus individual decisions and strategies embedded within German households or families where the live-in care work is performed. An analysis of women's narratives show deep insights into the everyday struggles and journeys back and forth of migrants, involving values, beliefs, attitudes, gendered hierarchies, practices, emotions, services and commodities. Particularly, I am interested in multiple relationships that elder care workers form with their colleagues, care recipients, their families and employers – job intermediaries and recruitment agencies.

Personal relationships constitute a special area of enquiry in the literature on domestic and care work migration. In my research these complex relations in diverse specific settings between persons who often do not know each other and do not work with each other because of the rotation system, give rise to several important questions. For example, how care workers conceptualize and manage their relationship with colleagues has important ramifications for their motivation for work, their working conditions, their well-being, and the quality of care for the elderly they provide. Furthermore, I pay special attention to these relationships because live-in care workers are exceptionally and unavoidably exposed to establishing intimate and personal relationships with the people in whose homes they work. Basically, there are two main reasons for this. For one, interpersonal encounters across cultural and national borders sometimes undermine and sometimes enhance boundaries that divide them. Secondly, elder care work involves tasks that are very personal: feeding, changing clothes, bathing, cleaning, cooking, taking care of their private belongings, taking care of the health and wellbeing of elderlies. Hence, it involves a high level of intimacy – even if it is unwanted, undesired or rejected (often in the cases of elderly people who suffer from mental difficulties as I show in Chapter 5 and Chapter 7).

To examine the micropolitics of negotiations of personal boundaries, be they physically intimate, cultural or social, I look at "the strategies, principles, and practices we use to create, maintain, and modify cultural categories" (Nippert-Eng 1995: 7). Christena Nippert-Eng (1995) discusses how employees negotiate the home/work boundary by organizing realm-specific matters, people, objects, and aspects of the self. Feminist literature on domestic and care work has pointed out structural patterns of exploitation between, for example, maids and madams, in case of Filipina domestic workers (Parreñas 2001), domestic workers in Los Angeles (Hondegneu-Sotelo 2007) or domestic workers in London (Anderson 2000). These different researchers and their observations show different preferences and strategies of employees and employers either formulated as "personalism", "benevolent maternalism", "strategic personalism" or "cycle of dependency". These are the ways in which both parties involved, negotiate social distance or closeness in distinct ways and for various reasons. In my study, I find that is important and interesting to show how boundaries along different divides – cultural, ethnic, social produce interactive dynamic of reproducing, negotiating and contesting social inequalities among parties involved. To achieve this, I outline several analytical typologies of structural factors (class, job tasks and time-space in the care working settings) that enable me to get a better understanding of how to care receivers and their families and care workers create variety of approaches to negotiate structural factors to explain their distinct preferences toward certain types of boundaries negotiations. These structural factors knit together a complex map that coordinates a variety of subjective dispositions shaping the interactive dynamics between employers and women care workers which can be recognized in their narratives on personal relationships with their employers. This dynamic demonstrates the effects of territorial citizenship and racial, ethnic, and national stratification on everyday personal interactions. Although we could say, referring to previous numerous studies, that domestic and care workers are marginalized in host countries through politico-legal regulations and the cultural discourse of racism, nationalism and even sexism we cannot generalize their everyday interactions with employers and host families as mediated by the construction of class distinctions, ethnic stratification, and spatial inequalities. However, the local practices of "boundary work" or production of boundaries (Lamont 1992; Lamont, Virág 2002) in a household is a constituent part of reproducing structural inequalities in the global economy.

The multi-level analysis is inevitably connected to ambivalent relationships between agency and structure. Whilst I am setting an analytical framework that incorporates agency, I also avoid problematic constructions of "choice", "resilience" or "entrepreneurialism", which can reify domestic-care workers as ambassadors of (neoliberal) economic growth and forms of self-making (e. g., Morokvasic 1993). Instead, my ethnography demonstrates how everyday experiences of elder care workers are part of the global domestic labour regime enabled through government ideology and policies, cultural and social norms, and modes of social reproduction. My focus on quotidian activites in process of care labour moblitiy rather than a broader labour regime analysis, allows for a dialog within debates on exploitation, agency and resistance whilst looking beyond scholarly discourses on care migration that reduce care migration to economics.

We cannot simply state that migration and mobility bring material prosperity and empowerment in any respect. This is important because, within the literature on gender and migration, scholars frequently assert that migration is a somewhat liberating experience. This argument has also been made in reference both to professional/skilled female migrant workers such as nurses and to low-wage migrant workers in the child and elder care sector and domestic workers. For example, I find the argument that migration empowers and improves the status of migrant women quite evident is under certain circumstances problematic. However, migration can at the same time have the opposite effect, which is not considered when one only looks at the increasing income of the women's household. These scholars base their perspective on two arguments: 1) women's greater income-earning power leads not only to their greater economic contributions to the family but also to more decision-making power in the household; 2) women have greater access to the public sphere upon migration. However, empirical ethnographic evidence challenges these generalizations. Studies on South Asian migration have revealed that migration might reinforce traditional gender norms (Gardner 1995), but also improve the education of non-migrant women, or that migration might have both negative and positive effects on gender relations, as demonstrated by Petra Dannecker's (2005). Her study revealed that whilst on the one hand migration strengthened Bangladeshi women's networks, on the other hand, it introduced sexist imagery. Similarly, Näre's study on the post-Soviet migration from Ukraine to Italy demonstrates that migration strengthened Ukrainian women's social capital and collective social remittances (Levitt, Lamba-Nieves 2010), at the same time as they had to struggle with sexualised stigmas of being 'prostitutes' both in the everyday of their work in Italy, as well as in Ukraine (Näre 2014).

Despite the turn towards transnational studies and multi-sited ethnography in contemporary studies on female migration, scholars who claim that women are empowered by migration are rarely interested in their background, mobility continuum and personal biographies to document or study physical mobility, agency or decision making in those spaces. Making scientific claims about female labour mobility as the transfer of one system of gendered inequality to another leaves no space for deeper insights into how inequalities are challenged; when, where and why they are maintained or strengthened.

Finally, the question is how to explain the relation between structure and agency, or between domination and resistance? As this book demonstrates, women care workers internalise particular dominant constructions of their gender roles (which are not separable from economic and social structures) that would require them, for example, to stay put or to migrate following their male kin, but at the same time, they challenge and defy these dominant representations. As Henrieta Moore has suggested, individuals hold multiple and contradicting positions. The subject is, in fact, a site of differences "which constitute the subject and are internal to it (1994: 58) and the crisscrossing of gender, ethnicity, citizenship, age, and education produces a multiplicity of diverse and subjective positions. At the same time, however, Moore suggests that how subjects adopt one position instead of another is not simply a matter of personal rational choice. Instead, she proposes the idea of "fantasies of identity" which are "ideas about the kind of person one would like to be and the sort of person one would like to be seen as by others

(1994: 66) and which consciously and unconsciously propel individuals to challenge or to achieve different positions. Moore's contribution is particularly useful for reaching and understanding how women elder care workers develop their decisions to move, the choices that make within the process of labour mobility and how they conduct their lives in that process. Freedom to move or to travel to another country can be understood as a movement to another world and culture (which they are familiar with) and as the expression of a new life emphasises women's "fantasies of identities", which however are never autonomous from women's social and economic backgrounds. As Bourdieu teaches us, subjects are involved in reproducing social meaning through practice. Even a minor change in everyday life and habits offers possibilities for interpretation and re-interpretation (Bourdieu 1977). For women from my study, mobility for care work presents a radical shift, a life important event (negative and positive at the same time, or empowering and disempowering) whereby facing new circumstances of everyday life as live-in elder care workers in the German households provoke their thoughts and reflections about themselves, their roots, and their cultural habits.

Chapter 3
Making a Care Labour Mobility
Researchable: *Ethnography of Movement*

Before I present how, why, where and when I collected the ethnographic data that this book is based on, I would like to start with a few simple arguments that support and essentialize my methodological approaches and methods of data gathering presented in the following sub-chapters.

The first argument is that ethnographic research that involves extensive and immersive fieldwork is a "slow science" (Salazar, Rivoal 2013: 181), slow but methodological and thoughtful processes. The second argument is that fieldwork is interwoven with the social and personal circumstances of the researchers and that their everyday lives impact the fieldwork process, whose dynamics might or might not produce ethnographic discoveries. Hence, in this chapter I am going to reflect on specific sets of situations, i. e. „fieldwork encounters ", which affect the research by "disturbing" its course or taking it in new and unexpected directions. There is no part of the fieldwork as a "total" experience that informs the analysis and the writing process which can be dismissed or trivialised as unscientific; any factor that influences the fieldwork process needs to be considered throughout the entire research process, which usually starts with the choice of a research topic and ideally ends in a written book. Reflecting on my own experience of ethnographic fieldwork, in this chapter I present the specific methodological challenges and opportunities that arose from circular labour mobility-related research and ask how these created a specific and new approach to research and analysis. In doing so, I want to provide a more nuanced understanding of the conditions in which my fieldwork was carried out and ethnographic knowledge is produced. Whatever position I am taking in the debate on postmodernity and constructivism in the social sciences, reflecting on fieldwork practices and how they influence the nature of the knowledge produced, generally leads to critical reflection on the effects of power – domination, reification, reduction to silence, normalization (Burawoy 1998) or on the effects of my subjectivity, particularly in the formalized moments of producing data. Hence, to set out the methodological approach to the *ethnography of labour care mobility*, my third argument is that the conditions of my presence as a researcher in the field and the presence of my respondents have both spatial and temporal implications.

Doing ethnographic research on im/mobility for care labour creates specific challenges and difficulties that have a constitutive power of what I call an "ethnography of movement". Thus, my fourth argument is that the mobility of the researcher is essential for a full understanding of im/mobility processes. Researching *peripheral labour mobilities* and "potential for mobility" includes following activities: a) to be immobile and observe those who are mobile; b) to be mobile and observe those who are immobile; c) to be mobile and observe those who, with oneself in movement, are mobile. Over two years long ethnographic research I found myself in all previously mentioned situations along with the process of interviewing. But these are not only "situations". They become approaches to care labour mobility aimed at understanding the tension between mobility and immobility, between travelling and being temporarily immobilized, which shapes mobility processes. It is not a question of opposing these "moments" to one another, but of understanding the relations that unite them as two aspects of the same process.

The issues of mobility of researchers concerning mobility of those who are researched – haven't been much problematized in studies of gender and labour mobility and migration. As labour mobility is above all a movement, it implies a continual change of natural and social contexts – both researcher and research participants. Considering this, studies like mine must allow for the instability of the social forms such as variations in social relationships of individuals, the continual (re)negotiation of their relationships, and the adaptation of their actions. Therefore, my research aims to achieve a full understanding of the journeys of women care workers which are the combination of stasis and movement – required my mobility. From a methodological point of view, this mobility is twofold: mobility in the field and "mobility" as fieldwork. One of the ultimate challenges of my fieldwork certainly was the precarious and vulnerable position of my respondents due to the irregularity of employment and lack of residence permits in Germany. Questions about living and working arrangements in the grey zone of domestic and care work were viewed as an intrusion in their private life and arose suspicion. Therefore, great sensitivity and ethical behaviour from the side of the researcher was required. The interviews were carried out at different locations in the former Yugoslavia and Germany. When my mobility was not possible, I conducted some the interviews using Skype. To achieve the trust of my respondents, I initially immersed myself in participant observation: I spent many months with these women, observing them working and travelling and listening to their stories – about the way they went about getting jobs, establishing networks, disseminating information about living arrangements and counterfeit legal obstacles, problems in performing care work, and more.

In detailing the ethnographic methods used in the study, I also want to provide a genuine account of my ethnographic encounters and how my background and identity affect the fieldwork. As a person who share the same language, and cultural background (or at least, I thought so), I came into the field without expecting cultural or any other barriers. But the fieldwork revealed unanticipated challenges and shattered my assumptions about the women I was interviewing. As a relatively privileged, cosmopolitan, doctoral researcher enjoying favourable conditions of free mobility, backed up by a German residence permit and University funding to cover costs of travelling for research, I was in many respects, a representative of some unidentified "otherness" – being neither one of them, nor one of the people for whom they work. In the eyes of my respondents, I am from Serbia, I am Serbian, but I am certainly not "like them". Sometimes, I represented a link to potential employers. Because of my perceived proximity to potential German families who need a care giver, I was for some of my respondents a member of the German society. Their assumption about my privileged position made them sometimes instrumentalize our relationship as researcher-participant hoping that I will be useful in finding them (a new, better) job. In a few cases, it happened that as soon as they realized that was unlikely to happen, they stopped communication with me.

· Despite the prevalent assumption about me as a privileged person in comparison to my respondents, I could not neglect institutional, occupational, political circumstances and my personal issues that drew the contours of my research project and its execution. Although, ethnography is often cherished in feminist research for its capacity to valorise lived experience and the multiple axes of the personal as political, I have found it to be a methodology that – if "properly" conducted – would require the researcher to be an independent, autonomous, mobile subject, capable of devoting her life fully to research during the intensive periods of fieldwork. Paradoxically, a methodology cherished by feminist research would require a "good" researcher to be a disembodied liberal subject, without the commitments and relations of care. One could say that I was this subject, yet my status as foreign student, academic migrant taking care of herself in a foreign country, constantly struggling with changing intellectual environments, places of living, insufficient fieldwork funding, health issues, coping with a scattered field sites and ad hoc participant observation when and where I get a permit to do so – become salient factors in how my field was built, what kind of methods I used and quality and quantity of ethnographic material I accumulated.

Following the tradition of reflexive ethnography, I tell a "confessional tale" (Van Maanen 2011), a type of writing that is intended to show how my research work came into being and how my life, as fieldworker is lived. A confessional tale is writing that is concerned with how "the fieldwork odyssey" was accomplished by the researcher (Van Maanen 2011: 75). In confessional writing, the ethnographer opts for a personal style, presenting emotional reactions, unexpected occurrences, and one's expectations and experiences of the fieldwork. In the following sub-chapters, I describe and analyse how I entered the fieldwork and negotiated access to respondents, both as an "insider" and "outsider" and how an incident that happened during fieldwork induced my emotional reaction and decisions I made during that process. I want to scrutinize what impact unexpected situations and unexpected presence of certain people may have on the process of data gathering and data analysis. Also, the "tale" that follows in the next sub-chapter, is aimed to unfold the process in which my positionality, multiple roles and emotional experiences complicate methodological discussions on the diversity of ethnographic fieldwork procedures, as well as the multi-dimensionality of fieldwork that guided the process of research and its outcomes.

3.1 Ana's Case

I started my fieldwork on the bus between Belgrade and Munich when I met Ana for the first time. She became my first respondent and – as it turned out – a key respondent. My academic mobility situation was complicated at that time because I didn't have a German visa. I was applying for a German visa, which was the reason for often travelling between Munich and my hometown, Belgrade by bus. For me, like my respondents, life was less fortunate at that time. Difficulties in finding proper accommodation in Munich forced me to stay with my friends, which meant that I was staying in several places during the first two months of settling down in Munich.

During the repeated travels and by listening to conversations I became aware of how many women working as care workers travelled on the bus. I met some of them during the breaks at the petrol stations and on the way to the toilet, but I did not develop any communication or consider them as potential respondents. Since I travelled mainly during the night, I did not have time to communicate at all, or the people were inaccessible and not very friendly. However, with Ana, I started the conversation by accident. She was sitting on the seat in front of me. She often asked me if I had enough space for my legs and if it was okay for me if she adjusted the seat into a sleeping position. As she was very kind and considerate, I decided I will start a chat with her at the next break. Firstly, it was a chat mostly about long-distance bus travelling issues, and then we started talking about personal things – where did we go, what did we do for a living, and so on. After she told me that she had been working for three years as an elder care worker in Germany, my curiosity as a researcher instantly started to grow. I had asked her questions, but very cautiously, so as not to jeopardize her openness.

In the beginning I was not honest, and I did not tell her the topic of my doctoral project. I told her only that it dealt with labour migrations from Serbia to Germany, but not that the focus was on women like her. In one of our later subsequent encounters, she admitted that she had assumed that my inquiries about her life were not of simple personal curiosity but professional ones. Anyway, during our first encounter while travelling, I did not disclose my research intentions. After we arrived in Munich, we exchanged phone numbers. She admitted that she was very lonely and that there was nobody in Munich and that she would love to meet sometimes and have a coffee with me.

As promised, we started to keep in touch regularly, at least once a week. Compared to my other respondents, Ana's working arrangement as a care worker was unique and at that time seemed to me, far fortunate. She worked taking care of an elderly and very sick man in a very wealthy family in Munich. She had lived in a separate one-room apartment owned by her employers and a few streets away from where she worked. This kind of luxury enabled her to have privacy and to sleep during the night without being disturbed. However, she was not allowed to bring visitors, she had to be quiet in the apartment, she was not allowed to use a common washing machine in the basement, nor to use the kitchen (because she used to eat in the house of employers where she also cooked), nor to listen to the TV at a loud volume, and she could only switch on heating when it was necessary. She was also never permitted to communicate with neighbours or to reveal her identity. As she was working without a contract, she was non-existent as a person. Also, her apartment was officially vacant. This kind of life of isolation and informality, with the constant fear that someone would report her to the police and that she would then be deported to Serbia without the possibility of returning, had caused various fears and frustrations for Ana. Although she worked only until 6 p.m., after which she was free, she did not go out and walk around the city. The apartment she was staying in was in the affluent residential area in the Munich centre from where she could easily reach the historic part of the city and walk along the river. When I suggested that we could walk together one afternoon, she said:

"No, I do not prefer to go out. Can you come to my place? I can make a coffee. Thus, you can see where and how I live. We just must be quiet, you know, because of the neighbours."

I had visited her 4 months after we met. I came to her apartment, and I remember that everything seemed to be like no one was living in that flat: everything clean and white, with new furniture. I then decided to tell her what I was doing and what my research was about and to ask her for an interview that I could record. She replied:

"You know, I have a child at university. My younger son is finishing his studies, and the older one already has finished … I do know what it means to study and write papers. I'll tell you everything I know … there's rather a lot … enough to write three theses, not one. Well now, how does this work? Do you have a voice recorder? Where should I start from?"

She spent much of the interview talking about her experiences with two previous employers, unhappy marriage, patriarchal behaviour of the family of her husband and the complex relationship with his family. I guess that she shared these intimate details with me because I am a woman, but of course, I cannot know for sure if she would have told that story to a male interviewer.

That interview lasted at least three hours. She seemed very happy to have someone to chat with. Reflecting on this interview, I realized how our different age/generation and her role as a mother created moments of empathy and rapport. I got insights into her personal experiences as an informal care worker in Germany but also learned about the person she was doing a rotation with Helena, who was the second worker in the same household. When I did a follow-up interview, I had got to know Helena. I expected that either Ana or Helena will introduce me to other women, their colleagues or, at least provide the channel of information about how to reach them. It was obvious that neither of them wanted to help in my search for respondents. At the end I got an explanation that both provided me with:

"Look, we mind our own business. We don't want to ruin our position within the network. You know women do not trust someone that they don't know that easily. What you do … it's really nice … and I know why you do it and for whom, but they will not understand it, so please do not ask us anymore."

I was convinced that I had reached a dead-end and that I must end my research before I even started. As an interviewer, I was assumed as an outsider whose access to their colleagues should be limited. Unlike in the previous situation, where I was assumed as "an insider" being recognized as a student, someone's child or simply a person in need of help with whom one should empathize, asking them to recommend me to other women created tensions and sense of distance.

Despite my disappointment about the perspective of my fieldwork, I continued to see Ana. After several months Ana became the only employee in the household. The old gentleman for whom she was nursing had died. His wife, Frau Müller, was old but did not need care. She lived a normal, healthy life as senior person. She needed a house maid more than a care worker. Ana was very happy that she left her old life of constant mobility going between Germany and Serbia every three months and she was determined to persuade Frau Müller to make a contract and hire her regularly. In addition to the Serbian passport, Ana possessed a Hungarian one (based on the Hungarian origin of her husband), so that she could remain in Germany for an unlimited time. As an EU passport holder, she didn't need a visa to reside in Germany. That meant she stayed regularly, but she worked irregularly. During that period, we had seen each other every two weeks. I lived only a few blocks away so, on the way from the library to home, I would have stopped by and had a cup of coffee with her in her apartment. Then she told me generally about the working conditions, but she felt that Frau Müller was putting too much psychological pressure on her by being very demanding, often capricious, and demented. Since she was no longer a care worker, her household tasks changed: she cooked, cleaned, served the guests, fed the cat, went to the post office to send letters and parcels, and did the shopping. Most of these new jobs were unknown to her, and she began to go out and move around a city that she did not know so well. At this point my role as a researcher grew into a friendship. I helped her with tips on where to go, which public transportation to use, where she could buy certain things, and even to translate from German something she did not know herself. Frau Müller told her that if she was satisfied with her work, she would keep her and make an employment contract with pension and social benefits. I was quite aware of how important this was to Ana which is why I tried to help her as much as I could. I also knew that that kind of job opportunity would not come up probably ever again.

The weeks were passing by, and Frau Müller did not mention a word about the contract. Ana felt more and more isolated and lonely. Besides me, she did not have anyone else in Munich. She missed her family and many other things, including her favourite food. Since she could not cook in her apartment, her diet came down to only what she cooked for Frau Müller which was usually potatoes and salad. I used to invite her for dinner sometime. She enjoyed the food and even offered to cook something by herself at my place.

The event that caused a twist not only in course of the fieldwork, but also in my private life, was the car accident that happened to Ana. One evening at about 10 o'clock, I received a call from the police to come to the hospital because the person who referred me as an emergency contact had had a traffic accident. They told me her name and asked me to confirm whether I knew that person. At that moment I knew that Ana could not say where she worked or for whom, because it would have legal consequences for both her and Frau Müller. They told me that Ana was conscious, but they did not know how serious her injuries were because the doctors were still examining her. With a mix of fear and sadness, I went to the hospital. I waited an hour before they let me see her. In the meantime, the police asked me many questions since they found her unconscious and without any documents. They asked for my ID and residence permit as well. I lied for her. I gave them an explanation that she was my guest, a friend of my mother, visiting Munich. Finally, when they let me enter her room, I was shocked. She was all blue and her face was hardly recognizable due to the swelling and bruises. The doctors told me that there was no internal bleeding or head injury, but that they wanted to keep her for observation for two or three days in the hospital. I was barely waiting to finish my conversation with doctors to go to the bathroom to cry. This traumatic experience had triggered in my grief and pain, and then anger. I was enraged by the fact that the women who work and care for others have no protection, and no one cares about them. I could not talk to her that evening. I went back to the next morning to the hospital, and she told me what happened. On the way back from Frau Müller's house around 9 o'clock, she was crossing the street and did not see that green light change to red. When she stepped into a marked crosswalk, a car came and hit her. She was very upset. She cried and held my hand. Although her health condition was still critical, she was thinking about her job and Frau Müller who still did not know what happened. Ana's main concern was not her health but how she was not at work and how Frau Müller would be angry because she did not get breakfast in time. I asked her to give me her phone number that I could call Frau Müller and inform her about the accident. I did so. My German was very poor at that time, so I talked to her in English, which she spoke very well. Frau Müller was very confused. She kept asking questions about who I was and why I was calling her, but in a very suspicious way. When she finally realized that the situation was more than serious and that she could trust me and rely on my discretion, she said she would come as soon as possible. Frau Müller came to the hospital an hour later. Very worried and shocked by Ana's condition, she repeated that she would pay the hospital expenses and hire a nurse at her home after she left the hospital. Then she took me aside and asked me what I told the police and if her name was mentioned and in what context. I said that I did not reveal anything, but it would help a lot if she would start to think about legalising Ana's status in her household. Since that moment, Ana's life had changed, and my research took an unexpected course.

3.2 Multidimensionality of Ethnographic Fieldwork

What does count as a "field" in ethnographic research? This open-ended and continuous question has been part of debates in anthropology and ethnography for the last three decades. Traditional ethnographic studies tend to focus on a single locality, with the assumption that cultures are coherent, integrated isolates bound with specific spaces and communities. This model of culture has been revised 30 years ago under the influence of globalization. "Flows" and "networks" have replaced "systems" as the new metaphors of culture. The contemporary picture of global flows (of peoples, capitals, commodities, practices, ideas, etc.) accelerating and complicating contemporary life in unprecedented ways, and markedly since the 1980s, has provided the backdrop for a wide range of studies from a variety of disciplinary angles and backgrounds (Giddens 1991; Harvey 1989; Appadurai 1996; Clifford 1997; Marcus 1998; Sassen 1998; Bauman 2000; Sheller, Urry 2004; Cresswell 2006; Urry 2007). Even those who conducted research in the fixed locality like Anna Tsing, for instance, were forced to abandon the geographical locality of the field and follow her respondents, whose communities can be understood only "within the context of … mobility – from daily visits to annual field movements to long-term trajectories across the landscape" (Tsing 1993: 124). It is important to remind, that there have been key technological and social changes that affect how people, things, and ideas move – so even we chose to study people or phenomena in a single site (like in a hospital or research institute) we are forced to visit a variety of spatial and cultural sites accessible via computer (various databases, websites, social media, etc.), or to leave the space to make the local trip to conduct the interview. The point is, we cannot say with certainty what that "locality" is – it can be understood as trans-local, bi-local, multi-sited, multi-local or "network of localities" (Hannerz 2003) or "deterritorialized ethnography" (Merry 2000). Based on my own fieldwork experience, the question "What locality or site is?" or, "Where it is?", depends mostly on the research questions, researcher's relationship with respondents, the quality of that relationship and the duration of stay in the field.

From the very beginning, I methodologically framed my study as a multi-sited ethnography (Marcus 1995). George Marcus's celebrated "multi-sited ethnography" deals with the idea of how combined field studies in several localities could illuminate wider social and cultural interrelations. The way I understand this methodological program is suitable for the investigation of culturally connected, but geographically dispersed, phenomena (Clifford 1997). However, Clifford made clear distinctions between multi-sited ethnography that recognizes the many locations of culture, and multi-local fieldwork that requires field study in many locations. Of course, this dissonance can easily be solved by Hannerz's solution of *translocality*. The point is not that much in the fact that we are at localities (because we are always somewhere during the fieldwork) but how these localities are connected – "what happens in one locality influences what happens in the other, whether that is and can be foreseen or not" (Hannerz 2003: 21).

From the start of the research process, I was asking myself how to do fieldwork on labour mobilities of care workers, which is inherently transient, unstable, and difficult to set up in space and time? How such field-site(s) should be determined, delimited, or constructed? How to catch up with a subject of research who are constantly in existential insecurity, the uncertainty of the next location where they will perform their job, the uncertainty of remaining at one workplace, being mobile between two places? Or, how to follow them in immobility or stillness while acquiring motility for labour, waiting for a job contact, learning a language, or gaining knowledge about care work and their/regulations related to border crossing? To answer these questions, I begin with a few theoretical considerations. First, for a long time, migration was studied in terms of migrants' places of departure and arrival. Similarly, as I argued in the previous chapters, studies of domestic and care work migration rarely focused on actual movement between departure and destination. As a result, migration studies were based on the description of fixed places and fixed moments. Yet if we consider care labour mobility as a process and the focus of research, one that has movement at its heart, this needs to be reflected at the methodological level.

To start with the more obvious facts what my fieldwork was. My research setting consisted of gathering places of care workers, their apartments, working places (households of their employers), parks and gardens, coffee shops, bus stops, travelling with them in trains and buses. I followed them wherever they might be by keeping in contact via Skype, Viber, social media and so on. All these different settings prompted me to think about what do places mean to people – and why? Do certain forms of spatial organisation or place-attachment foster particular kinds of social relations – or vice-versa? And does place matter all that much, does it make such a difference – especially today, amid the whirlwind of communication technologies that help us to defy distance?

It was not enough to use multi-sited methodology, which tends to examine the ontological status of "the local" and offer a more careful contextualization of sites within networks and flows across diffuse time-space. This kind of methodology is less concerned with the physical traces of movement. To overcome this methodological obstacle, I turned to proponents of new methodologies of mobilities and their volume "Methodologies of mobility" (Salazar, Elliot, Norum 2017) that illuminates how to produce ethnography based on travelling with respondents, movements of respondents by themselves, and understanding mobility on a number of levels, ranging from questions of space, scale, and time to bodies and materiality. This methodological and epistemological turn in ethnography was valuable for me as an anthropologist and ethnographer who documents ways in which physical mobility for labour transform social and cultural life and depict the lifeworld of the protagonist of that ethnography. Editors of the volume mentioned above summarized the contemporary study of mobilities and its methodologies in one main question: "How to make meaningful research whilst allowing research problems to guide which methods we use, and not the other way around?" (Salazar, Elliot, Norum 2017: 15). It is also true that the choice of research methods evolves during the research process.

In Ana's story one could see that duration and frequency of contact with my first respondent and quality of the emerging relationship is more related to time than to space. Shifting this focus from place, space and locality to time makes a lot of sense when seeing my field as a temporalized entity. There are two reasons for this. One is the fact that any fieldwork experience is structurally limited in time, resources and conditioned by the rules of funding institutions, research institutes, universities or other external factors. Secondly, every fieldwork itself entails its own pace and rhythms, and it is marked by temporal ruptures like waiting, repetition, delays or simply a time when nothing happens. Constant delays of fieldwork trips because of the cancellation of the interview appointments (sometimes because of mistrust of the potential interviewees and more often because of impossibility to get the time off work), long breaks while I was searching for new ones – made my fieldwork being discontinuous and coming "in drops". As just as my respondents' mobile lives were changing in chronological time, what constitutes the field site also changed in my understanding, when I connect events in the process of analysis. I can see on the one hand, how my field has been transformed by incorporating new ethnographic aims, my academic mobilities, different localities I visited to gather information and relationships I developed with each trip; on the other hand, how biographical temporal cycles of my respondents, temporal aspects of border regimes and spatio-temporal configuration of performing informal care work (waiting periods of preparing and searching for a job, getting the job and time within period of working) were shaping and re-shaping my field sites.

Making a parallel to the notion of "multi-sitedness", Steffen Dalsgaard and Nielsen (Dalsgaard, Nielsen 2013) to avoid demarcation and definitions of the field anchored in tropes of locations and spatiality, call for extension of the notion with a conceptualization of multi-temporality of the field. They invite us to think towards temporally oriented ethnography, which, according to authors, unpacks the multi-temporality of the relationship between fieldworker and the field. The term multi-temporality means that what ultimately constitutes the field entails different temporalities depending on the rhythms of social life that one is studying, and how these may emerge or transform as the fieldworker becomes increasingly embedded in social relationships. This process certainly need not be necesserely linear or chronological.

Dalsgaard (2013) provided an account of how his relationship with the field emerged over time, what different temporalities were at stake and what they meant for relationships developed. In the next sub-chapter, I will give a brief timeline of my fieldwork. The temporalities of my field will show how the field is conceptualized, how research questions and methods of inquiry were changed, and how unexpected events related to personal circumstances were crucial in access to the field and its setting.

Time in the Field: Temporalities of My Field Site

My fieldwork stretched over 2 years (2016–2018). The first phase or pre-fieldwork phase was aimed to making inquiries about doctoral studies in Munich and to find the supervisor who will be willing to support my project. During that time, in 2015, I visited Munich, twice as a holder of the BAYHOST research grant. These two separated research visits, I used for gaining an initial glimpse into the stratified labour market of migrant domestic work, to use the University libraries and collect relevant literature to write a research proposal. My journeys by bus between Belgrade and Munich turned out to be main source of information about mobilities of care and domestic workers. As I did not finalize research design and research questions for my doctoral project, at the time I did not conduct any interviews. However, informal conversations during the long nights of travelling by bus gave me an insights into phenomenon of irregular domestic and care work which served as my first field notes and first contacts. In one of these occasions, I met my first and key respondent Ana, now known from the story I told previosly.

In 2016 I officially launched my PhD project titled "The Micro-politics of Motherhood and the Transnationalization of Care: Experiences of domestic workers from former Yugoslavia in Germany" at the Institute for European Ethnology at the LMU Munich. My enthusiasm and hopes for successful ethnographic study were fading with an increasing impossibility to get funding for my PhD project.

Financial problems caused the first interruption in my fieldwork phase. My residence permit in Germany was at risk because I did not have financial means to support my living during doctoral studies. I was close to decision to give up on the project. I was lucky enough to get six-month research internship position at one of the research institutes in Munich. This paid internship allowed me to cover my living expenses but not cover expenses of the field trips. I had six months ahead to secure funding for the project and to set up the field in Munich. The gatekeepers of the field, to say, were Ana and her colleague Helena with whom I spend most of the time observing, doing group interviews, conversations during informal gatherings. When Ana became contractually employed as the only employee in the household of Frau Müller, she started trying to help other women who would coming to Munich to search for a job, providing them with an accommodation in her little apartment. That was an opportunity to get to know them and to make interviews with them in their initial phase of labour mobility. My fieldwork in Munich, time-limited and geographically restricted was comprised of social relationships that were emerging over the six months. As its result, I collected five in-depth interviews and numerous pages of field notes. This low number of research participants can be accounted for by availability of trusted contact persons for this particular group. It became apparent that networks of female domestic workers in Munich were particularly closed off and difficult to access. However, the most important result of the time spent collecting the stories is the discovery that women do who put themselves on the move for domestic and care work in Germany are mostly in their fifties and sixties years of age. Those women who had children (which was not always the case), turned to be without caring responsibilities as the children are grown-ups. Several differentiation categories came into my research focus. This is the reason why I decided to rework the research questions, targeted research subjects and overall aim of the PhD project.

Finally, I secured my research project by receiving a three-year Ph.D scholarship at The Max Weber Centre for Advanced Cultural and Social Studies in Erfurt. I found myself in a situation where I had to move swiftly from Southern to Eastern Germany. I left Munich, my friends, my supervisor and to some extent fieldwork network that I built up over time. As my project had been adapted, the new research questions and research aims came to focus. Instead of looking at the motherhood practices and discourses in process of labour migration for care and domestic work I rather switched my attention to a different category of women, in different stages of life, of different family statutes, age, citizenship, level of education, nationality, religion, ethnicity – how all these dimensions of social reality affect labour mobility, employment strategies and employment relationships. My fieldwork was significantly slowed down after I came to Erfurt in the autumn of 2016 due to adapting myself to a new academic environment, in the new town where I did not know anyone. Nevertheless, my Ph.D was made possible by a three-year grant that gave me the opportunity, as a young scholar, to "think, read and fail" (Rivoal and Salazar 2013) as anthropological process always requires.

In the first year of PhD, I had experienced a series of unfortunate unexpected events in my personal life – traffic accident and surgery. Due to poor health and physical immobility, I was forced to be creative in finding research participants. The original focus was on how mobility for care work constructs characteristics of working culture and the complexity of work identities. This emphasis on mobility and connectedness would have unavoidably led to conducting fieldwork in both places, place of origin of my respondents in the Former Yugoslavia and place where they work in Germany and in-between while they are on the move. Due to the mentioned circumstances, I had to give up on the original research plan and set up the field only in Germany. For the second time, my research project was revised.

Despite all difficulties, I had managed to conduct several interviews in different towns in Germany during my first year in Erfurt. As a spider in the web of irregular care market, I had to make journeys to a new site on very short notice. I never knew when and where the next respondent will be willing to meet me and talk to me. The central characteristic of this field is thinking about it in terms of a network because all of my respondents move between different families or different jobs through the network. Repeated brief visits, or "yoyo fieldwork" (Wulff 2002) served as a "follow-up interviews" in order to collect data at different points of women's labour mobility and their stay in Germany: right upon their arrival to the family (start of work), during the work and after the work ends. This means that depending on the circumstances, I talked to one woman, several times to get insights into her work-life world. When the conversation was not possible to be done "face to face" either because of my immobility or because of the unavailability of my respondents, I used Skype, Viber, Messenger or Facebook. With most of them, in a certain period of six months, I was constantly in touch. I was getting updates about how they are doing at work, how is their family, anecdotes they shared from their working environments, or they just wanted to ask how I was doing as someone who was perceived as a friend. It was a necessary gradual development of mutual trust with my respondents.

Spending more time with me (offline or online) had made them more open to talk about their experiences, especially those who tried to avoid topics of irregularity of care work or information about job recruitment in the first interview. The second reason for intense communication is the nature of the irregular live-in care work in German households. The extreme social isolation where social interaction is reduced to the care recipient and his/her family induces loneliness and depressive moods of women care workers. The need to maintain social and family bonds is met through frequent and regular online communication. In addition to this, as Facebook become the main niche for their entertainment but also the source of various information about the care labour market, it is only natural that connections and communication with them have moved online. Therefore, in the next section, I will show in more detail why and how social media platforms in my dissertation challenge conventions on how ethnographic data are generated when face-to-face relationships with informants are supplanted by online communication.

Moving the Field to Facebook

At the end of the 2017 when thought I did the last interview in the "offline world" with a woman who quit the care job, I feared that I exhausted all the resources in finding new research participants. She decided to stop commuting to Germany and she could not have recommended to me any new potential respondents. That made me feel restless because the number of interviews I had at the time, would not be enough to complete my research sample. She pointed me to Facebook telling me that there was an increasing number of Facebook groups where women who are looking for a job in the rregular sector of care work, particularly, in n Germany and Austria share job posts, jokes, discuss their experiences, sometimes useful advice how to perform the care work, etc:

Originally, my intention was not to analyse the content of the Facebook material. I, naively, believed that as a contemporary ethnographer trying to document cross-border labour mobility, I could avoid the use of rapidly burgeoning technology that threats the singular concept of the field. On the contrary, the scholars in social theorizing on social media have convincingly argued that online sites are by now so integrated into many people's everyday lives that it makes little sense to maintain a clear-cut distinction between online and offline life (Miller 2011). My experience of using Facebook in ethnographic fieldwork and paying attention to the multiple presences, the multiplicity of roles and identities, the multi-textured arena of experience helped me to bypass typical constraints of space and time in research on migration and mobility.

Yet, I have to explain why and how ethnographic practice mediated by Facebook impacted my research and forced me to re-consider the requirements of my methodology: the way how I collected data, what forms of digital data and how I will present them. The first clarification is regarding terminology. I have found that many authors have given different names to the same method. Hine (2000) called it *virtual ethnography;* Pink (2016), Horst and Miller (2012) and Postill (2010), called it *digital ethnography;* Puri (2009) called it *webnography;* Libin and Libin (2005) called it *cyber-anthropology*, and sometimes it's called *online ethnography*. Taylor, Pearce, Nardi and Boellstorff (2012: 4) explain that like many scholars, on occasion they conversationally use phrases like "digital ethnography", "virtual ethnography", or "internet ethnography". However, they see their selves as ethnographers conducting research in virtual worlds, not as "virtual ethnographers". On the other hand, Beneito-Montagut (2011) makes a distinction between virtual ethnographies, which may consist of observing gaming worlds such as "Second Life or World of Warcraft", and "expanded ethnography", which consists of online experiences as expanded enhancements of real relationships. Beneito-Montagut argues that the term "virtual ethnography" appears to be adequate "only if the inquiry takes place in virtual world, but not if we inquire into everyday communications and interactions carried out online but in fact intrinsically linked to the face-to-face communications" (2011: 719). I make the same important distinction. In my research, Facebook ethnography is a type of *expanded ethnography* – supplemental to the real interactions that come from real ethnographic fieldwork locations and fieldwork encounters. I have taken into consideration Facebook Groups used by care workers as a result of the perspective that suggests how online is part of offline contexts and cannot be considered separately (Postill 2010). This standpoint is backed up by the research that shows that the Internet may reinforce offline social relationships (Hampton, Wellman 2003), and that much of the people using social media, including myself, employ it to manage social relationships some of which are simultaneously mediated offline. As my experience with the involvement of Facebook communication with my respondents and insight into the communication between them shows, whatever appears on Facebook often does so with direct reference to offline phenomena or it is integrated with what appears in other (online) media. Also, we cannot expect one could rely solely on online data which brings us to idea of multiplicity of media that researchers can use or adopt "multimedia data collection methods" (Beneito-Montagut 2011). Madianou and Miller (2013) consequently coined the term "polymedia" to indicate that their informants saw the multiplicity of media not as separate channels but as a communicative environment of affordances. Their study of transnational families, who stayed in touch across distances through a variety of digital media, suggested that the choice of appropriate media for the informants had social, emotional and moral consequences for them as persons.

The question that remains to be answered is: How did I use online ethnography my research study? In her book, Hine (2000) explains that we can perform a virtual ethnography in two different ways. The first way is from the perspective of an observer where the ethnographer will not interfere or interact with the community investigated. In a second way, the ethnographer is actively participating in the community doing significant contributions. I decided to pursue an investigation without interference or interaction in the group, looking through posts that members of the group have published. Thereby, the behaviour of the Facebook group members is not interfered with by my participation as a group member. Baker (2013: 135) claims that Facebook can simultaneously be three seemingly disparate things: 1. *A tool or a communicative medium* (used to communicate with the participants across time and distance; 2. *a type of data* (including the participants' status updates, message contacts, photos); 3. *a context of research* (a shared, observable space that fed into and framed data collection). Thus, for me Facebook groups have a multiple functions. This methodological potential of Facebook groups I integrated into my research to initiate, foster and manage friendly relationships with participants, reduce distrust and suspicion and as a result of these relationships deepen ethnographic interpretation. As soon as I realized that an increasing number of my potential respondents use Facebook groups and since I had a Facebook profile as well, I had started to search for these groups. I used the term *Negovateljica* (Serbo-Croatian word for *Caregiver)* a search keyword on Facebook. The result was at least seven to nine groups at the time (December 2017) whose number of members was only increasing over the time I had followed these groups named differently as "Diary of a Caregiver", "Care workers from Bačka to Germany", "Care workers wanted in Germany", "Care workers from Bosnia and Serbia to work in Germany", "Care work 24h: Community of care givers from Italy, Austria and Germany". Most of them were closed groups. As an outsider and without the intention to pretend of accessing the group as a care worker or potential care worker, I had to negotiate with an administrator, the "gate-keeper" of the group. I decided to choose the group "FEMINA – Chit-chat room for caregivers from all former Yugoslavian Republics". This group was chosen because of the large number of participants; because they write a significant number of messages and comments, where members interact and exchange their experiences and information and because cover the region that was particularly of my interest.

This is the description of the group, rules and the goal written by the administrator:

"The group is intended to help women who work or want to work as care workers in the EU, in a following way:
– posting job advertisements of agencies from the EU
– giving advice
– German proficiency test (with me in inbox from 12:00–16: 00, all days except Sundays)
– Chatting among women who do hard work and are part of their families
– Members' posts of all kinds of content, jokes, funny stories
– Any offensive words according to one's nationality will be immediately banned
– You can add people you want, and you know
– You can also place the ads you find on your own, because the happiness should be shared with others
– I hope you will have a good time
– Don't post songs; for that, we have YouTube
– I will block all the posts and comments that induce conflict between group members
Your administrator XY"

I sent a request to join the group that was approved instantly. I realized that the group represent a community of care workers that allows them to come together around a common problem related to doing care work, express concerns and warnings about employers and brokers, share photos from their working places, post jobs, etc. The group is a "free zone" where the above-mentioned fear of irregularity of their statuses as undeclared workers was non-existent. It is a space where members can discuss and share knowledge without legal consequences on, for instance, about irregular crossing borders, irregular stays in the EU and be very transparent in sharing experiences related to semi-legal recruitment agencies and their intermediaries. It happens sometimes that the administrator of the group or some active members suggest a particular topic and others post comments. This form of "entertainment" seemed like my interviewing, only in the written form, like a survey. For example, they ask: "What has been your most challenging and most difficult patient (care receiver)?" Then members reply with very descriptive cases, often interacting with each other. Apart from the insights I gained from rich content of the shared posts, I became aware of the increased number of women who join groups usually to look up a job. For these reasons, I thought that this could be an opportunity to find new research participants. I approached the administrator of the group sending the message in her Inbox, introducing myself and explaining in a very honest manner that I am interested in the group for scientific reasons. In addition, I asked her for permission to post a little advert where I ask members to be part of "scientific research on female migration". She reluctantly agreed, saying that women might react suspiciously. She was right. The comments to my post showed again like, in my offline access to the potential respondents, distrust and anxiety. Some of them accused me of spying in the group while others proved that I was who I said I was sharing the link of my profile at the web page of my institution. Only one woman replied to my post sending a private message that she was willing to talk to me. This was an initial interaction with my first "Facebook" participant who over time become my face-to-face research participant. Soon after I became Facebook friend with more women that I got to know online but also with those I met later in the offline research situations. By utilizing the Facebook chat function (Messenger), I was able to ask questions that remained unanswered in the interview or, which was often the case, to be contacted by women themselves who were informing me about their new jobs, their mobility trajectories, or their lives generally.

The observation in the on-line field showed that for most of women, Facebook groups are fundamental support for their lifestyle in circular labour mobility. The Facebook group activities and contents opened room for thoughts and comment that I as an ethnographer could not have witnessed otherwise. And it displays who writes what. I had learned keywords, dichotomies, phrases, and formulations. While there was certainly bias to these data, this bias always revealed something about the group members and their mutual sometimes, conflicting interests, perspectives, and so forth (Hammersley, Atkinson 1995: 160). Facebook data, like all other forms of data, are produced socially. Therefore, when carried out in conjunction with offline participant observation, the textual and visual analysis of online phenomena is a valuable set of data that can bring out social relationships and patterns.

3.3 Doing Interviews

The main interviewing technique I applied was an "ethnographic interview" (Heyl 2001: 369). Doing ethnographic interviews is a practice that differs from other similar forms of qualitative research technique by two factors: time (duration) and quality of researcher-respondent relationship. According to Heyl, the core of ethnographic interview is "actually genuine exchange of views and enough time and openness in the interviews for the interviewees to explore purposefully with the researcher the meaning they place on the event in their worlds". The key definitional characteristic of an ethnographic interviewing is the craft of establishing respectful, on-going relationship that generates enough rapport for creating the conditions for a genuine exchange. Structured interviewing decontextualizes respondents by separating the individuals and their respondents from the context of their daily lives. Like structured, also semi-structured interviews, interfere with respondents' ability to develop detailed, coherent narratives and to describe how they have made sense of events and experiences. For the purposes of this research, I opted for the narrative interview. The narrative interview technique often used for the life biographies in oral history research, proved useful here because it does not set out a fixed agenda; rather it tends to let the interviewee control the direction, content, and pace of the interview (Scârneci-Domnișoru Florentina 2013). In addition, it creates an atmosphere that "imitate" regular situations of everyday life, wherein people often find themselves telling various things to friends, neighbours, acquaintances, etc. (Scârneci-Domnișoru Florentina 2013). However, I must stress that the narrative interview in case of my research was carefully guided. That means that I was highly aware of the flow and direction of the interview and its content during the interview. The interviews were thematic – I had a list of themes that needed to be covered in the interview but otherwise, I aimed for the interaction to flow freely and as conversationally as possible. The interview questions included themes regarding their background, finding work care in Germany, preparation for that work, changing workplaces, working conditions and work relationships, private and family arrangements. Finally, I always asked about their plans and hopes. Due to the sensitivity of the topic such as irregularity of working status, I learned through the research process to adapt the level of guidance regarding specific character or personality of the women I am interviewing, the context where interview is taking place, and their physical, emotional, and mental state at the moment of the interview. As the narrative interview generates data, rich in detail, complex, vivid, and very often covering a dozen of pages, I have accumulated 40 hours of recorded interview material. Every interview lasted 1,5–3 hours. A third of the interviews were followed up by an additional interview in different settings or during participant observation.

After the debates in social sciences over epistemology and the crisis of authority and representation emerged in the 1980s, the voices from feminist and postmodern critiques in anthropology and sociology during the 1990s highlighted issue concerning the relationship between the researchers and their subject and the issue of what can be known as the interview process. Following this trend I find that is necessary for the validity of the data and the transparency of the research process, to reveal how I did produce interview material and what was the characteristics of that interview process and its flows. As interviewing involves a complex form of social interaction with the respondent it is important to recognize and explain what the respondent chooses to share with me, and how this choice reflects the conditions of the interview situation and my relationship with the respondent. The crucial part of this social interaction according to Heyl (2001) is listening to respondents respectfully and carefully, developing ethical engagement while being aware of our role in the co-construction of meaning during the interview process. The knowledge I gained from the interview is influenced by how I managed to connect with the women care workers, how long and how often I talked to them and quality of relationship I built with them. Considering myself to be an "active interviewer" (Holstein, Gubrium 1995) I am focused on how respondent develops response including all hesitations and contradictions (sometimes without the coherent answer). This is the key in process of analysing narrative, which reveals how meanings are constructed from different identities and different positions.

The question of access to the field, that is to encounter care workers, as has been mentioned previously, proved to be the most difficult step in the research process. This is due to the obstacles I encountered in my efforts, firstly to find them through various channels of information that were at my disposal, secondly to convince them to give me an interview, and third to get their consent to use voice recorder. What type of interview the researcher chooses to apply in her/his study mainly depends on who are the research participants in the study, what is the topic of research and what are the interview questions? In my research, doing interviews with women of different ages and education, working informally, and thus often being in fear from disclosure of their undocumented status and identities, required to develop mutual trust through the relationship that had to be built over the period. On the other hand, it is not only the nature of their work that makes them uncomfortable to speak. The interview questions sometime require answers that are sensitive topics related to the profoundly intimate sphere of people's lives such as divorce, financial problems (debts), the problem with children, health problems, psychological problems, etc. In many cases, women felt reluctant to talk about them, sometimes they even felt ashamed.

This brings me to the central problem in the interview process: What is the motivation of my respondents to give me an interview? What does motivate women to talk about their experiences? To think about this question is crucial because it affects the course of the interview, richness of their stories, and decision on what kind information they want to share, and in what manner.

Once when contact is established either through my friend or acquaintance or through other respondent by her recommendation and respondent agrees to meet me, I usually get in touch with a person via phone to introduce myself and the project I work on. At that moment, I was finding women in different contexts: either they were at work somewhere in family in Germany working all around clock (having no time to talk for one hour or two), or they were waiting for job at their homes, or they were between two jobs, making the break. Those women who did not have a job, were more inclined to talk about problems of job networking, problems in accessing the networks, reasons for taking the job, financial deprivation, personal problems, and less about, for instance, working conditions in German families, difficulties in performing care work, attaining specific knowledge on care work, etc. Thus, some of them are motivated by the injustice they are experiencing being aware of the informal system of exploitation they are part of, or just unsatisfied with a colleague they work with. Worth noticing here, based on my careful conversational analysis of interviews, is that their motivation to talk to me is related to my social positionality. In some cases that can be their expectation to find them a "good job" in Germany or to send the message to the German society through my research about the elderly care system and its weaknesses. Above all, they are motivated undoubtedly to help and to contribute to the project. The respondents' willingness to participate in the project has been built over time. The research like mine that involves "hard-to-get participants" requires more collaborative approach in interaction with research participants. That means giving empowerment to respondents, for instance, by explaining in detail my research project, my reasons for doing it, my biography and how I am going to use the data. This kind of approach is a basis for genuine dialogue and rich narrative data as its outcome. However, building the trust takes time. The most successful interviews were those that followed up telephone or skype calls or intense messaging via Viber and Messenger. If I do not spend enough time with a respondent, the level of trust will be very low. Consequently, the respondents usually reply with a concise statement, with "yes" or "no". The difficulties in gaining information about processes of illegalization in framework the care work mobility are the best example. Respondents were selective about information they want to disclose. The unwelcomed questions could be an obstacle for the continuation of the interview especially if I didn't manage to keep the respondent talking about topics that are relevant to research questions due to respondent's self-censorship. In such situations, I had to invest a significant effort to stimulate the respondent to keep the narrative going with "clarification questions" or to make break re-directing their attention to another topic.

Below is an excerpt of the interview with a woman who at the time did not have much care work experience. She worked for two German families where she spent two months in each, because of the deaths of care recipients and was about to take up a third job). The interview setting is her household in Serbia. We had several Skype calls before interview to get to know each other and to schedule our meeting. During the interview, she was very enthusiastic, very generous in describing her relationship with families, care work, language barriers, daily tasks in the household, etc. In the middle of the interview, I decided to ask her about how the job is organized in the informal social network. I had already tried that at the beginning of the interview asking her how she had found the job, but she avoided to reply changing the topic to reasons for taking up the job. I tried again when she mentioned that she liked knitting and that she usually knits in the bus while travelling to Germany. That was an opportunity for me to ask more about transportation arrangements:

"T: How do you go there, by bus?
J: No, in the car.
T: By the car? So, who drives you?
     Her mood is slowly changing.
J: A driver ... It is organized. He picks us up and drives us home. He comes to my home, picks me up, and brings me to address Germany.
T: And you pay?
     She is getting nervous.
J: No, they pay for it. They pay for everything. Yes, so that's all ... about me, for now ... I'll tell you when I go there. We can talk after that. We can meet each other in Germany.
     I wonder who 'they' are. She hesitates to talk about it. She makes a distance and wants to end the conversation.
T: Yes, we can ... but tell me, do they charge you for finding you a job? Many people do it, I know that, right?
J: Yes, they do charge. I do not know how much I should tell you about this ...
T: It's ok. You don't have to.
     A long silence breaks. Suddenly, she continues:
J: It is understandable, isn't it? Oh, come on, nobody will work today without being paid.
     I explain to her that I know the nature of 'business' and that the prices of brokering are different. I tell her that I'm interested in what is her experience. After the short break, she continues:
J: First two times I paid 150 (euros). After that, each time 100 euros. But ... look ... Considering that they take care of everything, where is the driver, who is the driver, who needs replacement and where – it is quite okay. I do not care for the price. Even if would be constantly 150 euros – it's not a big deal ..."

This fragment of the interview illustrates how questions and answers were negotiated between the respondent and me and how gaining knowledge is a dialogic process. The silence of the respondent and unwillingness to continue the conversation were indicators of complex reaction to the obvious dubious relationship between her and me. Until I did not show to her my pre-existing knowledge about how the black market of care work is organized, she was sceptical about sharing the information with me. Once when I convinced her that I know a lot about the issue and that I am interested in her story, she decided to unveil her experience. In our second encounter, in Germany, I conducted follow up interview with her in the household of her employers. Then she provided a full account of care work brokering and self-regulation of the black market in the care sector.

Unlike in other studies focused on the same topic (for example, Bajt, Leskosek, Frelih 2018), in my research experience, concern about breaking an anonymity and fear about revelation of identity due to their "unique status" as irregular care worker, was less emphasized. This is because many of my respondents (especially those who are doing the job for a long time) know that all the stories of women who experience working 24-hours in German households are almost the same. This is how Fatima wants to ensure her anonymity while thinking also about accidental revelation of her identity:

"So, this is how we are going to do it: My name is Fatima. And for your research, as long as my name is Anja, Alma or else, I don't now ... everything is OK. Even if my story comes out, you write it, or whatever you say, women can recognize themselves and not me."

My respondents showed a very good knowledge of care work migration in Germany. They were aware of the intentional official ignorance of irregular care workers' presence in German households. They regard it as the "open secret" knowing that there are inconsistencies between the official welfare state policy on domestic work and unofficial reality – families and individuals in Germany prefer more informal care market solutions (Lutz 2010). In addition, they can see from theirs everyday experiences that the need for informal elderly live-in care workers is increasing drastically in Germany. However, the problem of fear and trust (which will be more discussed in Chapters 5 and 7) exists not only between the respondent and me but it is much broader and more complex. The success of the interview depends on several layers of trust: between the respondent and me; between respondent and the person who introduced (recommended) the respondent to me; between me and the person who introduced the respondent to me. Only few respondents I got to know through my personal contacts (friends or colleagues) and others by the snowball sampling. It was usually two or three women in the "chain of trust". The women I contacted through Facebook groups did not know each other.

The flow of the interview and openness depends on many factors. Apart from the rapport mentioned above, these factors are certainly age, education, the level of experience in doing care work, material and psychological conditions in which my respondents find themselves at the time of the interview. Respondents with more experience are more likely to be free in telling their stories, providing detailed descriptions of their working lives. Question order is important for substantive reasons. Nevertheless, in the case of my interview process that was not possible. I rarely got an answer to the question straightforwardly. I had to encourage them, by asking for small work-life stories, that usually began after initial questions like *"How are you doing? How is at work?"* or (in cases where woman is waiting for a new job) *"Any news about new job?"*, *"How was at the previous one?"* Starting with kindness, respect and showing care for them at the beginning of the interview makes them feel more comfortable to talk. If I ask the question *"Any news about new job?"*, more likely that I will get the answer about process of recruitment, struggles to get into the network, relationships with colleagues and so on. If I would start with *"How are you doing, how is work?"* I usually hear the story of job tasks, relationship with a family of care receiver, day structure, and so on. This line of questioning respondents allows for the space where they can revoke episodes, emotionally experienced moments, individual practices, detailed opinions and ideas and attitudes explained. Very often experience of "illegality" and informal working arrangements were the themes that came up only when we finished formal interview procedure. In these cases, I often write the notes down instead of using voice-recorder. I avoided the themes such as extremely precarious working conditions, brokering, irregular border crossings, mental and physical violence, etc. until the point in the interview when respondents feel free and safe to tell these experiences. After the initial question I ask for more stories about the themes tackled in the initial narration, following the order in which they were dealt with and turn to interview's words. Then, other topics may emerge which will be subsequently approached. Alternatively, respondents decide to provide the other story that is associated with a previous topic in the narrative. After a preliminary analysis of the material collected hitherto, I identify unmentioned topics and answers that might seem has nothing to do with the narration and bring them up in the follow-up interview.

Sometimes it happens that we cannot make sense of the respondent's narration due to often-contradictory statements, unarticulated speech with a lot of breaks and incoherent accounts. That happens usually at the beginning of the interview. The interview excerpt below describes that. I start the interview with Milica Jeremić opening it with the usual questions *"How are you? How is work?"* before I asked for permission to record the conversation. Milica, who had been working for two years in the same family express her current state and mood as follows:

"Go on (she is pointing to the voice recorder permitting me to turn it on). Not the problem at all. It's good, it's good … it's not hard for me here, do you understand? It's just a bit hard psychologically … I mean, when you are away from home … Especially me … I leave children behind … there are some days when I feel really bad … catastrophe, disaster … it's not that bad for me … nor it is hard but … sometimes it can be … but now the time comes when I must pay for everything … with my health. The first two months, sorry … the first two weeks, are always tough to get through … until I get used to it and then it is fine. The last week is the hardest, I am in a crisis. It is not difficult for me, I am not nervous at all. It Is nothing. It is more personal. I only think about when the time will pass, when the time will pass."

Referring to what has been said above about an active interview, the researcher should be annoyed and confused by this recount interpreting it because of emotional distress or other mental condition. However, my research topic and the respondents require an extremely sensitive ethnographer who considers biographical and situational aspects in the process of interviewing. I interpret the interview excerpt as Milaca's struggle to describe how performing the work is not hard or bad, but it is personally hard, emotionally hard because she is missing her children. She makes a distinction between work itself, the act of work and the consequences of that work that affect her mental state which will be later in the interview much more elaborated. It is important to stress that all respondents have never been subject of any academic study or been in a situation to give a formal statement or the view on the matter. An exception was the student of psychology, Ivana Petrović who already had done some interviews as a student's assignment. During the interview, she often used the expressions like *"Was I clear enough? Just interrupt me at any time if you don't understand"* or *"So, I will now explain it to you better"*. Even though, she sometimes jumps from one topic to another while providing an answer to the more concrete questions.

3.4 Observation with Limited Participation

"Participant observation", that *intimacy of detail*, is sharing the same space with respondents, events and day-to-day living is at the heart of ethnographic research (Okely 2012). Due to the nature of the care work that my respondents perform in the privacy of German households, in the majority cases, it was not possible for me to participate in their daily activities. In the studies like mine, where ethnographic focus is on the process of care labour mobility, participant observation includes visiting and inhabiting various sites and situations where the researcher is not always allowed to observe or participate in (for instance, changing diapers or feeding the elderly). Although my research involvement due to the ethical issues was not possible, there were situations like activities outside of households, travelling or being at home searching for a job where I could have taken different roles and chosen levels of participation in them.

Many authors (for example, Bernard 1994, DeWalt, DeWalt 2002) pointed out that including participant observation in cultural studies increases the study's validity. DeWalt and DeWalt (2002: 92) argue that "the goal for the design of research using participant observation as a method is to develop a holistic understanding of the phenomena under study that is as objective and accurate as possible given the limitations of the method". Being able to conduct interviews in the households where women care workers lived and worked facilitated my involvement in sensitive activities – negotiation of job tasks, salary increase, and other work performing strategies in which I generally would not be invited to participate in. This helped me to improve the quality of data collection and facilitated the development of new research questions.

The opinion, that participant observation is the first step in ethnographic fieldwork (Schensul, Schensul, Le Compte 1999) which serves to connect with a participant, achieve rapport and gain access to the field, in case of my research it turned out to be opposite. The participant observation was only possible when trust and rapport were already developed. The essence of participant observation in my research was the relationship between my respondents, as collaborative researchers who, through building solid relationships, improved the research process and improved my skills to conduct the research.

According to Gold's (Gold 1958) classification of researchers based on the level of their involvement of researcher in the activities of respondents, I would appear as *the observer as a participant*. This position enables the researcher to participate in the group activities as desired, yet the main role of the researcher is to collect data, and the persons being studied are aware of the researcher's observation activities. In this stance, I am an observer who is not a member of the group and who is interested in participating as a means for conducting better observation and, hence, generating more complete understanding of persons' activities and behaviours. This "peripheral membership role" (Adler, Adler 1994: 380), allowed me to observe and interact closely enough with women care workers and to establish an insider's identity without participating in those activities constituting the core of group membership.

Participant observation in the context of care labour mobility would yield results only when it takes place over long periods and I as a researcher become part of the everyday setting. However, my fieldwork, which I labelled as *fieldwork with limited and selective participation* that was not the feasible for two main reasons.

The first is the privacy of families where women care workers perform their work. One could assume that employers of women care workers, that are elderly and their families, wouldn't allow my presence in the household due to mistrust and suspicious about my intentions. I was quite sure that even mentioning my role as a researcher, would endanger women's position in the household and probably their job position. Despite this perceived obstacle, I was visiting women in several households, which I described and underlined in their portraits (see Chapter 6 and Chapter 7). These visits to the households where I was introduced as a friend of woman care worker helped me to get more nuanced understanding of social relationships, working conditions and women experiences of performing elder care work. Observation with limited participation for example was occurring when I was witnessing interaction between care workers and care recipients, between care workers and family of elderly person they take care of, between women care-workers between themselves. Also, I had an opportunity during the interview to accompany care worker to her house or accommodation, assisting her with her work in the household she works in, travel with her, and other situations that I thoroughly described in empirical chapters.

The second reason is the necessity of abandoning *par excellence* of traditional ethnographic practice, that is spending extended periods in one place, in favour of multi-locality of research design. The multi-locality of lives of my research participants as previously pointed out required my own mobility. To answer the research question "how motility for care work is built", I had to move together with my respondents and observe labour mobility processes and mobility flows from the inside. Doing research between stopover points while travelling with women that is, within movement, allowed me to access different phases in the formation and reconfiguration of my respondents' plans, routes, and interruptions. Working within labour mobility flows makes it possible, for example, to witness the ephemeral moments of contact between care workers on the move and various non-state and state actors (for instance, border police). Sometimes I was moving randomly taking the routes where travel opportunities led me. The advantage of this type of *ethnography of movement* is that it prevents the researcher from being guided too much by preconceptions and provides the possibility of researching in places other than those initially identified, thereby allowing new avenues for research to emerge. Being participant and observer in crossing the border and experiencing "illegalization" of myself, allowed for investigation of border crossing practices, the events would be invisible or at least unverifiable and indescribable without making "mobility" my fieldwork. It also makes it possible to perceive nascent sociability during the encounters that care labour mobility offers and entails.

Relationships of trust, closeness, and friendship, built up through several interview encounters with the same women, made it possible for me to take participation in some aspects of their daily lives. These usually included commuting from one town to another, doing the shopping together, visiting them at working places (where family agreed to host the careworker's guest and when my respondent had time and freedom to include my presence in their everyday activities). The most intensive presence and my involvement with care workers and their patients occurred in two cases. The first, is my key respondent, Ana. Since we lived relatively close one to another in Munich, my often visits to her, chatting with her and her colleague Helena helped me significantly to become a "cultural member" that facilitated a closer look into their behaviours and activities. A distressful accident that happened to Ana, triggered unexpected developments in my relationship with her employer, which in turn made my presence at Ana's working place more intense and more durable. During Ana's stay in the hospital, Frau Müller invited me to her house "for tea". I was surprised and curious about the motives behind the invite, but I knew that she wanted to get to know the only person Ana knew in Munich. After a long introduction of myself, she showed admiration for my education and career-oriented goals asking why I am so close to Ana alluding that we don't have much in common – different age, education and interests. I told her that Ana was a friend of my mother, that she was kind, honest and hard-working woman with complicated family history and that she deserved to be happy. Frau Müller replied: "Yes, she does, and I can make that happen." We spent the rest of the time talking about her husband, family, her social position and capital and the wealth in her possession. She also told me a story about how she had "found" Ana, which gave me an insight into the how employers perceive and use the informal domestic and care work market, which enriched my ethnographic material and induced a new questions. Since that encounter, Ana used to invite me to Frau Müller's house when she was away. Since Ana was not allowed to leave the house during Frau Müller's absence, I was coming to visit her and make her company during long hours when she did not have anything to do. These visits provided me with a deeper insight into domestic work choreography, caring tasks, knowledge about relationships with other people related to that household.

Similarly, with other respondents, I had more interacted in "hanging out situation". "Hanging out" is the process that De Munck and Sobo (1998) called the "intimate stage", during which the researcher has already established a relationship with the respondent to the extent that he/she/they no longer has to think about what he/she/they says. There is more to participant observation than just hanging out. It sometimes involves the researcher's presence in the everyday activities of the respondents. During these intimate interactions, I learned about the nonverbal expression of feelings, determined who interacts with whom, grasp how my respondents and their colleagues, care recipients, and other persons involved in care work communicate with each other. However, participant observation is conducted by a biased human who serves as the instrument for data collection. The researcher must understand how his/her/their gender, sexuality, ethnicity, class, education may affect observation, analysis, and interpretation and reflect on it which is the topic I moving to in the next sub-chapter.

3.5 Reflecting on the Ethnography of Care Labour Mobilities

Reflexivity in the research process, discussed by social scientists for many decades, is informed by interpretivism, feminism and critical discourses (Mauthner, Doucet 2003). The question of how our social positions shape access to participants, data, and field sites is a central concern of many qualitative researchers; however, being reflexive does not erase potential conflicts that occur in the field interrogating our positions as researchers remains an essential task of qualitative research because reflexivity affects both writing up the data and the data's status, standing and authority (Brewer 2000: 127).

Reflexivity, particularly in sociological and anthropological research can be understood as the idea "that the orientations of researchers will be shaped by their socio-historical locations including the values and interests that these locations confer upon them" (Hammersley, Atkinson 1995: 16). Taking the idea further, Bourdieu has called for epistemic reflexivity (Bourdieu, Wacquant 1992: 36–47) or participant objectivity (Bourdieu 2003), which refers to scrutinising the researcher's positions and practices not only in the research site but also within the specific epistemological field (Bourdieu 2003: 283).

According to Bourdieu, to "practice reflexivity" means turning the analytical gaze to the researcher by "situating him [sic] at a determinate point in social space-time – and so acquiring a more acute awareness and a greater mastery of the constraints that can be exerted on the scientific "subject" through the links which bind him to the empirical subject, his interests, drives, and presuppositions" (Bourdieu 2003: 119–120). Carrying out social research, especially face-to-face encounters with participants, encompasses numerous complex and shifting boundaries. Research that requires communication of opinions, feelings and experiences from the participants to the researchers needs to understand and negotiate, at least temporarily, the boundaries that may shape and impede that communication. These boundaries may be physical, temporal, ethical, linguistic, socio-cultural or religious and thus will be influenced by the gender, age, ethnicity and social class of participants and researchers. Reflexivity can help to reveal the complex dynamics that underpin the research relationship. Through an awareness of the dynamic rhythms of our multi-positionalities, we can appreciate the complexities and contingencies of the stories that are shared and understood through the various qualities of interactions in fieldwork encounters.

On the other hand, there is a point to the argument of over-emphasizing the need for self-reflexivity. I argue that good research practice must be somewhere in-between the two extremes of researcher neutrality and self-centred reflexivity. I understand fieldwork as constituted by a set of relationships and embodied practices, which requires focusing on how the research participants and researchers are socially situated (Haraway 1989). I fully acknowledge the importance of situating oneself in the academic field as well as in the research field. In such complex research setting, reflexivity means being sensitive to the power relationships involved in the research process and adjusting the research methods accordingly. It also means reflecting upon the theoretical tools and concepts applied in the research. In the next two sections, I will provide an account of my own reflecting on three points by providing an examples from the field: a) power imbalance in the researcher-researched relationship, b) emotional response of researcher and risks that researcher face during the research process and c) strategical use of our multiple positionalities.

Insider-Outsider: Multiple Positions of the Researcher

Ever since Merton's (1972) classic essay "Insiders and Outsiders" there have been ongoing debates about who can speak for whom and who can research whom. Researcher's status as "insider", one who studies people who are similar to themselves – or "outsider", one who study people who differ from themselves has been for a long-time fixed category. There is an implicit assumption of a clear fixed collectivity, usually defined through ethnicity or nationality, of which one is either explicitly inside or outside. Such an assumption not only underestimates the multi-layered identities of researchers and participants, but also the dynamism through which varied dimensions of identity may be enacted during an interview. Each research encounter involves multiple positionalities including gender, age, class, religion, nationality, migratory experience, language, parental status, etc.

Although we all retain both characteristics because we have multiple statuses (Merton 1972) "being outsider within" (Collins 1986; Zempi, Awan 2017), social science researchers have a long history of focusing on the question – what or where are we inside or outside of? During my fieldwork, I was eager to establish a relationship of trust with the people whose lifeworlds I wanted to explore. However, at some points, I had the feeling that I was the one who was being studied. They usually ask a lot of questions about my statuses (marital, professional, economic, residential, etc.), my personal history (Where I was born? Where my parents are from? Where did I live in my childhood? How did I decide to come to Germany to do my Ph.D.? Which class my parents belong to?) I was an object of general curiosity wherever I went and whomever I met, but more than that – why I am doing this research, was of even more interest. The very fact that my study took place at different places with persons who live in double "illegality" (lack of work and residence permits) greatly contributed to problems of gaining access or getting close to care workers. My questions and observations about routes into mobility, negotiations with employers, access to information about available jobs, salaries, networks, process of recruitment – are viewed not only as an unwelcome intrusion but also arouse suspicion about my identity as a researcher which was sometimes understood in terms of someone who works for the German officials like border police or the immigration office.

My gender identity, indeed, has implications for my researcher's position, but my cultural and social background also creates assumptions and expectations about who I am and affect how others perceive me. I could have heard very something like a critique or even advice with a good intention:

"Why are you doing this to yourself? To talk with us an uneducated woman, to listen to hard life stories and to chase women who do not want to talk to you – you can choose so many other topics for your thesis. You are a child from the nice family, you didn't used to listen such hardship and problems. You better go, find husband here. Here, in Germany."

I realized how my professional and private identities would get mixed together, since I was from the same country/region but from different class and of better education. Often the interview atmosphere became more relaxed when I created a connection to the circle of women who were connected through close friendship or history of good collegial relations. I felt that being entangled in such a web of social relationships and the clash of expectations regarding my close friendship with them was harder for me to claim the role of a "professional fieldworker". On the one hand, I was a friend, when they did expect certain help in finding a job through my connections. On the other hand, I used to be seen as a selfish researcher who wants to exploit them taking their stories, misuse them and build the academic career based on their private lives. While some of them have viewed me as a threat, that is being able to reveal their identities, others raised the question about influence of my study on structural conditions of employment and how my research could help (or not) change their position in German policies on migration and employment.

Although sharing an "insider" identity as a Serbian woman, I found that my class position, education, and urban lifestyle defined me as an outsider; marking a boundary between the disadvantaged women, I sought to interview and myself. However, my position as a friend of someone's friend who recommend me as a person of trust appeared to facilitate access and cooperation with potential respondents. This resulted in shifting positionalities as I was negotiating multiple standpoints through research encounters with different participants. Thus, shared nationality or ethnicity, even when combined with shared gender, was no guarantee of mutually accepted "insider" positionality. Overall, I am convinced that my identity, gender, where and how I was raised, my personal traits – influenced whom I met, what was confided to me, and how I interpreted what I heard and saw. I am sure that my academic status opened the doors to Frau Müller and helped me gain access to information and views on informal domestic and care work regimes and how, for example, working on the black market of care became culturally

150　　PERIPHERAL LABOUR MOBILITIES

perceived as a "normal practice", one that is economically convenient both for employers – who save on taxes and for employees, who can earn a higher salary.

Getting Personal: Friend or Key Respondent?

In contemporary ethnography, there has been considerable concern with the personal experiential aspects of research. Various terms have been used to describe this phenomenon, such as reflexive ethnography, autoethnography, or personal narrative (Davies 1999; Ellis, Bochner 2000; Hedican 2001; Reed-Danahay 1997). Although it could be said that descriptions of the various dimensions of the field research experience have become plentiful in recent times, an analysis of the core aspects underlying and shaping researchers' experiences have only begun to receive specific attention. It is also an interesting matter that despite the importance of the role of experience in fieldwork, there is a dearth of critical discussions, aside from the various descriptive accounts of this phenomenon.

Through my experiences of doing multi-local fieldwork in different settings, I became familiar with care workers' relationships with each other, their work routines, their attitudes toward employers as well as their attitudes towards me. All these different relations, reminded me, again that who can be a knower, what we know, how we know, who speaks for whom – depends on the politics of our multiple locations and intersections of identities and social structures that construct these locations. This was especially important in doing participant observation and doing in-depth interviews. A Serbian educated, unmarried woman from middle-class urban nonreligious family from the political left, studying women who work in German households who are from varied racial, ethnic, religious, educational backgrounds and of different ages, from different class with diverse migration histories and diverse motivations to put themself on the move for care work. In this kind of setting, reflexivity in anthropological fieldwork is understood, as the idea "that the orientations of researchers will be shaped by their socio-historical locations including the values and interests that these locations confer upon them" (Hammersley, Atkinson 1995), must be addressed. Since the 1970-s there has been a philosophical debate within and beyond the social science about the nature of knowledge and scientific enquiry (Harding 1987). The basic of such knowledge has been questioned by calls for re-examination of dichotomies of masculinity/femininity, objectivity/subjectivity, mind/body, reason/emotionality. The intellectual movement of the 1990s captured by postmodernism and post-structuralism has added fuel to this debate with an argument that there are no universal truths to be discovered, and that all knowledge is grounded in human society, situated, partial, local, temporal, and historically specific. As Ann Oukley, a British sociologist (Oukley 1981) suggested that contrary to an objective, standardized and detached approach to ethnographic interviewing, the goal of finding out about, in this case, women irregular care workers' experiences need to be understood and told – is "best achieved when the relationship of interview and respondent is non-hierarchical and when the interviewer is prepared to invest his or her identity in the relationship". However, this romantic perspective has been criticized highlighting that gender and personal involvement may not be enough for full "knowing". Reflections of the inevitability of power differentials within the research have extended into discussions of the dangers of the illusions of equality in research relationships, the ethical dilemmas involved in conducting research with marginalized vulnerable women, as well as larger epistemological issues involved in attempting to "know" others.

The truth is that we cannot escape the necessity of developing rapport and a level of intimacy during the pursuit of prolonged fieldwork. In fieldwork, professional relationship has a personal quality. Fieldwork simply will not generate good data and interesting analysis without personal investment in the relations of the field. Establishing field relations also has certain limits and boundaries. Sometimes we need to establish relationships with social groups or people with whom we have explicitly very little in common. It is also possible to experience situations where at first there are genuine shared views and personal engagement. In both cases managing the consequent relationships, both personally and professionally can be challenging. During ethnographic fieldwork, we develop relationships with key individuals. Some field relationships built up into the field, last well beyond the fieldwork. These are long-term friendships based on trust, rapport, respect, personal commitment, sharing mutual interests, feelings and so on. During my research, I engaged in conversation with respondents whose views I particularly despise, that made me feel uneasy. There are also situations when we should not pursue the argument, clashes, or misunderstandings in a way that we might do with our friends or colleagues. Maintaining friendly relationships in research, many social scientists consider as damaging effects of a research technique that encourages friendship to focus on private and personal aspects of life of the respondents. Judith Stacey (1988) argued that although "the ethnographic method appears ideally suited to feminist research when it draws on those resources of empathy, connection and concern that many feminists consider being women's special strengths, it is ultimately unclear whether the appearance of greater respect for equality with research subjects in the ethnographic approach masks a deeper, more dangerous form of exploitation". Postcolonial scholars like Said (1978) have been particularly critical of privileged position of researchers and potential exploitation of the researched (specially developed in the discussion on ethnography and issues of representation).

My involvement with respondents during the research process proves that fieldwork is more a messy experience (Marcus, Fischer 1986: 22) than simple exploitation/collaboration dichotomy based on equality. Imbalances in the degree of trust, commitment, and personal investment can lead to potentially exploitative or unbearable situations, for both sides. The reliance of fieldwork on our personal relationships also places us at risk of vulnerability, exploration, and hurt. If we go back to the story about Ana, we can see that power imbalance can lead to potentially exploitative or unbearable situations, for both researcher and respondent. During the research process, I realized that the success of my fieldwork relies on my personal relationships with women who are very often in the grey zone of legality starting from the journey they take to Germany to the work they perform in German households under the threat of abuse, lack of any right and of health and accident insurance. I couldn't have anticipated risks and troubles I could have faced. I knew, though, that I have a power when I act as a researcher, which was very often appreciated by my respondents whose respect I gained as someone who "succeeded in life" and therefore can earn their trust. On the other hand, power can be in the corner of my respondents who perceive my research activities as a "fishing expedition" for law enforcement agencies to gather information on an irregular work in Germany and thus deny my access to the field.

As Ana's case demonstrates, Ana certainly earned my empathy that I felt not only as a researcher but also as a human being. My emotional response to the distressing episode led me to the right decision despite knowing that concealing Ana's real status (not the irregular care worker, but my guest in Munich) to the police could potentially place myself and her in legal danger. The risk I took by protecting Ana by giving the false statement to the police, could jeopardise my legal status as a foreign academic in Germany, my freedom of movement and my future career prospects. This kind of "edge ethnography" can cause experience of a variety of risks within the categories of physical/health, emotional, legal, and personal/professional. While making an argument for discussion about privileged position of researchers and potential exploitation of the researched we must bear in mind the complexity of situations where these risks take place and where both sides are equally involved. The experience with Ana led me to face ethical dilemmas regarding my own level of intervention in the life of the subject in research. One of these issues involves a feeling of ambiguity in certain fieldwork situations and how to respond appropriately to them. Evidently, our training in qualitative methods do not provide sufficient sensitivity to situations in which there is an ethical or moral dilemma. We cannot expect hard and fast guidelines for all fieldwork situations, but in my personal case, I felt a rather intense conflict between the professional desire to gather information regardless of the sensitivity of the situation, on the one hand, and at personal side, wish to help her to overcome unexpected traumatic situation she was in. All this urges us to understand fieldwork process in terms of the dynamic rhythms of multi-positionalities. Such an approach enables researchers to be reflexive about the instability and contingency of empathy, understanding, and rapport, and how these need to be continually negotiated across layers of power differentials.

The expected ethical concerns related to protecting the respondents and the data were awarded my full attention. Special care was given to establishing trusting relationships by following the model of a so-called "working alliance", which was developed as a good practice for researching migration and integration processes via a biographical narrative interview method (see Apitzsch, Siouti 2007). In interview transcriptions and fieldwork diaries, all the names were anonymized, as pseudonyms, especially since some of the respondents were anxious about disclosure of their personal information. Information like name of the village or town where women were working, name of the family they work in, names of family members, are strictly asked by my respondents to not to be revealed in the study. It is important to stress that research that deals with a marginalized and vulnerable participants like refugees, asylum seekers, or persons who work without work permit like women in my study, faces the problem of limited extent to which we can keep anonymity. This is because the biographical parts of interviews and the history of women's mobilities and trajectories pose a special challenge, because anonymization appears to run counter to the idea of biography itself.

Nevertheless, I used all research ethical tools to prevent anything that would allow backtracking a sensitive statement of my respondents that could negatively affect their legal status, personal dignity, and their privacy. I always first asked for the permission to record the interview. Then, I informed my respondents about the study: its objectives, benefits, and its importance. This was not only a matter of following a procedure, but also to ensure the commitment of the participants to the study. It was crucial to be responsive and receptive to the sensitivity of the interviewed women and their life stories without being intrusive in their life. To prevent "invasion of privacy", they were informed that they can choose to terminate the interview or their involvement in the research whenever they wish. Murphy Elizabeth and Robert Dingwall (2001: 339–351) describe a set of ethical principles that I followed in my research: non-maleficence; beneficence (that research should produce some positive and identifiable benefit rather than simply be carried out for its own sake); autonomy, and self-determination (the values and decision of research participants must be respected); justice (all participants should be treated equally). The same ethical principles can be applied to virtual ethnography. Wilson and Peterson (2002: 461) argue that anthropology online is substantially the same as any other sort of anthropological research. Although above listed ethical principles in research do not address IT and internet communication directly, showing respect for participants in my study, protecting their dignity, their anonymity or giving them proper credit, and obtaining their informed consent, I applied online as well as in face-to-face contexts.

3.6 Short Biographical Portraits

Before I embark on the explanation of the geographical, political, and socio-economical context where my study took place, I would like to provide background information on the elder care workers whose stories are explicitly referred to or quoted in this book. As an anthropologist, I am interested rather in documenting and understanding the variation of situations and actors, than identifying what is typical or average in my study. To ensure the diversity of the sample, I aimed to gather perspectives and stories from women care workers who are different in the respect of:

1) age,
2) family and marital status; caring responsibilities,
3) citizenship; nationality; ethnicity,
4) educational attainment,
5) employment status,
6) financial status: (in)dependent,
7) German language knowledge.

1. *Ana Wendl* is 54-year-old and she has been working as an elder care worker in Germany for over 4 years. Married into a German minority family in the Northern Serbia (Vojvodina) Ana speaks German fluently. Her husband works as a long-haul truck driver. They both hold Hungarian and Serbian citizenship based on her husband's employment in Hungary for over 10 years. She has two sons, both grown up, living separately in the big city in Vojvodina. The oldest son lives with his wife and twin daughters and works as an agricultural engineer. The youngest finishes their studies in electrical engineering lives with his girlfriend and still financially depends on Ana. In the country, Ana has a big family house and the land where she is coming back from Germany. Although still married, Ana is emotionally and physically separated from her husband. When he is not driving the truck, he resides in Hungary. Ana is taking care of two family houses in the village, land, and a big orchard. She works in Germany to earn the money to buy her own little apartment in the city and to finance her pension fund. Ana has a secondary education and most of her life was a housewife with occasional employment in the sale and agricultural sectors.

2. *Fatima Hodzić* was born in 1980 in Bosnia and Herzegovina where she lives with her second husband her child from the first marriage, and two children in a big family house that she shares with her mother. The children are aged 12, 6, and 1. She's been travelling to Germany for care work 4 years. She learned to speak German over the years and today she speaks it fluently. She has a brother and sister who run a family floral business importing flowers and owning the flower shop. While Fatima's father was still alive, she was involved in family business working occasionally. Fatima is professional ironer and before she started elder care work in Germany she was working as an ironer in the textile industry in Bosnia. She quit the job because of the sexual harassment and the low salary. While she is in Germany, her husband takes care of children with a help of her mother.

3. *Gordana Tasić* lives in a village in Vojvodina, Northern Serbia, in an idyllic family house surrounded by the big vegetable garden and orchard. She works as a teacher in the local primary school. She holds a degree in German language and literature. In the age of 46, Gordana has two children (9-year-old and 6-year-old sons), an employed husband and apart from her tetheir aching job, she produces organic vegetables. To improve family budget Gordana tried to work as an elder care worker in Germany during the school holidays, sick leaves, and days off. She didn't manage to work in Germany for more than six months.

4. *Helena Telban* is 48-year-old mother of two sons (age 18 and 23). At the time of the interview, she has been working as a care worker for a year already. After 15 years of working as a laboratory technician in the soap and detergent manufacturing industry in Norther Serbia. As the industry closed down in the post-socialist economic transition, Helena lost her job in 2005. Between 2005 and 2016, she didn't have a stable job or income. In the meantime, she divorced her first husband based on domestic violence. During that time, she was a single parent working in different sectors: sales, beauty salons, and service sectors (restaurants and bars). She decided to travel to Germany for care work in 2016. She remarried in 2014. Helena was born in the former Yugoslav republic Slovenia (todays the EU member country) but she never applied for Slovenian citizenship.

5. *Isidora Bašić* is a 53-year-old mother of three children and two grandchildren. She gave up on her permanent white-collar job in the hospital where she was working in administration for health insurance for almost 30 years. Struggling to meet ends and finance life in the big house with children (who still need parent's handouts as she says). Isidora's husband is retired as a former construction worker. His pension and Isidora's salary were not enough to sustain monthly spending which forced them to take a bank loan that she must pay off. As she was born in today's Bosnia and Herzegovina, she holds dual citizenship and two passports that allow her to work in Germany for more than three months on tourist visa. Isidora speaks German fluently.

6. *Ivana Petrović* is a 31-year-old student who is one final exam from obtaining a bachelor's degree in psychology. Ivana lives with her brother, also a student and her mother pensioner in a family house in the town in Southern Serbia. She's been taking various student jobs, mostly in the NGO sec-

tor. Ivana is feminist activist involved in a several projects in the local NGOs. When her father died, her mother with one pension and two students with occasional jobs struggled to survive which is why Ivana decided to take a care job in Germany. Ivana doesn't speak German. She speaks English fluently. She worked as an elder care worker for an elderly blind woman for more than a year. After that, she quitted travelling to Germany, finished her studies, and found a job as a psychologist.

7. *Jasna Pajević* is unemployed artist, sculptor with university degree, who dreams of buying her ceramic furnace to create ceramic figurines. She is a 57-year-old single mother of 21-year-old son. She holds Serbian citizenship and lives in Northern Serbia, in her house with her son. She has no German language skills, but she speaks very good English. Prior to care work in Germany, she worked in a studio for stained-glass windows. She has been working as elder caregiver in Baden-Württemberg for eight months. Jasna has survived breast cancer and the fire that almost destroyed her house to the ground.

8. *Marina Jovanović* holds a full time job in the hospital as a scrub nurse (surgical team assistant). 49-year-old Marina lives in Eastern Serbia in the family house in the country an extended family that includes her, her husband and her parents. Her son finishes his studies at the University of Medicine and Pharmacy, Timișoara in Romania where he has been living for the last three years. Marina proudly talks about educational achievements of her son. Marina uses holidays, days off work and unpaid leaves to travel to Germany to take care of the elderly. She says, she needs a money for her son's education and to pay a mortgage for the apartment she and her husband bought in near town. The family is occupied with agriculture and land. They produce their food. Her husband is employed and they both drive cars. Marina starts to learn the German language when she applied for the German-Serbian recruitment program for nurses and doctors. Initially, her idea was to migrate to Germany as a skilled worker in the health sector. As her plans failed, she found a way to juggle between her nursing job in Serbia and travel to Germany every three months.

9. *Milica Jeremić* and her husband are war refugees from Croatia, living in Northern Serbia, Vojvodina. As a teenager, Milica fled with her parents from the border zone between Croatia and Serbia where most of the military op-

erations during the Yugoslavian civil war were taking place. Milica was born in 1979. in Croatia. According to the post-Yugoslav citizenship law she was entitled to holding two citizenships, Croatian and Serbian. As Croatian, she is a citizen of the EU member state, which improves her chances to find a declared and contracted job in Germany. Milica has two children, daughter (18-year-old) and a son (13-year-old). Her husband is employed. They do not own the property. They live in rented apartment in the city. Milica holds a secondary education. Through life, she was taking various jobs, mostly in sales (supermarkets and cloth stores). Being not able to finance everyday life in Serbia, she decided to take an elder care job in Germany. She has been working two years for a German family, taking care of an old woman as a care worker with contract and social benefits. She speaks German.

10. *Nada Marković* is a 61-year-old, twice divorced (a long time ago) single woman and mother of two daughters and three grandchildren. She lives in capital of Serbia, in her own apartment. She is pharmaceutical technician with a secondary education. After 20 years working in the biggest and most successful pharmaceutical industry in the Former Yugoslavia, she lost her job due to the redundancy and the industry collapse in the post-war Yugoslavia. For the last 13 years Nada has been striving to sustain a basic income by taking jobs in different sectors far from her professional occupation (in sales, restaurants, cafes, clothes industry, etc.). Her younger daughter, single mother lives in the same city in her own apartment she rent. Having a good paid and stable job Nada's daughter needs her for taking care of a small child. Nada's older daughter lives in Germany with husband and two sons. They are both employed. At least 4 months a year Nada travels to Germany to help with kids of her older daughter. Without stable job and income and without qualifying years to be entitled to pension Nada doesn't want to rely financially on her children. She wants to improve her financial situation and opts for the elder care work in Germany. She has a basic knowledge of German that she learned during visiting her daughter in Germany.

11. *Sanela Mehić* is 48-year-old unemployed geriatric nurse from Bosnia and Herzegovina. She has been taking care of the elderly professionally in nursing homes for the last ten years. She has been taking care of an elderly man in Germany three months. Sanela is a mother of three children, and grandmother of one granddaughter. She lives with her husband and two sons (age of 18 and 21) in their house. Her daughter is married and lives in the same

town with her own family. Sanela's husband is unemployed, and her sons work from time to time. They don't have a stable income and are in debt due to taking a bank loan for some time.

12. *Snežana Kemeneš* worked over twenty years as an accountant in the financial department at the city council and other government institutions. When she was made redundant, she got fired. Since then, as a woman in her mid-fifties she couldn't find job at the formal labour market in Serbia. Snežana is 58-year-old woman who is not entitled to pension because of the lack of qualifying years. Since her divorced husband died, her financial troubles have been growing. She is mother of 18-year-old daughter who lives with her boyfriend, and she is still financially dependent on Snežana. Snežana owns the small house in the middle size town in Vojvodina (Northern Serbia) which she currently cannot afford to keep warm because she has no money to buy firewood. She doesn't have any source of income. She feels tired and depressed. Currently she travels to Germany for care work every two or three months. She recently has started to learn German language. She is able to communicate basic things related to care work.

13. *Suzana Mitrović* is a 40-year-old from Central Serbia. Married. She lives with her husband and two children (16 and 13 years of age). She holds a high school diploma. She doesn't speak the German language. She has no previous experience in care work. Suzana owns family business in agriculture and runs the local café bar. The first time she worked as elder care giver in Germany was in 2013 for 6 months after she stopped and never tried again. For a decade she worked in the local furniture industry until it was closed.

14. *Vera Jelić* is a 59-year-old married pharmaceutical assistant. She worked for 28 years as a pharmacy assistant. She is from Serbia and holds Serbian citizenship. She lived as a migrant, for a few years, in Sweden where her husband was working. Knowledge of the German language is on a communication level. Not entitled to pension. Lives in a family house with her husband and a 30-year-old daughter who is unemployed. She has been working as elder care worker a year and a half.

15. *Zorica Milić* is a 42-year-old from Central Serbia. She holds a degree in economics. Since she lost her job as an economist in the town administration due to redundancy eight years ago, Zorica is unemployed without a stable

income. Her husband is a mathematical engineer currently without a job as well. They live in their apartment with a son of age 12. For the last four years, Zorica has been working occasionally as a babysitter in Switzerland and Italy for migrant families from Serbia. She recently started taking elder care jobs in Germany. She doesn't speak German. She has a modest knowledge of English.

Chapter 4
Contextualizing Care Work Mobility from the Former Yugoslavia to Germany

4.1 Snežana's Case

4th of August 2018, 17h (from my Messenger log/fieldwork diary)

"Hi Tanja, I got an aggressive dementia patient with her mentally retarded daughter. They said one patient. It turned out it is two of them. They said she was demented and not movable. On the contrary, she is like a whirligig toy and very aggressive. I am pulling through my sixth day here. I should stay 21 days. Fuck my Serbian passport! When I make the Croatian passport, I will be able to choose the job I prefer. I do not know how to do it, but I will do it. All the jobs one can get with a Serbian passport are not worth even telling you about. Disaster!"

5th of August, 00.20h (from my Messenger log/fieldwork diary)

"Are you awake? Here it is like working in a psychiatric ward. She howls all night long."

These are just two out of dozens of messages that were fired at my phone almost every day and sometimes during the night, from the different respondents I was in touch with during my fieldwork. Such frequent messages, follow-up interviews in transit situations and permanently keeping contact with women care workers via Skype, Messenger, or Facebook over a longer period were constitutive part of "mobile fieldwork". Sometimes women contacted me often to find a mutual convenient time for meeting and sometimes they reached out to inform me about their jobs or just to have a chat. I had been in touch with Snežana via Skype and Messenger for almost a year. In our first interview via Skype in April 2018, Snežana told me the long and painful story of her first experience commuting to Germany for elderly care work. Within just a few months she had worked in 7 different towns and villages in Germany caring for elderly individuals in 7 different households. Snežana is 58-year-old, a divorced woman from Northern Serbia who worked for over 20 years as an accountant in the financial department at the city council.

162   PERIPHERAL LABOUR MOBILITIES

"The reason why I started to travel to Germany is – I lost the job in Serbia. I am not entitled to unemployment benefits or even to be registered as a job seeker at the National Employment Agency. I don't have enough qualifying years to retire. Then, the Employment Law changed and now I cannot even get early retirement. Until last year I was paying pension contributions on my own. This year I gave up because I can't pay it anymore. I spent a fortune on pension benefits and still cannot retire until 65 years of age. When I realized that I cannot afford myself a 'piece of bread', I started to learn German and search for a job as a care worker."

Snežana divorced her husband after he had a heart attack and stroke. Long before he got sick, Snežana's marriage broke down irretrievably when she realized that he was not the same man she had married. In the meatime, her husband got diabetes and his personality changed radically. She narrates her situation as follows:

"I don't know how I dared to divorce him. I was unemployed, without any income, with a child in high school. I have no idea how I handled that situation. I lived without money, 'on grass and water', without money even to buy firewood to heat the house. When he died, I paid for his funeral with the money he had in his account. He has two children from a previous marriage and an inheritance settlement at the court is to be held. With all the money I had, €500, I paid the lawyers, just to start the process. And … my daughter is so angry with me, disappointed. I don't even know why. We're out of money. The land my husband and I owned together, he sold and got €36,000. €10,000 remained in the account, but the bank account is frozen until the final resolution at the court. My daughter inherited his pension of Serbian Dinars 15,000 and I pay €100 for her apartment rent. The man, her boyfriend, who she lives with, is an unemployed, problematic guy, with debts … horrible, horrible."

After the divorce her daughter started high school and her husband took her to live with him. Then he sold the land they owned and spent all the savings they had earned together. When her husband died, they had already been divorced for 5 years. During these five years, after the divorce, she was taking care of him as his health condition worsened and she wanted to protect the daughter from caring for the sick father, who was living with him at the time, and went to the university. Her husband paid for the education of her daughter and was very generous with her allowances. Snežana was, as she says, fighting against her husband who was spoiling her daughter with the money, which turned her daughter against her. This emotional and financial hardship and her broken family forced Snežana to look for eldercare work in Germany:

"It has been two or three years since I started looking for care jobs in Germany. At the time, there were no Facebook groups and alike. Everything was by word of mouth. You ask around, you get to know a person who goes to Germany, and then ask for a recommendation or contact person … nobody wants to tell you. It was a big problem for me until I got into the network and figured out who sends women and who organizes the job."

This is how Snežana describes the 7 jobs she moved between over the 6 months.

"The first job I got was through my daughter's friend's mother. I should have stayed two months. Instead, I worked only seven days. The woman I was replacing came back. At the same time, my father died … so I had to come back anyway.

The second job, I found through a former office colleague I had worked with. He had a female friend who does elder care work in Germany, but she was recruited through a Hungarian recruitment agency. They needed more women at the time. I went there and the old lady died in 8 days. I had to wait 4 days for the driver to come to pick me up. I spent four nights in the house where granny died. I was told that I would be paid for these 4 days and that I should rest. Rest? How to rest? I hadn't slept a wink. Horror!

The third job … the neighbor from my street came to ask me if I would replace her for six weeks because her daughter had a surgery. I said yes, went there and … what can I tell you? It was hell. The woman screamed, yelled at me … You know what was the most humiliating? After I had served the dinner at 6 o'clock, I would climb the stairs to my room to get out of her sight. If she needed me, she would switch on the light on the ground floor and that would be the sign that I have to come down. If I did not see it, she would scream. She treated me like I am a hunting dog. After five weeks, the woman whom I was replacing returned because she made a deal with an old lady. My replacement had been working for a long time there and she was the one who organizes who will replace her and when … at her convenience. Because she was the first one in that position.

The fourth job was also as a replacement. The woman who worked there searched for a replacement and I jumped in. The old man, I call him Shaman, he was a hippie after the war, 90-year-old, he reads tarot cards and does other prophet techniques, running some practice for alternative medicine; he says he visited the Dalai Lama. The old lady, his wife I was taking care of, was 95. A very strange house, very strange business. The house had been in the family for four generations. It was so dirty that I was disgusted. During the six weeks, (the time I spent there) I cleaned the whole house from the bottom to the roof. The salary was €1200, and an additional €100 if I spoke German perfectly. I do not speak German perfectly. In the end, he paid me €1500, explaining that €1200 is the salary, €100 for travel costs, and €100 for a good German. I argued that my German was not that good, but he said that I understood everything, and he understood everything I wanted to say, even from reading my gestures and facial expressions. For cleaning up the house he gave me €200 s. The old lady lived in a room that looked like a Chinese temple, and his room was like an Indian church … Tanja, just imagine how it felt to spend time in these rooms … The Indian bells ring every night … so strange, so odd …

The fifth job, I found on Facebook. One of our women from Bosnia was married to a German guy so they looked up someone for his old mother. The granny had cancer, so they sent her to the hospital. However, as it happened, she fell and broke the collarbone. She got surgery and then she was released from the hospital and sent back home. The old lady died in my third week there. Her daughter, when she died, was in Egypt on vacation. She was the one who should have paid me. The house was in the Black Forest and I had to stay four days longer, waiting for them to give me the salary. I would never have been paid if it was not for their neighbour, a well-off lady who put pressure on her sons to pay me my salary. I got €100 less than we agreed. Then the lady paid €100 from her pocket. She was so kind to me. For the last four days in the house, there was nothing to eat and drink. No shop or market to buy the food. She was bringing me food every day. The driver who was supposed to pick me up came after midnight, instead of at 21h as he said. I was waiting fully dressed for four hours. I couldn't wait to leave that place.

For the sixth job, I was called by a woman who needed someone with an EU passport. The client was a man in Germany who needed a care worker for his mother. It was urgent because he was too busy and there was no one to stay with the granny. The call came on Saturday, and already on Sunday, I was on the way there. The first thing I realized, when I g[o]t there, was that there is no Internet in the house. Then the patient, granny, who was described as depressive, turned out to be suicidal. On the third day of my stay there I was told by the family that due to special circumstances they must ask me to leave. They don't need my services anymore. The day after, they called the driver to come to pick me up. He didn't show up. I was waiting one day and one night until I could find my own transportation back to Serbia.

At the seventh job, I had a sexual harasser as a patient. The woman (broker), the one who sent me there, didn't mention that the man was inclined to sexually touch women who cared for him. I was told that he is grumpy man, a "special case", and can be hard to deal with, but nothing about sexual harassment or similar. There is a big difference between saying someone is grumpy and someone who could sexually touch you. Anyhow … I got there … and when I spoke with my colleague on the phone, when she realized that I was in Neuhausen, she asked me if the name of the man was Peter. When I confirmed it is, she told me that her cousin worked there and ran away because he tried to touch her between her legs, her breasts, and her bottom. Black humour … I said to her: 'I am so skinny that I don't have a bottom anymore, or boobs, I lost weight for the last a few months so that he has nothing to touch.' But, the very next day, when I was in the bathroom with him helping him to get dressed, he reached with his hand between my legs. I instinctively jumped back and slapped his face as strongly as I could. After that, I called the woman who found me the job and explained what happened. Her reaction was: 'Well, he is demented.' I wanted to leave the house as soon as possible. She told me that I had to wait for a few days because her son-in-law (who drove women) is currently busy. I told her that I agreed to stay only if the man stopped touching me. Then I confronted him saying that he cannot do that and that if he were in the hospital or a nursing home, they would kick him out. He said: 'I will tell my daughter what you did. You came here to make money and to do what you are told.' Can you imagine, Tanja? I have no idea how I dared to slap the man, in a foreign country, in an unknown household. You are not going to believe it, but I got 350 euros for seven days and covered costs of transportation to Germany and back to Serbia." (Skype interview, 3/4/2018)

Unlike other women, Snežana does not have a stable position in the sense that she rotates with just one other person, usually every 6 to 8 weeks. Snežana is, as widely used at the informal market of elder care work, a *Springer*, person who is called to jump in whenever some other woman needs time off, when someone gives up on the job or when the patient or family is so difficult that no one wants to take it. This ethnographic case is the most extreme example of live-in care work arrangement: unstable short-term mobility for care work, unequal power relation between care worker and broker, and between care receiver (patient) and care worker, total control of the broker over the care worker's mobilities, unpredictable and emotionally and physically demanding tasks and situations, absence of any kind of agency or ability to negotiate her position. Although, Snežana's case is the most unique one that I have come across during the fieldwork, it could be said, without risking generalization, the model of organization and distribution of care work between the former Yugoslavia and Germany, make care workers vulnerable to various forms of discrimination and abuse throughout the labor mobility: lack of access to information about the job and the patient (client); exploitation and extortion by the job recruiters; denial of rest periods, sick leave and holiday leave; overtime work and non-payment of wages; ad lack of knowledge about the travel routes and uncertainty of safe traveling. These are only some of the features of mobility for care work where "motility", or a capacity for that mobility depends on different factors. Before I embark on the analysis of other ethnographic cases and stories that illustrate women's strategies to resist and overcome mentioned characteristics of doing care work, in this chapter I will identify the main structural factors that induce the increasing incorporation of women from Yugoslav countries in the constantly expending irregular care work market in Germany: restrictive migration and border regimes, social and economic background and specific complexity of citizenship in the former Yugoslavia countries and German contradictory policies, inconsistencies and paradoxes between the official welfare state policy on elder care work, and the reality in German households. These macro-condi-

166   PERIPHERAL LABOUR MOBILITIES

tions provide a coordinate within which the research questions in this book will be answered through subsequent empirical Chapters 5, 6, and 7.

4.2 Geopolitical, Social, and Economic Contextualization: Post-Yugoslav Gendered Labour Mobility in Germany

Followed by the civil war during the 1990s the break-up of the former Yugoslavia resulted in the establishment of seven states with different citizenship regimes and a very similar period of economic, political, and social transition in their societies.

The former Yugoslavian countries (Serbia, Bosna and Herzegovina, Croatia, Macedonia, Montenegro, Slovenia, and Kosovo) underwent a two-decade-long transition to a neoliberal economy and western-style democracy characterized by economic, social, and political re-engineering accompanied by austerity measures. This process created many uncertainties and led to mass impoverishment, lack of employment, government cuts in the area of social welfare, education, and retirement benefits.

The independence of Slovenia, Croatia, and Macedonia in the early 1990s, followed by the constitution of post-war Bosnia and Herzegovina, and the gradual disintegration of the Federal Republic of Yugoslavia into Montenegro, Serbia and Kosovo constitute what is now known as the "post-Yugoslav" space. In 1992, Serbia and Montenegro jointly proclaimed the Federal Republic of Yugoslavia (FRY). In 2006, after a successful Montenegrin referendum on independence, Serbia was the last Yugsolavian republic to declare its independence (map 1).

The transitional period in most of the former Yugoslavia countries is reflected in the loss of employment security, which was considered as the largest achievement of the socialist economy. Instead, movement and changes in the labour market in the 1990s caused by dissolution of Yugoslavia, wars, and destruction of industry caused massive unemployment due to work force redundancy. At the same time, opportunities for new employment decreased and that situation affected women to a great extent. During the 1990s, the largest female unemployment rate was in South-eastern Europe countries, like Bosnia and Herzegovina and Macedonia (around 40 per cent), Croatia, and Yugoslavia (between 22–26 per cent). From 2000, due to privatisation and entering Serbia and Montenegro in transitional processes, the

Map 1: Picturing the break-up of Yugoslavia. Source: https://reportingbalkans. com/the-bbc-break-up-of-yugoslavia-timeline/

unemployment rate increased more and more. While in Serbia and Montenegro this rate was 21.6 per cent in 2006 in the countries of the Eurozone, which in 2006 included 12 EU members states, the unemployment rate was 7.5 per cent. Unemployment rate of women in Serbia was significantly larger (22.8 per cent) compared to man (18.5 per cent) in 2006 (figure 1).

As most women in my study are from Serbia, Bosnia and Herzegovina and Croatia (or holding dual citizenship) I will briefly focus on the economic conditions in Serbia and post-Yugoslav region in attempt to show the rise of women poverty and economic disadvantage, which is one of the main reasons for labor mobility for care work to Germany. As we can see from the chart, female unemployment reached its peak twice – in 2006 and 2012. At the end of December 2006, Serbia had 916.257 unemployed persons. 191.864 were older than 50 years of age. Among them more than 83.700 were women, many of them did not have any working experience or did not have experience in the field in which they were educated or trained. Although, when I conducted my research from 2016 to 2018, there was no statistical data that shows the age of unemployed women, more than half of the women I interviewed or came across during the fieldwork were above 50 years of age.

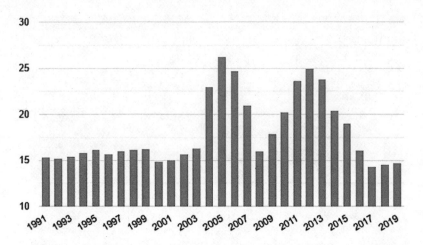

Figure 1: Female unemployment 1991–2019 in Serbia. Data Source: The World Bank. https://www.tradingeconomics.com

Today's employers have no interest in these women. If we take into consideration that women over decades constitute those segments of population that have the highest percentage of unemployment, it is easy to find explanations for the extremely precarious position of women which especially culminated in the last ten years. One of the the reasons is certainly employment in the sectors of social reproduction like health, education, and care where government austerity measures are mostly applied. In addition to this, on average, women are waiting longer to get the job than men do, and in the time of economic, social, and political crisis they are the first ones who lose the job and source of secure income as being employed in less profitable branches. Not having control over family budget and financial assets and often without any savings, they must turn to alternative source of income which is usually situated in informal economy. In case they become widows or get divorced, they are often left without any financial security and must find way to make fo living.

The co-existence of the informal economy can no longer be considered a temporary phenomenon. Since 1990s all former Yugoslavia states have been facing a high rate of unemployment, low wages, and non-payment of salaries that have led to the rapid growth of informal employment. Examples of informal work that combines employment in the remaining public sector can be found, for example, in the case of teachers and nurses. Informal economy activities are usually undertaken due to the low purchasing power. The nurse who travels to Germany to work as an elder care worker three times a year, is one of the cases in my study.

Most of the former Yugoslavia countries is experiencing an "existential" crisis – a crisis in the reproduction of their living workforce – which makes them most unequal countries in Europe, in terms of its labour force, also the cheapest. For a starting illustration, in the case of Serbia, the average income by month is less than a month's worth of consumption. According to the Statistical Office of the Republic of Serbia, the average household spending per month in 2016 was €554, while the average monthly income was only €375. According to *Eurostat*, Serbia has a highest rate of inequality of income distribution in Europe. According to another report by the same Statistical office, every fourth citizen of Serbia is facing the risk of poverty, which, at the most recent and current threshold is set at €132.26. According to a study, about half a million people, or 7.2 per cent of the entire population, lived below even such a most extreme level in 2017. Yet, according to the same study, in South Serbia, "The Capital of Poverty", as it has been nicknamed, poverty levels rise above 12 per cent (even by the extremely low Serbian standards).

The period of transition from a socialist economy to privatization of state factories, industries, and properties from 2000 onward in all former Yugoslavia Republics very often led to bankruptcy leaving former workers without jobs, often without roofs above their heads. The small salaries, unemployment, and decades of gradual financial deprivation of the population impelled many people to take mortgages and credit card loans (sometimes to finance everyday living costs) with the highest rate of interest dictated by predatory lending financial actors. Deepening indebtedness in Croatia for example (see Mikuš 2019), led to the boom in household debt and thus when debt is non-payable to debt enforcement proceedings that may encompass monetary assets as well as movable and immovable property.

The current economic projection for Serbia seems to be optimistic given the fact that the unemployment rate was increased to only 9.5 per cent (Statistical Office of the Republic of Serbia). Official data shows that the employment rate in Serbia is rising despite the national income declining or stagnating. This seems like an interesting paradox. The positive assessment of the International Monetary Fund (IMF) on the development of economic circumstances and management in Serbia is being expressed in a politicized atmosphere. The government's leading party wants to partially alleviate the effects of austerity policies by slightly increasing salaries and pensions, even though austerity is a condition of the Stand-By Arrangement with the IMF. This slightly changes the statistics but not the reality in which people live. The numbers do not match the existing situation that I could come across during the fieldwork in Northern Serbia – in the several villages I visited almost every household sends its members to Austria and Germany, men and women, to work in irregular job markets of construction and care work. One could see the entire streets or neighbourhoods are being emptied as result of intense cross-border labour mobility.

Mentioned economic conditions forced a considerable number of female populations from Former Yugoslavia countries to migrate searching for a job. Women in my study are those entering Germany after 2009. In November 2009 the Former Yugoslav Republic of Macedonia, Montenegro, and Serbia were granted visa-free travel to the European Union (EU). In May 2010 a proposal was launched to grant the same privilege to the remaining two Balkan countries of Bosnia and Herzegovina and Albania. Since 2009, when liberalization of the visa regime allowed Serbian citizens to travel to the Schengen zone, women have been able to easily enter Germany as tourists. Moreover, they may now enter and leave Germany every three months, based on EU freedom-of-movement regulations.

Therefore, the "flexibilization of labour" in Germany and the "liberalization of the visa regime" in the former Yugoslavia resulted in an increasing autonomous migration and mobility for work in European countries where they perform often non-declared and non-contracted work in the feminized and ethicized sectors sectors of agriculture, domestic work, care work, and service economy. As we look at their status, they are entitled to stay in the European Union without a visa, but they are not entitled to work. In this sense, these persons are perceived as "illegal" in terms of employment status. Most of the women interviewed were between thirty and fifty-nine years old, single mothers, divorced, widowed, married women with small children, or women with adult children, grandchildren, and extended families. They had been factory workers, teachers, nurses, housemakers, pharmacy technicians, etc. It is worth keeping in mind also that women migrate not only due to economic reasons but also on political, social, and sometimes emotional grounds (for example when society does not accept them as individuals due to their life choices, lifestyles, etc.). As I have already stated, one of the main motivations that encourage women from post-socialist countries in transition to migrate is unemployment and household debt, factors combined

Map 2: The map of the Former Yugoslavia countries, with bullet marked areas where care workers come from. (Screenshot) Google Maps

with changing welfare structures in Western European countries caused by increasing aging populations and demands for elderly care – put many women on the move to Germany.

It is important to note that in comparison to earlier periods of female migration – especially in *Gastarbeiter* period in 1960 and 1970 when women were the followers of men, today spatial movements are predominantly self-directed and independent. They have a certain distinguishing characteristic: 1. Women who migrate are much more educated. 2. They are either middle-aged women with grown-up children; or young women without children. 3. Women become breadwinners in the family. The motivation to gain economic independence very often helps women to escape from an unhappy marriage, domestic violence, the dominant patriarchal discourses, to negotiate their gender identities and/or to fulfil their desire to try out something else or undertake a new life.

The novelty that makes a central role in the new patterns of labour mobility is the increasing usage of information and communication technologies and mobile applications. My study shows that social media like Facebook and various chat applications (Messenger and Viber) become indispensable tools for facilitating distribution and organization of care work. Facebook groups have provided an unprecedented potential for supporting the entire irregular market of elder care work. Use of Facebook created a fertile ground for building small businesses in the sector of informal care. Undeniably, it has become the overriding means of organizing and distributing elder care work. Relatively affordable gadgets like a smart phone, tablets, iPads enable daily, habitual, and ritualized nature of using Facebook which serves as a platform for social interaction, information seeking, passing time, entertainment, relaxation, communicatory utility, convenience utility, expression of opinion, information sharing, and surveillance or knowledge about others.

4.3 Citizenship Policy in the Post-Yugoslav Space

The possibility of cross-border rotational mobility for care work in Germany is facilitated not only by liberalized exit laws but also by the consequences of the political events that took place in the former Yugoslavia during the 1990s.

Over the last three decades, the geographical and political space once occupied by socialist Yugoslavia has been subject to fragmentation, which in turn has gradually yielded new sovereign states. While rooted in the same political, constitutional, and economic set-up as the socialist Yugoslavia, these states have had different post-partition experiences, ranging from (relatively) peaceful secession, transition, and European Union (EU) integration, to conflicting, prolonged state transformation, and domestic and external contestation. These dissimilar experiences, driven largely by the interplay between national identities and statehood, have shaped the citizenship regimes of the seven new states in South-Eastern Europe.

Since 1991, citizens of the former Socialist Federal Republic of Yugoslavia (SFRY) have been subjected to frequent and unpredictable changes in their nationality and citizenship status. The new citizenship laws of the successor states affected considerably a significant number of individuals, often with dramatic consequences for their everyday lives and personal destinies. Citizenship is generally considered a basic precondition for political, economic, and social rights, as well as a legal ground for many individual rights (e. g., property, housing, health care, employment, and social benefits). When a state dissolves and is succeeded by new states, the redefinition of citizenship becomes an issue of crucial importance and the safeguarding – or restriction – of previous rights. The situation is complicated further when the new state favors a certain ethnic group, usually its ethnic majority, and thus discriminates the others, who by their origins cannot conform to the dominant ethnic character of the new state, and whose loyalty to the latter is questioned.

Since citizenship of former Yugoslavian republics did not have any practical consequences, and since federal citizenship was a strong guarantor of the rights of citizens living outside of their native republics, the residence became the most important factor in the everyday life of Yugoslavs. For more than four decades, the benefits of Yugoslav citizenship established personal and family ties across republican borders, whereas economically motivated migrations and the resettlement of federal administration personnel resulted in a considerable number of individuals living outside, and even very far, from their republic of origin; it also led to a certain degree to the modification of ethno-demographic balances in the Yugoslav republics.

After democratic changes in 2000, and Croatia declared its willingness to satisfy all conditions for joining the EU, the situation has improved considerably. Although many issues related to events in 1990s remain unresolved, for instance, Croatian Serb refugees (those who fled Croatia during the war) face no significant obstacles today in acquiring Croatian citizenship. Their return to Croatia and the full restitution and reparation of their material goods are some of the most important political conditions for the success of Croatia's accession talks with the EU. Croatia grants citizenship through cultural links to the nation. This implies that such "claims of cultural belonging" can be exerted by descendants of expatriates, yet not through the link with a person, but through that with the state. Such a policy is clearly an outcome of the uncontested dynamic between state and national identity. While the general expectation has been that differences across the post-Yugoslav space would be starker, they are mirrored in the legislative detail that excludes certain categories of applicants, while offering facilitated access to others. In sum, states whose cultural imagery spills over their borders (Serbia and Croatia) rely on ethnonational policies and facilitated access on grounds of cultural claims. That is, their citizenship regimes are ethnic and expansive. In the case of Slovenia, where nation building is coherent, citizenship policies are ethnic but restricted by their emphasis on territorial belonging. How does this practically apply to the situation of women care workers and their "motility"? For instance, women who belong to Serbian ethnic group

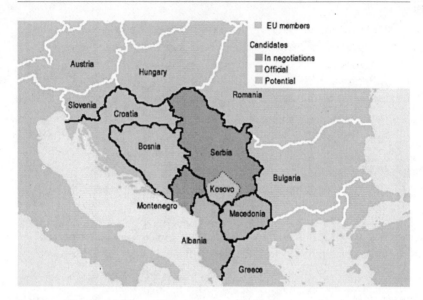

Map 3: Map of the former Yugoslavia countries and its neighbouring countries in relation to the EU. Source: https://www.oscebih.org

and who fled the civil war in Croatia frequently acquired dual Serbian-Croatian citizenship. As Croatia became part of the EU in July 2013, women who poses Croatian citizenship can work regularly in Germany and enjoy all benefits stemming from European citizenship. For the women interviewed in my research, possessing a Croatian passport means that they not only benefit from visa-free travel to the Schengen zone, but opportunity to get a contracted job of the care worker in Germany.

Furthermore, an undesirable side effect of the EU's external borders is the fact that Serbian citizens can obtain citizenship in those states that it is surrounded by. Countries as Bulgaria, Croatia, Hungary, Romania, and Serbia are kin-states (Brubaker 1999) that have strong co-ethnic citizenship policies grant preferential access to citizenship to wide groups of co-ethnics (e. g. descendants of former citizens) and on very few conditions (e. g. exemptions from residential requirements).

That means that women, respondents in my research, who live in Serbian villages in the Bánát-Bácska (in Northern Serbia) can claim their right to Hungarian citizenship based on their Hungarian origins, or, more frequently, based on their husband's origin, or that of their ancestors. Thus, the access to labour mobility is highly circumscribed by geopolitical limitations. Their motility depends on the possession of the right passport, which enables them to travel without a visa for an unlimited period, to build access to social networks and to consolidate their position within these social networks. Heterogeneity of population in multicultural region of Northern Serbia, called Vojvodina adds another dimension to different chances and opportunities for women – this region is the result of the specific historical and demographic circumstances described as a territory where peoples, cultures, languages are fantastically intertwined.

4.4 Care for Germany: German Welfare, Gender and Migration Regime

Gender relations – embodied in the sexual division of labour, heterosexuality, gendered forms of citizenship and political participation, ideologies of masculinity and femininity, profoundly shape the character of welfare states. Likewise, the institutions of social provision, the set of social assistance and social and health insurance programs and universal citizenship entitlements which we refer as "the welfare state" – affect gender relations. On the other hand, neoliberal strategies argue that labour market deregulation and the retrenchment of social welfare programs will lead to economic growth. Without state interference, markets theoretically work more efficiently. State actors have used neoliberal ideologies to justify lowering state costs for care; restructuring is then a political strategy that draws on economic ideologies. Neoliberalism shapes care work in both sending and receiving countries. As states have withdrawn from social care provision, women's care work requirements have intensified. Economically disadvantaged women migrate to provide support for their families, while wealthier families solve their care needs through hiring foreign care workers. Rather than states taking responsibility for aiding families, neoliberal strategies have led to an international division of care work that places the burden for care on the least powerful (immigrant women workers). States have privatized care (sending care provision to private, non-profit, and voluntary sectors) through marketizing state care provisions (contracting out services and care provisions and withdrawing state support from certain provisions). They have moved from providing care services to encouraging the development of low-wage private sector services.

Consenqunetly, partial outsourcing of social reproductive work to paid workers in private households become the trend in most of the Western European countries, including Germany. These individualised care arrangements are mostly established in the private realm with highly informal and semi-informal character. Over the past two decades, many European countries have seen major long-term care reforms with impacts on the distribution of long-term care responsibilities between the family, the state, and the market. Reforms included extensions in long-term care coverage and the introduction of *cash-for-care payments* and went along with market-based care approaches with a reemphasis on individual responsibility. But even extensions in public support, strong family orientation and the difficulties in reconciling work, family and care obligations have increased the demand for comprehensive service alternatives (Lewis 2001). The topic I want to tackle in what follows makes a basis for presenting the German case situated within intersection of disparate socio-economies, "welfare cultures" (Pfau-Effinger 2005), and notions of care as a public good that underpin the contrasting policies for supporting care.

The German care regime is based on the ideology that families (i. e., women in families) care for their elderly and that those elders prefer to be cared for by family members. This premise implies that family members of two or three generations live in the same household and that, therefore, a few hours of caregiving per day is sufficient. Placement of elderly in nursing homes is socially rejected by much of the population. Pfau-Effinger (2005: 13) has therefore asserted that the "official political semantics" are characterised by a family-oriented culture of care for dependent family members; the political discourse reinforces the cultural desire that care should be provided by the family at home.

In the early 1990s, long-term care insurance in which care is financed through an insurance system, not tax-financed, was introduced; it provides, however, for only partial insurance coverage, requiring citizens to buy additional insurance privately. In other words, full care in the nursing home is too expensive and not covered by the average insurance policy. Family members who look after care recipients at home receive transfer payments for their work, while private nursing services are directly paid by the government. However, the money allotted by the government for a person who needs 24-hour care is insufficient to pay for arrangements as provided by nursing services. Another disadvantage of the commercial arrangements is that they involve a permanent change of caregivers. Thus, the mediocre financial support for commercial caregiving, along with "uncontrolled" direct transfers to families seem to be the key elements of German care policy that boost employment of live-in migrant caregivers in private households (Theobald 2009).

In order to better understand the complexity and complicity of German migration policies and care regime, I apply the framework provided by Bridget Anderson which conceptualises the various legal "spaces of (il) legality" in the employment of migrants and acknowledges the complexity of perceptions and functions of these spaces from the points of view of migrants, employers, and the state. This approach breaks the dichotomy between legal and illegal employment and looks at them in combination with rights of residence and rights of employment. Thus, Anderson and Ruhs (2010) differentiate between *compliant, non-compliant* and *semi-compliant migrants*. Compliant migrants are legally resident, sticking with the conditions attached to their status, while non-compliant migrants lack the right of residence in the host country. Semi-compliant migrants are legally resident but working in violation of some or all the conditions attached to their status. They are an important source of flexible labour and yet as subjects of migration control and border police whose employment needs to be closely monitored. Semi-compliance is a distinct and contested space of (il)legality that allows employers and migrants to maximize economic benefits from employment while minimizing the threat of state sanctions for violations of migration law. Semi-compliance exists, and is likely to persist, in part because it constitutes an equilibrium, which we show, serves the interests of migrants and employers and in practice is difficult for the state to control.

Translated into the German elderly care situation, semi-compliance seems to be characteristic of the situation of the former Yugoslavian care workers. However, not all of them equally. Slovenian and Croatian elder care workers as citizens of the EU countries are entitled to work as domestic help or care assistants (as unskilled workers). They are employed by the commercial intermediate agencies (according to the freedom of service rules of employment regulation in the EU member states (2006/123/EG) and entitled to pension and social benefits. As the bureaucratic procedures and administrative barriers are to be complicated to overcome, both for families of elderly care workers and care workers themselves rather opt for undeclared jobs. In addition to this, for care workers declared work is an economically less desirable option because they can earn more without job contract. Those women who are from non-EU former Yugoslavia countries as unskilled care workers have no working rights, nor residence permit. They are allowed to stay on tourist visa up to 90 days and then to leave the country. Performing the elder care work in German households that is not declared to competent authorities (non-taxable work) is not illegal, but it could be punishable. So, in this case, the violation of rights is restricted to labour law and not to residency. However, overstaying in Schengen territory is punishable. Despite that there is not a common policy for all Schengen Member States on the overstaying penalties, each of the states applies different types of penalties. Germany is known to have the strictest immigration laws in the EU in this direction. For overstay penalties are: paying the fee (in amount up to 250 *euros*), being banned from entering the Schengen for 1–3 years, and being deported. In case of getting caught engaging in paid activity while overstaying tourist visa or engaging in illegal activities, it will be most possibly that the person will be taken into custody where s/he will wait for the trial.

The German state's approval of a flexible and unregulated care market helps to overcome the gap which exists in (affordable) professional care services and statistics that yield increasing needs for elderly care work. As there is no reliable data of how many persons work in German households as not declared care workers because they are invisible, there is calculation that illustrates misleading statistics data. Helma Lutz and Palenga Möllenbck illustrated this paradox by showing the following: according to the Federal Statistical Office there are 1.45 million elderly Germans registered as needing care and who receive benefits from the government to be used for their own care arrangements at home. As this homebased care is provided by family members (70 per cent) or by a combination of family members and nursing services (30 per cent), one gets the impression that care is mainly carried out by family members. However, migrants often replace the declared kin care either alone or in cooperation with a private nursing service. The fact that 40 per cent of those who are officially declared as "kin carers" are fulltime employees, the likelihood that a large percentage of these family members is outsourcing their care responsibility (to a migrant worker) is high (Lutz, Palenga-Möllenbeck 2010). Although this calculation might seem outdated, still it is a proof that administrative ignorance and statistic inaccuracy promote and encourage informal care market and irregular, not declared jobs. If we add to this the fact that allowances (cash-for-care) that go to family members for home caring of their fragile, sick, and old, are not monitored in regard how this money is spent, then we have a rapidly growing uncontrolled market where state payments are used for hiring women, like

Map 4: Map of Germany, with marked areas where my respondents are employed. (Screenshot) OpenStreetMap, https://www.openstreetmap.org

those from the former Yugoslavia countries. A strong public discussion about the "care crisis" in Germany and "the state solutions" shows that the German state ignores the problem of increasing commodification and deregulation of the care market where private employers are prosecuted for the violation of labour laws in the private sphere because it is treated as a minor offence. It seems that system shows understanding for the hardships faced by families and, as a result, the employment of undocumented care workers is not perceived as punishable. Although, as the result of my research demonstrates, women care workers see this situation as win-win ("they get a care for their parents, we get the money") whilst private households are becoming a workplace and home where an isolated atmosphere and insecure working conditions could be unfavourable, and even dangerous, for both sides – those who give care and those who receive – as Snežana's narrative vividly describes.

Chapter 5
Routes into Care Labour Mobility

As the title of chapter indicates, the ethnographic material will be analyzed to show the different routes into elder care work, strategies, and decisions that women make to build their potential for sustainable movement across the borders. As the routes into care work mobility characterize their work experiences, in this chapter these will be scrutinized in relation to their impact on working lives and the interplay of opportunity structures and agency. These routes spring from the dynamics brought about by changes of border regimes in the last decade that among other factors gave an impetus for women to work in the informal sector of elder care work.

Following on Kaufmann's work my main argument is that "motility" or potentiality to move for care labour is comprised of motivation and aspirations, attitudes, towards mobility for care work and performing the work, and networks that women build or use those already built up. The main question arises: How mobility for care labour is built and how such mobility is sustained? Further, what are the factors that facilitate the sustainability of "being mobile"? This chapter seeks to address several interrelated questions: if mobility does indeed play a constitutive role, through what means such mobility is sustained. What are the factors that hinder or induce sustainability of care labour mobility for care sustainable? My central argument is that the sustainability of cross-border care work mobility depends on three factors: geopolitical context, organization of mobility for care work (transport and distribution of work) and the way how women deed, consider and evaluate experienced care work for the elderly in German households. These processes of labour care mobility build the chain made of the following events:

preparation for travel ↔ travel ↔ household destination in Germany ↔ residing for care work ↔ travelling back ↔ travelling again

Each of these events interact and they are mutually constitutive but can be interrupted, broken or not realized. For example, a person can prepare herself for a job in Germany: to learn some German language, gain a basic knowledge of working with elderly immobilised persons with Alzheimer disease, find a position in a certain family where she will take care and then to learn that the person or agency who promised her a job, gave the job to someone else. In other cases, the care worker can also experience involuntary immobility by being in the household, at work, where elderly person all of sudden dies and she must remain there until she finds another job in another household in Germany. In other words, the way care work across the border is organized, directed, and distributed, determinate different practices of mobilities and different care practices, as well as attitudes, behaviors, and relationships between subjects involved in elder care work mobility. Considering this, in following sub-chapters I want to explore: what social and cultural practices, social relations, forms of sociality are developed during the labour mobility process mentioned above. Thhort-term mobility pattern entirely relies on private care arrangements and the state care regimes in two respects. First, care makes mobility possible – if there would be no demand for elder care workers in Germany, women, probably would not travel. Care work deficit is, thus a precondition for mobility. Secondly, care is an activity that comprises consideration, affection, interest, feelings of concern, and protection. As such, care work is the generative force through which the sustainability of care labour mobility and women's experiences are created.

The next question I want to explore is what are the factors without which the mobility trajectories of women care workers would not start and continue. For some women, without access to communication technology and computer literacy that allow for finding the right channel of information, becoming mobile in the first place would not be possible. Drawing on the women's testimonies of their experiences this chapter answers the question: why for some women becoming mobile for care work is more difficult than for others. What are the factors that not only encourage mobility, but also potentially block mobility, or make it impossible?

Drawn on Kaufmann's model of "motility" its three constitutive factors, I structured this chapter around three sub-chapters. In these, I analyze ethnographic cases, ethnographic portraits and interviews to provide empirical evidence for answering the questions I set above. I will start with an explanation of how I understand these factors and apply them in my study as a slight modification to Kaufmann's original model introduced in

Chapter 2.3. The most important factor for my analysis is *appropriation*. According to Kaufmann, *appropriation* encompasses three aspects that are underlined in my analysis:

1) *motives and aspirations* that are intrinsically linked to women's internalization of values, perceptions, and imaginations as motivators of movement, but also are induced by the movement;
2) *appropriation* refers to how people consider, appropriate, and select specific options. It is also how skills and decisions are evaluated;
3) *attitude towards mobility* in Kaufmann's conceptualization refers to the ways people approach commuting or travelling, or in my case, how women care workers perceive, approach to, and deem commuting back and forth – and, in particular, how these are linked to attitudes towards performing elder care work and care itself.

The second factor I will be looking at is *access t*o mobility. What does labour mobility make accessible to women? Kaufmann includes the spatial distribution of the population and infrastructure, including transport. Beyond this Kaufmann refers to access to resources and opportunities. In structuring this chapter, I opted to pay the most explorative attention to motivations and aspirations, access to mobility (including significance and function of social networks), and attitudes towards care work. All three factors that frame women's experiences are considered dependent on namely social and cultural contexts within which people live, stretching beyond migration, mobility, border, and labour laws and regulations. These may include: cultural norms; encouragement or discouragement of mobility by family members, social networks; personality traits concerning reaching out to other people and places; one's sense of responsibility regarding balancing between the freedom to move and other values, wants and obligations; and previous and current social relations and labour mobility experiences as encouraging or blocking one's mobility.

Considering previously framed questions, this chapter is divided into three main sub-chapters. The following sub-chapter tells a life story and care labour mobility history of Ana Wendl. Further on, sub-chapter 5.2 investigates the construction of aspirations and motivations understood not only in relation to "movement through the space", but also through the time and within specific contexts. The sub-chapter 5.3 discusses factors behind unequal *access* to labor mobility as the one of constitutive elements of "motility". Here, the accent is on variations of mobility experiences linked to

184 PERIPHERAL LABOUR MOBILITIES

geopolitical constraints or limitations created by the spatial dynamic of networks, communication and transportation. I refer to "migration networks" (definition provided in Chapter 2.6), to analyze narrated women's strategies and negotiations as individual responses to the limited access to information and networks, responses to regional disparities in permeability of border crossings, and border regimes. In the final sub-chapter 5.4, I explore women's attitudes towards care work mobility, their performance of care and their evaluations of skills and knowledge. The chapter reveals how elder care labour mobility exposes different cultural understandings and meanings of what constitutes care work and care of and for someone. It also analysis and discusses elder care work as essential for organization of care labour across the borders, and the complexities of relationships between different actors, but also the dynamics of power that interweave these.

5.1 Portrait: Ana Wendl

„(…), people like it when you're unwell, they don't like it when you're good. It's better to say that you are not well, even when you are doing fine."

It's August 2016, the end of a warm late-summer afternoon. I am in a small village in Northern Vojvodina in Serbia and it is plum harvest season. While I am thinking about how I ended up in this village and why I am picking plums in the orchard of people whom I barely know, I hear the voice of Ana telling me to hurry up because it's getting dark: "Tanja, you need to speed up. All the plums have to be picked today. Tomorrow we are going back to Munich. This is it."

Ana, her younger son, and his girlfriend are picking the plums quickly and efficiently. They have three times as many baskets as I do. As I arrived just two hours before the start of work, I didn't have time to properly meet Ana's family apart from a quick introduction. Ana's youngest son (32 years old) and his girlfriend are explaining the workings of the plum business to me: "Now that mama is permanently in Munich we sell the plums to the people who produce Sljivovica,[2] but we keep a small amount to make plum jam for our family." Ana listens to our conversation and shouts at us from the other part of the orchard: "Come on people, it's getting dark, let's hurry up.

---

2 Serbian brandy made of plums.

We are making plum jam tonight and baking pancakes" (Fieldwork Diary, 26/8/2016).

Ana Wendl is the first respondent with whom I had contact for this research project, and I have already introduced her in methodological Chapter 3.1. At the point when I made the diary entry quoted above, I had already known Ana for more than a year. Ever since I met her on the bus on the way to Munich, we had become close, particularly after the accident. By August 2016 I had done several interviews with Ana as well as some participant observation. But I had always wondered what her life must have been like before she started to work as an elderly care worker in Germany. I finally got the opportunity to learn more about Ana's life in August 2016 when I decided to visit my hometown, Belgrade, for a few days before the start of the academic semester in October. At that time, Ana was on a short 7-day vacation in her village. Even though, at the time, Ana was a contracted worker with her right to holidays and specific working hours written into her employment contract, Frau Müller was always finding an excuse to negotiate (or even question) these rights. Despite this, Ana managed to get the 7 days of vacation she needed for what she refers to as "business at home". Since we were both in Serbia at the same time, and planning to return to Germany on a similar date, Ana suggested that I should come to visit her in her village and that we should then travel together back to Munich. I agreed to the plan. I was curious to learn more about Ana's family for personal reasons, but I also wanted to gain deeper insights into the social and cultural background of my respondent for research purposes, to understand better the complexity of family relations and the seemingly mundane practices through which the terrain of caring worlds (in the country of origin and across the border) are made possible and crafted, as well as to understand how the effective encounters that are an easily overlooked element in making mobility possible, are produced and sustained. The following stories contain everyday, ordinary, seemingly banal forms of sociality, which help to make this portrait into a valuable ethnographic jigsaw piece within a bigger puzzle.

My impression of the village as soon as I got off the local bus was of a remote and deserted place. This was quickly followed by the surprise of seeing Ana waiting for me at the bus station in her car. It was an old car and Ana had never mentioned her ability to drive. She explained to me that it wasn't possible to live in the countryside without a car. As soon we set off for her house, Ana started listing the things that she must do before the following day, amongst which was paying the registration fee for her car. We drove

186 PERIPHERAL LABOUR MOBILITIES

around for some time because she wanted to show me the village and narrate both its history and her own story of coming to the village. Most of the houses, I noticed, looked abandoned, and, since the village is surrounded by agricultural land and agriculture and farming are the main sources of income for the villagers, it was surprising that everything seemed so dead, with hardly anyone to be seen on the streets. Ana explained:

"This is because only the old people have stayed in the village, and everyone who can work is in German or Austria. Men work in the construction sector and women in the care sector."

The northern province of Vojvodina provides a perfect example of the complex and diverse nature of interethnic relationships between Danube Swabians and Hungarians among others. Due to complex historical events during the time of the Habsburg Empire and before and after the Second World War, regional identity makes itself felt in the high number of inter-ethnic marriages. While I am thinking of these historical facts and the historical conditions that have shaped patterns of ethnic distribution in Vojvodina, Ana draws my attention to a house at which we have stopped, and which I assume does not belong to her. It is an old, apparently abandoned, traditional Swabian house with closed shutters, surrounded by uncut grass with a large tree in the yard.

"A: Do you see that house?
T: Yes.
A: Well, it's the house of my deceased father-in-law and mother-in-law. I came to that house when I married Gerhard. Do you see that tree in the yard?
T: Yes, what kind of tree is that?
A: An oak, 200 years old. That's the tree my mother-in-law hung herself on 10 years ago. I found her. Come on now, I do not like to stay in this place for long. It takes me back to a hard time in my life."

On the way to her house, which is the house that she and her husband built together, she recalls the past:

"I got married young, at the age of 19. I came from Bosnia and married Gerhard. I knew nothing about life. His mother was a very harsh and insensitive woman … patriarchal in a way. I worked with them on the land and raised children. Nobody ever asked me whether I was sick, if I were happy, how I was doing or what I was thinking … three days after I gave birth to my first son, I had to work in the field. What a job, what a career. Nothing. … We worked in agriculture and did the farming and that was it! Now we have two houses where no one lives. None of these houses or land is mine. The house is my children's home. Now that they're gone, I have no reason to be here. I don't want to live here in this village anymore. I don't want to die here."

At the time of the interview, Ana was 55-year-old, and still married. She said: "Our marriage only exists on paper." She resented him. "I don't want to divorce him. Not yet. I fear that my kids will not inherit the land."

Ana has two grown sons. The youngest is graduating from university and lives with his girlfriend in the city. The oldest one has started his own family and works and lives in a big city in Serbia. None of them lives in the village anymore. Ana is in Germany and her husband is a truck driver who is constantly on the road or living in Hungary where he has a small, rented apartment. They have a shared house, which they built together. Her husband inherited his parents' house, as well as a good-sized farm. She says:

"The land and the house – none of that is mine and it never will be. My children will inherit everything … I hope unless Gerhard changes his mind and leaves everything to someone else. He is now in a relationship with a Hungarian woman, that's what I heard. She has children as well. You never know with him."

Ana describes her life as very. Her husband is known for his adventures with other women. Ana says she was humiliated because everyone knew what he was like. He even used to bring his mistresses home, presenting them as colleagues or acquaintances. Divorce has never been an option for her. Having experienced this domestic environment, with its traditional family hierarchies and power relations, Ana's biggest motivation has become financial and physical independence. Her dreams of buying a small apartment in the city motivate Ana to work in Germany. She has already saved a decent sum of money and pays contributions to private health and pension funds. She also takes care of her 80-year-old mother who lives in Bosnia on a pension of 87 euros. Ana sends her money every month and she says that, although she has siblings, she is the one who offers the greatest financial support. DespiEven though Ana's husband is the owner of the properties, land and houses, she is the one who takes care of everything. In our conversation during my visit to her village, she told me that she keeps everything running because her husband is not interested in the house or land.

"I am doing all of this for my children. This is their future. It belongs to them. Wherever they decide to live in the future – they can always come back here and rely on this land."

"Keeping everything running" means that Ana takes on a lot of tasks and responsibilities paying taxes and bills, leasing the farmland, housekeeping,

188   PERIPHERAL LABOUR MOBILITIES

and paying a person to maintain the houses and land while she is in Germany. This is how Ana describes her situation in relation to other female care workers:

"Someone rarely decides to stay in Germany … I mean, almost no one does it. They all do rotations. I stayed, but they all want to come back home. I mean … my goal is to … what am I supposed to do at home, alone. Just to work until I die. I want, as long as I am able, to earn more money, to do something with my life and not to travel back and forth every few months. Most women do this. They come and go. They are satisfied with it. Then again, you have women who are well-off, but who need the money for a particular purpose … for a new car or a house repair. And, some of them use the money to survive. It takes you 5 years to pay off all your debts and to satisfy some needs. What we earn in Germany sounds like a lot of money, but a lot of this money is spent. Whenever I come here I just pay the bills […] My youngest told me: 'Mom, I don't know how you are managing it … it's the same when you have money and when you don't have it.' Even if I didn't have money, I would manage to cover everything. You know, if my parents-in-law were still alive they would share the costs of taxes and bills. It's worse for me now, because I am alone and have to manage all my finances on my own … every two months bills come … and there are two houses that nobody uses."

After picking the plums, we spent the evening cooking the jam in a big pot on the fire, in their garden. Ana's son and his girlfriend made pancakes. During the evening, I realized that I had learned a lot about the different relationships in Ana's family: the absence of her husband, her supportive sons, the caring neighbors, and about the obvious and deeply rooted gender segregation in the environment where Ana has lived most of her life. I have witnessed how Ana makes plans with her son about where money will be invested. Ana is the one who is now the head of the house. She speaks proudly about her grandchildren and already plans to set aside money to buy them birthday presents.

When we were left alone after dinner, Ana told me the story of how her previous experiences of labour mobility and the complexities of citizenship had played a role in her more-recent care labor mobility. Changing her citizenship and getting an EU passport meant becoming independent from care work agencies and the black market, greater material security, and the opportunity to establish her own independent life.

Ana's husband, Gerhard Wendl, belongs to the population of Banat Swabians, who historically inhabited present-day Serbia, Croatia, Hungary, and Romania. Since Gerhard had Hungarian citizenship and had worked and resided for several years in Hungary, both Ana and his children qualified for the naturalization process. The main requirement for getting Hungarian citizenship is 8 years of continuous residency in Hungary, but a preferential procedure is available for applicants with Hungarian parents or heritage, or for those with Hungarian spouses or children. With a Hungarian passport, Ana could live and work in Germany without any problems. This is how Ana explains her history of mobility concerning her EU citizenship:

"I only got a Hungarian passport in 2014. When I went to Germany to work as a seasonal worker in asparagus fields in 1992, it was still Yugoslavia and we could have traveled without a visa. But we got a work permit so that we could work there for 3 months. [...] Everything was organized – they took our passports and stamped our work visas ... that was in Frankfurt. We had an extra 10 days to prolong our stay in Germany. I made a big mistake then ... we planned to bring our children to Germany right after the working season and to apply for German citizenship for them on the basis of their father, my husband's German background. However, I made a mistake. At that point, my post-work visa had another 15 days remaining, and I could have gone home to pick up my children on my passport and bring them to Germany. But I didn't. Soon after that, the civil war in Yugoslavia started and the borders were closed to us for the next 18 years. My husband worked in Hungary in the meantime, so we had one-month visas for Hungary, and we were able to visit Hungary and my aunt who lives in Achen. I could have obtained a Hungarian passport much earlier if Gerhard had not been so tight with the money. It is very expensive to get Hungarian citizenship. You have to pay for residence in the country for 8 years, pass the language test, and submit piles of documents and proof of marriage and children. Finally, he signed the papers and I applied for citizenship. The language was not a problem because I already spoke Hungarian and German – we used both at home with my parents-in-law. I got Hungarian citizenship on my third attempt."

Between 2010 and 2014, before she got Hungarian citizenship, Ana worked in Germany as a care worker with a Serbian passport.

"I was commuting for care work between Germany and Serbia on a one-month rotation – one month at home, one month in Germany. The better option is three months there, three months here. But then you use up more days than you are allowed to stay. I had 7 days overstay in the EU ... they didn't say anything to me at the border because I was calm and quiet ... so I didn't have any problems with them, they let me go. I needed a Hungarian passport because I was always scared ... Gerhard told me: 'Ana you shouldn't be afraid, your passport is legal ... and you shouldn't let some Monika (job broker) from Hungary threaten you that they will send police to the border to get you caught.' Can you imagine Tanja, how it feels when she calls and says: 'Does your employer know that you have a Serbian passport? I'll send the police to the border.'"

190 PERIPHERAL LABOUR MOBILITIES

The kind of threats and blackmail described above were a regular part of "informal care work arrangements" at the time when Ana started building her networks in the "care work chain". The threat of sending the police was a common mechanism used by recruiters and job intermediaries to control and discipline women workers, to prevent negotiations about salaries, working conditions, or transportation and to prevent any questioning of their authority or decisions. Whilst staying in Ana's village, I tried to picture how business in the informal care sector could be undertaken in a place, which is so remote, with no internet and almost no transport links between villages (except for the local buses that run just a few times per day). This is how Ana describes one of her first experiences:

"A: I didn't know anyone, but I was nosing around until I managed to find the contact. You know how hard it was at the beginning to get in touch with the right people. It was impossible. That Radojka, my friend – she is, for example, a different type of person … she already knew everything … when someone had been going one month we asked everyone who, where, how … We asked everyone, asked for the contact, but no one wanted to give a contact. You know how that works in the village, rumor has it … for example, that Ildiko went to Germany to take care of the elderly. We were waiting for her to get back. She got back, but she didn't want to reveal who sent her to Germany. But Radojka somehow found out from her sister who that person was.
T: And what is the reason for not sharing the contact? Competition?
A: Yes, because they're afraid you'll take their job. Envy. Radojka hangs out with Hungarians more than me. She gave me a phone number from Monica. Of course, I was more than happy to find the contact. I needed money desperately. I immediately called Monica. She tested my German language skills. She says something in Hungarian, and I need to translate it for her into German. At that time, I was trying to speak German more than Hungarian with my family and with my German neighbors in the village. She tests me like this: She says for instance: 'Here's your wallet, you go to the store and what do you say there?' And I have to say it in German. Then she asks me where I learned German and so on. I was impatient so I was texting her. She said not to press her but I couldn't do that, I needed the job. It was important to them, however, that you had a better knowledge of the German language than just being able to say Guten Tag. Some women said they knew German, but when they came to the family, it turned out that they only knew how to say Ja, ja. They used to send them back home. Some families were tolerant and more patient – the language was not a big issue. When Monika finally called me, she said: 'Ana, we've got you a granny. Her daughter is a little bit strange …' But before she offered me a job she asked me about my preferences: what price I will not go beneath, whether I want a male or female, mobile or immobile, wherein Germany – Stuttgart, Munich? I said,

Munich. And yes, as a salary I'm not going below 1200 because I already worked for that salary. I have experience. (Interview, Munich, 14/2/2016)

Ana found her first job through a person whom she met in Germany in 1992 during the asparagus harvest.

"Marta told me it wouldn't be right away. I have to wait. She said: 'It won't be right away – you must wait between 3 weeks and a few months.' However, I got the job in two weeks. I went as a replacement in Mainz. But it wasn't realistic and fair. You know, when you replace someone for one or three months they shouldn't charge you commission for the job. Usually, you pay 200–300 euros for the first job – that's the commission. That woman Marta was the indirect mediator, so I had to travel with her husband. The deal was that her husband would come to pick me up at my address in Serbia, drive me across the border between Serbian and Hungary to the Hungarian village of Baja, and then from there another person would drive us to Germany. I was thinking 'why should I do this when my son (my eldest was not married then, he lived with us) could have taken me?'. He could have taken me … I didn't have to pay that much. Okay. I agreed to that. It does not matter.

Then later, during one of the travels, to Germany, I met a Hungarian woman, Katika on the bus. We got close. She found a job in Gräfelfing and offered me to be her rotation partner. However, she made a big mistake: she was too honest … you must not be. As my children said to me: 'Mom, people like it when you're unwell, they don't like it when you're good. It's better to say that you are not well, even when you are doing fine.' That job, that was the best job place … ever … just to be there … nothing else. Well, I don't mean that I didn't do anything, but it wasn't demanding: the old lady was physically in a very good condition, she was independent, but she had started to suffer from dementia. So, I had to remind her to do things … For example, she did the laundry by herself, and a man came to clean the house. My job was to cook and organize the household, do the shopping and so on. The old lady had a very good pension. She had worked for BMW for 35 years. I lived in a separate little house and the salary was 1700 euros. But then, Katika brought her 'friend' Edika, another Hungarian woman, to visit her. She showed her the house and gave her a landline number. At the time, Edika was working for another family in Bayern, where the person she was taking care of, died. So, Edika used the contact she had gotten from Katika and called the old lady offering her services. Since the old lady knew her from before, she agreed for Edika to come to replace me. And I was out. Lost the job! (Interview, Munich, 16/2/2016)

Between 2010, when Ana started to travel to Germany for care work, and the end of 2015, when I met Ana for the first time, she changed jobs several times, moving between different households mostly located in Southern Germany. Over the years, increasing demand for care workers in Germany (and Austria) and the country's proximity to Hungary and Serbia created an army of women willing to put themselves on the move, rapidly expanding both the "migration industry" and the network within which they were able to become care workers and/or (over time) labor recruiters themselves. Although Ana had, over time, learned from her own experience how "business" works, she says that she wouldn't be able to do that.

"Well, you know how it works … now … I'll show you … here, look at these … Hallo München Anzeigen … you can find here private advertisements from people who need an elderly care worker for someone from their family. I could find 20 grandmas on my own. You get in touch with them … ask questions, they ask you … and there you go – you are already an intermediary and you find jobs for others. But no, I'm not like that. I could do that, but I'm not the type of person … It is too complicated. You find a job for someone, then that person turns out not to be satisfied or the family is not satisfied … no. I want to do my job and that's it. You see, the problem is that women cannot do this by themselves – they don't know the language well enough to build such networks. But after two or three years, every tenth woman becomes independent, becomes able to find a job for herself. Now I am in this family, and I think they love me because I am good to them. When they no longer need me, they will find another family for me … you know not to go through the agency of intermediaries. Because I am in a better position if I do not depend on the agency or other people." (Interview, Munich, 25/5/2016)

In May 2016, Ana decided to become independent, to leave Frau Müller because she saw better opportunities to make money in other sectors such as cleaning, working in shops, bakeries, etc. During several of our meetings between March and September 2016, she complained about psychological harassment from Frau Müller and about how she was becoming more demanding in terms of weekly working hours. At that point, Ana wanted to improve her German to be able to pass the test and get a B2-level certificate of German language knowledge, so she enrolled herself in the language school. To do this, she needed Frau Müller's approval since the language course took place every day from 8–9.30 p.m. This meant that she wouldn't have been at Frau Müller's disposal on weekday evenings. Frau Müller did not agree easily with her decision to attend the course because, regardless of Ana's working hours, she expected flexibility from Ana.

Ana also found an extra job because she wanted to have a job to make a start with when she left Frau Müller. Ana was repeatedly saying to me that she wanted to leave because she deserves more and something better in her life: "I have served enough. I have always been doing what others wanted from me in my life. Now it is time to do something for me" (Interview, Munich, 15/5/2016).

The biggest reason for this decision was the social isolation of the job and the constant focus on Frau Müller and her life. As I mentioned earlier in Chapter 3.1, Ana could not have guests, could not access the internet, or adapt the small apartment in which she lived to her needs. She always complained about the expensive Biedermeier chest of drawers that was in the center of the room. Ana was anxious not to damage it because she knew she would have to pay for it. She wanted to have a sofa where her guests could sleep and she liked that she could have guests: sons, relatives, and friends. Our conversations became almost entirely focused on future work possibilities and the opportunities that Munich and Germany could offer her. Working in a neighborhood bakery, cleaning for cleaning companies, or a job in sales became her new goal in life and she started looking for these opportunities in newspapers.

Having started in a situation of financial and emotional dependence with very little or almost no chance to care for herself, since she was always caring for others, she managed to earn enough money to secure her future and thus the future of her children. When I finally asked her what she wanted the most for herself now, Ana quickly replied: "Freiheit!"

5.2 The Construction and Contextualization of Motivations and Aspirations

Much of the scholarly attention has been focused on socio-economically disadvantaged female migrants. Particularly, the literature on domestic and care workers has been predominantly occupied with migration motives and aspirations of women who are often pictured as impoverished, from poor families, countries, and communities, exposed to violence, often forced to domestic and care work without any other option to sustain their lives materially. My concern is that such perspective might be an obstacle in creating a new approach to more nuanced and sensitive analysis. To illustrate my approach, I have opened Chapter 5 with the portrait of Ana Wendl. Her case is a very good example of how within very narrow horizon, women can find spaces for agency and self-realization. Her developed mobility capability or motility, along with capability for navigation through the informal sector of care work offers her a powerful new personal and social identity. Striving to unchain herself from emotional and financial dependence on her husband

and his parents which is her strongest aspiration, Ana turns her achieved power towards the management of family economy, deciding how to spend money and who will benefit. She is aware of her economic power and proud of her capacity to improve the living conditions of her and her sons and to ensure her pension and a good life in old age. Based on the developed skills and knowledge that Ana has gained through mobility, her self-esteem is strengthened, and her social status is lifted.

In what follows I aim to provide more ethnographic "in-detail" evidence that will help us re-thinking of how elder care workers challenge "ideals" of silence, passivity, and invisibility. This starting point disputes pressing motivations and aspirations of care workers as essentialized family's economic wellbeing or survival. Herein the underlying assumption is not that labour mobility is necessarily reduced to escape from poverty and hardship expressed in materialistic terms, but that the development of motivations and experiences during the period of mobility exposes other hidden motives and aspirations rather than those income induced. These could be revealed only if the researcher: 1. Deploys immersive ethnography with follow-up interviews and series of encounters with research participants; 2. approaches the shifting character of aspiration for mobility from a temporal perspective. In order to avoid above mentioned homogenized social constructs of women care workers, these two approaches are necessary for understanding aspirations and motives not only through space (as migration researchers usually do) but also through time and within specific contexts. These aspirations are influenced by structural dynamics, but also constructed through the individual meaning-making of the interviewees and shaped by their actions that counter structural conditions. It needs to be highlighted that I conducted the interviews in various stages of mobility of my respondents. Sometimes the interview took place prior to mobility, during labour mobility, and sometimes when mobility had already taken place and are therefore constructed in the context of already experienced migration. Utilizing a temporally sensitive approach to motives and aspirations I show that the experience of labour mobility contributes in both material and emotional ways to changing roles and statuses of women and changing the way they understand who they are, what they want to achieve in their lives, what are their desires, dreams, and plans for the future.

In migration research, especially the long-term international migration, scholars examine and frame aspirations *before* migration which in turn result in understanding of "choices" that individual "agents" make about their "actions" to achieve future goals (De Haas 2010). This approach is widely used in the sociology of migration and migration policy research. However, recent scholarship (Boccagni 2017) suggests the need to examine aspirations as imaginative, emotional, and mutable during migration and mobility and that they refer to plans, ideas, and goals but also relate to matters of agentive will, cognition and emotion. As such, aspirations and motivations for mobility relate not only to present-oriented calculative decisions but also involve a range of feelings such as anger, bitterness, curiosity, hope, excitement, avoidance, and fear, and emerge in present material circumstances (Boccagni 2017). Boccagni suggests that scholars should pay attention to the content of aspirations, the manner that they find in relations with people and places, and the horizons of future possibilities that aspirations are crafted around. Read in this way, aspirations are about the emotional dimensions of the future – how we feel the future might and should look like based on our experiences of the past and our present circumstances (Boccagni 2017).

In the pages that follow, consideration is given to the respondents' reconstructed aspirations over time, the activities and realizations and the evaluations as conveyed in the interviews. Their understanding of mobility motivations will have changed throughout these trajectories and through their reflection. However, the interviewees referred to what they understood as the initial plan or rationale behind their decisions, and how they reflected in retrospect upon this process and their previous life experiences and life situation in the time of the interview.

The content of the interviews where respondents are asked to give an account of their reasons, motives, and aspirations suggest that their biographies differ in the following dimensions: material (economic) situation, living situation, personal circumstances, individual identity constructions, social networks, working situations and initial plans for mobility. These variables reveal different mobility aspirations are formed around three different constructions:

1. Aspiration and motivation for mobility are a result of highly precarious lives without a stable income. Mobility for care work is aimed to sustain life and it presents the only source of financial means. Thus, mobility is a necessity to overcome the existential crisis of a single women or a whole family and household.
2. Mobility for care labour is driven by personal and specific aspirations. Here, plans and dreams are part of aspirations and motivations for per-

sonal achievements or the realization of specific goals and personal, family, or collective projects.

3. The women are aspired and motivated by curiosity and adventure. Mobility is seen as an opportunity that should not be missed, but from which person could if something did not work out as expected. It is framed as an attempt associated with the idea of trying this new opportunity and seeing where it leads.

The aspirations and motivations framed within these three interconnected categories can certainly not depict a deeper understanding without seeing how they overlap through the different times and phases of mobility. While some interviewees perceive care labour mobility as the solution to economic difficulties in the context of a family strategy, such as paying debts and credits, other women are drawn to mobility from problematic marriage relationships or on the contrary, because they want their family to sustain and to improve their livelihoods together.

Economic Survival as an Aspiration

The consequences of economic transformation had an impact on the working lives of many of the interviewees, who often directly referred to their perceptions of these changes. The experiences of the changing economic system together with their labour market situation were manifold and were mainly determined by their age. Nada Markovic is a typical example of a "victim of post-socialist transition" due to the collapse of industries and factories in the former Yugoslavia. Nada lives in Belgrade in her apartment that she earned during her life. This is how Nada narrates her reasons and motivations for care work in Germany:

"Well, I do this simply because I am not retired, I do not have a pension and I don't want my children to support me. I could not stand it, because I've supported my children all my life … One can think, well, you can give birth, bring children to the world … but they are my children, and I cannot let them think whether I have enough for living or not … or not at all. I got divorced from my husband very early when I was 28 years old. I raised both my daughters alone. They were 'never hungry or walked barefoot'. I do not complain about my life and I have never complained even when we had only margarine and bread on the table."

Nada lost her job as a pharmacist in 2006 after almost 20 years of working in one of the biggest and most successful pharmaceutical drug-makers in the Balkans. I remember as I grew up in Belgrade, that those who worked in "Galenika" (name of the company) were usually well-paid and privileged workers. Nada was working in the department of electronics and had a good salary. When the company lost the mentioned reputation due to financial collapse, many employees became redundant, among them Nada. Since 2006, she did various jobs from cleaning to waitressing in restaurants.

"I lost my job when I was in the middle of building a new apartment. It was built on an already existing building like a loft (under the roof) you know ... I was saving money all my life for that place. Before we moved into a new apartment, my two children and I lived in 18 square meters. We lacked nothing, we were happy."

Nada's older daughter lives in Germany. The youngest lives in Belgrade.

"My youngest daughter is a single mother. Until recently, we lived together in our apartment. Then, she decided to move out and pay the rent. I sold my old apartment and bought a smaller one. The rest of the money was spent mostly on financing everyday life. My daughter in Belgrade spends a lot ... more than she can earn and she has a very good salary. Therefore, I cannot rely on her. At some point, I found an administrative job in the police. Not a very good paid but stable job. Then my daughter got a child and I left the job because we lived together and it was more sensible for me to look after my grandchild than to send her to nursery ... because we together lived at that time. So, I will not have a pension. I will be entitled to the state pension when I turn 65 ... but that will be around 200 euros, not more ..."

Nada's main motivation is to make her own living and to avoid being dependent on her children whom she so proudly brought up single-handed. Further, in the interview she explains that she very often comes to Germany and stays with her daughter who has two children:

"Why should I go there? I don't feel useful. I sit in the house ... but that's, you know ... from my house to their house. I do nothing ... of course, I am with my grandchildren, I cook, I clean, do the laundry ... but I don't earn money."

Similarly, to Nada's case, Snežana a single mother, divorced, and in debt, found herself in the informal elder care job market. The exclusion from the formal labour market in her country due to her age, the loss of her qualified employment, the death of her husband followed by an emotionally difficult relationship with her daughter, and the absence of any income gave her a feeling of despair and pressured her to opt for care work as an only chance for survival. I have described Snezana's case in Chapter 6 where it is clear that her exposure to labour mobility and aspiration for mobility are related to the basic economic survival of her and her daughter whom she still financially supports.

While the previous two cases, where women are in their sixties without a chance to retire, young women with families like Fatima from Bosnia and Herzegovina are motivated for several reasons. As the excerpt of the interview below shows, Fatima identifies herself primarily as a mother, she uses motherhood as a social role to make sense of her labour mobility and to legitimize her absence. Her narrations are seemingly permeated with "the rhetoric of sacrifice": she is working to fulfill her "mission" that is guaranteeing the economic well-being of her family and in particular of her children, neglecting her well-being.

"I am 38 years old. 4 years ago, when I first left, I had two children already – Amar was 8 and the younger was 2. The youngest is a little princess; she is turning one year now, in a few days. Well, let me tell you ... I have been working as a care worker for the last 4 years. I know many women who are leaving such small children. Believe me, either you leave a small child or a 20 something child – it is the same. I mean, it is not equally hard, but it is difficult to leave your child at any age. Even those who are married and have their kids. When I had only two it was hard, I cannot say it was not ... but now when I have a little one, only one year old, my heart is bleeding. I will not be at home for her first birthday. I am sitting here poisoning myself with anti-depressants and crying. But, I am doing all this for them."

As the conversation goes on, Fatima's narrations of her biography reveal that aspirations are changing from purely sustaining family livelihoods to other aspirations: preserving her dignity, purchasing power to meet cultural expectations in the religious community, and reinstating a life standard that she had before financial problems came.

The event that Fatima describes as the turning point that forced her into care labour mobility:

"You ask what the motivation is. Four years ago I sat at the table with my husband, we had coffee and I told him: 'I have nothing to cook tomorrow.' Let me tell you something Tanja ... my husband quit his job three days ago because my mother is not mentally capable of taking care of my children anymore. After the death of my father, she had a little nerve break down and she never recovered entirely ... she loved my father so much and she couldn't have coped with life without him. So, my husband and I had to make a decision about who is going to leave the job me or him. Somebody had to. But his daily wage is 25 Bosnian Marks and mine is 75 euros. We lose a lot if I quit. And, then we decided that if he left the job, is somehow better for the time being. But the director of the company where he worked, told him that when I get back from Germany that he could take his job back. I have now decided to take a small break of two months. But it is not easy for him … I cannot say … with three kids, it is not easy for him at all.

Fatima's frames of aspiration for care labour mobility can be seen in terms of cost-benefit calculation and thus are constructed as a form of household decision-making to improve their common situation by maximizing common income. However, we should not read it as a mere household decision where the household is seen as a homogenous decision-making body, but it is one influenced by internal power structures. In Fatima's case, family structure and negotiations of power relations are crucial for her decision to commute for care work in Germany. The continuation of the interview describes this tension in the process of decision-making:

"Now Tanja, to make things a little bit clearer to you – I am a dominant woman. My husband … I must say … there were problems … I can't say that I didn't have problems with him but my husband knows that I cannot be burdened with more troubles than I already am. I cannot carry the burden of the family alone … So I asked him: 'Do you want to have a nice life?' Yes, right? Then, please make the sacrifice, as I make it. So, we split the burden. Because he knows … if he would complain about the situation … you know, I can't do this, I can't do that okay … I wouldn't go to Germany to take for elderly. I would stay at home and look after my kids. But you see, my husband is not a resourceful man and he would take all responsibility for the family.

Well, he would carry a complete family on his back … and he couldn't make it. He knows that I think so. My husband is a wonderful person and, believe me, I have a perfect relationship – from raising children together, conversations, friends, sex, everything. So, I am satisfied in any respect. There is only one thing: When the problem arises, he shits himself. Then, I am the one who holds the bridle reins … and has a solution for everything at all times."

The opportunity to act, to become mobile is linked to Fatima's controversial role of family breadwinner which is in collision with gender ideologies of her cultural context where a conventional version of fathering means to conform to norms of breadwinning and male domination in the family. Consequently, like many "transnational mothers" of small children, Fatima often expresses through the interview feelings of deep sadness, depression, and even guilt about "abandoning" her children despite the fact that labour mobility was prompted by a sense of obligation to provide their children with education, food, clothing and a lifestyle they could not otherwise have afforded.

However, very soon after this Fatima tells the story of why she left the job she had before care work. She decided to commute to Germany for elder care work she worked in the textile industry as a professional ironer. This is how she describes the reasons why she left her job:

"Actually, I had my job ... I was employed but quit the company. Because, I couldn't stand it anymore ... the first thing, I couldn't stand is being paid 250 euros. The other reason was the mobbing and sexual harassment in the factory. I was one of the best workers. In a company with 1200 women I had the highest salary until my boss decided differently. He was forcing me to have sex with him. When I refused, he started with blackmails and threats. My salary went down and in the end, I was earning three times less than before. I found out later that he was doing that to other women as well."

Her accounts of sexual harassment at work were compounded by pride and dignity. She quitted her job. At the time, Fatima's parents and her brother were running the "flower business" (import of flowers from abroad), which was the family business for the last twenty years. Fatima was part of that business until she got married and got her children. The death of her father affected the scope of the family business. They worked less and only for the local market.

"My father paid for the house where I live today. He also built houses for my brother and a house for my sister. He was a great money saver and he believed that money should be invested in real esta and so he took care of us all ... My mother lives with us, but she has her owapartment on the top floor of the house. My brother lives two streets away and my sister lives in Sarajevo. But we're all one big family ... when a problem comes up, we all jump to solve it together."

When I asked her about the support of her family (parents and siblings) at the time she lost the job Fatima answered in a hasty way insisting on identity related aspects like self-respect, autonomy, and dignity:

"Oh, woman, I had nothing to eat, do you hear what I am saying? Nobody knew, I didn't tell my brother or sister or mother. I couldn't have.
T: Why didn't you? They would have helped you, wouldn't they?
Well, I know all that ... but you do get to that point of shame where you have a man and a woman in the house who are incapable of making ends meet ... you know ... and we used to live with enough money, even luxuriously. All of sudden, it turns out, you have nothing. At some point, I gave up ... I couldn't have gotten out of bed. My husband makes me a coffee and breakfast and says: 'Get up ... look I made the coffee, let's eat ... come on ... at least drink a coffee.' I say: 'I don't want to, leave me alone.' My brother comes as well, but I send him out of my room. So, that period in my life ... again, I say ... that's how God wanted it ... to bring me to that situation. Because, you know, I quit the job, my husband didn't work ... we had nothing. And you must think ... how to earn the money ... where, with what ... when you

do the math: loan installment of 500 KM (250 euros) I have to pay monthly and then I wonder what I am going to do, how to climb out. I cannot afford to not to pay off the installment … I am never late … not a day. All these debts were a huge burden I had to carry …

On the other hand … to be honest with you, I spend a lot, as well. The first two years of working as a care worker in Germany were only to pay off debts. I have one more big credit that has lingered for a long time … with God's help I will pay it off as well. I came to the point where I can afford myself to go out for lunch with my family, you know, let's go to the restaurant today … you know … Another thing, you do know that I am Muslim … it is important to me that I can afford the Qurban for the health of my children and my family. Before we got into financial troubles we were going to the seaside for holidays every year … and then it happened that we couldn't afford to have a coffee … you know? And then, God gave us that opportunity, directed me to that woman … my boss … well, she is not my boss, I have nothing to do with her … the woman who finds me jobs … I owe her for lif.. I cannot thank her enough. If it was not for her, I could not have afforded anything for my kids today. I am simply in that position today that my kids have everything they need. Maybe it sounds ridiculous, but my kids have learned what the branded goods mean … and the little son of 6 years says: 'Mama, mama, buy me a Nike, Adidas, or Asics.' And I say to him: I buy you a piece of shit, do you hear me?"

The other interviews can be summarized in two cases where lack of prospects induces future-oriented aspiration. 42-year-old Zorica bitterly complained about the situation in the country:

"I always say it is better to go abroad to wipe someone's ass than to be forced to join the party and to go from town to town promoting them and their politics. Why do women decide to leave the country? Here is why … Take me as an example. My husband is a mathematical programmer, I'm an economist, and let me tell you, I was unemployed for eight years, without money, without any source of income, we barely managed to buy food for ourselves. So of course, I decided to go to Germany …"

Similarly, 48-year-old Sanela was guided by earning the money to give her reasons for care work in Germany:

"I simply must work. My husband does not have a job. I have two sons. Also, I have a daughter. She is married. I have grandchildren. On top of that, we are in huge debt. I must earn the money to pay it back. I am going to Germany while I still can do it, while I am healthy. I must think of the future. It has been 9 months since my last job in Germany. I can't find one. I see the advert, I respond but it's already gone."

"Who Needs a Sculptor These Days?" Personal Goals and Desires as Mobility Aspiration

Unlike previous examples, narratives in this section presented by women care workers have two central elements. Mobility for care work is a result of the difficult economic situation for all women in general: no job opportunities and being constantly in debt that they cannot pay off. The second element is personal problems that come after economic problems but are more valued and better articulated in the interview. Women from this group frame themselves as independent and active agents with a specific goal they want to achieve in the short or in the long run. They are aspired by more meaningful life goals led by the ideas of fullfilment of their personal desires and dreams.

Jasna Pajevic is a 57-year-old unemployed sculptor, a single mother of a 21-year-old son. Her son is not employed and does not study but he takes various jobs from time to time. Jasna's approach to raising her son is more "laid-back" approach, relaxed, and easy-going:

"He is a good kid. I don't want to pressure him with his studies and career. He is still young and without a clear idea of what does he want to do in his life. He needs more time. So, I will support him as much as I can."

Jasna has already developed her little business. She created her artistic internet webpage where she advertises her art. She became moderately successful on the art market by selling her ceramic figurines across the world. However, that is not an income that she can rely on because it comes irregularly and in drops. She must have found more reliable sources of income to maintain the life of her and her son. When I had the first interview with Jasna, she already worked for two German families as elder care worker. Being asked how she decided to take the challenge of such a radically different job, Jasna framed her motives for labour mobility in Germany like this:

"I am new to this business, as I told you … what motivated me was, as you will have guessed, of course, money. I am a professional sculptor. I have a degree from the Academy of fine arts, but who needs a sculptor these days? I had worked with ceramics for a long time. I had worked at 'Stanisic studio', very famous, as you maybe know, for making stained-glass windows and mosaics. They expanded their business all over Europe, so I did several German churches as well. However, the work ran out. In fact, the owner of the studio had changed, and the job had become more expensive: the electricity had become more expensive, the colors had become more expensive, and I had become expensive for them as well. So, I found myself in the middle of the winter without a job. At that point, I started to think about it (going to Germany) … since many women from my street go to Germany. A lot!"

Six months after the first interview I visited Jasna in the household in Germany where she worked for an old woman she cared for. Although she seemed to be content with her job and working conditions, she quickly came back to the topic of her profession. She strongly expressed another reason for doing care work – her desire to make her art and to work as an independent artist that costs money that she must invest at the start:

"I like to make these ceramic figurines … and now I am going back to my art again. With the money I earned here, I can take enough time to relax and to do my things … not commercial, not to be pressured by other people's tastes. I will work until I earn enough to buy my ceramic furnace."

When I asked about her plans for continuing traveling to Germany and the retirement plan Jasna gives a straightforward answer:

"For now, I am doing fine. I go to Germany, I change the environment, I earn some money, I help someone. I feel good when I help them. I feel good spending time with these old ladies. I don't know, in some sense, I look at it in its human aspect … As for pension … oh, I haven't accumulated any pension entitlements at all, not a single day. I am not entitled to a pension. I will work for as long as I can, and however much I can. When I won't be able to work anymore, I won't exist. I am 57 years old. That means … you know … maybe a couple of years more, and then I will not need to travel to Germany anymore. I am not going to go there to take care of someone younger than me!"

It is clear from the statement above that Jasna has no plans for her old age, but she is also not frightened of not having them. Her future is wide open. However, aspiration for future elder care mobility is constrained by the time pressures of the life course like an old age and aging. In the case of Jasna, it seems that professional aspirations in the first place and personal (family and well-being) are aspirational factors in her mobility experience.

The portrait of Ana Wendl, however, gives us a more complex account of aspirational aspects of Ana's labour mobility. Following Ana's journeys from the early days of her care labour mobility to her first steps into the world of other job possibilities in Germany others than care work. Ana has managed to overcome a series of traumatic experiences through the years of care labour mobility, which in turn determined some of her life choices. As a woman with adult children and without caring responsibilities, mobility for care work provided her a way out from unsatisfactory marriage, the hardship of everyday life the patriarchal gender order in the family of her husband.

It is evident from Ana's portrait that her aspirations were always connected to a very strong determination to emancipate herself not only financially, but also emotionally from her husband with whom she doesn't share anything, but the common children and the estate that he inherited from his parents. Ana's specific economic goal was often combined with the aspiration for independence, for example when the living arrangements, in Serbia, did not provide for a self-determined way of life. Unlike others, Ana is very future oriented in her planning. She works to accumulate enough money to buy herself a little apartment, to design it and furnished it as she wants, and to put aside put aside some money for her old age, given that she is not entitled to Serbian pensions are very low.

In all of the cases mentioned above, aspirations for mobility, take shape in relation to sustaining livelihoods and in cases like Jasna's case, to realization of personal professional fulfillment. The reasons for mobility that interviewed women provide first are common to most of them: the necessity to earn a living and to maintain the standard of life that they perceive culturally acceptable in their contexts and according to their personal preferences. Children's wellbeing and education are not given priority in their narratives. In this respect, the case of 49-year-old Marina Jovanovic, scrub nurse (surgical team assistant) from Eastern Serbia differs from others. Aspiration for care labour mobility is constrained by Marina's full-time job in the hospital. However, she is using her vacations days, days off and for the last two years, the opportunity to take unpaid leave to be able to do rotation shifts in the care work in Germany. Marina's aspirations are mostly revolving around the desirable progress of her son's future life and career. Asked about her reasons and motives for traveling to Germany, Marina openly expresses her frustration over her low salary and unfair employment practices in Serbia:

"Doctors are paid very well. Of course, there is bribery, corruption, and everything else. They earn very good money. I, personally, as a nurse … don't have money for the education of my son. Despite the fact that we live in the village, own the house, and produce our own food, we are still short of money. My husband is employed as well. I also take side jobs, seasonal jobs. I went to pick apples, cherries, etc. It's petty money … it doesn't help that much. We have a mortgage to pay for every month."

Only later in the interview, Marina told me that she and her husband bought an apartment in the nearest town that explains the mortgage payments and debts she has to pay.

"Before I took the decision to go to Germany my salary was about 250 euros. My son studied in Timişoara, in Romania – every month I have to send 200 euros to my son, plus 200 euros for the mortgage … I am telling you, God sent me this woman from Negotin (town in Eastern Serbia). She had surgery in my hospital. I didn't know her before. I asked her for help. I explained to her that I need money to pay my son's university fees and that I couldn't live with a negative balance on my credit card all the time. She found me a job in Germany."

It seems that Marina constructs her motivations and aspirations as a dedication to solve her financial problems and pay back the debt, which she had accumulated to buy an apartment, son's university fees, and his student allowance. However, in the interview Marina revealed her intentions and plans to pursue her further professional goals in Germany. She tells her story with a tone of disappointment and anger. Seeing the root of the lack of money in nepotism, in the lack of the state's funding of the public health system in Serbia, Marina utilizes these structural conditions as a powerful motivation to make use of her qualification and migrate to Germany as a skilled worker:

"But before all this … you see, I first tried to get a job as a professional nurse in Hanover. There was a program for skilled health workers because of the agreement between Serbia and Germany at the time. The program offers you the opportunity to take unpaid leave and to study German for 6 months there. I would be on probation and have a mentor. If they were not satisfied with me, I would return to Serbia. However, my hospital wanted to prevent nurses from going abroad (because we already have a shortage), so they came up with a new policy – anyone who wants to take an unpaid leave to go to Germany will be sacked with immediate effect. I was revolted and angry … because I paid for the German course A1 level and was looking forward to it. Until then, I hardly heard any word in German, not even on the TV. Nevertheless, I was persistent to go to Germany … either to go to babysit or to earn 500 euros per mon or look after elthe derlyth … it was not a problem for me. Many of my colleagues, despite of all them, are leaving the hospital next year … mostly nurses, but doctors as well. I would go as well. Although, I must admit that they raised our salaries … now I earn double, around 500 euros per month. Even so, I would leave immediately. Because, because … you know, it is not only about salary … it is about organization of work. In Serbia as a surgical assistant, I do everything in operation theatre from cleaning to assisting surgeons. In Germany, you do the job you are qualified for and your tasks are very clear … I like that system very much."

As Marina decided to not to leave her secure and permanent job in the hospital, she opted for commuting for elder care work for a few months during the year when her job in the hospital allows her to do that. This is how Marina describes the German family where she is caring for an old lady:

"I think the world of these people, and the Germans in general ... their culture, manner and behavior and how they respect other people ... they are wonderful ... I am speechless ... Plastic bottles recycle system! When I saw that ... and you know, Germans are very careful with garbage disposal ... Everything has it's own place ... I like that very much. I am thrilled with life in Germany ... for that, I would quit my job tomorrow. But then, my parents are sick. I must take care of them, too. My mother supported me. She said: 'Go my child, you need the money.' My dad is sicker than my mom, but that's how it is. But if it weren't for them who supported me ... well, my husband supported me anyway ... if it weren't for them and my son, traveling to Germany to work would not be possible. You know, the family I am working for, they are trying to make it easy for me ... with a language. They repeat sometimes the same word 15 times if it takes, just for me to understand. But, for me it was enough just to see the word written down and I would understand ... it was nothing scary ... I have the internet there too. They offered to pay for the German course to improve my language. When I arrived in the family first time, I immediately talked to my husband and son on Skype. My son speaks German perfectly. He studied at two Universities. He enrolled at one, then the other. As a student in the German language and literature, he was fluent in German, so he was always there to translate or explain to me something I didn't understand. At the end, my son graduated from both the Faculty of Philology and Pharmacy. Nothing of this could have happened if I had not gone to Germany to work."

As Marina's account demonstrates, aspiration is regulated by external, institutional forces that at the same time hinder her mobility and make her more determined to realize it. Her aspirations to maximize her income intersect with ideas and perceptions of the Other, in this case, Germany is associated with the order, reliability, and certainty and the German people as a positive culture. An envision of Germany as a better living place is filtered through Marina's personal experience.

When I asked her about her plans for the future, Marina gives a vague explanation:

"T: Do you think you will continue traveling to Germany?
M: I don't think so, because my son finished both Universities. But you know how it is, there is never enough money. For example, to renovate a bathroom, I need €2000. For my son to go to Germany, to search for a job, he also needs the money for the start. To raise that amount of money here in Serbia is impossible. No way. I still pay for the mortgage. My son never got anything from this state, a scholarship or something. And even though he graduated with the highest grades he has no future in Serbia. Of course, he will go to Germany ... it is a little bit difficult but on the other hand, I don't want him to suffer as I do here. He has no prospects here absolutely."

Marina's contradictory statement demonstrates that her goals and plans for the future of her son and her family never stop. The way she is looking at the future doesn't exclude further trips to Germany for doing care work which confirms that aspirations for labour mobility cannot be understood as emergent at a singular chronological instance. Rather, they need to be understood as they emerge and develop across time and are subject to constant transformations, disruptions, and dis/continuities.

"Intentional Unpredictability". Adventure as an Aspiration

Interviewees who construct their aspiration as an adventurous undertaking are usually guided by the question: "Why not?". In their perception, they are "embarking on a journey" to see what would happen. This construction known as "intentional unpredictability" (Eade, Drinkwater, Garapich 2007: 7) is a phenomenon of viewing the mobility for labor as a venture and desire for a new life experience, an episodic life event rather than planned activity as an outcome of facing pressuring existential hardship. This is how 40-year-old Danijela narrates her route into labour mobility:

"One of my cousins recommended me to a family in Nuremberg. One day she texted me asking: 'There is a family in Germany who needs someone to take care of an old lady. Can you go?' I said, 'Why not? I will talk to my family … and will let you know.' At that time, my children were relatively independent. My daughter was in her first year at the secondary school, and my son in 7th grade at primary school … you know … that's what I want to tell you … and then I come home and tell my husband … he knew how my character was and what kind of person I was … He went: 'I don't want to say anything … you should decide for yourself. If you think you can …' and I said: 'I would go and try … For God's sake, that's only 3 months, not 30 years. If I can do it, I will do it – if not, then I won't go anymore and that's it.' But, you know Tanja, I was quite convinced that once I start, I will continue with the work … and that's how I left for Germany."

Although Danijela expressed a strong sense of responsibility towards her family and concern about how her husband evaluates her decision, she made an autonomous decision regarding mobility. At the time of the interview, her attempt to work as a care worker in Germany was behind her and she started to run a local café in which she has been quite successful. Further, in the interview, while reflecting on her experience working as a care worker, her previous determination to continue with care work, she gives reasons for taking a "go-and-see" approach:

"They (the employers) think that I must be poor to take this job … but, you know, I can tell you, I live under normal conditions, I live in the countryside, I own land, we produce our food … however, on the other hand, my children are going to school, and maybe later they will go to university. I wanted to help them. Indeed, this job is often taken by women who have nothing, and no one to help them. I have everything … a car, a house, my husband has a job, I have a job … okay, I lost the job, that is true … because I worked in the furniture factory until the factory was closed … shut down … you know how it is here. What I wanted is just to go and try, to see if I can do it."

A similar example is the case of Ivana Petrović, a young woman, unmarried without caring responsibilities, who expresses a more individualistic attitude by refusing to sacrifice her life and work as a live-in caregiver for a long period. At the time of the interview, Ivana was no longer working as a caregiver. Soon after obtaining their bachelor's degree in psychology, work and started a new job in one of the NGOs in her hometown in Serbia. The moment that triggered Ivana's decision to go to Germany to take care for the old, blind lady, was the death of her father.

She was in the last year of studies, and she found herself, her mother, and her brother in the financially disadvantaged situation:

"Two students and one pensioner with a pension of 200 euros is very little money. My brother and I did some part-time jobs that helped us to finish our studies at the University. These part-time jobs did not allow us to live normally … we didn't spend that much or needed luxury … but we lived in the house and the house needs repairs, maintenance and wood for heating … we heat the house with a wood stove and the fireplace … it costs a lot. I made the decision to go to Germany when we no longer had the money to buy firewood. I was the one who made a decision and said: 'Okay, now I am going.'

So, I went to Germany. I went there also because of my age. When I turned 30 I realized that I had no job, no prospects, and when someone offered me to earn that amount of money in a short time which would solve some of my problems that year – I decided to go without any further thinking."

Originally, Ivana's plan was to spend a year in Germany and then to fo finish her final exams at the University in a more relaxed financial situation. Ivana's aspirations for labour mobility are a result of her desire for achieving her educational goal and for the improvement of material situation of her family. Ivana's account of her care work experience in Germany is compounded by a sense of degradation and de-skilling:

"After a year, I realized that this job was not for me, that I was too smart for this stupid job. That I can find a job without being harassed and humiliated even though it wasn't so bad as it was for other girls who have gone through much wors experiences than me. I do not want to put myself in a position to be bullied by some who do not deserve me."

Retrospectively, Ivana found her experience very negative and hard but on the other hand, she switches very quickly on recollection of her experience of travelling to Germany for other reason than working as a care worker:

"I think, if I came back to Germany, I would come back with a B2 or C1 German language certificate to work as a psychologist. I would not go back to elder care work, babysitting, and stuff. I would go there to work with my qualification. Or, to do other things that aren't so degrading. The problem is that German is too rough language for me. Germany is OK … to visit it. But not for living. This year I was in Berlin for 10 days on a youth exchange and that was my first visit to Germany after a year and a half … since I left my care job in Frankfurt. I could have seen and felt how familiar was all to me … So after my experience working as care wora ker, I am going back to another city and all of sudden I explain to young people from Serbia who have never been in Germany, who do not know how the public transport work … you know how the system works. I was impressed with my knowledge that I could have shared with others. And then a little incident happened … I lost my passport when I was on the bus. Luckily, they found it, because that happened at the last stop and because it is very common that bus drivers in big cities in Germany inspect the bus at the last stop. My point is, that with my broken German I was able to explain to the receptionist in the hotel we were staying what happened to me, after what she made a call to ask if the passport has been found. I was surprised that I could have without dictionary to remember the words and communicate, rather fluently. I realized that I would have learned German more quickly than I had to do it under the pressure of her 'royal highness', Elizabeth (the old woman Ivana was taking care of). When I left Frau Elizabeth and Germany I didn't have the desire to continue learning, improving the language …

I experienced a lot of diversity in different cultures … I did travel a lot … well, maybe not as much as I would have liked, I didn't know many things I wanted to know. Anyway, the experience of living in Germany, in an authentic German family, with traditional German values, in a rich Frankfurt family is unique. I mean, I left my comfort zone and went into the unknown. I faced many fears – thinking whether I am involved in human trafficking … because I didn't know much about the person who found me the job … then, being alone in a foreign country … I was challenged by the questions like how much I can endure loneliness, how much I can endure listening to a language I don't understand and not go crazy, etc. But you know, I discovered a lot of cultural differences. On balance, I benefited so much from that experience and in addition to that, earn the amazing sum of money in a short time.

So, my care work experience wasn't entirely the only negative ... I lived in Frankfurt am Main ... and I always tell people to travel. I was posting some photos on Facebook for my friend to see something that they have never seen without visiting Frankfurt, some little things in different parts of the city or for example, the moment when the sun goes down at 22.00h which we cannot see in Serbia. You know, little things fascinated me ... as drivers stopping at a pedestrian crossing, people who are kind, that whole system works and everything is in order ... such small things I keep in my memory and I am very fond of these memories and moments. I miss mostly looking at the planes above me and I miss their sales ... I love clothes that I bought there, good quality clothes that I paid ridiculous money."

Ivana's recollection of her life in Germany demonstrates emotional dimensions of her experience where we can recognize how her aspirations were shifting from "earning easy money" to a desire to get to know another culture and to become able to re-imagine her future. The interview echoed this aspiration wherein Germany serves as one of the West European countries where she gained intercultural competency, learned the language, and made the money that helped her to finish her studies. In addition to the motivations of having specific goals, there was another narrative in Ivana's story regarded that acquiring social and cultural capital, such as living abroad for a while as a positively valuable experience in the country where young people do not travel as compared to those from Western Europe. Ivana justifies her decision to take care of old blind lady by cultural apetites for a new language, an exciting journey, a way to discover the world, to be a "vagabond for a while". In addition to changing aspirations over time, Ivana's case confirms an important ambivalence felt by all care workers with aspiration for education and with a sense of vocation – the "contradictory social mobility". This is a good example that highlights why well-being cannot be reduced to calculated income but requires respect, meaningful work, and decent working conditions, the topics I will elaborate on more on in Chapter 5.4.

5.3 Access to Care Labour Mobility

Access to mobility is one of Kaufmann's stone corners of "motility", potential for movement understood as socially unequal not randomly distributed ability to be mobile or immobile or to move other people and things. Access to different forms and degrees of mobility is conditioned by the geopolitical and spatial limitations, different means of transportation and communication, the technological innovations, logistic, services and equipment. It can be constrained and limited by the spatial dynamic of social networks that affect potential movers depending on their socio-economic positioning within social network hierarchies.

As mentioned before, in the elder care labour mobility, elder care work is organized through system of rotation, whereby female colleagues, friends, and relatives replace each other, organized, monitored and directed by ever growing number of employment agencies, individual job intermidiearis and informal networks that can be transnational, national or specific region, or even community.

In this chapter, alongside the structural aspects of access, I am focusing to the level of the individual – I look at various behaviors and strategies that women care workers use to negotiate structural obstacles to their mobility potential, on both a social and a spatial level, according to their different contexts and possibilities. In the process of gaining access to mobility, women care workers are taking part in labour moblity that is network assisted. These networks consist of a complex interaction of different actors, such as job intermediaries, drivers, care worker colleagues, and other individuals who are involved in care labour mobility. To understand these processes, I use the Goss and Lindquist's notion of the "migrant institution", a mid-level concept that refers to "a complex articulation of individuals and organisations which extends the social action and interaction between agents and agencies across time and space (Goss, Lindquist 1995: 319). Furthermore, as authors explain, migrant instution is "the pattern of communication between individuals and organizations that allows the boundaries of social practice to stretch and interact in time and across international borders (ibid.) In context of care labour moblity, recruitment agencies that act within formal and informal economy, job intermidiaries are gatekeepers who manage modalities that condition access to cross-border labour moblitiy. These are crucial in analysis of the strategies and constraints that women care workers face in access to labour moblity along with: technical and communicational elements; access to transportation; freedom to choose between different types of transportation; permeability of state borders; possession of the right travel documents. In narratives about women experiences of way into the labour moblitiy I look to answer the following questions: How do women care workers perceive their potential and capability for labour mobility? Under what conditions do they act and move, and how do they perceive their freedom to be mobile? Under what conditions access to mobility is denied to them and what kind of barriers to their movement they face? The selection of ethnographic case studies informs our knowledge about individual responses to the socio-legal regulations of border crossings and differences in geopolitical positionality that besides creating socially unequal "motility", play a central role in creating the forms of exploitability the informal care sector. This will reveal how to care labour mobility is distinct from other forms of labour mobility in terms of socio-spatial inequalities and their associated complexities and tensions. In addition, questions around how women perceive, evaluate, and respond to their access to mobility will inform us about the factors that shape a particular pattern of labour mobility as a self-feeding process in a given geopolitical context.

Factors behind Unequal Access to Mobility

During my field research, on several occasions and in different geographical settings, I had the opportunity to travel with women care workers and to observe their interactions with other people, as well as their different perceptions and reactions during their journeys to Germany. The following excerpt from my fieldwork diary illustrates how inequality in the access to mobility experience of women is one of the factors that influences their choices, options, and decisions regarding how to move and stay mobile.

"It is a sunny but cold early spring day. I am heading to Fulda Central Railway Station to meet one of my respondents, Isidora. Today we will travel together. She is waiting on the platform with two large suitcases. The son of the old lady she cares for brought her to the train station in the car and Isidora is very excited because this is the first time she has traveled by train in Germany. On her journeys from Serbia to Germany and back, Isidora normally travels by mini bus, a transportation business of a semi-legal nature, organized in connection with the informal care work market between the two countries. As Isidora is not bound to any particular job recruiter or broker, she can usually choose which mini-bus company she wants to use. But this time, she decided to visit friends on her way back home and to make a stop in Munich along the way. The reason I am taking this unusual 'fieldtrip' is to help Isidora to reach Munich, where she has a friend to visit before continuing the journey back to Serbia. A month before this trip, she asked me if I could help her with buying the train ticket. Without any knowledge of transportation systems in Germany or of how to use a ticket machine, and without a proper credit card, she cannot buy the ticket (…) She knows about the different discount possibilities available, but she does not know how to search for them on the internet. We are on the train. Isidora sits on the seat opposite. She is looking through the window and smiling. She looks very happy. Since we set off, she has repeated several times how much she likes the train and how excited she is about the trip. She is impressed by 'the cleanliness, comfort, punctuality of the train, the Wi-Fi access, and the beauty of the landscapes we are traveling through'. She thanked me and says that next time she will try to make the trip on her own. Apart from her lack of knowledge about train travel in Germany and her lack of financial tools such as a credit card to pay for the ticket, an additional problem was her fear of getting lost or getting on the wrong train. She confessed that, although she understands German very well, she is not sure that she can understand the voice announcements at the railway station. She could easily get confused about times, departures, and platform numbers. So I bought her a ticket and we agreed that I will pick her up in Fulda and travel with her to Nuremberg where I am getting off the train. She continues her travel to Munich alone, where her friends will be waiting for her at the train station." (6/3/2018, Fieldwork diary notes)

When asked about their previous experiences in traveling abroad, the majority of women, like Isidora (52-year-old), confirmed that they had very poor mobility potential and mobility experience. When traveling to Germany for care work, their freedom to choose their mode of transport is constrained by how care work is organized and arranged by recruitment agencies or individual job intermediaries. The main factors which women described in the interview are their previous knowledge and experience in traveling, their geopolitical positioning and proximity to the European Union border, the accessibility of information and networks, their position within these networks, and possession of the right travel documents and linguistic competence.

The Geopolitical Context of Mobility – Border Zones

Whilst, for some people, movement across national borders and settlement in or travel to a new place is relatively fast, safe and smooth, for others, cross-border travel can be dangerous and highly unsafe. Unlike the speed and safety of travel within the Deutsche Bahn (German Railway Company) network, travel across Germany for care work is often full of uncertainty, immobility, and sometimes even danger. Generally, women care workers have several modes of transportation at their disposal. Some of them travel using bus companies, while others use individual private transportation by mini-bus, which is organized on a more local level and is legally in something of a grey zone; and some travel using a service organized by the job intermidiaries. In this section, I will examine differences in the experience of travelling across three different border zones: in Northern and Central Serbia and Bosnia and Herzegovina. Territorial constraints such as border regimes have a crucial role both in the freedom of women to organize their journeys and in reducing potential risks that they face in doing so. Such risks include the potential to be refused permission to cross the border, the rising cost of transportation, and the psychological effects of travel such as fear, anxiety, and immobilization which can be the result of limited control over the movement.

With the following ethnographic cases I want to emphasise that, despite the efficacy of the regulatory mechanisms of the border regimes, women care workers are active constructors of the mobility worlds which they both inhabit and navigate. Instead of describing the knowledge and strategies different women deploy in crossing the border, which I will discuss more in Chapter 6, in this section I focus more on the interaction between women's practices, social spaces, and the social relations interlocked in territorial dynamic of potential and actualized mobility.

Snežana (58-years-old), who I have already introduced in Chapter 4, lives in Vojvodina. Vojvodina is an autonomous province and the northernmost part of Serbia and is bordered by Croatia to the west, Hungary to the north, and Romania to the east. Snezana describes the limitation on her freedom to choose her transportation options in a somewhat bitter and angry way:

"These women, the job brokers, don't let us travel by plane. When I went to Frankfurt, I found on the internet a return ticket to Serbia for the price of 60 euros. I could have taken a flight to get back. But I was not allowed … because I am tied to a Hungarian broker and her transportation. Most women are. In Northern Serbia women who speak the Hungarian language, they work with Hungarian intermediaries. But you can never get in touch with them. There is always another person between the two of you. That person gives your phone number to the Hungarian broker and then she calls you to check your German. So, she has your number, but you don't have hers. Once she finds you a job, she just sends you information about when her driver will come to pick you up in a car."

The Vojvodina region of Northern Serbia is a border zone with multiple border crossing points (see the map below) and forms an important transit zone between the Balkans and the rest of Europe. In the past decade, the Serbo-Hungarian border has become one of the busiest borders. Known as part of the "Balkan migration route", the number of border crossings has exploded due to attempts by refugees from Syria, Iraq, and Afghanistan to enter Europe and claim asylum in European states. In 2015, the exit points along the Serbian-Hungarian border were closed by the Hungarian authorities, with the establishment of a 174 km long fence along the border. Despite this measure, the combination of the refugee camps which had already formed along the border (on the Serbian side) and the illegality of the "business of bordering" induced a wide spectrum of activities ranging from human trafficking to an illegal transportation industry caused by the proliferation of border technologies and repressive border police. Within the context of increasing harmonization of European migration policies, the emergence of the European regime of mobility control, and the externalization of borders that has accompanied such processes, the Serbo-Hungarian border, as an external border of the European Union, represents the most corrupt and thus problematic border. Alongside a recent process to immobilize the refugees and the accompanying "migration industry", border activities such as petty trade, goods smuggling and human trafficking date back to the mid-1990s, when the European Economic Community imposed an economic embargo on Serbia as part of the UN and EU responses to war and ethnic cleansing in the Balkans. These conditions prompted cross-border petty trade and individual responses such as "suitcase importing" that created a new set of social relations between ethnic groups in Hungary and Serbia. After 2001, when economic sanctions on Serbia were lifted, the introduction of customs controls, and import and export tariffs meant that drug, cigarette and alcohol smuggling, sex trafficking and labour trafficking become frequent border activities.

Ana Wendl gives us a more detailed account of what role the Serbo-Hungarian border plays in her experiences of commuting. She recalls how her first journey was "stopped" before it even started:

"In the beginning I didn't know anyone but I was trying hard to get some information … it was almost impossible. For example, my friend and neighbor, Radojka, is a different kind of person … she already knew everything … who goes for work, for how long and so on … We asked everyone where, who, how … Finally, I managed to find a job through a nurse who was working with a Hungarian agency. At that time, women used to go to work for a very short time, two or three weeks. And there weren't many of them then. She gave me the name of a person with whom I could get in touch. The salary was much lower than the nurse had promised. But I agreed. The arrangement was like this: I would have to cross the Hungarian border and travel under my own arrangements to Baja (a Hungarian town) where the driver would wait for me and drive me to Germany, to the address of the family where I was supposed to work. I was tricked. I crossed the border into Hungary and no one came to pick me up. They told me to come at half-past six. My eldest son, Daniel, drove me there. I remember it was December, very cold and I didn't feel well. We arrived at 6.10 a.m. but no one was there. We called the driver. He said: 'Didn't they tell you not to come?' I said: 'No, no one informed me.' That is how things happen. You know, each of these job intermediaries who finds us jobs has either a son or a husband or a brother who are drivers. Something like a family business. We are forced to travel with them! The arrangement depends on a deal with the German family. For example, sometimes I have to pay for transportation with my own money, in advance, and, when I arrive in Germany, the family gives me the money for the travel. Somewhere else it works like this: when I travel back home from Germany, I get the money from the family, both for me and for the person I rotate with – that means they pay for my departure and, for example, for your arrival. So, it means that I bring money to you in Serbia, so that you can pay for the transport organized by those who found us Stelle (Germ. job position). And the third option is that drivers collect the money from the family when they bring us to their doorstep. So the majority of women from Vojvodina who travel to Germany do it in this way. This Hungarian connection is mostly known around Sombor (a town in Vojvodina)."

Although Ana's first attempt to go to Germany was unsuccessful, she went on to travel to Germany for care work in 2014 and 2015 through her broker, a Hungarian woman named Monika:

"I traveled for a year, maybe more, with the Hungarian job intermediary Monika. Her husband would drive us to Germany. Sometimes it was her son or a cousin. Anyway, it was always four women in the car alongside the driver. If I wanted to go with someone else or use regular bus transportation, I would have to pay him 170 Euros, and then I could travel with 'Touring' (the bus company). Then I would have to pay both, the bus ticket and 170 euros to her husband, just because she found me the job. Apart from the additional money I have to spend, I am forced to travel with her husband for the rest of my life (or as long as I continue working for her). In addition to this, I have to pay her 250 euros as a fee for finding me a job, alongside the 170 euros. On top of this, I have to pay for travel from my house to Baja – either with my car or asking someone else to drive me there. That was a lot of money … not to mention the fact that I cannot arrange how long I want to stay, I must not get sick, and I must travel with her husband. So many conditions … This is blackmail. It's as simple as that. However, I had to do it. There was no other option."

I was curious about how such a frequent border crossing does not raise any suspicions with the border police. When I asked Ana about this, she answered:

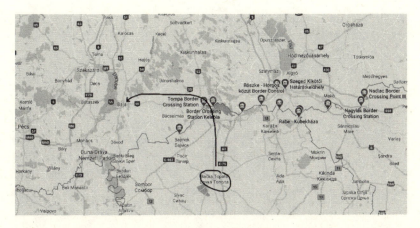

Map 5: The border-crossing point along the Serbo-Hungarian border shows the route that Ana was taking. (Screenshot) Google Maps

"Ah, Tanja ... they know about us. Well, if they see, for example, four women in a car traveling to Baja ... they know what they are doing ... that is an open secret. And corruption, of course! Tanja, do you know that you can cross the Hungarian border without a passport? You just have to pay 200 euros to the border police, and there you are. I mean, my husband is a truck driver ... he knows that very well ..."

Ana continues telling me about her experience of travelling:

"But you see, it wasn't that bad with Monika. That travel arrangement was better than the journey I made after I stopped collaborating with Monika. Her drivers would stop over in Germany to sleepover. They would take breaks. With the others after Monika, I was always afraid before traveling ... because my life was at stake. They sometimes drove 36 hours without sleep ... just drinking energy drinks and loads of coffee to stay awake. Sometimes it happened that they fell asleep ... you would speak to the driver but he wouldn't hear. When I started to work for Frau Müller I didn't want to travel with them anymore. She agreed to my new arrangement, and, since then, I have traveled by bus on the Serbia-Munich route. Frau Müller pays for my travel ticket."

Ana gained her independence to travel how she wanted because her working arrangement with Frau Müller was not in the hands of Hungarian job recruiters. After Frau Müller's husband died, Ana was no longer needed in the household and Ana did not have to pay the commissioning fee for jobs to intermediaries. However, Ana's emancipation from Hungarian job broker Monika didn't happen quite so easily. As the job for Frau Müller was considered to be a prestigious one, Ana had to pay Monika 250 euros out of her monthly salary. It is often the case that such positions are in high demand, and Monika had someone else in mind to continue working for Frau Müller. But Frau Müller wanted Ana to stay with her after her husband died and to continue to work in the same rotation system with another woman called Vesna, also from Serbia, with whom Ana had already worked. When Vesna realized that Frau Müller wanted to keep Ana without informing the intermediary, Monika began to threaten Ana and Frau Müller with the police. The threat was mostly directed towards Ana's safety while she crosses the border. Monika's blackmail was straitforward: if Ana did not give up on the job for Frau Müller, she would report her to the bordeborder police. Ana explains how this developed in an interview:

"Frau Müller was angry when she heard about the blackmail, and we came up with a plan. She created a little theatre play. Vesna and I were both in Munich because I had just arrived to take over my three-month shift and Vesna was about to travel back. Frau Müller invited us both and told us that she doesn't need our services. Her husband died and she will need only the cleaner from time to time. She has a daughter to take care of her. Vesna believed her. Frau Müller informed Monika and nobody suspected anything. I said to Frau M: I want to travel by bus. There is a bus from Munich to Serbia every day … and so it was … No one suspected anything. I cut off all contact with my colleagues and deleted my Facebook page. I didn't tell anyone. I told my children that if anyone asked about me in the village, they should say that I was with my aunt in Aachen. In the end, you know … it's Frau Müller's right to choose whom she wants. She does not depend on them. They did not find her. Frau Müller found them and paid them to find her a care worker. And I don't owe them anything either – I found a job for myself because Frau Müller wanted me. It's between the two of us. Frau Müller tricked Monika … ha, what do you say Tanja? The old bat … is clever (Ana laughs). So, you see how everything started … We women doing this work, we are fighting through it … as we are able and as we know how …"

The pattern of mobility that Ana experienced was the dominant model of cross-border recruitment for care work in Germany from 2014 to 2016. Since 2016 I have witnessed the flourishing of informal care businesses and the spread of small unofficial transportation services. With the advent of the first Facebook groups that advertised jobs, contacts, transportation, and a range of other services (for example translation services, German language courses, etc.) the care mobility industry has developed into a set of services that are not only tied to Hungarian job brokers but which have become increasingly lucrative economic activities on the Serbian side of the border as well. Thus, mini-buses have become available to all care workers who commute to Germany. The central actor here is the *vozač*, which in Serbian means *driver*.

Routes into Care Labour Mobility

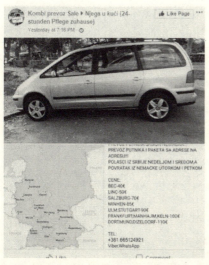

Figure 2: Screenshot of Facebook post, advertisement for minibus transportation services that displays destinations and the price list. Facebook, January 2019 (The link is witheld to protect the privacy of the respondent)

"The driver" is a person who owns a car. Drivers themselves or together with a couple of other partners, drive care workers for a fee from their hometowns to their workplace and back. The women who use this transportation know about it through networks of care workers or friends. The drivers can be independent of job intermediaries and agencies but, in most cases, each of the job intermediaries has one or two drivers who work for them (or who are, as Ana explained above, part of the family business). The driver often comes from a town or village next to the place where intermediaries are situated. For example, in Vojvodina, the center for elder care work agencies and individual job brokers is the town of Sombor, where the whole town from city administration to local businesses is part of the labour mobility chain to Germany and Austria. In this Facebook post, one of the job intermediaries advertises the Town of Sombor as a center of "informal care work business".

Unlike Ana and Snežana from Northern Serbia, Marina, (a professional nurse) from Eastern Serbia describes her journey to Germany as constrained by more individual reasons. Here Marina explains her lack of travel experience while describing her travel arrangements:

"T: How do you travel?
M: I mostly travel with Nikovic's Transport (the official bus company) or by minibus. These minibusses are much faster. The return ticket costs 200 euros. That is far better.

Figure 3: Screenshot of the Facebook post. Facebook, January 2019

Phenomenon SOMBOR!! In our business, this is the town with the largest number of care work brokers, agencies, and transportation companies. I heard that job intermediaries are coming from Belgrade (capital of Serbia) to rent their offices so that would be closer to the border crossing point and transportation. I am quite sure. Apart from Vrsac (a town in Vojvodina), Sombor is the "alpha and omega" in this business. I am 100% right. Everything starts here!!!

T: And why wouldn't you travel by plane? Do you know about the low-cost company Wizz Air? There is a flight from Nis to Hanover. That would be very convenient for you.
M: I have never traveled by plane in my life. Um … Well, I should. That would be the first time. I guess I will go, with my son. I have never flown … if you can believe me. I have not travelled around the world and this is new to me, especially the first time when I left for Germany. To go back to traveling … yes … You see, when I travel with Nikovic by bus, that is never-ending … very slow, it drives me crazy. That bus runs every day from Zajecar and runs to Frankfurt. In Frankfurt, I have friends. I sleepover at their place and then, the next day, I take the regional train to Giessen. The trains run every hour. And there, at the train station in Giessen, my family [the family she works for] waits for me. It is nice that I can sleepover in Frankfurt and all that. But I am tired. I leave Zajecar in the evening, at six pm, and we arrive in Frankfurt the next day at 6 in the morning. It is awful! 12 hours of traveling! So, it's far easier to travel by mini-bus and I'm telling you, I've never traveled by plane before. I hope I will travel with my son soon because it makes a difference when you travel with someone who knows."

Although Marina organizes her travelling independently, unchained from imposed costly services of the job intermediaries and agencies, her transport options are limited by her knowledge and experience in traveling and in the

Map 6: The route from Eastern Serbia to Germany Source: Google Maps, 2019

same time backed up by social networks, friends in Germany where she can make a break during the long ride.

Most women from Central and Eastern Serbia I came across or/and interviewed commute to Germany using official bus companies or mini-bus companies. Compared to their colleagues from the North, they are freer to choose their mode of transportation. This is influenced by three factors. The first is their geopolitical positioning since they are a long way from the EU external border crossing into Germany, a region where local networks of job recruiters, rather than transnational networks, direct and condition the movement of care workers. Secondly, this type of recruitment is untypical, and it is related to Eastern Serbia as a region populated with *Gastarbeiter* or guest workers, a historically important economic phenomenon in the former Federal Socialist Republic of Yugoslavia, which had a major social and economic impact on the area. Eastern Serbia was demographically depopulated due to economic immigration and is a traditionally poor agricultural area which therefore became the source of a great deal of migration into different European countries: Austria, Sweden, Germany, France, etc. At the beginning of the 1970s, economic migration from Yugoslavia, particularly to Germany and Austria reached its peak. After working for 30 years abroad, for the past several decades many *Gastarebeiter* has begun to return to their homeland. The extensive ethnographic research among Serbian retirees conducted by Dragana Antonijević and Ljubica Milosavljević, from the Department of Anthropology and Ethnology at the University of Belgrade in Serbia, fills a huge gap in scholarship where this topic has largely been neglected.

According to their research, some of the first generations of *Gastarbeiter*, who have now retired, are coming back to their homeland due to the very low German pensions they earned but that is insufficient for a good life in old age in Germany and Austria due to the high living costs. Others do not want to come back to Serbia because of the lack of entitlement to welfare and health insurance in that country. Those Gastarbeiters who do come back not only lose their social welfare status in Germany (mainly health insurance and extra social benefits in case that pension is very low) but in Serbia as well. Retired Gastarebeiters who choose to come back to Serbia usually are alone as their families, children and grandchildren live and work in Germany and Austria. They present a frail, vulnerable group of people that can easily fall through a support gap. Milosavljević and Antonijević show that the families of retired *Gastarbeiters* outsource their responsibility for the care of their parents or grandparents, tending to place them in domestic nursing homes. Another important strategy is hiring a local woman care worker to take care of an elderly person's day-to-day living activities and provide them with basic health care (Milosavljević, Antonijević 2015: 351). However, as my interviews show, caring for retired Gastarbeiter is economically less attractive, because they cannot afford to pay very much. Marina describes the economic reasons for her care labour mobility to Germany, comparing her situation there with what it would be like to perform the same work in Eastern Serbia:

"From just my village, ten women have already left for Germany to take care of the elderly. They do not go through the agency … I never went through them, but I do know about agencies and transport companies from Sombor and Vrsac. In this part of Serbia, it is different … you see, I know six women from my village who go regularly to Germany in a three-month rotation system – and that is far far better … otherwise, the only option they have is to work the land, to dig the vineyards for little money. Those who cannot go to Germany take care of elderly Gastarbeiters with German pensions … to change their diapers for 300 or 400 euros per month and to be humiliated and abused … It is misery!"

This is a very telling example of how current labour mobility for care work takes shape in relation to historical dis/continuities in labour migration over the last six decades. The social ties with those who still work in Germany represent an alternative source of information about potential employers in Germany for women care workers. Accessibility to care work and mobility is thus based on the possession of "movement capital" – privileged access to information that circulates through inner circles. This access is influenced on the one hand, by the level of trustworthiness that has been established between German families and women care workers and, on the other, by patterns of solidarity and reciprocity among women. Marina sums up this process:

"Women that go to Germany through agencies, especially those from Vojvodina … they work for 1200 or 1300 euros per month or even more. I heard that one German family pays both the agency and the women just to keep them coming back … the women pay the recruitment fee to the agency of around 350 euros for the first time and then 100 euros each month. However, the problem is that these agencies provide no guarantee … you know, if a woman does not fit into the family or is not suitable for them then the agency sends her to another family … but here, women who commute to Germany … they are very satisfied and the families are satisfied with them. Most of them work with the same family for years. They rotate with a cousin or neighbor, so it is always someone from the village who is … you know, known to others and reliable, not someone from the agency. Um … you see, it is difficult to get into this system … women usually bring their friend, cousin, or neighbor … because these women are unemployed. When the elderly person we take care of dies, their children find another job for the woman care worker through their friends and relatives. There is always someone who needs care for their old parents … so the German family secures your next job and that means a lot to us … also because it is a kind of security for them."

The system of rotation and commuting for care work that Marina describes above not only provides freedom of choice regarding transportation but also reduces the risk of exploitative relations between job intermediaries that we saw in Ana's case. In addition to this, women are working in a circle where they are empowered by the trust of former employers, which in effect reduces their chance of being stuck between two jobs or facing an uncertain situation of involuntary immobility.

A third example of the influence of geopolitics on labour mobility can be seen by taking the case of Bosnia and Herzegovina as a starting point of mobility. The interviewed women were aware that they could be turned away from the border if they were suspected of having declared a false reason for

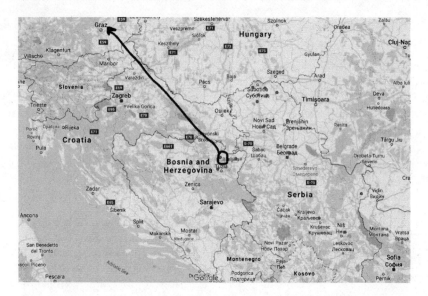

Map 7: The route from Bosnian towns through Croatia and Slovenia Source: Google Maps, 2019

their journey, lacking appropriate financial standing, or of lacking the proper travel documents. In contrast to Serbo-Hungarian border crossers, women from Bosnia and Hercegovina must cross two EU-borders: Slovenia and Croatia. Both borders are rigorously monitored, with a border regime that is much stricter than the Northern Serbian border zone. In the interview, Sanela described her route into mobility:

"Oh, you know how the Bosnian system is … you can go … and you can stay 3 months. I was there in May last year. Now it is almost a year since I've been there. However, it happened that the woman who is leading us (the job broker), always recommends her sisters. I was allowed once to go, and I am now trying to find something, a new job, a new family. But there is a possibility for going again in May. (…) Because that was the first time in my life that I went to Germany and crossed the border. I was there 3 months upon the recommendation of one of my colleagues. (…) So it wasn't through the agency … we went to … well, it was illegal … you know … black market."

But you know the problem for me is that I have no one in Germany who could register me at their address. I need an address. Just to report to the border police where I am going … just that … then I can cross the border, do you understand? I can say, for example, that I am staying only 7 days, just visiting, but the police will ask for an address. For example, now I am crossing the Slovenian border … the last time that I was crossing, the border police asked several people where they were going ... one of them was a young woman who told them that she was going to her cousin's wedding in Germany, and they asked for an address. She gave them the address, and they trusted her."

Later in the interview, Sanela explained that being allowed to cross the border depends on the arbitrary decisions of the border police. Appearance and age play a role when crossing the border. According to the border regulations, each person who enters the EU on a three-month tourist visa must show sufficient financial standing and travel health insurance. The required sum is 50 euros per day and the minimum sum required is 300 euros per person. If the person is unable to present such a sum when crossing the border checkpoint, the border guards have the right to refuse them entrance. The women commuters have to find different strategies to bypass this requirement, which they are generally unable to fulfil. As the required sum is high for women, especially those who are travelling for the first time, they usually borrow the money. In addition to the problem with the EU entrance requirements, access to labour mobility for women from Bosnia and Herzegovina is complicated by the fact that the informal care market is influenced by the proximity of Croatia, where job broker agencies operate within a semi-legal framework, and are the only chanell for job recruitment and only option left for women who want to find a route into care labour mobility.

"Networks of Care". Making and Sustaining Care Labour Mobility

It is revealing that in each of the three previous cases, with Ana, Marina, and Sanela, their experience of the journey is linked to the mode of job recruitment, their proximity to the border, and their empowerment as women through the trust of their employers. All three factors intersect in one location: in their access to social networks. Crossing the border several times per year, feelings of anxiety during the journey, arriving at unknown people's homes, and residing in these homes for care work requires the ability to strategize their movements. These strategies may depend on the length of time they are staying with the family, their level of spoken German, their nationality, citizenship, etc. However, to start the journey, they need access to information about how to get a job, how to develop mobility potential, and how to sustain labour mobility. Whilst some of the social networks and ties are created as a result of spatial proximity, as is the case in Northern Serbia (see e. g. the case of Sombor, mentioned above), others are created online on social media such as Facebook or simply through networks of friendship and family or ethnic networks.

At the time when I interviewed her, Sanela had already been working for some time in nursing homes in Bosnia and Herzegovina. However, the job is underpaid, and the working conditions are very bad, which is why Sanela decided to take the chance in Germany. Sanela described limited access to information and networks due to poor access to communicational technology as the biggest obstacle in pursuing this path:

"It is harder for me because of communication … in my family, we have only one tablet shared between the five of us. When the children come home in the evening, I cannot do anything."

Access to information automatically means access to networks. For example, access to social media means access to the information that is shared by the members of a certain Facebook group created for this purpose, alongside all kinds of assistance such as advice on certain problems related to care or border crossing practices.

Regardless of whether they are part of networks on social media or not, the majority of women in my study reported difficulties in making first contact with someone who could potentially find them a job. To gain access to more information about the potential job means to become involved in a complex interaction between different actors, such as friends and acquaintances, job intermediaries (brokers), drivers, etc. Demographic and social factors, such as age, stage in life, level of education, language competences and previous work experience all shape access to information and social networks. For Sanela, these obstacles are multiple:

"Now you see, for example, when I ask a friend, 'How did you get to go to Germany?' She said that she went through one woman. 'So', I ask, 'please can you give me her contact details, I would like to try as well.' She answers: 'I don't have that number at the moment.' In Bosnia, 'I don't have' means: 'I don't want to give you the number.' And then, another friend of mine told me about Predrag, the man whose aunt is a broker, but Predrag requires very solid knowledge of the German language. Then, I searched for him on Facebook and realized that his aunt is an intermediary, she is Hungarian. That doesn't work for me, because I cannot speak Hungarian with her and, as I am from Bosnia, I cannot travel with them."

When I asked Sanela about the possibility of finding a job through Facebook, a forum that has become an increasingly popular mode of communication among care workers over the last few years, she reports:

"Look, I do come across the adverts on Facebook. And I did get in touch with one of these women, Vesna, who advertises jobs on Facebook. I called her. She asked me where I was calling from. I said I was calling from Bosnia and that I could stay in Germany only for three months because of my Bosnian passport. She checked my German … I understood most of the questions … she said: 'OK. That could work.' Then she asked what kind of jobs I am prepared to do: shopping, cooking, and cleaning. She asked about my height, weight. In the end, she told me that I should travel to Zemun (a municipality of the city of Belgrade, Serbia) to sign a contract that I pay 100 euros. After I signed the contract, they will search for a German family for me, and for every month I stay with that family to work they will charge me 100 euros. All of this was very suspicious to me. I told her: 'Madam, I have no money to pay in advance. Can you find me a job where I can earn my first salary and then I will pay for your services?' She replied: 'We don't work like that.' I said: 'Thank you and Goodbye.' It was the first job advert I responded to. I called a few more agencies but they mostly look for people with EU passports or with residence in Croatia, since they are predominantly Croatian agencies. I would love to go through an agency. It doesn't matter to me. It is difficult for me because of this passport and the language."

In a similar manner, Snežana explains her difficulties in finding a route into mobility:

"The main problem in Serbia was that it took me a year and a half to find an initial contact after I had decided to travel to Germany for work. I could not have found the name of the women brokers. Can you believe it? Because I did not swim in those waters, and because of the extent of the competition, no one wanted to share their contacts.
T: How did you get into the network if you did not have an initial contact? Via Facebook?
S: Now you have this Facebook, but that was not the case before. It (Facebook) has been here now for a year and a half (…) When I started looking for a job and made the decision to get in, which was five years ago, there was no Facebook, because there was no need for that … business was not that developed like today. What did I do? I asked friends and acquaintances from my town who were traveling to Germany. When I found someone, I asked, 'Who sends you?' Then she says, 'a friend of mine'. I say, 'Please ask who the intermediary is', and so on. Since I did not get into those circles it was a big problem to find out where to get the right contacts. My first job came from the mother of one of my daughter's friends."

Lack of knowledge, isolation from social networks, unreliable job intermediaries and employers, and limited support networks can frequently push women into having to agree to exploitative working conditions. Their narratives reveal that these exploitative conditions carry risks that range from not being paid for work to being psychologically or physically abused. In the interview excerpt below, Sanela illustrates this by showing a willingness to take any job offered to her:

"It is very difficult, Tanja. There are a lot of us who want to go to Germany to work. For example, there was a colleague of mine who gave up on the job because she got an old lady who was mentally ill and she couldn't cope with it … Then I called the agency … it was through the agency … I said that I would gladly take the job. They said: 'Madam, this is a very difficult case. The grandma is now in the nursing home.' I told them: 'There is nothing I can't do, nothing that is too difficult for me.'"

The women who are in the most insecure and vulnerable position are those like Snežana who changed jobs seven times in six months (see Chapter 4). The jobs that Snežana was taking on were usually those that nobody wanted or where the women who did them had left as soon as it became clear that working conditions were dangerous or undesirable. Hence, women have different and unequal access to resources, information, or people as a result of their positioning at different levels of the network hierarchy. In contrast to Snežana's case, Jasna's closeness to Irena, a woman who acts as an intermediary between German families and care workers and who organizes jobs increased her chances of finding decent and fair working conditions:

"(…) But, my case is different … because I knew Irena from before. She keeps telling us to take care of ourselves and not to overwork ourselves. Well, Maja (Jasna's rotation colleague) and I don't have any problems here. But, in other places, women suffer from harassment and mistreatment. With Irena that is not possible, she is very protective. Every time she travels with us she visits the family we work with and makes sure that we are OK and well paid. Irena lived here in Germany as a child. She returned to Serbia at the age of 15. Her parents were here and she speaks German fluently. Over the years she preserved her connections with Germany and stayed in touch with the people here. There is a doctor who tells her which family needs a care worker and so on …"

As this example demonstrates, social networks where women can develop familiarity and closeness to job brokers or job intermediaries, result in more-predictable working conditions (payment, workload, etc.), security, access to privileged information (e. g. about new and better jobs). Moreover, Jasna's case proves that intermediaries' social networks are crucial "migrant institutions" for care labour mobility. The job intermediary is thus someone who provides an important link between German families and care receivers and women care, workers. The better the position that an intermediary holds in her German network of reliable and fair employers, the bigger the chance that women care workers will have secure and good job positions. This is how Jasna explains it: "It is also in her (Irene's) interest that the family is satisfied with us and that we are satisfied with them."

This shows that the person who acts as an informal job intermediary also must have trust in recommended care worker. This is important for the maintenance of her reputation as a trustworthy intermediary by meeting the expectations of the employers. Jasna knows that when she is recommended to a German family as a reliable person, Irena also strengthens her own position in the eyes of the employers.

The uneven distribution of information and access to social networks influences the capacity of a women to build up their potential for labour mobility. However, despite this, women nevertheless use their individual social and cultural capital, including personal connections, and other resources that facilitate mobility to allow easier access to social networks. These resources could include linguistic knowledge, specific skills, experience in care work, and so on.

Gordana is a 46-year-old married teacher from Northern Serbia who studied the German language and German literature and speaks it fluently. Gordana's mobility is constrained by her job as a teacher, so she can travel to Germany to do care work only during the school holidays. As a teacher with a low salary and two children, Gordana wants to earn extra money for her family.

"How did I find out about this job? How did I find the job intermediary? Well, I give German lessons, so one of my students, a woman, happened to be familiar with these networks of care workers. I told her: 'I would like to go to Germany to take care of an old lady for two or three months, so perhaps you could put a word for me with someone.' So, she asked around and one of those intermediaries who coo with Germans was interested … because, you know, sometimes a German family asks explicitly for a woman who is fluent in German. For intermediaries operate, it is important to have such women on their list. Within two or three days, she called me and said she had a job for me."

Gordana's case demonstrates that the need to use networks depends on how much knowledge is required for the mobility potential someone has. The better the knowledge is, there is less need to rely on the network. In that sense, Gordana's cultural capital offers a substitute for Kaufmann's "movement capital" which, as we have seen, mostly relies on social networks and

230   PERIPHERAL LABOUR MOBILITIES

information. According to authors such as Górny and Stola (2001: 177–178), for circular migration, social capital is usually located in the migrant's country of origin. My ethnographic material shows that the women I interviewed build up their social and cultural capital using their flexibility to adapt to changing circumstances, their use of different sources of information in Germany, and their ability to access different support networks across the two countries. Here my focus is on how knowledgeable women like Ana Wendl can employ their understanding of rules of interaction and exploit their access to resources within the migrant institution in order to find a job:

"Well, you know how it works … now … I will show you … here, look at these … Hallo München Anzeigen … you can find here private advertisements from people who need an elder care worker for someone from their family. I could find 20 grandmas on my own. You get in touch with them … ask questions, they ask you … and there you go – you are already an intermediary and you can find jobs for others. But no, I am not like that. I could do that, but I am not that type of person … It is too complicated. You find a job for someone, then that person turns out not to be satisfied or the family is not satisfied … no. I want to do my job and that is it. You see, the problem is that women cannot do this by themselves – they do not know the language well enough to build such networks. But after two or three years, one in ten women becomes independent, becomes able to find a job for herself. Now I am in this family, and I think they love me because I am good to them. When they no longer need me, they will find another family for me … you know not to go through the agency or intermediaries because I am in a better position if I do not depend on the agency or other people."

This excerpt from the interview shows that, although Ana possesses a high level of "motility", potential for mobility that that has been built up over a period and comprises gained linguistic competence, care skills, travel documents, and developed social networks – she rejects the idea of becoming a job intermediary herself. Moreover, she could exchange her "mobility capital" for economic capital, gaining financial benefits from brokering jobs but, as she asserts, "she is not the type of the person" and she doubts that she could do that job because "it is too complicated". This is an indication that job intermediaries are mainly perceived as actors whose primary commitment is to maximize individual gain, and who therefore are deemed untrustworthy and morally ambiguous. However, in the women's interviews, the figure of job intermediary is presented vaguely, sometimes villainized as a human trafficker or criminal, and sometimes portrayed in a more positive role as a "patron" who facilitates the process of mobility. How and why women care workers perceive and act within the intermediary-client relationship, which is an asymmetrical relationship characterized by unequal access to information and different resources, is a question that I will return to in more detail in Chapter 6.4.

As I have previously shown, in the case of Marina a self-organized system of rotation has an important role in freeing women from agencies and intermediaries as well as the risky and exploitative work arrangements that come with them. As the more women rely on one another and make their networks, the less they become exposed and vulnerable to sexual harassment and abuse, excessive working hours for no additional payment, and poor living conditions. The development of the potential for mobility is thus not determined only by unalterable macro factors such as border regimes, the possession of an EU passport, and labour laws but by solidarity, reciprocity, trust, and free circulation of information. Based on that, the rotation system is an important "migrant institution" embedded in cross-border labour mobility because it consists of care workers who rotate, job intermidiearies and employers. Developed as a response to the risks of overstaying a Schengen tourist visa, system of rotation is a work and life routine. But it is also a strategy that can be used by women who are new on the scene: by replacing another woman, these women can develop ties to other women care workers and potential new employers. The content of ties here is tremendously important for explaining evolution of labour mobility networks and mechanism that makes labour moblitiy self-feeding process.

Whilst, in rotation systems that are organized by job intermediaries, the "circulation of information" is controlled by them, in self-organized rotation, care work starts with one or two women who disseminate information to others as Marina explains:

"As for these agencies and intermediaries, you see, once I figured out how the system works and when I become close to my family, I started giving contacts to my colleagues in the hospital, women in my village, my cousins and friends … I wanted to help everyone who wants to work. Because, as I said to them: 'Go to Germany, save yourself, because there is nothing here in the country of Serbia.'"

Marina's access to her employer's network in Germany guarantees a certain routine and stability of employment, which was essential for the sense of security felt by the care worker in a climate of insecure, undeclared work. An additional advantage of self-organization is that women retain a certain amount of agency and can open new pathways and new routes. On the other hand, such a system requires mutual trust between women. It introduces other risks such as potential competitiveness and conflict between care workers.

The character of ties between rotation partners can also introduce risk within the rotation system. Weak ties involve relationships between acquaintances, while strong ties reflect relationships between close friends and relatives. The interesting question is what kind of ties are played out in the working rotation system. According to Granovetter (1978: 1361), "the strength of a tie is a probably linear combination of the amount of time, the emotional intensity, the intimacy (mutual confiding), and the reciprocal services which characterize the tie". Strong ties are characterized by time commitment and the psychological strain of consistency. However, when it comes to the rotation system, weak ties increase the risk of losing the job. That occurs, for instance, when employer/s are more satisfied with the replacement worker or (as they are called) *Springer* than with their usual employee. A paradigmatic case of this kind of relationship between employer/care receiver and rotational partners can be found in Ana's experiences which I described at the start of the chapter. Let us turn back to these cases.

As she described in an interview, Ana found her first job that was free from job intermediaries through a weak tie. After she got to know the Hungarian woman Katika during her travels to Germany, Katika offered the chance to rotate with at a very good job position:

"The old lady had a very good pension. She worked for BMW for 35 years. I lived in a separate little house and the salary was 1700 euros. But then Katika brought her friend Edika, another Hungarian woman, to visit her. She showed her the house and gave her a landline number. At the time, Edika was working for another family in Bayern, where the person she was taking care of, died. So, Edika used the contact she had gotten from Katika and called the old lady offering her services. Since the old lady knew her from before, she agreed for Edika to come to replace me. And I was out. Lost the job!"

As the story illustrates, when dealing with a less intimately known rotation partner, women may find themselves without work. By introducing her friend to her employer Katika, perhaps unintentionally, created potential competition for Ana that put her job at risk. The employer, who has the power to decide whom to employ, preferred Edika over Ana based on her previous connection with her. In this case, strong ties between Katika, Edika and the old lady proved to be the key to finding and keeping secure employment.

However, Ana's experience in the rotation system of work also shows a different case. Although, in this case, the rotation system was organized by a job intermediary, nevertheless, it is an illustration of how an employer's trust in the honesty of woman care worker, in her character, appearance and age, as well as trust in the quality of care service provided, are important factors in securing the job. Before Ana came to work for Frau Müller, she was taking care of a very sick and very difficult old lady. When the health condition of the old lady worsened, she was sent into the hospital and Ana wasn't needed as a care worker until the old lady came back from the hospital. As she was left without a job, Ana turned to her Hungarian job broker (who had found her that job) and asked for a replacement:

"So, I asked Monika if there is something I could jump into, maybe for three weeks … it doesn't matter how long. She said: "It might be something for you … That is how I came to Frau Müller. Her husband was dying, he was really sick … But it was different, I wasn't staying there during the night and I lived in a separate apartment. My work as replacement was only for one month, but Frau Müller told me when I was leaving that she and her husband wanted me to stay if I agreed. They knew that I worked in another family and that the old lady was in the hospital. So, they said: 'It is up to you.' Okay, I chose Frau and Herr Müller. When I informed Monika that I am not going back to my previous workplace she said: 'Who do you think you are? You stole someone else's job. Do you think that she should work too?' I replied to her: 'You know, I don't know if I have stolen her job. But I can't go back there. I can't endure it, I don't sleep, the old lady wakes me up 20 times a night. I am physically exhausted; my immunity has dropped; I wake up 20 times a night. I can't take it anymore!' That woman, Maria … I didn't steal her job. They just didn't want her. Whenever Maria entered the room, Herr Müller would send her out. She wasn't their type. She just didn't fit there. That is all."

In her story, we can recognize both that Ana refuses to be seen as a competitor who shamelessly steals other women's jobs, and that she justifies her urge to leave her previous poor working conditions. My interviews so far describe situations involving weak ties and limited access to social networks as in the case of Snežana who changes jobs every month. Jobs found through weak ties are usually in remote villages in Germany, involving hard and complicated health conditions on the part of the elderly, difficult characters, either in the form of the elderly people themselves or of family members, and bad working and living conditions in the household, etc. What appears in most of the interviews are three categories of strong ties: 1) strong ties with a job intermediary as in the case of Jasna; 2) strong ties with the German family who offers employment as in Ana's case; 3) strong ties on the level of community such as those found in villages where women operate their own rotation systems like in Marina's case. These three types of social relations are ingredients of the "migrant institution" that produce a rotation system enabling the sustainability and certainty of labour mobility, which in turn build "mobility capital" of women care workers.

5.4 Feeling, Thinking and Doing Care Work

This sub-chapter is set out to explore women's attitudes towards care work mobility, performance of care work and its meaning and how they evaluate, and appropriate skills and knowledge required for such work. By appropriation of skills here I mean how women interpret their own skills, experience, and knowledge and how to they act upon perceived care skills. Attitudes towards work are generally expressed based on evaluation of working conditions, relationship with care-receiver and his/her family, their own physical and mental preparedness and reaction to care work they perform.

When we are talking, thinking and writing about care, we must ask what kinds of doings do caring refer to. As I underlined at the beginning of this chapter, I argue that care labour mobility across the borders and between nations can reveal what constitutes caring and its significance for social organization, the complexities of people's relations and forms of sociality and the dynamics of power that interweave these. In the literature on "care", there is a variety of conflicting perspectives, definitions, understandings, and meanings. As Fine (2007: 24) pointed out: "Care is at once profound and deeply philosophical, and at the same time experienced as a basic everyday activity and a common attitude concerning all manner of things that people value."

The main conceptual distinction that appears in political and social theory of care, among other aspects, is dualism between care as a doing or set of the practices in material provision of care (embodied, physical, and corporeal care) and care as affective, emotional and cognitive practice and care as an ethical disposition. In my analysis I avoid this dualism by thinking of care as both, corporeal and affective, charged with values and attitudes – that, as appears in the analysis in women's narrative that follows – are intertwined and inseparable (Twigg 2000; Wolkowitz 2006). In our everyday relations, care is expressed as both *caring about* another, a disposition or concern for the well-being of another person, and *caring for*, the work involved in supporting another (Graham 1983). In practical terms, care may be thought of as the most intense expression of social support, involving not just affective concern for the other but the performance of care work and an expression of personal relationships (Chappell 1992; Rummery, Fine 2012).

The other conceptual concern crucial for analysis of elder care worker's experiences is understanding care as a *culture*. That means that the need for care and response to that need is always shaped and in turn central to culture:

"'Culture', in our usage of the term, interweaves an analysis of action (both intended and actual), meanings (ideologically received and more personally derived), and patterns of social resources and relations. It centres on the life worlds of carers, meaning a contextualised account of their experiences, drives and motivations." (Chamberlayne, King 2000: 5)

According to Fine (2015) the concept of cultures of care covers three distinct but inter-related domains:

– the ideals and approaches to care associated with different traditions, national cultures and ethnic groups;
– the practices and values associated with particular workplaces, organisations and professions;
– the care practices, values and behaviour produced as a response to national welfare and labour market regimes.

Following Chamberlayne and King's approach and concept of culture of care outlined by Fine, in analysis of women's experiences of elder care voiced in their narratives, I will regard care culture as a creative and living production, as a practice. By focusing on culture as revealed through everyday life and work – what women care workers do, how they talk about it and respond to constraints and make use of available resources – will allow for deeper explorations of relationships between actions (agency), structure, meaning and values associated with these actions.

Attitudes towards Care Work Mobility

"You have to turn on the switch when you cross the border. I switch into another mode. I am a totally different person when I am at home. Because I live their life, not mine and I am aware of that. I cannot change them just for me to feel better. I will be fine only if I want to be fine."

In this short interview excerpt above Milica Jeremić (40-year-old) who summarizes her attitudes towards work through identity position: necessity to be aware of who you are and to be prepared for another world where other rules play out and to leave the person who you are on the other side of the border. Here, the border has symbolical meaning and transformative effect – when you cross it you are becoming someone else. Strategy applied in Milica's case is only one of the coping mechanisms:

"When I started to think about taking this job and commuting to Germany, I was questioning myself so many times – can I do it? I wanted to meet new people, I wanted to see what kind of job is that , to experience it. People were always saying 'That is a hard work'. So, when I made decision to do this job, I knew it would be hard. First, separation from the family is one of the psychological disorders, so you automatically have a problem. People cannot understand, when you come to do this job, you are forced to live their lives, because you cannot change the way these people have been living for years. For example, you certainly would not allow someone to come to your home and change your habits, right? I think that, actually, many women are not ready for this job and they take the job thinking that this is easy way to earn big money ... you know, like someone gives us money for nothing. But it is not like that at all. Look at me, for example: I work in the garden all year round. Look at my hands how they look like ... my skin is sometimes peeling. But it's not hard. I live here. I want to make it nice ... for me. As long as I'm here. And the other thing, these people have accepted me. In return, I want to do my best for them, to give my maximum while I am here. But many women don't ... many women are just bad ... When we travel to Germany in the mini-bus you can hear some of them saying: 'I only work for rich people. I do not want to go to the poor. I don't want to do this; I don't want to do that ... Hello? We are all here for one thing – we wipe other people's arses. We are paid for that. I am not a model, I am a maid. I know who I am, and I know why I came here. And I act like that. That's why it's good for me.'"

Milica's work ethic, sense of commitment to her job, elderly person she takes care for, and the way she modulates her attitudes towards work make an anticipated hard work easier. For Milica, being aware of who you are and where you are going is a key prerequisite for of mobility for care work.

"I put the granny and the 'Rollstuhl' (Engl. wheelchair) in the car and we go shopping. We look around the supermarket together ... she sees people and things and she is happy ... then she laughs. That is priceless, that smile of hers ... and when she puts her arms around my neck. After the bath in the evening I put her into bed and sit next to her to talk to her a bit. She never goes to sleep right away. She is not my obligation, she is my hobby, she is there to fill my time. I really love her. Not that I love her like I love my family ... but I always say ... she's not my job, I didn't come here to work. This is family, this is someone's life, do you understand? We come here to live someone's life. You come here to prolong someone's life ... at least that's what I think. I didn't come to bury her, but to help her to spend rest of her life as well as possible … to make her laugh sometimes, and even if she doesn't know how to laugh, she laughs.

The way Danijela narrates her situation and attitude is in the contrast to Milica's experience:

"Well now … look … I liked the idea of going to Germany to work. But no matter how much you mentally prepare yourself for all of that, and no matter how hard working you are, how valuable your work is, and how profitable doing this job is – I had all these thoughts in my mind when I was going there – I couldn't stand him, the husband of the old lady I was taking care of. Terrible man! The other thing was – I had no freedom. Listen, I used to work 10 hours a day. But after those 10 hours a day you have your peace, you get some rest, you can do whatever you want. As a care worker in that apartment, I've been there all day … you have to put up with that situation, you have no other choice. I mean, he is the boss, you have to accept it as it is – you came to work for him, he didn't come to you."

Both women have several factors in common: they are of the same age, both married, both have two children of the same age (10 and 16), they both care for the female old person suffering from Alzheimer disease, have a very poor command of German language, and they both live in the household where they perform care work. Regardless of these biographical similarities, to understand Milica's and Danijela's extremely contrasting attitudes towards care work mobility we need to grasp different contexts where Milica and Danijela perform care work and how that work is organized. In the contrast to Milica's attitude, Danijela's negative attitude is linked to two factors: Danijela has very low aspiration for care labour mobility because she is not pressured by economic situation (as I showed in sub-chapater 5.2); second factor is a mode of job recruitment: Danijela found this work through, what I previously called, "weak ties", that provided her a job of poor quality. Danijela was taking care for immovable dement old lady in three-room apartment in the residential building in one of the German cities. Although she had her own room, she didn't have much privacy. Live-in care work arrangement, generally speaking, combined with the nature of care work, means spending most of the time inside the household, which can lead to isolation. When asked about her free time, Danijela reports:

"Yes, I had free time, but I didn't go out. Well, you know, I didn't know the city that much. I went out with them (the family she worked for) several times … we were taking a walk to the city centre … Altstadt, right? In the meantime, I learned how to go out alone. Then I went to out with their daughter. So, I knew very little about where I could go … but I never went far away … you know, I was afraid I would get lost. And most of the time, when I went to the parts of the town that I didn't know … like, you know … just as an experiment … I was always trying to remember the way back, so as not to get lost. It is difficult, you know, I don't speak the language, I don't know the people … I mean, ok, I could try to find some people from our country, and go out with them … but who knows who I could run into … the mafia, drug addicts … someone could kill me or kidnap me, and who knows what they could do to me …"

Danijela had confined her personal world for extended periods (in three months rotation system) to the restricted environment of her employer's home, and in this case apartment where she is permanently available and visible without possibility for privacy can be highly psychologically strenuous. Furthermore, through the interview Danijela stressed how such a relationship, while close, compassionate, and affectionate could be demanding and exhausting. Danijela's case shows how so called, paradox "immobility in mobility" as a result of the constrained movement, doesn't have to be necessarily imposed by the members or the household (or employers) but it can be a result of lack of the language knowledge, lack of social relations and local social network which results in feelings of fear and insecurity.

Unlike Danijela, Milica works for the big family in the Southern German countryside. She has her own room in the big house with a garden where she, as mentioned previously, spends her free time. The husband of the old lady and their son also live there. A few streets away lives the other son, his wife and their two children.

The second interview with Milica I conducted in the house of her employers where I had an opportunity to feel the atmosphere in the household and to observe household members' behavior towards Milica. My first impression was family's kindness and openness to me as foreigner in their house. Introduced as Milica's friend from Serbia, I was served with coffee and cake, and soon after the old gentleman showed me the garden being proud of Milica and her work. In the meantime, the whole family gathered so that I could see spontaneous and relaxing behavior on both sides, where mutual respect and understanding is shared equally among family members including Milica.

My ethnographer's observation convinced me that Milica's commitment and familial attachment to the family (that sometimes can be faked in the interviews with women) in her case, was not only genuine, but also was mutual. Being treated "as a family" member in Milica's case does not really fit the myth we often find in the literature – domestic/care workers and employers manipulate each other either to perpetuate inequalities or to resist the inequalities. While we could agree that the mechanism *"one of the family"* enforces, aggravates, and perpetuates unequal relations of power between maybe in the case of Filipina domestic workers in Rome and Los Angeles (Parreñas 2010) we cannot make generalization that each relationship in the realm of informal care work is exploitative. After analyzing how Milica has been negotiating her relationship with the family for the last four years, I can conclude that her compassionate view towards performing care work where intimacy gives rise to a familial attachment to the members of the family is a strategy to cope with the demands of care work. That doesn't mean that relationship is strictly exploitative or of the reciprocal nature but that a household where care work is performed is a site of constant negotiation between parties. To be able to grasp such processes we need to change analytical lenses by problematizing the notion of care as duality between obligation, burden and service and on the other hand social relations, emotions, and affect. The provision of care in the context of irregular care work must be understood in its multiple dimensions as a cognitive, bodily, affective, and emotional practice. Moreover, care is socio-cultural practice that connects not only the elderly who receives care and her/his care giver, but also collectivizes (producing collectivity rather than individual actions or identities) entire communities and nations. As such, care has capacity to shape (and to be shaped by) and maintain social bonds across the borders. I will elaborate these complex processes in the case of Milica Jeremić at greater length in the Chapter 7.2.

Cultural Conceptualizations and Perceptions of Elder Care Work

In the narratives below I have identified two sub-themes. The first, is characterized by cultural conceptualizations of care work and its value that are entrenched into experience of doing care through women's life course. The second theme is how women react both cognitively and emotionally to unprecedented working conditions.

With the informal care market being extremely flexible, the situation the women care workers from my study is particularly precarious. The interviews show that informal paid care workers perform a wide range of care activities, from intensive care to physical labor, cleaning and household chores. They may be hired to do work in rotation system of three months and sometimes

240 PERIPHERAL LABOUR MOBILITIES

4 weeks. They are hired as live-in care workers performing their duties on a 24/7 basis. Not only that such work is "illegalized" and "criminalized", but the care workers are completely unprotected, having no labour rights or any social and security with regard to their years of service, pension, and health insurance. In regard to the status of elderly person in the household and household structure we can differentiate several arrangements:

- taking care for elderly people who live with an extended family – with their children and grandchildren under the same roof where care worker has her own room/or sleep with a care-receiver in the same room,
- taking care for elderly people who live in the extended family, but in the separate living unit (part of the house, or separated house) where care worker resides as well,
- taking care of elderly people who are on their own, living only with a care-receiver and are visited by the family members or relatives from time to time.

Elderly care-receivers often are in their 80s or 90s, with developed dementia or Alzheimer's disease and require twenty-four-hour watch. Some of them suffered the stroke or bones breaking and recovering at home after being released from the hospital. There are cases of care-recievers who suffer from cancer or multiple sclerosis. A crucial difference in this sense is distinction between those people who are entirely dependent on the caregiver, immobile and those who are mobile or need an assistance in movement (like blind persons). In the case of immovable persons, the caregiver performs strenuous tasks of keeping hygienic and sanitary care, lifting the person up and down, turning and repositioning feeding and dressing up. Depending on living arrangements listed above, care workers apart from taking care of elderly person perform other tasks like shopping, clean the kitchen and go for a walk with the elderly person. Sometimes caregivers, not only take care of the elderly person but all of the household and its members. The tasks that require physical contact with a care-receiver, such as proper lifting up and down, bathing, changing the diapers – are tasks that usually need to be learned before one starts the job. As women from my studies have no training or any (medical) knowledge how to perform these tasks, they are facing sometimes difficult and as we can see below sometimes impossible and dangerous situations. My interviews show that care work performance depends not only on women's physical and mental preparedness. How women will cope with new unknown and demanding tasks of caring for sick elderly person depends mainly on the quality of information about the elderly person that they get from family of elderly person, job intermediary or colleague they rotate. Except two women who are medical professionals Zorica Milić and Sanela Mehić, no single woman I interviewed have previous professional experience of care work. Their main experience that qualifies them enough to work as caregivers is experience with sick and old members of their families. If we put aside economic aspirations, elder caregiving is driven by gender-related role expectations of women as care workers, "double socialization" and family backgrounds. German sociologist Regina Becker Schmidt (1987) calls it *"double socialisation"* of women referring to dual orientation of women to family and work which under existing conditions leads to a situation where the responsibility for housekeeping and for minding , caring for and bringing up children, as well as caring for older family members result in them being seen as women's tasks, to be performed in addition to women's professional employment. Women from my sample are the generation of women socialized in the Former Yugoslavia where despite working outside the home, women were seen as primarily responsible for domestic work and care Yugoslavian women's identity was summed up in the term *"working mother"*.

According to some researchers, the "working mother" gender contract was abandoned in the 1990s, with the state no longer providing support and guarantee of employment. However, woman's obligations continue to be linked to the family, while men are still seen as less bound by and responsible for family tasks. Neither education, occupation, nor participation in the informal economy had a significant effect in reducing this; only the presence of an older female in the household measurably could have reduced an employed woman's participation in the "second shift" (Massey, Hahn, Sekulic 1995). This is how Snežana narrates her previous experience:

"My mother-in-law had cancer three times and a heart attack, my father-in-law had multiple strokes, my husband had a 'brain stroke', my mother-in-law's mother was a very ill person – and all this spilled over onto me. Even if I did not have these experiences, necessity forces you to do something."

As a student of psychology, Ivana, utilized her experience of working with blind people along with experience of caring for her poor father:

"My dad died at the age of 72, so I got used to sick and old people. Before he died, he had been living with the consequences of a stroke for 12 years. The person I looked after was a 91-year-old lady, blind but mobile. I was supposed to clean, cook and to go for a walk with her ... when you hear this, you might think that it doesn't sound that complicated or hard to do. I had already had contact with blind people, I knew how to work with them. The only question is: how long can you endure; how much can you take? I got through 10 weeks when I went there for the first time. I could not wait to get back home."

Milica Jeremić framed her suitability for the role of care worker based on the theoretical and practical knowledge that she gained while taking care of her husband's family:

"I took care of my husband's grandmother, but not in the way I do care work now. She had diabetes. I wanted to know more about that illness, so I went to some lectures that the hospital organizes to educate the families of diabetic patients. I talked to the doctors, I kept asking what to do with such a person. Now, by chance, the old man here also has diabetes. I know a lot … of course, he is trying to trick me by eating crisps and chips secretly (she laughs) I know what he is doing … he cannot hide that from me. Now his blood sugar level is stable, about 7. It used to rise to 15, 16 or even 20. But with me, he is more careful what he eats."

No matter what kind of previous care experience carry with them, many women I talked to stated that elder care work is emotionally and physically hard work where certainty about conditions and job tasks is very low. This means, that when women care workers arrive to their destination in Germany and step into the private household, majority of them enter unfamiliar terrain, culturally, socially, linguistically and they are usually in for a surprise. Until they see elderly they supposed to take care for, in most of the cases, they do not know in what kind of mental and physical condition she or he is. Taken by surprise of specific care tasks, household structure and household dynamics, character of persons close to elderly (family and relatives), health issues of elderly person, women learn to accept such radical new situation and to find their own way to deal with it through creating acceptable working conditions and negotiating with a family. This is how Jasna answer to my question about the knowledge about the elderly person and the job prior to coming to Germany:

"I knew nothing. Nothing! Because I didn't know what was waiting for me. I let myself to go with the flow … I thought if I go around among people and behave in a decent and kind manner … as a human … nothing bad can happen. You see, I was left alone with a granny … alone in the house, somewhere in Germany. However, there is a tablet and phone … I have the internet. So, I can always call if something goes wrong. Every house, every family where women go to care for the elderly must have internet. At the places without internet, they had to set it up."

Although Jasna found her job trough "strong ties" and reliable and trusted job intermediary, she couldn't have known what situation she will face. However, communication technology affordances give Jasna certain level of security. An extreme case of uncertainty regarding job is the situation when job intermediary is a sub-recruiter of multiple German agencies to which they "deliver" women care workers and are paid for each recruit deliver. Women who are part of such legally controversial business deals are not even aware of such arrangements. Gordana narrates her bitter experience as follows:

"I spent only 15 days at my first care job. In fact, those women who work as intermediaries … I don't know how many of them are in the network … you can't figure out who is working for whom. They are very dangerous. The woman who found me a job didn't tell me the truth. When I turned up at the family in Germany, I found that the old lady I should have been taking care of was completely immobile. I asked specifically for a person who is mobile and emphasised that I cannot work with someone who is immobile, simply because I don't have the experience but also because that is a huge responsibility. So, what I found there was a totally immobile granny whom I was unable to approach from any angle. As I am, luckily, fluent in German, I got away from the situation by explaining to the daughter of the old lady that it was not that I didn't want to work or that I changed my mind, but that the Serbian intermediary simply deceived me. These intermediaries are very dangerous – they just want to take a commission, money, and they don't care what happens to you in Germany. I didn't even know who else was involved in connecting me with this German family … until the granny's daughter told me that she had found me through a German agency named 'Fuchs'. They are a semi-legal agency that collaborates with our local women who, probably in return for some money, recruit women from Serbia. I found out later that I shouldn't have gone to that place because I was explicitly looking for a mobile person, but that the woman intermediary placed me there because the woman who had been taking care of the granny gave up on the job. The family needed someone urgently, so she just transferred me to that place without me even knowing where I was going."

Vera Jelić, Gordana's collegue confirms Gordana's experience:

"We met, Gordana and I, last summer. They didn't tell her the real truth about the old lady's condition. She did not tell her that she was totally immobile, but only said that she was demented. Gordana didn't have enough strength physically to deal with the granny … there was no stairlift in the house, and the woman who had worked there before her had her own way of working which wasn't adequate, medically adequate … you know what I mean? This was the fault of the woman who found that job for Gordana. Their main goal is to take money from us, as far as I can see, say 150 or 300 Euros …"

Vera (59-year-old) continues describing her situation where relationship with a patient demands a high degree of tolerance, emotional balance, sensitivity, and negotiations with an elderly person's family:

"But, in my case ... I had a different problem. When the old lady I was caring for got sick, she was sent to the hospital for 2 weeks. I was in the hospital with her the whole time, except during the night. That hospital was in another town ... so I used to go by bus. Sometimes her daughter used to drive me there. She wanted me to be there with her, to feed her breakfast, lunch, and dinner and then I would return to the apartment in the evening. The first time she left me without any money. I didn't even know that I had to stay in the hospital ... You see, everyone thinks you're going to Germany to earn money ... it's all money earned with sweat and tears, believe me. But I approached the work and the person completely correctly. That granny (she has died recently as I heard) once took my hand and kissed it. I said to her: 'Oma, das ist große große Geschenk.' So, she appreciated my work. And the poor thing couldn't talk, she had some deep stress from her daughter, and she lost two sons ... one killed himself and the other died. I figured it out myself. She would tell me something sometimes, but I couldn't understand her entirely. I could understand something. While I was bathing her, I would talk to her all the time. She loved that. I paid maximum attention to her ... I would get up early and prepare the food and then from 9 o'clock, when everything starts, I would be dedicated to her."

Vera's perception of care work collides with an overall expectation in her community that doing care work in Germany leads to earning "big money". However, Vera's narrative demonstrates that such work doesn't have only a monetary dimension. Moreover, Vera's attitude towards care work and the elderly person reflects that although care workers, as by rule, are attracted to this job by the amount of money that they can earn in a short time yet, profit and self-interested rationality, care market exchange are not the only factor that shapes the quality of care work and care relations. On a more general level, I can argue based on women's experiences that at the bottom of "informal care chain" when all persons who are mediators like agencies, job intermediaries, families are gone, and care worker is left alone with an elderly, there is a micro-cosmos of relations where cultural and social worlds of both parties interact creating a space for negotiation and reconciliation around care work and its value (see more in Chapter 7). Vera's attitude towards performing care work reveals that care is regarded as genuine, mindful, and compassionate activity that goes beyond its economic value. Her account resonates well with the understanding of care as value which is always morally loaded and entrenched into cultural norms of the person who performs work. In Vera's case, obligation (or duty) to take care for the closest kin reflects traditional values of care, as emotionally warm (Hochschild 2003), altruistic, based on conventional conservative ideals in which care is provided by women as mothers, wives and daughters is seen as an unpaid familial duty:

ROUTES INTO CARE LABOUR MOBILITY

"After some time, she started having pain, she moaned all night. How could I leave her? I would come into the room and try helping her this way or that way … horrible. I told her daughter to take more care of her because she's not well. She was coughing terribly and choking from the cough. I said to her: 'Take her to the doctor.' Her daughter replied: 'It's normal. She is old.' I replied to her that that was not normal, and that it was not true, that she was very sick. I really suffered with that granny … but they didn't appreciate that work … I don't think her daughter appreciated it. I can't understand that. From my parents, when they were alive, if some someone greeted them kindly, I knew how to appreciate that. They don't. There is no love there. She drove me to the hospital and didn't go upstairs to see her own mother. Say no more."

What Vera's emotionally loaded narration shows, but what also appears in other interviews, is a high degree of respect for elderly people. Like Vera, women care workers frequently drew parallels between their experience of looking after their own family members and looking after the current elderly person. As Arlie Hochschild (2003) pointed out, emotional labour is practice of recalling inner feelings of love and attachment deriving from family situations and applying them to new working contexts. This is directly linked to appreciation of such performed emotional work. Acknowledging rewards are perceived as those that send the message that care worker is trusted, respected and appreciated by the family of elderly person. Most of the women when asked about their perception and attitudes towards what they are doing, they never answered directly to the question. The answer was always framed around personal characteristics of an elderly person they take care for and the members of the household and their relationship with them. Then, they do not only discuss the challenges of caring and negative aspects of care work but often highlight the pleasures and satisfactions derived from caring. Sanela was working as care worker for an elderly man in the small village in Bavaria. She describes her experience:

"The son of the old man had been always saying: 'Oh, since you arrived, I found some rest and relief.' When I asked him how so, he said: 'Well, now I am free to go out and not to think about my father all the time.' The son was very correct and respectful towards me. Every time when he wanted to sleep over at his girlfriend in Munich, he always asked if I was okay with that. I always said yes to that. But his sister (old man's daughter) lived nearby, and we talked every day, either she stopped by or we talked on the phone. We were texting each other via Viber as well. For example, once happened that the old man was unstable on his feet. I called her immediately and she said that she was on her way to us. You see, I realized that they work a lot, that they don't have time, they are very busy with their lives and work … which is why they called me to come to them and paid me for my duty. I accepted that.

But also, I received a huge gratitude from them, at least that what I felt, and I know it was so.

Sanela's perception of family appreciation is based on their assistance with caring for their father and consideration of her wellbeing. In such accounts, women often express appreciation of their work as a sense of achievement, fulfilment and sense of purpose and pride. Some of them, as Isidora, for the first time in their lives comes across someone who values and rewards their housework and care labour:

"And Tanja, literally every week when I get paid, I say to Robert (the son of the old man I look after), thank you, and he replies: 'No, I thank you!' I mean, that brought me to tears … because during my 33 years at work, I have never experienced that, that the boss or a colleague says to me: You did it good. There was no 'thank you', nothing … I couldn't believe it … It was the same at home … I never got paid for cleaning or washing or thanked for making lunch or doing something else for my own family, my kids, and my husband."

Cultural ideals commonly assigned to the concept of care as a gendered unpaid labour that has been always taken for granted travelled together with Isidora to Germany. However, Isidora's experiences in paid elder care work not only that made her acknowledged and respected for what she is doing, but her unpaid care and housework gained weight and valued in the manner that she never experienced before. The appreciation and rewards from families and care receivers can come in different forms. Through the course of my fieldwork online, women used to send me the photos of letters, small gifts or letters with money attached as an expression of gratitude and reward for their good work (see the picture below). These small emotional and material exchanges convinced me that "care" should never be reduced to financial incentives and monetary rewards. Even when is commodified as elder care work, "care" carries a meaning that is always contextualized account of experiences, drives and motivations. Material culture of care labour mobility that I gathered during my fieldwork shows that material objects of affection and gratitude from employers (elderlies) can be money but also goods like watches, silk skarves, or pieces of jewelry. These objects never come alone. They are always featured by emotionally charged writings demonstrating a confirmation of successful relationship and are incentives for the future, to ensure that person – woman care worker will come back.

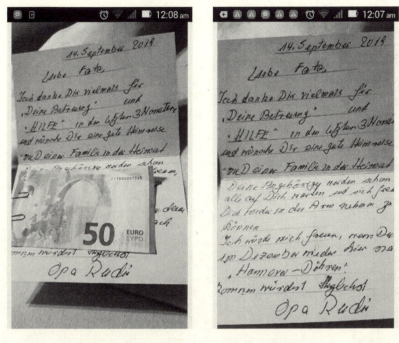

Figure 4: Letter of gratitude (Source: Picture by the author)

Corporeal Aspects of Elder Care Work

Elder care work is often regarded as "dirty work" due to its association with dysfunctional, decaying, and diseased bodies. Graham's (Graham 1983) work points to both the embodied dimension of caring and often hard physical labour that this entails, as well as foregrounding the affective labour that caring encounters comprise. What is usually missing in the literature is the interrelationship between these two. Indeed, the embodied aspect of caring is an issue that has overall received scant attention in the extant literature. Furthermore, those who have focused on such issues have pointed out that as well as its embodied character, what is generally referred to as care work, is in large part concerned with "body work" (Gubrium 1975; Twigg 2000; Wolkowitz 2002), that is tending to the physical needs of another. Such labour often involves a high degree of intimacy with another person: washing, cleaning, toileting and so on. It is these aspects of care, that Twigg (2000) argues, have led to care as paid work being frequently denigrated as "dirty work" (Anderson 2000; Jervis 2001). Twigg points to the "schizophrenic" orientations that can be exhibited towards care, in that it is also lauded as a "special" kind of work, involving supreme virtues of "love" and selfless devotion (Graham 1983). The perception of care work as "dirty work" goes someway to accounting for its extremely socially and financially devalued status. However, according to a number of writers, is also attributable to the fact that it is perceived as being unskilled and not requiring any special qualifications or proficiencies, because despite the major advances made by the feminist movement, care is still generally seen as something that women are "naturally" socialized to perform (e. g. England 2005; Schultz 2006). In the contrast with the many findings of study on domestic and care workers where sensitive nature dealing with intimacy and "dirt" induce feelings of disgust, shame, my respondents never voiced such problem. When they are asked about their attitudes towards bodies, they seldom engage with their feelings of aversion towards body of elderlies. Fatima asserts opposite:

"I had two sons, but I rarely wiped their bottoms, not because I was disgusted, but because I couldn't do so because of health problems. It is more like a health condition: any bad smell makes me vomit. Not just a normal amount of vomit, and not something that I can control. When I was changing the diapers of an old lady, I held the bucket I was throwing them into with one hand and cleaned her up with the other. You know, that was the worst thing for me. But over the time, I used to that somehow and now it's okay …
T: And she was, I assume, immobile, so you had to change her diapers and everything?
F: Immobile. Everything, everything … I accepted her like my child because she had dementia. There were moments when she so much got on my nerves that I could have blown her up! I was sleeping in the room next to her. But our beds were separated only by a wall. So, she used to knock on and hit the wall all night long. When I came and asked her: 'What do you want?', she would say: 'Oh, please come to scratch my back a little bit, it is itchy …'. In the end, I couldn't have stand it anymore, I needed sleep so I took her bed and moved it away from the wall to another side of the room, saying to myself 'Now knock to yourself, granny'. (She laughs). While doing this job you experience a lot of different things and problems that you must solve …"

Women's preparedness to perform care work depends on their different experiences and attitudes towards the physical body that stems, for example, from their professional dispositions. This is how Jasna Pajevic evaluates her own abilities, comparing herself with other colleagues:

"Some women give up at the start. Some of them don't want to do the job, some of them are not able do it. Some find it disgusting to change the diapers and clean the bodies. I don't see the situation in this way. You know, I am a sculptor, an artist …

a good part of my professional life I spent watching nude people, life models in academic settings who posed for us … all sorts of people: drunk, people with mental illness, homeless, dirty bodies … and so on. So, to me, the naked human body is not a problem to look at, not even when it is really repulsive. I have this attitude towards the body. I don't think it is disgusting or ugly … it's just human. These old people are in trouble … and it's not their fault!"

The strategy frequently used to eliminate feeling of disgust and intolerance to intimacy women usually compare care recipients with their children:

Isidora : No … oh, come on … There was a time in my life when my every meal was with a poop and peeing. I had three small kids, what do you think?!
T: Well, you had three children. But these three children were not all your life in diapers, right?
Isidora: That is true. But shit is a shit. It is either children's or elderly's. Yes, but you know … I had been getting kids one after another … I can't feel uncomfortable Tanja. There is no job that is disgusting or hard to do … My goal depends on this job.
T: And the goal is?
Isidora: Loan payment – zero!"

However, what is striking that in the each interview where physical and health condition of care workers is discussed, sleeping disorders or sleep affectations are one of the main features of performing live-in 24 hours care. It is directly related to a lack of control over working time. Women are often unable to rest because of nocturnal care-giving demands. There were no limits to their work hours, and sleep deprivation added up, leading both to exhaustion and to learned sleep alterations.

Further on Fatima gives an account on the condition of her own body and health:

"It happened when I arrived at my shift … it wasn't too long after I arrived. Maybe 20 days. I realized at some point that my period was late. There was a nurse who would come every morning to give granny insulin. I asked her: 'Would you please buy me a pregnancy test?' She brought me 2 tests the next day. She told me: 'Now go pee on it, I will wait in front of the bathroom.' Both tests showed I was pregnant. Oh man! I am 2,000 km away from home. What I am going to do now? And I could barely cope with my two previous pregnancies at home. I was in the hospital. I could not have stood it! But God gave me the strength, and I endured it for three months. During all that time in Germany I was lifting, turning the granny, changed her diapers and I was almost 5 months pregnant on the way back to Bosnia. I didn't dare to work anymore. And that was too much for me. I didn't dare, because I had already been through two risky pregnancies. I gave birth prematurely to my girl … and left her behind when she was three months old."

As Fatima's case shows, women are going through different personal experiences in different stages in life. Each of the cases I came across are highly individual and depend on age, general health, care mobility aspiration, health status, and educational attainment and so on. When asked about their view on how mobility for care work affects their lives and well-being, answers are highly diverse and sometimes contradictory. Jasna views and attitudes towards the benefits of care work are highly positively valued:

"I tried to explain to her how it is … at least with those women I know. First, they are all women who have reached a certain age. Most of them are working for a miserable salary. They all have grown-up kids. All of them are fed up with their husbands, who only wait to be served. That's it. And then, they decide to move for work, leave their husbands at home, with cooked food in the freezer for them to eat while they are in Germany. They come back with money. I can tell you, I do not know how many of these women you have talked to, but I got to know these women … actually, I would not have decided to go to Germany if I had not seen all this – before Germany, they all complained: I feel pain here, I feel pain there, I am tired, I am depressed. Right after the first or the second time travelling to Germany, they all feel better, as if they were born again, and there are no complaints anymore. It's all great, it's all ok. And you know … for young people, it is harder. They have small children, and they can't leave them behind. But these women with kids who are grown-ups, married with families … so, these women basically sitting at home doing nothing, having no money … then, it's better to go than to sit at home. I am telling you from my own experience, and from how it is in my surroundings."

Snežana evaluates situation radically different:

"Now I will tell you in short what are the consequences of performing all around clock live-in care work: 1. Highl level of stress causes irregular or missed menstrual periods. After three months working in Germany women lose their menstrual periods and not having them two or three months. 2. They have sleeping disorder. When they come back to their homes they cannot sleep for days although they are tired and exhausted. 3. They either lose or gain weight … that is result of constant stress that affects hormones. 4. They become emotionally unstable. 5. They never smile. 6. They are all the time under the huge stress: when they are travelling to Germany because of long travelling, lack of sleep, uncertainty about what will wait for them in the household, stress as if a job intermediary will charge her additionally for the services, stress of losing the job … I think this is enough to get a picture how is to do this job."

Appropriation of Knowledge and Skills

In the institutional context of care, like nursing homes, care labour involves competences (skills, knowledge, and expertise) and standards that must be acquired (e.g. hygiene, routines, timing) and it is often related to technologies like procedures, devices, equipment, knowledge, skilled personnel, etc. When it comes to informal care work in the household, my study shows that the knowledge or minimum of that knowledge required in elder care is entirely developed over the time and out of relationship with elderly persons. Thus, the competence required is experience-based, and that experience emphasizes the relationship, rather than the knowledge gained from a formal education. I found that, for women the use of knowledge was part of a process where knowledge was created, and knowledge was shaped. The analysis of my field notes I was making during observation in several households identified the themes of "a feeling for work" and "artistry and improvisation" as components of tacit knowledge in elder care. Because the processes of knowledge and job execution were closely intertwined, they were difficult to separate or even understand without deeper insight. Knowledge in practical professions is often called "silent knowledge" or tacit knowledge as discussed by Polanyi (1983).

The tasks that women usually perform are bathing, feeding, changing diapers, dressing up, giving medicines, insulin, if person is mobile, they do the regular walks or to accompany person at the social events, if a person is immobile than care worker must reposition person from time to time. Those women who live alone in the household with an elderly person (or with persons if there is a living spouse) are responsible for cooking, cleaning, and maintaining the whole household. Knowledge and skills in elder care work are gain and developed using different strategies that are dependent upon the various actors involved in mobility for care work: intermediaries, families, care recipients and relationships with colleagues. The focus on tacit knowledge was initiated because the care workers had drawn attention to it. The knowledge how to care about elderly is mostly gained informally and privately. As none of the women I interviewed had experience for caring of elder people with cognitively impaired or with impaired physical mobility, the knowledge about how to perform above mentioned tasks is based on improvisation, combination between medical knowledge that came as a result of studying a certain problem, collecting information or it is simply shared among care workers. The most common problem that an immobile elderly person is facing is "decubitus ulcer" or skin ulcer that comes from lying in one position too long so that the circulation in the skin is compromised by the pressure. These are practically open wounds on the body that cause a great pain. As I learned from my respondents these wounds are very persistent and difficult to treat successfully. Isidora narrates her experience:

"My previous granny had a terrible problem with decubitus wounds, she was poor thing constantly in pain. That was not my problem or my job task … because for medical problems were responsible nurses, Pflegedienst and doctor who was coming from time to time to treat that decubitis. So, what he did basically, he used to clean the wound, ok with some special liquid … and on the top on the wound he put the cotton pad and seal it with a sticky bandage. That did not seem to me very logical because that was even more pressuring the damaged tissue. Despite of these doctor's treatment, granny was in pain. Then I decided to try something that I heard from other women care workers. I told the family what I think that would work … I mean, it doesn't hurt to try. The worse thing that might happen is that doesn't work. Do you know what are green wheat capsules?
T: No, I don't.
I: It's a kind of food supplement … I was taking them to make up for lack of minerals … it's kind of superfood rich in antioxidants, minerals, vitamins and enzymes … anyway, what I did … I cleaned the wound with a liquid prescribed by the doctor, let it dry and put a very thin layer of the powder from the capsule and Pflaster on the top … not the plastic Pflaster … to let the wound 'breathe'. In only two days the wound began to close and healing got started … with every day she was less and less in pain until the wound had entirely disappeared. I am so happy and so proud that my granny died with a 'baby bottom' … really … it was spotless."

The process of gaining knowledge and skills for care workers can be often psychologically and emotionally challenging processes. Although most of the women would not speak directly about the feelings of fear while facing a new and unknown caring task yet, one could expect that especially those women whose work involves care of persons with limited mobility are aware of the physical strain and potential for injury that they faced in tasks of helping their charges to bathe, dress, and move about the household. This often involved supporting the weight of the other person's body or moving the person from one place to another. Jasna was taking care for an elderly 87-year-old woman, heavy and immobile. One of the job tasks was transferring an old lady from wheelchairs to bed or armchair. As she lived alone with this lady in a big house, she didn't have any assistance in performing these tasks. This how she narrates her attitudes towards care tasks:

"I think that they are just as scared as we are. When someone first comes into the house, you do not know what to expect. I say that they are old people. I see them as old people who are in need for help. I do not see them as someone who pays me … well, among other things, I am here in Germany because of that. I make it easier for myself by thinking that I am here to help them. I would dress and change the diapers of the first granny I took care of because she had limited mobility. I have never had that experience in my life. I never cared for anyone in this way. But, just before I travelled to Germany, I got in touch with a woman from a nursing home to show me a couple of tricks and tips … for dressing and changing clothes … you know, how to do it properly and whether there are any tricks for getting them changed, and that helped me a lot. I was dressing her like a little child."

Throughout the interview Jasna was indecisive about expressing her feelings of fear. In the first sentence we can recognize that she was also "scared like they are" but in the rest of the interview excerpt below, she asserts that "she didn't have a fear". Reading the interview transcript thoroughly I have noticed that she was often repeating her denial of fear. One reason for understating her emotional state was a strategy to convince me either that she performed her job well or, that the job itself was not difficult for her. However, as she was switching from one position to another many times during the interview, my impression was that she was concerned about insecurity in performing task:

"I didn't have a fear of moving her, lifting her up or repositioning her. I kept telling her that she had to trust me because I wanted to help her, and, when I had to move her from the bed to the chair and so on … to put her arms around my neck properly not only her fingers … which is what she did at the beginning, very shyly and reluctantly … she was afraid, naturally (…) But really, it all depends on how you approach your job … Some women give up immediately. They simply cannot do it. They don't want to do it. Some of them are disgusted by changing a diaper. As for me, I say I don't look at it in that way. I look at them like people, like babies. They are helpless. They just cannot manage themselves and that's it!"

The matter of self-confidence and trust, that Jasna raised in the previous interview excerpt, in relations between an elderly persons and women care workers comes up very often in narrations about women's attitudes towards care work. The interviewees however, though not obviously, concede that trust between caregiver and care receiver is not something that happens suddenly; rather, it is a gradual process. Important characteristics of the care worker for building this trust are flexibility, availability to changing schedules, and situations because the care needs of the care recipient continuously evolved, making care approach modifications necessary. That is especially visible in the cases when woman work as a caregiver for one person three or more years and watching and experiencing ill deterioration and overall decline of wellbeing of an elderly person. The care receivers, thus, must trust in care workers. However, this trust is not unconditional. It must be earned by women care workers who must adapt to the new working relationships. The adaption means to have an open attitude toward learning and flexibility in the given working conditions, which are both necessary for adapting to an elderly's condition. My interviewees highlighted that the ability and attitude of adaptation of the caregiver were important. The knowledge and skills necessary to perform these tasks are left to them either to learn from the other woman (colleague) with whom they are rotating or to be instructed by the family. The importance of networks and being lucky to get the colleague you rotate with, is crucial in learning how to do the job. Usually, the person who comes first to the household transfers the knowledge about the tasks to her colleague. As women come without any professional knowledge about, they are using different strategies to prepare themselves for this job. Milica explains her way of coping with a new task:

"My granny has Alzheimer disease. That was dementia at the beginning which wasn't treated properly. The first two years … I would say … they were hiding the fact that she is ill … they simply didn't want to accept that. And then, she was taking a lot of pills that literally almost buried her. When Katarina (colleague of Milica with whom she did rotations) and I came two years ago Ursula (granny) was totally immobile … today she can walk, of course with my help, she can walk for an hour, when we go for a walk. I admit, I forced her telling her: 'Come on, you have to, you have to walk, that's healthy.' Now when she can be standing, it is also easier for me when I shower her in the bathroom … I wash her, put a diaper on and put her into bed. And then, there are days when she can't do anything. Today, her eldest son barely dragged her to bed. It's such a disease … today everything is great, tomorrow she can't do anything. I also learned that disease has various stages, that there can be aggression … Before I came to the family, when Katarina informed about the granny's health condition, I read a lot about Alzheimer disease. She explained to me everything about her illness and her behavior before I came to Germany. She told me to prepare myself because Frau Ursula's illness causes unexpected aggressive behaviour like hitting, pinching, scratching, hair-pulling or biting. I experienced all of this with her … but you know, these are moments … she does it, but she doesn't understand. In these moments I am trying to calm her down and say: 'You must not do that granny anymore.' When she comes back to herself, when she realizes what she did, she apologies: 'Sorry, sorry … I will never do it again.' But she does. That is illness, not her …"

As we can see Milica's knowledge on caring skills comes from two sources. One is her rotational partner. Transfer of knowledge in this case usually relies on willingness of the rotational partner to share information about how to perform certain tasks in effective and accurate manner. The other source is Milica's personal effort to adopt more medical theoretical knowledge by reading literature about the disease. The third way of learning about the work is to ask professionals for assistance. In the excerpt of the interview below Jasna Pajevic, not only that she asked for help, but she also spread awareness among women about importance of learning elder skills. When I asked her about support by the intermediaries, she replies:

T: Do they contact you to check how it is going, do you have any problems?
J: Yes, they do … they call to ask if there are any problems, do I need any help, can I understand everything … you know, because of the language, is there anything that should be translated, stuff like that. But I did not have any problems. I did not need anyone. I mean, I didn't need them at all, but I had to report that everything was fine. Only, when I came to the first family, it wasn't clear enough if the old lady was mobile or semi-mobile … sometimes she can get up from bed, sometimes not … I mean, I didn't mind if she was an immobile patient. Even better. Because you know where they are … they cannot wander off … When it turned out that the granny was semi-mobile, I called that woman, a geriatric nurse from the nursing home, to show me how to treat someone like this. I only had that one, let's call it lesson, and I suggested to the woman who organized this job for us that she should organize some classes for all the women who are travelling to Germany for this job. I do not know … but I think that we need some kind of instruction, something before going there. But I am quite sure, I am telling you, that what these old people need the most is to have company, someone to be with them, so that they are not alone. In the nursing home they are alone again. And they are not in their own home."

The role of the family or persons in immediate surrounding of an elderly person is one of the most sensitive and crucial aspects in the process of women's adaptation to a new role of care giver. The relatives played a decisive role in this aspect. Because of a great effort, including continuous collaboration and intervention when needed, the family tries to achieve harmony, care and safety. I interviewed Isidora just a few months after she took over the job in a new family. She was still adjusting to needs of an elderly lady. The biggest problem is that she couldn't have slept during the night which keeps Isidora awake all night. Isidora explains how she dealt with the problem:

"I gathered all her family and discussed the problem with them. I said: 'People, listen up, this doesn't work. I can't do this. She sleeps in her armchair during the day, and I have to be awake all day and to do my job. I know that you do not expect me to do thorough cleaning and tidying, but even the things I have to do, I can't, because I am tired and cannot concentrate.'

Her son said that she can rant as much as she likes, but that she must stay in bed. She listened to him and stayed in bed for five minutes, and that was that … she wanted to get up again. Then I called her son again. He came back and told her furiously: 'Lay down and shut up. It is very selfish of you to believe that all of us should wait upon you hand and foot.'"

Isidora continues:

"Tanja, they are not doing it because they love me. What would they do if I left? What if the other woman doesn't come? Or, if she comes, and then leaves? What are they going to do with her? The nursing home costs 5000 euros. That is the thing. They know that very well. I am not saying that they behave badly towards me, or disrespect m… but by treating me well, they are mainly protecting themselves. The granny is really spoiled … Her behaviour drives me crazy. I said to her: 'My own children were not allowed to behave like this.' She replies: 'I am not your child.' I said: 'No, you are not! You are a grown woman.' I don't know what to do with myself. I am having long discussions with her during the night, as if it were the middle of the day. And then her daughter-in-law comes down and says: 'You (to me) – switch the lights off, and get out, and you (to granny) – sleep! End of discussion!' The woman gets up at 5 o'clock in the morning to go to work … she cannot listen to all that …"

This interview excerpt highlights Isidora's attitude towards the relationship between her and the family who employs her. Stressing that the family helps her out of "pure economic interest" does not fit into the frame of "disposable workers" – which is how migrant domestic and care workers are labelled in most of the literature on domestic and care work. Being protective to her and protecting themselves still means that family values woman care worker, especially if that person is performing very good job and is connected to family and care recipient which makes her hardly replaceable. To find a suitable person who will care for an elderly parent, that fits into the household, willing to adapt and to learn is very difficult. From my observation during the interviewing when I had opportunity to meet the family of an elderly person, I witnessed in the several cases admiration and respect toward the care worker. In such cases the key is a deep interpersonal relationship between the care workers and care recipients that involves intense emotional labour on the part of the woman care worker. Emotional labour is here a form of tacit knowledge that can be achieved only from deep interpersonal interactions in work of caregiving, complex deployment of self-management of emotions. "Knowing how to care" has a personal dimension and it is developed through the relationship of "family-like" intimate quality. In such instances care workers perform activities that are beyond physical tasks (bathing, repositioning, feeding) made an effort to be affectionate and accommodating towards care recipients. In their descriptions, as in the interview excerpt below illustrates, women care workers are physically and emotionally immersed into a relationship: they do massage, they do conversation, sing and use non-verbal forms of communication such as holding hands or hugging to show empathy or psychologically support elderly person who is in emotional and physical pain. As a result of long-term intimate relationship with an elderly person and the family women learned about their personal histories, families, habits, what an elderly person likes to eat, or where to sit, what to watch on the TV and so on. The extract of Jasna's interview illustrates

Sometimes during the night, my granny used to wake up, sit up in bed and just to stare blankly. Then I would come downstairs (because at that time I was sleeping on the second floor). I called her Maja the Bee … you know that cartoon character? Yes, Maya, because she would wear a T-shirt with yellow and black stripes … anyway, I would come to her and ask her: Maya, what is the problem? Does something hurt? Are you sad? Are you in pain? She wouldn't respond. Then I would say: 'Come on, let's kill the animals.' She had a feeling very often that something was crawling on her back. I would take some massage gloves and rub her back. We would call this Hochglanz … as a joke, rubbing the 'Speck' (eng. Bacon) on her back. She liked it very much. The first time when I did this, she asked for It … she asked me to 'kill her animals'. After that, it became a pleasure for me. I would do it without her asking. I know that I am doing it because I want to … not because someone ordered me to do it. I know that makes her happy. Then it is a pleasure for me as well."

Thus, tacit knowledge about how to perform elder care work is difficult to transfer to a new rotational partner for several reasons: firstly, it is the knowledge that is built throughout care work over a certain period of time; secondly, it a as result of gradual development of intimate relations; thirdly, it is the knowledge that reflects the complexity of the physical and mental problems elderlies are facing. Such accumulated knowledge is highly valuable so that woman who posses this knowledge is less likely to be replaceable and more likely very much respected and appreciated by the family.

According to the interviewed women, language skills were one of the basic advantages that decreases the risk of not finding a proper job, not properly doing that job and not be able to negotiate working conditions and thus not to keep the job. Depending on the health condition of the elderly person they care for, frequency of communication with their family and their social surrounding, usually, proficiency of German language is not requirement from the employer's side. If the elderly person is disable and cognitively impaired as result from dementia or Alzheimer disease, verbal communication is necessary for getting instructions from the family, doctors, nurses (medical care sevices like *Pflegedienst,* for example) about how to handle elderly person. In these cases, German proficiency is required by the family, especially when family doesn't live with the elderly person in the same household. Milica Jeremić (40-year-old) who lives-in the family house where she takes care for an elderly lady recollects her start:

"When I arrived without knowledge of the German language, I'd been working for three weeks, I did not know how to speak – I think I've said five sentences for three weeks. Even what I knew, when I arrived, I did not know anymore. You know, in this part of Germany, they speak Schwäbisch ... even today I cannot understand them clearly ... the dialect is very difficult to understand. They helped me very much at the beginning. We were communicating using our phones ... I said that I didn't want that. After some time, I told them: 'I am giving up ... I cannot type the words in google and translate then. It never translates correctly. Makes no sense ...'.
T: Did they know that you were coming without any knowledge of German?
M: Yes. They said that knowledge of the German language was not crucial ... it was more important to them that someone does the job properly.
T: How did they tell you what to do if you couldn't understand them?
M: Well, look, you have to know something ... so, I knew. I knew how to speak maybe, now let me say, 30 per cent but I understood 60 per cent. When they talk to me slowly, I understand everything. I was lucky to have a colleague who came before me, who introduced the job to me. She knew German very well. She was born in Germany, but later she married a Serbian guy and lived in Serbia. She told me what I should do, and how ... she explained my daily tasks and daily routine. She told me what I should cook, who eats what, who doesn't like what, where is this, where is that and so on. It worked well. I was doing my job properly ... and after three weeks they told me that they would like me to stay with them. I only came to them as a Springer, to replace another person and to go to another family. But, luckily, I stayed with them."

Very often families where women work could be very supportive and encouraging in the process of learning language. Fatima (40-year-old) narrates experience similar to Milica's:

"You know, bit by bit, day after day ... my German was getting better. But at the beginning was difficult. In the first family granny was very sick and she died. I had to go back home. After that I went to the family where I had a granny who literally walked step behind me carrying a notebook and pencil saying: "Take this and write: der Tisch, die Decke ... come on ... write it down, here ... when we are done, go to your room and learn. Tomorrow morning, I will check what you have learned". You know Tanja, I didn't know how to say Guten Tag. I am grateful to her because she forced me to learn ... and now it has been four years since I started to travel for Germany. I learned to talk normally, communicate with everyone ... when I have free time we go sometimes for a coffee or so ... with this family I have been for a year. I am lucky ... people like me wherever I go (Fatima laughs)."

The support in certain cases comes in practical and material terms:

"They (the family) offered me to pay for the German course. That far they are ready to go! But you see, it is because of this man, the son of the old lady, who is married to a Colombian woman. He knows how hard it is to get used to new language as a foreigner (...) they tend to repeat 15 times the same word for me to understand. Normally, it was enough for me just to be written down. By the way, it's nothing scary. If I don't know something ... internet is there!"

In the work surrounding where women intensively socialize with the family, where they feel welcomed and acknowledged, and where they are developing closer relationship with members of the household, they are more motivated to learn German language in comparison with those women who are isolated and lonely. However, what I found surprising is that women in their 40s and 50s years of age are ready to learn German language and they do that through the course of care labour mobility, with more or less success, that usually depends on encouragement in social environment and their satisfaction with a working conditions and employers.

The following excerpt reveals how Zorica Milić evaluates her German language competence:

"They realize that we don't know the German language, but they see what we do for them ... for example, when I feed an old lady, I do it slowly and carefully, making sure that she swallowed the food, then offering her warm tea ... or, when I noticed that her nails needed to be cut, usually after her bath, I would cut them with precision, so as not to go too deep and cause pain or injury. Or, when I would change her diaper, I would say 'Warten Sie' ('Wait, please'), clean her, and put on another diaper. Believe me, I received kisses after changing diapers, because they were so happy to have someone who was so gentle and considerate. I do it because I did it with one of my own parents, and one day I might be in a similar situation myself."

This highlights how care and domestic work skills can be used to compensate for a limited knowledge of the German language. Indeed, the former are more important and highly valued than the latter. In this sense, the women that I interviewed identified several skills that are crucial in caring for the elderly: patience, empathy, emotional intelligence, management skills, a high tolerance for frustration, trust – all of these being key qualities for caregivers, despite often being underestimated and economically undervalued.

Chapter 6
"Illegalization" of Everyday Life and Work in "Elder Care Labour Mobility Industry"

Elder care work, domestic work and child minding are occupations that are, in the broader literature on gender, migration and policy, often coupled with different attributes: informal, illegal, irregular. To avoid the further confusion through this chapter that is aimed to analyse how "illegality" is embedded in lived experiences of elder care workers, I would like to draw defining boundaries of the above-mentioned adjectives that are ascribed to elder care work. The term "informal work" is an umbrella term, which may often lead to confusion. Followed by words such as "economy", "sector" or "activities", the term "informal" is used to describe different phenomena. When referring to the term "informal economy", sociologists usually envisage non-market work, in some cases with reference to "black economy" or "grey economy". "Informal work" has been used to denominate work that is not declared to official censors or the tax system and may even include unpaid labour in the household. Consequently, these incompatible uses constitute a source of misunderstandings and confusion, particularly in policy contexts.

Informal-sector theories use the term "formal", to refer to waged and salaried labour in the sense of being employed by someone, while "informal" refers to self-employment, one-person enterprises, artisan production and domestic service. It is worth noting that in this strand of literature both terms refer to paid, officially registered employment. The other terms used for informal work are "illegal", "clandestine", "sans papiers" or "undocumented", or "unauthorised". These forms of labour sometimes refer to a specific migration status, sometimes used in the wrong context and more often confusingly applied to different sets of phenomena. Expressions such as "undeclared work", "illegal employment", "clandestine work", "hidden work" appear in policy-related discourses describing a wide range of informality in the labour market, as they usually denote lawful work by its nature, but not declared to the competent authorities/or non-taxable work.

In the following analysis of elder care labour market I use the term "irregular care work" as the most suitable to encompass the complexity of the type of work which is not contracted, doesn't include social and health benefits, and it is not reported due to the tax evasion. In this way, I avoid confusion with a term "informal care work" that often in sociology, gerontology and aging studies means care work performed by spouses, community members, children, that can be paid or not paid (Arber, Ginn 1990).

However, certain authors sometimes use the term "illegal work" or "illegal employment". The term again, carries ambiguous meaning. Sometimes it is related to undeclared work in the black-market economy (for instance, cigarette vendors). In other cases, it may be linked to migration status referring to entrance and residence to the country without proper travel documents or/and residence permit. In most of the cases, the terminologies overlap referring to the person's illegality that stems from lack of residing status and work permission. As Cyrus demonstrated, such overlaps in the EU legislation debate complicate clear-cut distinction between irregularity and illegality in the case of domestic and care work (Cyrus 2008) as domestic and care workers can reside "legally" but perform undeclared work. In this book I define the term "illegal" as a state and policy mechanism for labelling mobile labourers without work permits who are a priori criminalised in political discourses on illegality. The idea of criminalizing people is often misleading and highly inaccurate because it conveys the idea of criminality, implying involvement with prohibited forms of work where like with elder care work, that it is not the case. In the line with my understanding of what and who "illegal" is, in this chapter I want to show how "illegality" and "illegalization" is also a "mode of being-in-the-world" and the process that shape subjective lived experiences of "illegality" of elder care workers.

Scholars as Balibar (2004), Papadopoulos, Stephenson and Tsianos (2008), Hardt and Negri (2009) treat undocumented migrants as "agents of social change" whose collective actions hold the potential to undermine and even overcome global capital. These accounts theorize migrants vis-à-vis the state and broader politics of citizenship, important features of the migrant's trajectory but they do not address migrants' first-hand understandings, experiences, and systems of meanings. It has by now been widely documented that migrants who live with unauthorized status build and live their lives in the shadow of society, take precarious and undesirable jobs with limited access to healthcare, social services, and legal rights. Mainstream migration scholarship, especially those focused on migration policy, had the tendency to treat undocumented migration as "a problem to be solved". In this chapter I follow on critically oriented scholarship that moves away from treating undocumented migration as problem towards tracing and understanding how changing social and legal contexts function effectively to "illegalize" growing numbers of persons and turn them into subjects who as such are vulnerable to exploitation. Thus, "illegalization "is defined as "legal production of migrant "illegality" (De Genova 2002). More importantly, De Genova argues that "illegality" is not only generated through laws and migration regimes but also the acts of diverse state and non-state agents. I am taking up this approach to look not into woman care workers who are working "illegally" or whose status as undocumented unskilled elder care workers makes them "illegal". Their "illegality" is thus, socially generated. In line with this idea, I will use the term "illegal" in quotes to emphasize the socio-political formation of women's "illegality". Instead of explaining woman care workers' livelihoods with a reference to social and political determinants within care and migration regimes, I rather shift the analytical lenses to the connection between an "illegal status" that emerges from lawfulness of care labour and lived "illegality" and its experiential, embodied and sensory dimensions. Hence, in in the following sub-chapters I offer an analysis of narratives to examine the condition of women's "illegality" considering above mentioned dimensions, from their own perspective. With striking interview excerpts and ethnographic vignettes, I want to demonstrate how women care workers develop unique modes of being "illegal" through their engagements with others in the process of care labour mobility. The second aspect of "illegalization" discussed in the literature is related to *agency* of migrants and undocumented persons who move across the borders. Moving away from studying undocumented migrants as distinct epistemic subjects, scholars frequently neglect the agency of these subjects. That means, while striving to expose and unpack workings of migration law and generally migration regimes, researchers lose sight of the intentional acts, cultural meaning systems, or outlooks of migrants who actively interpret and navigate challenging migration context (Bloch, Chimienti 2011).

To return to the quest of this book: Who moves for care labour? What or who moves women from one place to another? To answer these questions, I conceptualized this chapter through examination of women's narratives by setting the concept of "migration industry" in the context of irregular market of commodified care work that arises from German care regime where long-term allowance *(Pflegegeld)* provides autonomy and choice for its recipients as consumers of live-in elder care. This regime entails an unregulated, ethicized, gendered, yet legally allowed market of commodified care. Such a market is a highly diversified and competitive market that involves individuals and organizations mostly working in the shadow economy. Generally, in the literature, "migration industry" is defined as the labour involved in managing, facilitating and controlling migration that makes this an industry. However, different authors approach differently to defining conceptual boundaries of the term "migration industry". Also, the relationships between actors involved in that industry are differently conceptualized. For example, a structuralist approach is concerned with the exploration of the commercialisation of migration – how migration is mediated by businesses as diverse as brokers, security companies, transporters, and recruitment agencies on the larger scale of international migration. This approach suggests that commercialisation as juxtaposed to reciprocity and solidarity seems to be a defining criterion for what constitutes migration industry. The most known for their structuralist approach are John Salt and Jeremy Stein, geographers who introduced the term "migration business" (1997) and highlighted the ways in which migration can be seen as "business", commercial and profit oriented. The problem of this approach is the restriction of boundaries to those that benefit commercially from engaging with migration. I argue that "migration industry", and in this case "care labour mobility industry" cannot be considered functionally and conceptually separated from different social networks. The other problem with the structuralist concept concerns "illegalization". Salt and Stein themselves, proposed migration business as divided into two components: legitimate (legal) and illegitimate (illegal) (Salt, Stein 1990: 469). They argue, for instance, that business of human trafficking relies on complicity of corrupted immigration officials, playing an important role in inducing and sustaining migration. I am more inclined to see "migration industry" as a complex web of relations in which different actors liaise, objectives oppose each other, and roles overlap.

My approach to analysing "migration industry" falls between two approaches. On the one side I follow the labour market perspective that asks, "how mobility is made possible and organized by brokers, most notably in the process of recruitment and documentation" (Lindquist, Xiang, Yeoh 2012: 9). On the other side, I appreciate achievement of im/mobility turn extensively discussed in the Chapter 2. As I approach to elder care labour moblitiy as a journey that is produced before, on the move and after movement but not necessarily bound up by discrete beginnings and ends, my

"Illegalization" of Everyday Life and Work

anaylitical attention is directed towards what happens on the move as the way by which we can understand how the mobility itself is produced, controlled and what meanings are attached to elder care labour mobility. This approach moves my research away from the fixed notion of migration industry as it consists of clearly demarcated domains, separating government institution from private individuals or job intermediaries from non-profit actors. Therefore, this chapter concentrates on women's narrated experiences that illustrate dynamics of relationships between different actors in the care labour mobility industry (apart from job intermediaries) and strategies that women utilize in the process of acquiring and sustaining potential for labour mobility. The greater attention is paid to differences and connections between actors, demonstrating how these shape women's everyday lives in the course of care labour mobility. I show how these experiences voiced by women care workers reflect not only how care labour industry works for itself, but also how women perceive manifold relationships whilst trying to navigate and manage their im/mobility.

In the previous chapter, I carefully examined the varying factors of facilitation and obstruction in labour mobility process. In so doing, I showed the ways in which identities, aspirations and attitudes towards elder care workers and experiences of doing care work, may shift along the path of movement. Furthermore, I gained insights into how women care workers's mobility trajectories are impacted by the various ways different actors of facilitation and control liaise, bypass each other, or work in a continuum of practices. In this chapter, I want to show how peripheral labour mobilities like care work mobility is bound to specific space-time rhythms of movements that require a specific knowledge, creativity and resorcorsefulness on the part of women care workers. Additionally, the chapter explores women's connections and integration into "care labour moblity industry". Even though elder care workers are subjected to multidimensional insecurity (physical, emotional, financial, mental) and exploitation, I want to draw attention to accumulation of multiple skills and knowledge, or flexibility, is inherently contradictory and potentially creative.

6.1 Portrait: Isidora Bašić

"Someone else's house, someone else's life, everything is someone else's. But I know why I am here."

Isidora is waiting for me as I arrive at the train station in a small village in Hessen. Before this meeting, Isidora and I had been in contact via Messenger. It took us two months to arrange a meeting and the interview. We could have done the interview via Skype, but Isidora insisted that I should come and visit her. She assured me that the family would not mind since: "You are my guest, the only one so far." After I get off the train, I can't see Isidora right away, so I wonder whether I am at the wrong station, but then I see her waving to me from the opposite platform – she says that she did not know from which direction the train would be coming. I am stunned by Isidora's appearance because she seemed so different to her Messenger profile picture, and I have never seen her in person. She has heavy makeup on her face, red hair and a colourful outfit. The colour of her hair, her purple jacket, and her light blue jeans give the impression of someone who is cheerful and happy, and in a way she is happy, she is in a good mood. She greets me with a smile on her face. After I offer a compliment on her appearance, she says: "Well, I don't go out that much, except to Lidl for shopping. This is my chance to dress up a bit." She laughs and continues: "I don't remember when I used makeup the last time. And how are you, my dear?"

Since I am hungry, I suggest that we should go somewhere where I can eat and where we can talk. She says that I don't have much choice: "This is a village. People eat at home." I soon realize that the village is too small even to have a central area or a pedestrian zone, rather it has a bank, a döner kebab shop, and an Italian restaurant. There is also a small shopping centre located a couple of kilometres away. We decide to sit in the kebab shop, although it is tiny, with just a couple of tables. Inside the shop there are local men drinking beer and noisily watching television, in my mind not a particularly suitable atmosphere for conducting an interview. The difficulty of the situation is compounded by the fact that we are talking a foreign language, which marks us out as outsiders and leads to a degree of unfriendliness and glances indicating that we are unwelcome. I tell Isidora that I am not eager to go to the house where she worked, I don't feel comfortable. She says that this is not a problem, that we can stay here as long it takes. She has three hours before she has to go: "You know, today is Friday, and on Fridays Frau Renate is in the kindergarten for the elderly." She laughs. "On Fridays I am free from

"Illegalization" of Everyday Life and Work

10 a.m. until 2 p.m." We order our food, which cheers up the man, probably the owner, who has been serving us, and the next three hours of conversation pass quickly. When we are done, Isidora insists that I meet the granny and her family. Reluctantly, but with a degree of curiosity I accept the invite. We arrive at a modest middle-class German family home, with two floors surrounded by a garden and little apple orchard. Jörg, the son of the old lady Renate Isidora is caring for, is working in the garden as we arrive. He greets us kindly and Isidora goes into the house to see Frau Renate whilst I stay behind to chat with Jörg. From Jörg, I find out that he and his wife, as well as their two teenage boys live together on the second floor and that the two of them are both physiotherapists. The house doesn't seem particularly big, and soon as I enter the house, I realize that the whole of the first floor is dedicated to Isidora and the granny: the big kitchen, dining room, Isidora's room, the granny's room and a big bathroom. During our interview, Isidora had told me about the bathroom and about being impressed both by German health system and the system of long-term care insurance, especially its ability to cover the costs of auxiliary materials:

"The other bathroom is for us to brush our teeth, and so on. I take a shower in the same bathroom as her. It's just a floor with a drain and a shower, without anything else, so that the wheelchair can move around the space. So, everything is prepared and taken care of. The family is getting Pflegegeld. That's good for them. With that money, they pay me and they pay the bills. I have no idea how much it is. But I can see that they receive the money every week. It depends, probably, on the degree of disability. She was a housewife. Her husband paid social and health contributions to the state. She has a family pension … and, on top of that, she gets everything she needs from the state: complete mechanization – a wheelchair, a hydraulic bed, a toilet for the disabled – everything is covered by the health insurance. Even the adaptation of the bathroom was paid by the insurance. We were waiting for the bathroom to be renovated for three months, though. I had to bathe her with water and a sponge. They had to wait for the company that works for the health insurance … that takes time …"

During the visit I am most impressed by my encounter with the granny. After listening to Isidora's story about the challenges and (sometimes) pleasures of caring for Frau Renate, I can recreate all her stories and descriptions on location in the real-life situation. Frau Renate is 70-something years old, skinny, and wheelchair bound. She seems to me to be very fragile, and her eyes are small but lively and curious. As I enter the room with her son she asks: "Have you come to take care of me?" I reply: "No, I am Tanja, I am a friend of Isidora. I live in Erfurt. I study there." Then she asks: "Can you play cards?" I reply: "Yes, I can play some games. Do you mean any game in particular?" She asks me: "Do you know Doppelkopf?" Me: "No, unfortunately I don't." And then she says in a serious manner: "That's why you are not staying here." Frau Renate suffers from developed dementia and often her statements make no sense. Isidora tells me that granny is tired, and she needs to attend to her, and this is my signal to leave. Frau Renate's son and daughter-in-law, Claudia, apologize for the state of the old lady, and explain that she sometimes doesn't know what she is saying. They offer me a lift to the train station, but I decline their kind offer and walk to the train station, wondering what it must be like to spend 24 hours day, seven days a week with someone in a condition like Frau Renate.

The same evening, I text Isidora asking her whether Frau Renate ever asked her to play cards. Isidora tells me that granny has never mentioned any card games to her. Moreover, she has never played cards in her life, but her husband has, at least that is what family had told her. My next visit to Isidora was five months later, in September 2017 (Hessen, March 2017, Interview log).

While we are walking from the train station to the village, Isidora starts to narrate her story and experience by drawing my attention to a biographical object:

"You see this jacket I am wearing; it is from the previous granny I was taking care for. She had water in her lungs. She was in the hospital for 10 days, and died. But she told her family to send all her clothes to my address in Serbia. Now, I have clothes for the next 5 years. Look (she points to herself), everything you see on me is from her. Two big suitcases of clothes!"

Isidora came to this family in November 2016 from another family 20 km away.

"Frau Renate was healthy, and there was no need for anyone to take care of her. She was the one who took care of everyone, and now she is in such a state that she can no longer do it. She can't do anything. Like a new-born baby. I came to this family because Renate's daughter asked the previous family about me … if she could recommend me … That previous granny had 17 women who took care of her. The woman was sometimes a real devil. But I managed. We were very close. Of course, the first time was a disaster. After that … I could have stayed with her for the next 100 years. T: Was that job the first one?
I: Yes. I will never forget that. I arrived 8 hours late. They welcomed me like my own family – they had prepared a bed for me, warmed up the room, made dinner for me … they paid for Pflegedienst for two days, just to let me get a rest from travelling … you know … to not start with work immediately. There is nothing

that I wouldn't do for those people now ... nothing would be too much for me. They came here several times to visit me, to take me out for dinner ... it was on Christmas day ... I was invited to their house for dinner ... I really don't know what to say ... such incredible things ..."

Isidora is a 53-year-old woman from a mid-size town in Northern Serbia and, just like many of her colleagues that I have already described, her aspiration to travel to Germany for care work is the result of the need to pay off a bank loan. Unlike others, Isidora's route into labour care mobility was easier and less stressful. She wasn't recruited by the job intermediaries, but through private connections and friendships. At the time when I met Isidora, she was searching for a job via Facebook:

"But it turned out that the mother of my daughter's friend knew my story, and she knew that I wanted to go to Germany to work as a care giver. Unfortunately, she got breast cancer ... and the job was not an option for her anymore. She called and asked if I could go instead. I said: "Why not?" Then she put me in touch with a woman from Smederevo (a town), who knows the people I am working for now. And that's how I arrived here. How? Everything happened like in a movie. First of all, the decision – I am going away! Then, the information started to come in – information about the family I was going to. Then, learning the language, or, in my case, refreshing my German, because I had learned it at primary school and high school. I had never worked as a care worker. I nursed my own sick parents, who were not disabled, but they both died from cancer."

Alongside the bank loan, Isidora is the mother of three adult children, and wants, in turn, to help provide their children with education, good food, clothes and holidays, birthday celebrations, weddings, house reconstruction, new furniture, technical equipment etc. All this, Isidora couldn't have afforded without taking the loan. After 30 years she decided to leave her permanent job. This is how Isidora justifies her decision:

"I had had enough, because I had been constantly struggling financially. My husband had retired, and after 40 years of service, he has a pension of 25,000 dinars (which is about 200 euros), out of which 20,000 is needed to repay a loan from the bank. Secondly, my salary is 25,000 dinars after 35 years of service, which goes entirely on repaying the bank loan too ... I had had enough. I said I don't want to always be scrabbling to make ends meet. My children are grown up. I do not have to do anything for them anymore ... there is no need to wipe his or her ass, or to reprimand them when they do something wrong. They are grown adults. My youngest child is 22 years old. I have three of them – two daughters and a son. Also, I have two grandchildren from one of my daughters. And I said that I had done enough ... They are already mature, and I no longer need to be beside them. They still need me, of course. Mum is always needed, but not like it is with a small child. My husband is retired, so he is my fourth child now. Until he retired, I couldn't go to visit my daughter in Bosnia. He is terrified of administration. I had to do all the paperwork for the retirement procedure. I couldn't do anything until he received confirmation of his retirement. When he got it, I said – well, ladies and gentlemen, goodbye, I am off. Then, I started to search for the job, because that was the only way to earn that amount of money in a short time."

When I asked her why she had taken such a big loan from the bank, Isidora answered:

"All my life I have been refinancing. Two salaries: a construction worker and an administrative healthcare worker. Minimum wage. And I did not want my children to go without anything. I wanted them to have the basics. And you cannot do that with only two salaries of 30,000 dinars … When my husband was about to retire, we had to refinance the loan, because to retire, he had to pay 1,500 euros to the Ministry for social welfare. I mean, what can I tell you? The company he worked for didn't pay social and health benefits, so, when the time came to retire, he had to pay the money to get the pension. 40 years he got up early, went to work, worked very hard – and for what?! Nothing! At that point, I had had enough … so, we were buying clothes for the kids, like jackets and trainers, by taking a loan, refinancing the loan, and so on. We got stuck with the bills. In order to avoid going to court, prosecution and other stupid things … I had had enough … I said … Goodbye! They asked me, how could I quit my job after 33 years? But I could, with a big smile on my face. That is how I said goodbye to my job."

Isidora doesn't regret giving up her secure white-collar job in the hospital, even though she is aware of the fact that she will not get a full pension. When she turns 65, Isidora will be entitled to the state pension which is very low (no more than 200 euros). But she seems not to be worried about this:

"You see, Tanja, I still cannot get a state pension. But I don't care about the qualifying years I still need to be entitled. I don't care about pension. It wouldn't hurt to have it, but I don't need it. Do you understand? I know why I am here! I am very happy to have the opportunity to earn the money. And very happy to have the opportunity to get rid of the bank loan. I have been working for 6 months continually with just a one-month break … since November last year. Practically, I do not live my life. It is someone else's home, someone else's life, someone else's everything …"

As highlighted in Chapter 5 women's aspiration for labour mobility is almost always strongly grounded in financial difficulties, most often debt, which are the main source of stress. In Isidora's case that also means freeing herself to be able to have more meaningful and relaxing relationships with her family, her husband, and her friends.

"I can live at my home without a problem ... I can be with my children and with my family, but the bank sends me messages all the time reminding me that there is loan instalment coming to be paid off ... and I haven't paid even the previous one. How to live like that? I love my husband. What I love the most is to fall asleep on his shoulder ... I call him my safe house ... I love him the most, but I cannot enjoy it if the bank rings me every now and then reminding me that I have 4,500 euros to pay off."

Isidora projects her imagined future by making plans. Her second daughter is getting married next year, and Isidora thinks that she, as a parent, should share the costs of wedding. The material implications of labour mobility are inseparable from Isidora's dreams, desires, and hopes:

"When I repay the bank loan, then I can take my time to use all the money I have earned here for what I want, when I want, in peace – everything I ever wanted to buy for myself, for my family, as gifts for my friends. I will take my husband and we will go shopping like we've never done before. When I have paid off all my debts, the next project is enjoyment, travelling. The first thing I will do when I get back home is to go to the spa town Vrdink for three days. This is a surprise for my husband. I am tired, I worked hard for the last six months and I need to relax for at least 3 days. I have booked everything. He doesn't have a clue. He will probably eat himself alive at how expensive it all is."

While travelling to Germany to earn the money to pay off her debts, Isidora, paradoxically, leaves behind a house of her own which is bigger than the house of her employers. Isidora lives alone with her husband in a huge family house that her parents built for her and her brother. Since her brother has his own apartment and Isidora's children have moved out, she has to pay all the taxes, maintain the house, and cover the heating costs during the winter. These costs cannot be covered from her regular income – her hospital salary and her husband's pension.

"My husband and I have a 320 metre-square house to ourselves. The children are scattered around leading their own lives, and Jovan (her husband) and I can play hide and seek in the house (she laughs). But then comes winter, that's the worst, because we cannot heat up the whole house. We only live in two rooms; it is so cold that if you grab the door knob there's a chance it will stick to your hand. We don't need more than 50 square meters, so that we can sleep and have a bathroom, kitchen and dining room. The children come to see me, we chat, kiss each other, and say goodbye! We are slaves to this house ... but we cannot sell it ... it is the family home."

A specific theme which dominated the interview discussion with Isidora is her relationship with her husband. Although she talked with me a lot about her kids and their problems, she would always stress how these children are now grown-ups who can solve their own problems without her involvement. When I ask her whether she helps them financially, she replies that she likes to treat them with gifts, and to buy things for her grandchildren. When asked what her husband most wants to get from Germany, Isidora replies:

"What he most wants is for me to come back to him. He is lonely and has had enough of being on his own. So, what we decided is that we will try to find something for him here in Germany. In that way, he will not be alone, he will be close to me and he will feel useful. My husband, Tanja, is a very diligent man. What he could do here in Germany is for example, to take care for elderly, but without diapers and medical care. There could be someone who is old and needs someone to keep him or her company. You know, that's where he'd be perfect, he would be perfect for that because he can talk 24 hours non-stop and he speaks excellent German. He is very good with housework, garden work, he can do repairs, whatever. My husband also cooks. He can do anything, nothing is difficult for him, he has patience. More importantly, he has infinite patience, and he likes to hang out with old people. I think that the chances are minimal to find something like this. But I told him that if something comes up he should pack up his bags and come here. I told Jörg and Claudia to spread the word among their friends, so maybe someone knows someone, you know ..."

After almost one year of work experience as an elder care worker, Isidora, has developed a very strong sense of what it means to do care work. Many times, throughout the interview she reflects on her experience, pointing to the high responsibility that care work carries with it, an awareness which shows that Isidora takes her role very seriously:

"What I am going to tell you now is important ... as for age and experience. We women who do this job ... we are all in our fifties, late forties ... most of us ... because this job cannot be done by a young person. In my opinion, no one under 45 should do this: For this, you need life experience. For this, you need courage and wisdom. Because we don't have any professional experience and knowledge to take care of these people, no certificate as such. And there are consequences. For example, if an elderly person dies, we find ourselves in a position of great responsibility. It will raise a lot of questions: how did the person die? Who was there with him/her? Why did it happen and under what circumstances? Was the therapy administered properly? And, so on ..."

Isidora perceives care work realistically, as a dirty work, associated with dirt handling, a low-level occupation that puts the worker in a servile position in relation to the care recipients. She makes a conscious effort to be positive

"ILLEGALIZATION" OF EVERYDAY LIFE AND WORK 273

about a work situation that, as she says, is sometimes emotionally unbearable:

"You know, to be able to do this job you must have a strong motive. You need to have a clear goal that will always be in front of your eyes, because this is hard. As strong as I am, often I feel loneliness, moment of despair when I miss my children, my lovely husband, my house, my friends … I miss everything Tanja. When this moment comes, I think of my password 325 – that is the code that brings me back to life, and that's my weekly salary. Then I remember my salary in Serbia, and how I earn that amount of money here in a week. I just compare these two numbers and I immediately go back to normal. So, you must know exactly why you are here and why you are going through all the suffering you are going through. You also have to change your attitude and change yourself: you can't be disgusted by the human body, you can't get offended. Everything that offends your ego, it has to be put aside. For this, you need life experience, because it's not the same when someone insults you in your fifties and when you're thirty-five years old. You don't take it in the same way."

Isidora rationalizes the hardship of performing care work by stressing its intrinsic humanitarian dimension. Seeing her role as a human, compassionate and altruistic human being, Isidora puts into practice an emotional coping strategy: reciprocal relationship of mutual help and respect with a German family is an important motivator alongside her weekly salary as she stressed above.

"Another thing, in order to be able to do this job, I adopted an attitude and thought of this job as if it is a humanitarian mission. Here, I will tell you how. First, I help the family by taking on the huge burden of caring for Frau Renate. Jörg and Claudia are relatively young people and they need to live their lives, take care of their children, take care of each other, and take care of their house. Of course they look after the granny, they come and spend one or two hours a day, but they shouldn't be with her all day long, and they can't, I understand that. Secondly, it is a humanitarian mission towards Frau Renate, in the sense of improving her life and making it better, healthier, and joyful. I humour her, make jokes … to keep her cheerful. On the other hand, they are all part of a humanitarian mission towards me: they freed me from my financial burden, financial suffering and uncertainty. So, we all help each other and try to understand each other's needs. You know, I despise it when my colleagues say: we wipe other people's asses. I believe that we do much more than that. We do the most humanitarian work in the world. We give a hand to those who are helpless, those who cannot take care of themselves. We help them not to feel miserable, alone and abandoned. We make their lives easier. You know, Tanja, how many times Frau Renate has cried when I was changing her clothes or diapers? She kisses my hands saying: 'You don't take care of your own children, and you came here to wipe my ass.' That brings tears to my eyes. But then I try to cheer her up: 'Granny, if it makes it easier for you, here, I can give you some toilet paper, so you can wipe mine too.' Then she starts laughing and I laugh and then we both feel better."

Referring to "low occupation prestige" of elder care work, Isidora disagrees with her colleagues and their stigmatising image of care workers as being unimportant and invisible. In doing so, Isidora tries to upgrade the low occupational prestige attached to her job by "reframing" dominant perceptions. She uses the tactic of infusing elder care work with positive values of "greater good" where personal characteristics of caregiver like empathy and care for vulnerable people confer a positive meaning on performing care work. The last lines of the interview excerpt reveal the second coping strategy – humour. Isidora's sense of humour is a means to release tension, and it serves as a means of ensuring balanced and harmonious communication with the elderly person, and of maintaining a supportive relationship. It is clear that a focus on obtaining particular benefits as a coping strategy does not focus simply on economic benefits but also takes in affirmation of a carer's wisdom, maturity and responsibility, which in turn, in Isidora's case, contributes to a more positive sense of self (Hessen, September 2017, Interview log).

After six months, I meet up with Isidora in an Italian restaurant, in the same village. She still works for the same family, but her physical appearance has changed. There is no makeup this time, she has lost weight and she has changed hair colour from red to black. The lines on her face show the tiredness and exhaustion. Even her face looks slim. This time we are not alone; Isidora's new rotational colleague, Nada, joins us. Isidora will be leaving for Serbia in two days, and her shift will be taken over by Nada who came two days earlier to get to know the household and a new job. This is Nada's first job and her first experience in elder care work. They got to know each other through a third woman, a mutual friend on Facebook. This is the first time that Isidora has had a rotational colleague, because she only had to take a one-month break since her passport allows her to stay in the EU more than three months. During the one-month break that she used to make every fifth month she decided to find a reliable colleague through "strong ties", close friends and relatives. Not until I mention how her husband must be happy that she is coming does Isidora tell me:

"Oh, you don't know, Jovan is here, in Germany. I found him a job … two months ago. He wouldn't settle until I found something. He was annoying me … I told him that for men it is harder to find something. It takes time. But he was persistent."

"Illegalization" of Everyday Life and Work 275

Since she couldn't find him a job through her "strong ties" Isidora, found him a job through the Hungarian agency for home care recruitment. Like most of these shady, semi-legal agencies, they charge commission for the recruitment but very often do not provide accurate information about the "patients", as they refer to them:

"I talked to the owner of the agency and described what kind of person we need. He said that there is one possibility in Hessen – a woman two years older than my husband, she is 63 years old. They told me that she had had a surgery for brain cancer, but that she is recovering successfully. She can do everything by herself, but she needs help with climbing the stairs. Okay, that suited us great. When my husband went there, the woman was still in the hospital. She came home from the hospital two days after my husband arrived: barely alive. She needs help with everything, she can't do anything alone. In the end, her daughter organized that the Pflegedienst and medical assistants would come every day. They would come every day to administer her therapy and to bath her. He would change her diapers during the day. That wasn't a problem for him because he had taken care of his mother until her death."

I stayed in touch with Isidora through 2018 and the first half of 2019. Frau Renate died in 2018. After that, Isidora changed families twice through personal recommendations. Her husband endured three months at his first job. He continued to work as a care worker along with Isidora.

6.2 Border Crossing Knowledge

In sub-chapter 5.3 I showed how the ability to access transport is tightly connected to the territorial constraints of different border regimes and plays a major role in the strategies which women elder care workers develop in the negotiation of social and geographic space in relation to different territories and networks throught labour movements. This directed our attention to the way in which border regimes affect both the level of freedom in organizing journeys to Germany and the manofold choices and opportunities that can reduce the potential risks that these journeys carry. Such risks include the possibility of being refused the permission to cross the border, the rising costs of transportation, and the psychological effects of travel, such as the fear, anxiety, and immobilization, as the result of limited control over their movements.

If the border can become an obstacle and a resource only through mobility, then it should be stressed that access to mobility is a resource that is unevenly distributed among women care workers. Thus, mobility inequalities are intensified by the possession (or the lack) of the appropriate travel documents, by linguistic competence and by differing levels of access to the "migration institutions" that permit border crossings. By developing mechanisms that control mobility, borders consolidate inequality, reinforce power relationships, and materialize hierarchies. I strongly argue that human movements across borders are contested objects of knowledge. While recent paradigmatic shifts in border regimes studies focus on how knowledge of border regimes and migration is constructed and governed from above, I re-shift it to show how the knowledge about cross-border mobility is produced from below. I am interested to examine what narratives of women care workers can tell us about the actors involved in the production and transfer of that knowledge. Moreover, I am curious about whether and how borders act as barriers to movement, and how they can induce women's creative responses to permeate these barriers. I pay a special attention to the flexibility of routes, journeys and destinations. Because these are flexible rather than fixed, women's actions and decisions contain aspects of instability, insecurity and volatility, all which complicates building the potential for mobility or maintaining realized mobility. To successfully navigate their cross-border movements, women care workers must know where to find the cracks in the "other side's" control infrastructure and devise strategies to exploit them. As Creswell (2006) states, "some mobilities are acts of freedom, transgression and resistance in the face of state power which seeks to limit movement, police boundaries and inscribe order in space". The narratives of women which I relate in this sub-chapter demonstrate that there is no production of space or a sense of space without movement, and this movement inevitably involves power relationships, power games, transgressions, and adjustments. In short, and at least in this regard, it appears that the reinforcement of the border encourages mobility. A careful examination of what border regimes between EU and non-EU countries means in the experiences of women care workers – their agency in resisting borders, the conflicts and negotiations which they engage in and their inventiveness and resourcefulness in trying to circumvent border regimes and even use them as a resource – is able to highlight the main features which characterise the acquisition of motility or the potential for mobility. The knowledge of border crossing and related tactics of how to cross the border and how to stay mobile include, for example, "passport washing", having two passports on basis of dual citizenship, paying the penalty for overstaying, or bribery and corruption. To illustrate some of the range of strategies employed to cross borders, I present three cases which should not be understood as exceptional, but vital for showing the process by which "motility" or the capability to be mobile is acquired. With the increasing trend towards undocumented care labour migration to Germany in recent years, there has been a gradual increase in the knowledge of how to overstay in Germany without consequences among commuters. This has created a variety of different informal bureaucratic activities where legal loopholes relating to the issue of documents such as passports, documentation of citizenship, identity cards, birth certificates and marriage certificates allow irregular cross-border strategies to be used by individuals or small groups. Hence, women care workers, as cross-border commuters, are integrated into multiple social and economic systems of the "migration institution". Here, the focus is on the way knowledgeable care workers employ their understanding of the rules of interaction and exploit their access to resources within the migrant institution in order to find work (Goss, Lindquist 1995: 335). To add to this complexity, many recruiters "deliver" women care workers to multiple recruitment agencies and are paid for each recruit delivered. The chain of migrant institution consists of the family of the care recipient who pays the agency, the agency that pays the broker to find a care worker and the care worker who is paid by the agency and by the family (only transportation costs). All parties involved in this chain create an incredibly complicated and unstable network that embraces a wide range of people who earn their livelihoods organizing elder care work across Germany and former Yugoslavian countries.

One of the main concerns of the women care workers from my study has to do with the possibility of legally entering, re-entering and staying in Germany. The length of time for which women from ex-Yugoslavian countries (with the exception of Croatia and Slovenia as EU members) can legally stay in Germany is determined by the officially declared goal of their migration/mobility. Women can enter Germany as professional skilled labourers – usually qualified nurses – in order to stay legally in Germany with a work permit. Alternatively, they can possess a second passport. For example, they can be citizens of Croatia, which is an EU member, and of Serbia, which is not. These women can travel using special work permits, once they are declared by the German households in which they work to be "domestic helpers" *(Germ. Haushaltshilfen)* on a legal basis. The women from my study, however, belong to a category of border crossers who enter the country as "tourists". This means that they are allowed to stay for a maximum period of 90 days within any 180-day period. Upon exit from Germany, border guards check the date of entrance and the length of their stay. Initially, those who have overstayed are obliged to pay a fine. In those cases where overstays are longer than permitted or where individuals are found to have false travel documents, women care workers can be expelled and forbidden to enter Germany for up to one year. One of the unique features of care labour mobility in my research is to be found in its temporalities and temporal rhythm – the absence of security and the routines of employment combined with uncertainty about the temporary or permanent nature of their work can trap women care workers in extremely precarious and dangerous working conditions. This is how Snežana explained the ideal temporal rhythm of care labour mobility as dictated by bureaucratic time:

"You see, when I was travelling, I lost 2 days according to the stamps in the passport. I lost two days on the way to Germany, I was waiting for the transportation, and I was travelling two days. And we are allowed to stay 90 days. Now, I will tell you what women do. With a rotation every four weeks, we fit wonderfully in the regime of 90 days. That means, when you do the math, it is four weeks, or 28 days and two days of travel. If we leave in the morning and cross the border in the afternoon, we lose one day to get there and one day returning home, that is 30 days. During six months, we leave for Germany three times, so if you work for 4 weeks, plus two days in transit, you have 30 days. So, 30 days you are at home and 30 days you are in Germany and 30 days home and so on ... Usually, women who work for three months, they have a very good job and a good family ... so they can endure that length of time. Especially when you go through the agency ... the agency sends women for three months because in that way they save money on transportation, the organization of round trips and the rotation of women."

One of the main legal risks that women face was that of being forbidden from entering Germany. Not being able to enter the country means losing both the investments they have made in care labour such as the commission paid to an intermediary for job brokering or transportation fees, and the chance of future financial gain. However, as Snežana describes above, women's movements are not only limited by bureaucratic time but are also dictated by the organization of job intermediaries, drivers, and care recipients and their families. Women's room for manoeuvre in fighting temporal and organizational constraints depends mostly on the rigidness of border crossing regimes and practices at the borders. For example, the Serbo-Hungarian border, as I showed in sub-chapter 5.3 , is one of the most corrupt borders, enabling the easy negotiation of irregularities in travel documents and entry requirements. On the other hand, border checkpoints such as those between Bosnia and Herzegovina and Croatia (the EU member state) are much stricter. Although women can enter the EU zone as tourists, they are also obliged to provide, for example, evidence that they have compulsory health insurance (which in most of the cases they do not), a declaration about the purpose of their travel, evidence of their financial standing and official documents such as their passport and a letter of invitation from the German family where they are going to work.

In what follows, I describe and analyse the border crossing strategies which women care workers use to avoid overstaying their legal time in Germany and to avoid temporal interruptions to their rotational mobility pattern.

"Two-Passport" Strategy

Not being able to re-enter Germany because of the overstay in the Schengen zone means interruption of movement and temporary immobility which reults in losing not only the chance of future financial gain but also exclusion from the rotational system. One of the strategies used to avoid this is the possession of dual citizenship. As I discussed in Chapter 4, since 1991, citizens of the former Socialist Federal Republic of Yugoslavia have been subjected to changes in their nationality and citizenship status. The new citizenship laws of different successor states have resulted in a heterogeneous range of different citizenship statutes. Isidora Basic, who lives in Serbia and holds Serbian citizenship, took advantage of her political and civil rights to dual citizenship. Since her parents were born in and lived in Bosnia and Herzegovina, she is automatically entitled to hold a Bosnian and Herzegovian passport.

As we know so far from her ethnographic portrait, at the time of the interview Isidora had already taken a new job in Germany because the previous old lady who she had looked after had died. Assuming that Isidora, like her other colleagues, would be allowed to stay only three months I asked her how she had managed the temporal transition to a new job:

"T: Did you take a break after that?
I: Yes, a one-month break.
T: Just one? That means, soon after you found this one, right?

I: Yes, yes ... the daughter of an old lady who passed away called me, saying that her friend needs someone to take care of her mother-in-law ... that was Claudia ... I accepted a job offer and immediately travelled to Bosnia to get a passport with another security number. Well, what can I say ... what else can I do ... In such situations, I want to reduce the risks as far as possible.

T: What are the risks?

I: The risk of being checked at the border, and not being allowed to pass the border. What is worse than that?

T: Well, it is not a big deal, even if they send you back from the border ...

I: They cannot send me back. That's not an option. I don't want to let that happen. When I decide I am going, I am going.

T: But they cannot send you back from the border. These are two different states.

I: If I had just one security number and two passports, that would be suspicious. Then I am screwed.

T: What does that mean, you have two passports?

I: I have both a Serbian one and a Bosnian one. With each passport, I can stay three months in Germany. I get back home, get the other passport, change my clothes, and go back to Germany. It is a little loophole in the law."

Isidora's case is specific in several respects. First, she holds two passports from different former Yugoslavian countries which are not currently members of the European Union. As the rules regarding entering the Schengen zone are applied equally to both of these autonomous states, this means that Isidora can switch from one 30-day tourist visa stay to another without a period of "temporal passage" (30 days of immobility). To take the next job, Isidora would normally (without a second passport) have been forced to re-enter Germany earlier than she is allowed. For this reason, Isidora was urged to make a fast-tracked application for both citizenship and a new passport. Usually, this process lasts between 6 months and a year, and it can be very costly – involving the costs of travel, administration taxes and fees, registration at a new address, and so on. However, the prerequisite for all of this is that an applicant for citizenship must be on a list of applicants who have registered in advance. Because the list of applicants is long and many people apply for dual citizenship, the waiting time to begin the administrative process can take several months. Judging from the stories of other care workers I came across who are entitled to have a dual citizenship, I learned that, although the "two-passport"-strategy is the best solution for overcoming temporal limits to staying in Germany, it is not widely used because it is a temporally, financially and bureaucratically demanding process. However, for Isidora, this process went faster and more smoothly because her daughter lived in Bosnia and Herzegovina. She registered at her daughter's address, which saved her the money and time that she would have lost for renting an apartment or paying someone to register her at his/her address. The other reason for speeding up the process is, as Isidora explains, that:

"In Bosnia and Herzegovina, I have a different social security number. I have two identities. I got the chance to do it when someone who was supposed to be registered on the register of citizens died in the village where his dad was born before he could be registered. It was necessary for someone to be enrolled in the register of citizens, and this man died before it could be done, so there was an empty place. A friend of mine who worked in the citizen registration office told me: 'Hey, this is your chance, and who knows when you will get it again.' And I did it. You know our proverb: 'Until dusk falls for one man, dawn cannot come for another.' Everything fell into place …"

In the remote Bosnian and Herzegovian villages, citizenship registration is still done by the books of registration. That means that each village in the county has a registration book keeper, or registrar, who physically enters the data of new citizenship registrations into the protocol book ordered by numbers. Each registered citizen has a number which serves not only as number of the entrance into the book but also as a "folder" with a field where facts about the person are written (date of birth, occupation, marital status and so on). The man who died, created an empty place in the protocol register and his place was taken by Isidora. This ethnographic detail, seemingly uninteresting, actually demonstrates how bureaucratic loopholes created by outdated bureaucratic procedures and administration, are channels of opportunities and chances to avoid illegality and "three months of being immobile".

Isidora's case is a perfect example of how the changing historical dynamics of borders result in creative responses using "bordering knowledge" where some people, such as Isidora, find themselves in possession of "mobility opportunities". That is to say that cross-border mobility heavily depends on spatial inequalities that are result of uneven access to the ability to exercise the right to certain citizenship. Within the temporalities of care labour mobilities, the "two-passport" strategy for crossing borders is an insurance against uncertainty and becoming stuck. This underlines how mobility inequality is embedded in the control of time and the unpredictability of timing. Waiting for three months to pass to be allowed to move undermines care workers'agency and leads to a certain form of governmentality of "stuckness" regulated by cross border labour mobility industry and their actors.

"Passport-Washing" Strategy

Unpredictable timescales cause immobilization and experiences of "stuckness" during care labour mobility. Immobility, however, can be prevented by getting a passport "stolen" or by "accidentally" putting it in the washing machine so that stamps of entry are no longer visible. This is the most popular strategy used by those who have overstayed their legal time in Germany and do not want to be expelled when finally deciding to return to their own country. This is not an individual strategy as in the previous case and it depends on women's personal circumstances. While, in the previous case, the strategy was used to prevent overstays, the "passport washing strategy" was invented to remove the legal consequences of overstay. As I have shown in Chapter 5.3 women care workers rely on their social networks in order to mobilize resources for labour mobility, for gaining access to information about job offers, and for getting a job. When it comes to negotiation and overcoming borders constraints, the "migration industries" play a pivotal role, especially within the context of restrictive migration policies and border controls. Hugo (1996) and Castles, de Haas, and Miller (2013), advocate an analytical focus on the meso-level of migrant institutions, using the term "migration industry", that mediates between the micro-level of social networks and the level of the state. Care labour mobility is an interesting exception in migration and mobility studies because it comprises a whole range of actors on different levels, sometimes acting simultaneously. My research findings corroborate a structural interweaving of informal and formal structures in the facilitation and control of care labour mobility. As we have seen so far, women who do not have sufficient language knowledge, travelling experience, or access to information regarding where and how to find a job in Germany turn to intermediaries for finding them a job, for organizing transport and sometimes money (for example, when they cannot pay the commission to the intermediary). An ever-expanding networks in care labour mobility industry function both within and outside of the legal structures which are in place. This means that, in order to understand how women develop their mobility potential and the strategies which are at their disposal to overcome different obstacles, we need an explanatory approach that goes beyond that of social networks. More precisely, we need an approach that doesn't understand the "commerce of migration", job intermidiaries and other recruiting informal actors on one side and state representatives or state institutions, on the other – simply as worlds in conflict. It is necessary to call for the inclu-

"Illegalization" of Everyday Life and Work

sion of public sector actors in care labour brokering (Lindquist 2010; Spaan 1999). Moving on from this, I showed in the Chapter 5 that the "migration industries" and social networks are not substitutes for one-another but are, instead, entwined and operate simultaneously, as can be seen, for example, in the case of agencies who perate in grey zone care sector which use individuals as informal subagents within migrant social networks. I will return to more-commercial elements in sub-chapter 6.4. Here, I want to focus on the narratives of women which reflect their knowledge about how the "migration industry" within care labour mobility works as they provide information, products and services, thereby promoting, facilitating and organizing the process of care labour mobility. Snežana demonstrates the knowledge which she has built up as she describes one part of the process:

"These women job intermediaries, they are the problem. They organize the job so that you have to change your passport all the time. We travel in their organization with their cars and their drivers. So, we leave in the afternoon, and when we reach the border my passport will be stamped. For example, if I cross the border today, after 6 p.m. this day will count as if I spent it in the European Union. Instead, they could drive us later, because … you see from Sombor (the town of departure) to the Hungarian border takes only 20 minutes by car. So they could postpone the departure so that we cross the border after midnight. That would save an entire day. Then, you have those job intermediaries who have only one driver … of course, because one is cheaper than two … so, he sleeps over in Germany, so you have to wait for him and end up with a third day overstaying in the EU. The last time when I was crossing the border, a month ago, I crossed the border only 20 minutes late … only 20 minutes! … Can you believe it? … That counts as if I was a whole day in the EU. I crossed 20 minutes after midnight and started a new day.
T: What happens then?
Nothing. Then, I got a penalty, I have to pay the fine … 230 euros … or to get a new passport. The problem is that the Hungarian border police now enter all the data, because the passports are made according to a unique social security number so that they can track every person … how many passports each person has and when the passport is changed. Changing the passport is a criminal offence. And, you know, that could easily be avoided. But those who organize the job, who send us across the border … they only consider how to take the money from us, how to charge for their services and nothing else. At this last job I just mentioned, I had to change my passport every second rotation. To get a new passport costs 50 euros … now do the math: I earn 1300 euros per month, I have to pay the job intermediary 200 euros for brokering, pay 150 euros for transport, pay 50 euros for the passport. What is left for me? Netto, brutto …"

Snežana's statement that "changing the passport" is a "criminal offence" is not entirely correct. As long as passports are regularly issued by the Ministry of Internal Affairs of the Republic of Serbia, the activity of replacing an old, damaged passport with a new one is not generally legally controversial. Yet, in making this statement, Snežana underlines her knowledge about how the informal care market works. While knowledge usually represents an advantage and a form of agency, in Snežana's case her knowledge about the care market, coupled with her knowledge regarding how the migration industries effectively generates cheap labour and labourers is unfavourable among actors who facilitate cross-border care work:

"As an accountant, I have been working all my life with numbers, papers, finances, salaries and so on. I know a lot, which is why I am unsuitable to the job intermediaries ... I am a problematic one for them because of my knowledge. I ask them questions that other women wouldn't. That troubles them ... Do you understand?"

Here Snežana reveals a strong confrontational attitude towards and condemnation of the job intermediaries, something which might serve as a coping strategy, but which also places Snežana in the role of an outsider who questions the "system". This rebellious attitude towards job intermediaries and colleagues is an obstacle on Snežana's way to find and keep a more stable position rather than remaining in the role of "Springer" who changes families and destinations every two months. Looking closer at how the system of brokerage and job intermediaries works allows us to see the power asymmetries and inequalities that they create, inequalities that result not just in a range of different experiences but in the attachment of differentiated meanings and values to movement for labour. In contrast to Snežana's case, Jasna's understanding of the complexity of space-time rhythms of labour mobility shows a tendency to neutralize negative attitudes towards the role of job intermediaries:

"I can spend three months in Germany within half a year. But since we rotate every 6 weeks I have to get a passport four, five times a year. I have to get a new passport every time.
T: Why?
Look, if I leave for three months ... if I stay here in Germany for three months over the course of half a year, that is ok. It counts from the day I entered the EU zone. For example, I entered on the 4th of April and I am leaving on the 2nd of June – I have been here three months and that's the limit for half a year. So, July, August, September ... I wouldn't be able to enter Germany until October ... However, now we are going back to the old system that we used to work with – rotating every

6 weeks. After Sanja (her rotational colleague) comes here on the 4th of June and stays 6 weeks, in order to replace her I have to enter Germany earlier than I should. Well, then I have to get a new passport, and with the new passport I cross the border, as if I'd never been there before. If we could rotate exactly every three months, that would be okay. But in this case, we rotate every month and a half. And also, if we rotate every month, then after the second time, when I re-enter Germany for the third time I will have an overstay of three days ... which means I am in the red zone! Again, I have to get a new passport."

Even though the practice of changing the passport is not illegal and the fact that there is no legal limit to the number of passports that can be issued in any single year, Jasna nevertheless expresses a certain unease with the practice, demonstrating a cautious attitude:

"They know why we are applying for the new passport ... She even asks: 'Is this because of the overstays?' But I don't trust anyone. I never know if someone has reported to someone else. For example, this is very complicated and risky to do in the bigger cities like Novi Sad and Belgrade. Here in Sombor, it is common practice because half of the city goes abroad to work, illegally."

In the quote above, Jasna is aware of the potential risks involved in processing travel documents but justifies her behaviour by identifying with others from her town who cross the border and engage in irregular strategies to travel to work. Her voicing of the opinion that the state administration ignores the irregular strategies which are used in order to achieve labour mobility is a display of practical consciousness also voiced by many other women in the course of interview. Jasna knows that "passport-washing" and similar strategies are culturally accepted and normalized practice in her region. The excerpt below presents a striking illustration of the ways in which government and public sector institutions facilitate the organization of transnational rotational work in the sector of irregular care work:

"Actually, the state doesn't care ... it suits them ... the administration earns a lot of money issuing new passports ... but listen ... when I came with a bill that I had paid for issuing the passport, the lady who works on the passports said: 'Now, can you give me your passport and the form you filled out.' And then I started to tear up the passport. I washed it, but I wanted it to look like it had been totally destroyed. Then she goes: 'Oh , stop, stop ... it is damaged enough ... don't do that here.' She even laughed ... then a colleague of hers came, and they started to discuss the most efficient way to damage a passport ... they even gave examples of the ways that people do it ... There, on the spot! Nothing is secret!"

A Bribe

The third type of strategy that balances the risks of being refused re-entry to Germany and the resulting forced immobility is – that of a bribe. An important role in this strategy is played by bus drivers and the border guards at border-crossing points. In Chapter 5.3 I explained two possible modes of transportation which care workers use in travelling to Germany. The first is transportation by mini bus, in which the transport is organized and directed by the job intermediaries. This is used when either intermediaries are running the business of job brokering and transportation or when they use the services of private drivers (who officially call themselves "taxi services") which have mushroomed over the last 5 years due to the expansion of cross-border care labour mobility. The second mode is used by women who do not depend on job intermediaries but travel in a self-organized system of rotation using official private bus-companies who operate within a legal framework of transportation regulations monitored by the state. The travel with these long-distance buses to Germany, depending on the region, can last between 12 and 20 hours, sometimes even longer. The regular users of this cheap transportation over recent decades have been Gastarbeiter, retired Gasterbieter, students, construction workers, domestic and care workers. The arrival of low-cost air transportation and cheap flight connections is the result of new airports specializing in low-cost services in former Yugoslavian countries and has become a popular means of transportation for tourists, students, labour migrants, for those who know how to travel, have financial means to do it and who have no legal obstacles to entering Germany. It is not so popular, however, among domestic, care and construction workers who work in the shadow economy and whose legal status emerges from circular mobility across borders. I had a chance to speak with some of them during my fieldwork trips, they claimed that crossing the border by buses gave people a better chance of successfully getting through than travelling by plane. According to them, travelling by plane more often results in the refusal of entrance than travelling by bus because border guards and border police at the airports cannot be bribed. In the case of women care workers who are not tied to the transportation arrangement of their job intermidiaries, the reasons for not using this low-cost flight are various. They range form a general lack of travelling experience, lack of foreign knowledge, lack of financial power and knowledge of how to book a ticket on the internet, and, last but not least, the challenge of how to reach the family where they are supposed

"Illegalization" of Everyday Life and Work
287

to work once, they arrive in Germany. As care work relies on organized transportation from the women's towns of origin to the doorstep of the family where they work, crossing the border is the most critical point during this journey and is an event that involves a variety of different actors in labour mobility industry such as bus drivers, border guards, fellow travellers and job intermediaries. But also for those women who are travelling independently with cheap commercial bus companies. Within the border crossing mobility, the relationships between unequal individuals are the result of the existence of a hierarchy, understood here as a structure linking unequal persons in relations of dominance and subordination. These relations are the most visible in overcoming entrance barriers such as that of a "stamped passport" due to overstay.

Whenever the topic of bribery as a border-crossing strategy would come up during interviews, women were usually hesitant in telling their experiences. The interview situation, where the conversation is recorded with their permission, made them even more reluctant to talk about this particular cross-border strategy. They would only mention this "service" indirectly. Snežana is a rare example of someone who was open and outspoken about these practices:

"Usually, it used to be eight of us in the mini-bus. That was a lot of women. It was more suspicious because it was obvious that the women were travelling for work in Germany. Now they have switched to luxury cars because it's less obvious. However, they control it and they know, the cameras at the border register each car. I know, for example, many women who reported drivers to the police … you know because of fraud and so on … nothing ever happened … cases were concealed. Everybody knows about this business … our police, the border police, the German police …"

By "reporting drivers to the police", Snežana refers to the situation where women were tricked by job intermediaries and drivers in sense that they were not paid, or that driver didn't picked them up at the address of household where they worked or any other reason that broke "agreement" between parties. When I asked her about the "procedure" when someone overstays the permitted length of time and faces the consequences at the border Snezana said the following:

"Well, it went like this: you have to pay the border officer between 50 and 100 euros … it depends … but not directly to him. First, you ask the driver, and give the money to him if he agrees … because he is the one who negotiates with the police. The driver usually takes 50 euros for himself as commission for mediation between you and the police. Everyone has to earn something …"

Either the job intermediaries organize the bus driver, or it is a bus driver from the official bus company, bus drivers are experts who hold particular "border knowledge" and, for the travellers, they are there to guarantee a successful passage despite legal barriers. The drivers are professionals in crossing the border due to their passage routine through the border check points two or three times per week. The driver of the bus has a "financial arrangement" with one of the border guard shifts. Here is how Vera Jelić recalled her border experience:

"Well, you know how I don't have an EU passport, I have a Serbian passport, I have to be home for three months. The only thing is that I paid 100 euros to the Hungarians in January so that I could return immediately after a month. I didn't even want to, I wanted to rest.
T: Who did you pay 100 euros to? The Hungarian border police?
I gave the money to the driver, and then he gave it to the Hungarian border guard. He didn't stamp my passport. But you know, you can't do it with Hungarians anymore … you can't bribe. The Hungarians were replaced at the borders, so now no one can avoid penalties and paying fines. So, if you overstay you will be denied entry to the EU for a year.

During several journeys as part of my fieldwork, I saw for myself the presence of Austrian and German immigration and border police at the Hungarian border, which confirms Vera's story. My first-hand ethnographic experience leads to a similar but more-detailed description of the process of crossing the border. During participant observation in a regular bus run by a Serbian company while crossing the Serbo-Hungarian border in February 2016, I witnessed the highly complex procedure of crossing the border and the different steps which it involves. Perhaps it is important to stress that, on that particular occasion, it was me who had overstayed three days and anticipated the possibility of facing the consequences. Actually, the main purpose of my trip, besides participant observation research, was to go back to my hometown of Belgrade in Serbia to pick up my student visa from the German Embassy and to travel back to Munich. Since my visa had expired, and because my German language course had taken longer than it should have, I stayed in Germany two days longer than I was allowed. I left Munich Central Bus Station at 7 p.m. During the journey, it was very cold in the bus, and I couldn't sleep at all. When we reached the Hungarian border around 5 a.m. the temperature outside was -20 degrees. Crossing the border with the driver consisted of several stages. When the bus approached the border crossing point, the driver opened the doors and we all had to go outside. The next

"Illegalization" of Everyday Life and Work

step was waiting in the queue between two border crossing-points where we would encounter the border police at the checkpoint. My fellow passengers, with whom I hung out together during the trip, consisted of two men, construction workers and two women care workers. No one had regular travel documents. One of the women even had a passport that had expired. While we were queuing, the border police and customs officers examined the bus, and this is when the passengers prepared themselves for the culmination of the process. The driver approached every passenger in the queue and asked them to show him their passport and visas. I didn't know why he was doing that. My fellow travellers explained to me that he is checking if everyone is alright and that in case there is a problem with overstays the driver will "take care of it". When the driver came to us, I noticed that the four other passengers all handed their passports to the driver with the money inside. The driver walked away. After 10 minutes, he came back with their empty passports, signalling by a nod of his head that everything was alright. Then he turned to me and asked if I had any problem. I said that I didn't have any problem, I had only two days overstay. The driver said to me in a patronizing way: "You know that you will pay a fine or be denied re-entry to Germany." I said that I knew, but that I was a student with a visa waiting for me in the German Embassy in Belgrade. He said: "They don't care what is waiting for you in Belgrade. You have an irregularity now. If you want, I can talk to them. They will take something" (he meant money). I asked him how much and he leaned towards me and said: "I think 70 will be enough." I thanked him, saying that I didn't have the money and that I was going to be ok. I wasn't okay. I didn't know if I was shaking because it was cold, or because I was terribly frightened. The driver was not satisfied with my rejection of his services. Walking away from us he said to me: "I wanted to help you, but now you are on your own." The extortion of money from the passengers by threating them with bad treatment by the border police is the mechanism that drivers use to maintain hierarchy and control on the one hand; and to "act out" the role of gatekeepers whose credibility actually facilitates corrupt border practices, and thereby, also facilitates labour mobility on the other. From what I observed during the interaction with other passengers, drivers are keepers of information about passengers, their work and their migration status, which they use to control knowledge regarding the risk of different strategies for how to cross the borders. In this case, overstaying showed the development of a complex migrant institution with a number of participants: the bus driver (who gave the bribe), the passengers (who overstayed), the border guard (who would accept the bribe), and me.

After half an hour of queuing, I couldn't feel my legs anymore and didn't care very much about what would happen to me. I was the last in the line, and the border police officer was young with a stone-cold face as he looked at my passport. "You have two days", he said. I explained who I was, presented my student ID card and the confirmation that I had completed a German Language course. I said that I was going to collect my visa in Belgrade and that I had to come back to Germany. He skimmed the papers, returned them to me and stamped my passport. Before he gave my passport back to me, he asked: "So, when you are travelling back?" I said: "In four days." He smiled, saying: "Good luck with studies."

I have never in my life, and probably never will, felt more "illegal" than when I was crossing the border. What I learned from this experience as a person and as a scholar is that even when we have good arguments on our side, self-confidence and the courage to present them to authorities we feel vulnerable, filled with fear and powerless. Being "illegalized" involves the legal production of a person's "illegality" which is generated, as we can see, not only through laws but through the acts of non-state agents as well. Moreover, "illegality" is not only a juridical status and a socio-political condition but also an embodied experience of being-in-the-world.

6.3 Being "Illegal"

As I have already explained in at the begininig of the chapter, the consitutive aspect of elder care labour mobility is its illicit, undeclared or undocumented manner in which the work is performed. In addition to the fact that many of the women in my study regularly stay in Germany on a tourist visa, their "illegal" status is also connected to labour laws and the absence of working rights. The chosen title of this sub-chapter is not intended to label women care workers as "illegal" but, rather, to draw attention to the ways in which individuals' legal status affects their everyday life within the privacy of Germany households. "Being illegal" is the result of a process of "illegalization" and "illegality" which is sometimes equated with criminality. Being illegal is also an attribution that women care workers assign to themselves, as they talk about working on the black market (in Serbian, *rad na crno*, in German

Schwarzarbeit), although they often justify their position in the irregular l care market using the logic of demand and supply. Without falling into the trap of assuming that the stories of all irregular live-in elder care workers are necessarily stories of fear and distress, it is nevertheless the case that these are common characteristics of the lifeworlds inhabited by many of the women who work in different household settings in Germany, albeit, not only in households. The aim of this sub-chapter is to demonstrate, based on my respondents' testimonies and my own observations, how their interactions with different actors in the process of labour mobility activate and produce specific kinds of feelings such as fear, anxiety, frustration, and insecurity. This is important because different configurations of "illegality" not only affect the external structure of women's lifeworlds but can also extend their reach quite literally into women's "inward parts", profoundly shaping their subjective experiences of time, space, embodiment, sociality, and self. Because of their irregular working status, women care workers often cannot escape fearful situations that have the potential to undermine their livelihood. Hence, I am analysing women's stories to examine the condition of their "illegality" from their own perspective. I want to demonstrate how women care workers develop unique modes of being through their engagements with others in the process of care labour mobility. Willen (2007) suggests that the condition of migrant's "illegality" operates as "the catalyst for particular forms of "abjectivity", and only ethnographic research can reveal "the impact of "illegality" on every-day, embodied experiences of being-in-theworld. Building on this, I argue that becoming an "illegal elder care worker" is neither a passive nor a unilaterally imposed process, but involves visible dynamics characterized by recurrent threats and fears as well as women's ongoing strategies for coping with and overcoming the situations in which they live. Officially and more generally, women elder care workers become legally irregular in relation to labour laws because they engage in "illegal" employment that legally invalidates a three-month tourist and constitutes a prosecutable offence. Based on this knowledge, every woman I talked to believed that, if her working status would be disclosed to the German authorities, she would be deported and that both the care worker and the German family who employed her would be punished with a fine. These (partly) legal procedures and practices of making women illegalized care workers are forms of subjectivation of the women in the sense of Foucault. They develop and employ their own strategies of not being endangered or detected in this regime of governance and surveillance. In the interview excerpt below Isidora's strat-

292   PERIPHERAL LABOUR MOBILITIES

egy to not to talk about borders and transformation of the former Yugoslavia shelters her from possible subjectifivication of illegalization:

"When friends of her children come to see her'(the old lady), to talk to her, simply to visit her, they love to talk to me as well, and they ask some things that I'm not willing to talk about.
T: Why? What things?
I: Because it concerns politics. And that's ... I do not know enough words to talk about that kind of thing in German ... you know? ... I just say: Everyone should put their own house in order. It is what it is ... We don't have another home country, and that's it. I don't want to discuss these things. I do not want to go there. But then they start with other questions: What kind of borders are there between the Yugoslav republics now? Are they autonomous states? They were totally clueless. I told them that, for me, there was only one state. I don't want to talk about them as separate, autonomous states. Let's not talk about that. Instead, let's talk about lakes, rivers, mountains, about entertainment and such things, but not about politics."

In this chapter I put the emphasis on linking the social processes of "illegalization" with the ways in which women care workers – as socially situated, goal-oriented agents – participate in and, in various ways, contribute to the formation of their life and working conditions. In so doing and being an active part of the procedures of subjectivation, the following narratives and observation from the field will show how women navigate their unique status-related challenges in order to build meaningful and safe working lives in these settings.

Critical Incidents

Although the irregularity of the women care workers from my study is well concealed within the privacy of German households, they often cannot escape the fearful situations that threaten to undermine their well-beings and their jobs. Although, as I already mentioned in Chapter 4, state control of undeclared care work in the household is almost non-existent and largely ineffective, each of the women whom I interviewed was aware that almost any "slip-up" could lead to the exposure of their status. Most of the care workers stressed that they saw those activities for which they had no training, such as moving and repositioning disabled or immovable elders, as high potential legal risks, leading to a sense of fear that stemmed from their working status. Isidora's case typifies the way in which sudden incidents, usually related

"Illegalization" of Everyday Life and Work 293

to the health of elderly persons, remind women of their lack of the professional knowledge, and generate fears that pervade their everyday experience:

"It happened one morning ... when she got up, just like a million times before that ... I wanted to move her and place her on the toilet wheelchair. When she stood up, the healthy leg she was standing on just collapsed. She fell and pulled me down with her. In that moment, I tried to get under her, so that she wouldn't fall on the floor, but onto me instead. Both of us collapsed. I saw how she fell, and it was not good at all. There were no children at home, her children who live in the house had left to go to work. Only her grandson was at home at the time. I asked him to call his uncle and aunt, who live not far away from us. They showed up almost straightaway, and they are both physiotherapists. They helped me to lift her up from the floor. But seeing how she felt, I knew that she had broken a hip or a femur, there was no doubt about it. I was crying like a little child, I never, ever cried in my life, apart from when I was angry or feeling stuck. Anything could have happened. They were trying to calm me down, but in my head, I was thinking 'I am not a skilled worker, I don't have a certificate, I am working illegally – jail!' If they asked in the hospital how she fell, and they found out it was my fault ... you know, they have to go to the hospital, state what happened, and report the accident. But the family stated that she fell when she was with them. I do not care what happens to them, they'll get out of it. It's their country, their house, they'll get away with it, do you understand? So many things went through my mind."

From the excerpt above, we can see that the fear Isidora felt after the accident was related to the lack of trust that employers will protect her, and thus her awareness of being at risk of legal consequences. Thus, the level of trust established between women and their employers is a crucial element in women's experiences of "illegality" and the vulnerability, which is an outcome of these experiences. Furthermore, "being illegal" has substantial material consequences in the arena of medicine and health not only for the elderly people they are responsible for but also for women care workers themselves. As non-contracted workers without social benefits and health insurance they have no access to the health care system unless, in situations where they need medical attention, they pay themselves. If they were to need urgent healthcare for any reason, care workers would be subject to thousands of Euros in hospital costs. An extreme example of such a situation is the hospitalization of Ana Wendl after she had a car accident, the case I will turn to in the following section.

Dangerous Spaces – (In-)Visibilty

Although elder care workers remain largely invisible within the private space, they cannot remain invisible or escape public spaces. During the time they spend outside of the house (which is usually only a few hours a week), they visit supermarkets, bus stations, pharmacies, posts, and other public places as a part of their daily job such as shopping, buying medicines, doing errands and so on. Given the risks and dangers associated with moving through public space, many women reported being always on their guard, always looking around, and always keeping their eyes and ears open. Despite the fact that such caution may be irrational, for women care workers, the anxiety that stems from their status nevertheless perpetuates the above-described modes of somatic attention. Isidora describes her experience as follows:

"What does it matter to me, as long as I do not have to be scared if someone approaches me on the street, or if he or she smiles at me – that happens to me here regularly, and then I wonder who that person might be, or whether someone is following me, and things like that."

Having colleagues with good intentions in similar situations was important, as such people are able to understand women's predicaments, share their concerns and frustrations, and provide both direct and indirect advice about the best courses of action in potentially dangerous situations where women's identity might be revealed. Through their engagements with others, women care workers develop the strategies necessary for successfully navigating their "irregular" conditions through often-changeable policies and rules in the institutions and services which they use. These situations are best described with reference to the case of Fatima. Fatima, we met in Chapter 5, had been working for four years as an elder care worker in Germany at the time of the interview.

"(…) Now I am just thinking about how to send the money for a new bicycle for my son … because the situation has changed. Until recently, I have been sending money through this Western Union … you know what that is … yes … so, I was sending money every now and then … for birthdays and in case of some urgent financial situation. But now, I can't do that anymore, they changed the law. I found out because one of my colleagues here told me. You see, there are 5 of us here in the same village … we meet up when we have time … anyway … one of them told me that now when you send the money, they ask for your passport and they make a copy of it … but not only that … they also ask where the money came from, they ask for my address here in Germany and they store all of that on the computer. It was nothing like this before. You know … I used to send 200 euros almost every month … and it wasn't like this. It happened to one of our colleagues … she went to Western Union and they asked her for all this information … the woman ran out from Bank and never came back. It is good to know … otherwise, I wonder what would have happened if I had been caught … what would I do? Where would I go? Working without documents … I don't need problems … So now, whenever one of us goes home we send the money through her."

The household where women perform their work can also be a dangerous space. While it would seem that individuals who are privileged enough to live-out, who have living spaces separated from the care recipients and their families, have more personal freedom, in the case of Ana Wendl, her "home" was a place where she felt persistent embodied tension and anxiety. Ana lived in an apartment 25 square metres in size, consisting of one room, a kitchen and a bathroom, without a washing machine. The laundry room in the basement was shared among all residents in the building and, following a recent renovation, the apartment was very cosy with a new kitchen and kitchen appliances. Positioned in the very centre of Munich, only a few streets away from the house where Ana worked for an elderly lady, Frau Müller, the apartment was officially designated as "vacant". As Ana was an undeclared care worker, she couldn't register at the address, and in addition to that, Frau Müller wanted to keep the status of apartment as if nobody was living there. For this reason, Ana was "supplied" by Frau Müller with a list of instructions about what she should do and what she must not do in order to keep her life in the apartment secret. In no situation must she bring visitors into the apartment, she must keep quiet, she mustn't use the common washing machine in the basement, the kitchen or kitchen appliances (except the coffee machine and the toaster), she must throw out the garbage during the night, never listen to the TV at a loud volume, keep the heating switched off (except in the evenings) and never communicate with the neighbours. In order to follow all these instructions, Ana developed certain strategies and struggled constantly not to leave any bodily traces in the apartment or in the building. She performed these actions repetitively and almost obsessively: keeping the window shutters constantly closed, listening for voices before she left the apartment, waiting in front of the building to make sure that there was no one in the entrance before she went in, throwing out the garbage during the night, washing her clothes between 2 a.m. and 3 a.m. when she was sure that no one would be in the laundry room. Being constantly somatically attentive to her clandestine status, Ana developed a great deal of psychological distress, coupled with excessive, even paranoid behaviour. Since, as I described in the methodological chapter, Ana and I became close over the course of time, I had the opportunity to witness and observe changes in her behaviour. Ana would work every day during the week from 8 a.m. until 7 p.m. On Sunday afternoon, she was usually free from 1 p.m., which is when she used to invite me for coffee. Every time that I came to visit, the apartment would look like nobody had ever lived there. There were no personal objects or clothes, and the kitchen was as clean as new, without a single sign that it had ever been used. When we had finished with the coffee and dishes, she would scrub the counters and sink meticulously. When I commented on how hard it must be to keep everything clean, Ana told me that she keeps the apartment clean and tidy because she found out that Frau Müller would enter the apartment in her absence to check if everything is as it should be. Ana even told me that Frau Müller went through her personal things in the wardrobe and in drawers. When I asked her how she had found that out, she told me that, after she began to suspect something, she left a slipper behind the door so that she would be able to see if anyone had opened the door whilst she was out, and when she came back home the slipper had moved.

Ana's sense of *being-in-the-world* was fundamentally shaped by a range of different fears in relation to different people and situations: neighbours, mail carriers, caretakers, cleaning staff and Frau Müller as well. Ana struggled with experiences of social isolation, marginalization, exclusion from her immediate surroundings and profound worry that someone might discover that she lives there and report it to the police. In addition to this, as I described both in Ana's portrait and in Chapter 5, Ana was threatened by the job intermediary that she would report her to the police at the border when she decided to "cancel her services" after Frau Müller decided to choose Ana over the other care worker. Ana took this threat seriously because she was convinced that her safety while crossing the border might be compromised.

"Can you imagine Tanja, how it feels when she calls and says: 'Does your employer know that you have a Serbian passport? I'll send the police to the border.'"

Clearly, the weight of Ana's irregular working status and clandestine housing situation had crept into her unconscious. The anxiety and fear were so deeply entrenched in her mind that, after a year and a half, Ana started to suffer from insomnia, fatigue, and lack of concentration, all of which eventually led to the car accident in which she could have lost her life. I have described this event, my involvement in Ana's hospitalization, and the identification procedure carried out by the police in Chapter 3. The potential exposure of her irregular working status to the police was a "wake-up-call" for Ana and Frau Müller to regularise Ana's status as a contracted worker.

My findings, including Ana's experience, do not align with empirical evidence in the research literature that reports how "living-out" arrangement enables greater independence for care workers, freedom of movement, the possibility of emotional distancing, and opportunities for negotiating their working and living conditions. This topic resonates with earlier discussions in German academia on re-politization of domestic sphere among feminist sociologists during the 1990-s. Some authors like Maria Rerrich were assuming that the invisibility of jobs in the private sphere benefits many women working "illegally" by shielding them from discovery (Rerrich 1997: 20). On the other hand, Becker-Schmidt (1992) and Phizacklea (1998: 34) note that private zone has one main disadvantage: live-in domestic workers have minimal freedom to manoeuvre and to express their agency. "What is 'home' to affluent white women has an entirely different meaning for her domestic staff, who experience it as a place of social alienation and exploitation" (Becker-Schmidt 1992: 221). This is confirmed, for example in empirical evidence provided by Gioavanna Campani whose work on Filipina domestic workers in Italy shows that domestic workers, they can afford it, they rent shared apartments, where they meet during their free time and find refuge or social safety and comfort (see for example Campani 1993). In the more recent German empirical literature, the issue of re-politization of household is taken up by authors of younger generation of cultural anthropologists and sociologists of work. Hess and Puckhaber (2004) draw our attention to the racialized economization of the private sphere in case of au-pairs and reveal exploitative features of their specific workplace. Similarly, Karina Becker (2016) from sociological perspective investigates structural powerlessness of East European migrant care workers. With my own research I will turned to the problem of household as segregated social space, social relations and negotiation of social boundaries providing more nuanced evidence in Chapter 7.

However, despite living out, Ana was nevertheless constantly "available" to her employer's demands, and continuously on duty. Ana's case is the best demonstration that worker's wellbeing and level of dependency do not depend on the spatial organization of work but on the relationship between care worker and employer in which "illegalization" often leads to the formation of adverse psychological conditions, thereby making women care workers vulnerable and exploitable as cheap labourers. Thus, the space of the home can become a fragile zone of phenomenological safety not only leading to unprecedented forms of "illegalization" and humiliation but also of criminalization, as the following example demonstrates.

Vera Jelic worked as a care worker for an elderly lady in the household which also included the elderly lady's husband. Their daughter, who lived in the same village, would come to visit them several times a week. Over the course of time, Vera became less and less able to cope with the unfavourable working environment which her employers offered. She complained about the workload, which included many tasks unrelated to caring for elderly woman, and her poor diet. She wasn't allowed to cook and was entirely dependent on the food cooked in the house by the husband of the elderly lady. This was further compounded by the husband's drinking problems, his often-inappropriate behaviour towards Vera and an unclean and unhygienic working environment. Vera recollected how, no matter how hard she tried to maintain acceptable level of hygiene in the household, she couldn't do anything to prevent the odours of urine, trash and spoiled food in the kitchen, the constant messiness of the house due to hoarding and so on. Due to these reasons, Vera decided to leave the job. She informed the daughter of elderly lady, who was Vera's employer since she is the one who found Vera through an unofficial "agency" and was paying Vera directly. Vera voiced her reasons for leaving, mainly in regard to her health and physical inability to perform work. She did not complain about the working conditions or tried to negotiate them. From this point onwards, the space of home became a danger zone. Vera narrates her story like this:

"In that family I had a great deal of stress towards the end. Granny's daughter, when I told her that I wanted to leave … it was awful Vera makes a break and sighs … She came once to visit her mother and, when I saw that they would be busy, I said that I wanted to go out a bit for a walk to take a fresh air. She didn't say anything. It seemed very strange to me that she did not react at all to the fact that I wanted to go out. She usually says I can or can't or that I can do it later. When I returned from the walk, I realized that she had searched my entire room and gone through my things. The same evening, the police showed up at our door, saying that a theft had been reported and that they needed to check my room. I was terrified. They found a pair of sandals in my room, in the laundry basket. I said that I'd never seen them in my life, and I didn't know where they came from. It was instantly clear to me that the daughter had put them in there to incriminate me. And she did that while I was having a walk. Since she didn't comment my going out, I suspect, I had an instinct that she would do something bad … I don't know how to explain … She was an awful person. Her behaviour towards me was sometimes unbearable ... She would usually bring her dirty laundry to wash it at her parents'. I didn't mind that. She would put the laundry into the machine and leave, and then I would normally take the laundry out of the machine, fold it and iron it together with the other laundry. My job was to take care of her mother, not to do laundry, but okay, I didn't complain. When she came to visit her mother I would disappear and leave them to talk, you know ... to have some privacy without me around. One day the daughter arrived and I noticed that she went to the basement, and so I thought that maybe she had her the laundry with her. I came to her in the living room and just wanted to ask if she had put the laundry in the machine so that I would know to take it out later. She started shouting at me, slapping her hands on the table: 'Who do you think you are to go through my private stuff?' I couldn't move and I was speechless – I was just in a state of shock. Later she apologized, but for me that was the last straw, I couldn't stand it anymore. I was a stranger in that house, with no connection with the world outside; I didn't see the sun or the moon."

Vera's story points to the psychologically strenuous side of being a live-in care worker whose personal space and time are very limited. In extreme cases such as Vera's, women are not allowed to leave and return to the household however they please. Having to ask for permission to leave the home, being asked how long she would be away and being checked up on when outside the home is constraining for an adult who is not a family member. It must be borne in mind that free time is essential in order for women to build up their social capital and find out about different jobs and working conditions from other women. The live-in care workers I interviewed were isolated from people other than members of the household where they work. They have a little chance to meet other people, to develop ties, to create their own networks or to exchange work experiences with other women. This isolation limits possiblites to leave an unfavourable working environment. Also it leads to a constant sensation of insecurity and danger due to the absence of legal and economic guarantees. However, in Vera's case it was surprising how she, in a highly dangerous situation, nevertheless found courage and resilience to deal with it:

"I explained to the police that I never used the laundry basket because I put my dirty laundry in a bag and washed it by hand. I told them also that I did not know what was in the basket. The sandals were in a package which had been ordered by the daughter and delivered by Amazon, and the accusation was that I had stolen them. The police asked who I was and what I was doing in that house. I said that I work here doing Schwarzarbeit, I had to say how it was. Then they took me to the police station and took all my data. I felt like a criminal. I told them that I was a victim because I was suffering terror in that house. I told them that, as much as I was

guilty of working illegally, the daughter was equally guilty. In the end, I left, with no consequences. Only later I found out that no woman came to their house to take care for them anymore, only the Pflegedienst and Diakonie … the living condition worsened after me … it was dirtier and who knows what happened to them. I know for sure that they didn't have the money for a nursing home and couldn't hire women to work illegally.
T: How do you know this?
V: Because I stayed in touch with a Russian nurse who used to come to administer insulin and to check her blood pressure … She was really nice … she helped me to survive. We are still in touch via Viber, texting each other."

What is surprising in this story is that the daughter who reported Vera to the police was careless in not thinking that she might incriminate herself as well as someone who had breached the law. In Germany, generally employers have no incentive to declare the employment of irregular workers because the societal and cultural acceptance of informal work is a very high and the risk of labour Inspection is low. German labour inspectors are not permitted to inspect private households unless they have received serious information about suspicious activity. As Helma Lutz (2010) and Norbert Cyrus (2008) have argued based on their research of political and public discourse on care work migration in Germany, employers of care workers are rarely criminalised since the violation of labour laws in the private sphere is treated as a minor offence which, both in the eyes of the police and public servants, and in society more-generally, is not perceived as punishable. The case of Vera is an exemption of the unwritten rule that the household protects the undeclared elder care worker from the police and labour inspections. Whatever the reason that the daughter of the old lady reported Vera to the police might be, this case demonstrates how "home" can, paradoxically, become one of the most dangerous spaces, with the potential to play host to extreme forms of exploitation and psychological mistreatment.

"Being Someone Else": Strategies of Concealing One's Identity

Generally, through their engagements with other individuals they came into contact with in the course of labour mobility, women managed to develop the new understandings, strategies, and perspectives necessary for successfully navigating their "irregular conditions": they learned what to do, what not to do, who to speak to, what to say, when to say it, and so on. This learning practice can be self-imposed, but more often it is imposed by the employer

"Illegalization" of Everyday Life and Work

or elderly person that they care for. I often came across women who told me that their employers had changed their names in order to introduce them to others using a more acceptable variation of the same name: name Mirjana would become the German Miriam, Ljiljana would be transformed into Lily, and names such as Gordana, Dragana, Vedrana would be reduced to Ana.

In order to conceal women's identities, their employers give them guidance and instructions on how to conceal their ethnic and national background. In Ivana's case below she was asked to by employers to identify herself as Croatian. Croatia is a member state of the European Union which paradoxically doesn't change her irregular employment status in the household but in the opinion of her employers sounds more reliable in the eyes of social services.

"The granny insisted on me saying that I was from Croatia because Croats did not need a passport and did not need a visa, so she would be able to justify herself in front of everyone. Her own brother did not know where I was from, nor did her friends and relatives. The only people who knew who I was were her daughters, because they were around every day. When granny's granddaughters came for the first time since I had arrived in the household, I literally stood like a stone, not saying a word, just waiting to find out whether they would say I was from Serbia … I just didn't know what to say. The granny was scared, considering that she knew that the fine was 20,000 euros for hiring people to work illegally. Once, when a social worker came to the house to check if granny has a help in the house, her daughters told me not to leave the kitchen so that she would not see me. They told me to cook lunch, but if she came to the kitchen not to talk to her at all. If she asked me something … I should tell her … you know, we already had a story ready that I was from Croatia and that I was friend of her daughter who came to help while the nurse who takes care of granny is away."

The cyclical character of labour mobility meant that Ivana had the chance to reflect upon her experience in the household when she had to return to Serbia for three months. The excerpt below shows that, despite Ivana's knowledge about work regulations in Germany, her attentiveness to public space and psychosocial dynamics over time led her to adopt self-disciplinary practices and to experience a persistent feeling of uneasiness and watchfulness in front of unknown persons:

"I wasn't afraid that much because I knew the German system, and I knew that they do not care. As long as you don't really breach some serious rule, nothing can happen … they have so many foreigners working on the black market. But the first time when I was there I kept carrying my passport with me all the time in case the police stopped me. If, for example, I crossed the street somewhere where I should not, on a red light or something. I was following all the regulations. The second time I didn't care, and I was much more relaxed. But every time I met someone new from the family or some new friends of the family, and they ask me where I come from, there was a chance they might find out who I really am. For example, granny didn't tell her brother that I am from Serbia but from Croatia. All of sudden he started to talk Croatian to me … I was surprised because out of nowhere some German-born person says Dobar dan (Serbo-Croatian, Good afternoon). He told me that he worked with Croats for some years so he learned some of the language. But then, the problem came when I said that my family celebrate certain patron saints because we are Orthodox. Since Croatians are Catholics, he could have suspected that I was lying. I made up a story that I was from Vukovar (the town in Croatia) where the Serb community lives so that he wouldn't be suspicious."

This story shows how threats related to her status make her more sensitive even to those linguistic differences between Serbian and Croatian that a foreigner who doesn't know these two languages well cannot detect. The Serbian and Croatian languages are mutually intelligible with an identical linguistic system and can be hardly differentiated by the person who is not a Serbo-Croatian speaker. Yet, over the time Ivana became attuned to ethnic, religious and national aspects of her identity that might reveal her identity. In this way, care workers of preferred nationality or ethnic background who have more ability to respond to risks of working irregularly in the household are more welcome. This reproduces class, ethnic, national and gender spatial inequalities.

The ethnographic examples presented above have traced the ways in which women care workers constantly negotiate the tension between owning a body as object and a body as subject, or between their own embodied experiences of self in social context, on one hand, and the way their bodies are being "read" and construed, which is filled with gender, ethnic, and national signals that are associated with particular kinds of positive and negative values. The narratives of women show that risk is culturally constructed and there is no guarantee that the dangers they seek to avoid are those that will actually harm them most. The lingering fears of "being caught" and persistent feelings of precariousness causes continual self-disciplinary tactics intended to overcome these.

6.4 The "Care Labour Mobility Industry" – Business as Usual?

So far I have introduced several different terms in order to describe how the strategies of various actors in care labour mobility contribute to the mobility process, its disruptions, and its continuations. More importantly, I have described how social networks, migration institutions, and migration industries shape and facilitate or hinder women's motility and how they subjectify them to a wide-stretching moblity regime. In the following sections, I want to focus on the "care labour mobility industry" and the role it plays in women's mobility trajectories and their strategies of dealing with being subjectified as an "illegal" person. The different ways in which women respond to the "business of care", and the different conceptual and analytical implications of my ethnographic evidence related to notion of "migration industry", formed the major themes for the rest of this chapter. I have no intention of further interrogating the theoretical and analytical potential of the term that I have already discussed earlier. Rather I would like to focus on the meaning of the "care labour mobility industry" within the context of my study, and to suggest some ways in which my empirical findings can challenge and question the mere "commercial nature" of care labour mobility.

Before I do so, I want to draw attention to the semantic shift from "migration industry" to "mobility industry". I have made this shift for a number of reasons. Firstly, care labour mobility between Germany and the former Yugoslavian countries doesn't operate on the same large scale as international overseas migration. Secondly, my research explores both how care labour mobility and its meanings are produced and how they are controlled and constrained, understanding mobility primarily as multi-directional movement and ongoing process rather than a one-off event. Thirdly, I have held on to the term "industry" to highlight the various actors involved in processes of financial gain from care labour mobility; infrastructures that enable care labour mobility entail a large and developed network of individuals, entrepreneurs, small businesses, aboth in the formal and the informal sector. To understand the world of elder care workers on the move, I had to become sensitive to the presence of multiple mobility processes and to the actors and networks that facilitate them. The semantic shift from "migration industry" towards "mobility industry" enables a few empirical and conceptual interventions.

Firstly, it enables me to look at the operation of the "mobility industry" from a different angle, investigating how women care workers constantly negotiate their mobility or immobility. In the analysis that follows, I closely look into the positioning of different actors within care labour mobility and the different relationships between them. In doing so, I wish to demonstrate the ways in which the mobility industry works to shape care labour mobility flows and experiences of care workers within. Also, it is a question of impact of different actors and their roles on decision making, particularly with regards to questions of destination and who goes where and why they go there or not go at all.

Second issue with the term "industry", lays in describing it as a productive activity, thus begging for question of who or what exactly is being "industrious". In my study it concerns different types of "services" provided to care workers and to German families as care receivers, along with the complex relationships that exist among the various actors involved. Hence, I discuss the narratives and experiences of women to understand the social and cultural processes and meanings involved in the provision and exchange of the "services" that "grease the wheels" of care labour mobility such as job brokering and transportation. Thus, the industry is used figuratively to refer to the exchange of services, support, and favours in the processes of the "care labour industry".

The third intervention concerns the conceptualization of the relationship between women care workers and the "care labour industry". In other words, the question of who is seen as being actively involved in the process of "re/ producing" care labour mobility. For example, in Salt and Stein's account of "migration as business", the authors grant no active, participatory role in the migration process to the migrants themselves. In Salt and Stein's model of migration industry, migrants appear only in the form of "streams" that are "managed by a string of intermediate institutions". In studying the migration industry, scholars generally tend to privilege job intermediaries as the principal protagonists within processes of mobility. Such an understanding would fail to do justice to the various agentic roles that women care workers play within their mobility projects. While it can be said that they are exploited by individuals and institutions driven by the opportunistic desire for profit as previous chapters demonstrated, there is also a risk of conceptual objectification of women care workers when the "mobility industry" is taken as the principal driving force behind processes of mobility. We must, therefore, look closer into the potential meanings of "profit", and the different people for whom they are relevant. Given that Salt and Stein (1997) define migration as a business, it is not surprising that their account of the migration industry places the most emphasis on the profit motive in order to explain the behaviour of those who work in it. For these authors, all participants in the migration process are motivated by the desire for "commercial gain".

Contrary to the approaches to analysing economic activity taken by most anthropologists and sociologists, Salt and Stein seem to regard the migration business as almost completely disembedded from broader social relations and the norms and values that govern them. We should bear in mind that financial gain remains the principal motivating factor for labor migrations around the world; people move in the first instance for instrumental reasons – to increase their earnings, accumulate savings, and improve their material well-being. I argue that we also need to recognize that aid given for reasons of reciprocity within migrant networks is frequently governed by an instrumental logic of expected material benefits in the future, not by altruistic values. However, as the insights of economic anthropology and sociology suggest, economic activity is never "just" economic, and as sociologists and anthropologists we do not characterize any activity as being governed by a "purely" economic logic. Bourdieu's (1986) essential insight in propounding his "economic of practices" framework is that the resources which individuals and groups draw upon and exchange are social, cultural, and symbolic as well as material and economic. Moreover, individuals and groups constantly accumulate, exchange, and spend these resources as capital, including and especially across the material-economic and symbolic-social divide. Thus, as Smart (1993: 391) points out, it is difficult to neatly separate commodified relations involving economic capital from sociocultural relations involving social, cultural, and symbolic capital.

Actors

When we think of the elder care mobility industry, who do we imagine to be actively involved in the process of "producing" it? Over the last five years, the care mobility industry, led by job intermediaries or job brokers, has continued to facilitate a great deal of cross-border care labour migration. At the beginning of my research, I regarded job intermediaries, as those who operated the irregular care labour market between Germany and the former Yugoslavian countries. After extensive field research and a great deal of reflection, however, I become less convinced that the services they provide should be characterised in terms of the export of care workers from the former Yugoslavian countries into Germany. From the stories that different women care workers have told me, I have identified three distinct types of persons who are involved in placing women workers on the move for performing care work in Germany. First of all, job intermidiaries, that can be persons from different countries with different statuis and history of migration. They can be former migrants who came to Germany many years ago, as asylum seekers and refugees during the Yugoslavian wars in 1990s; or members of Gastarbeiter families who live in-between two countries or who lived that way a long time ago but have maintained their relationship to Germany. This is how Jasna describes her recruiter, or job intermediaries:

"Irena lived here in Germany as a child. She returned to Serbia at the age of 15. Her parents were here and she speaks German fluently. She has three daughters. Over the years she has maintained her connections with Germany and stayed in touch with the people here. Yes, she developed a business, why not? There is a doctor who tells her which family needs a care worker. She has a number of women in different villages in this region. But in this village, Maja (her rotational partner) and I are the only ones. There is no one else … because granny's niece found Irena through some woman from the village next to ours. Her mother is cared for by one of Irena's women care workers. So, the niece asked that woman for recommendations and that's how Irene brought me and Maja here …"

Jasna's testimony suggests that Irena's care labour mobility business depends on the symbolic capital of the word-of-mouth referrals and recommendations she receives from the German families in villages she is connected to. Jasna highlights that Irena's social capital is embedded in her knowledge of the German language and the social and cultural connections she established whilst living in Germany with her parents in her youth. Unlike Jasna's recruiter, Ivana's job intermediary has a somewhat different migration history. In answer to my question about how she found herself a job as a care worker, Ivana narrated this story:

"It was like this: my friend connected me to his girlfriend who was taking care of the old lady in some spa town near Frankfurt am Main. Since she needed a replacement for three months, he asked me to jump in, otherwise, she would lose the job. He needed someone who would replace her for three months, the length of time we are allowed to be there on a tourist visa … you know, so that she could come back and continue with a job. So, basically, I had someone from Serbia who put me in touch with someone who already had a job in Germany."

Ivana continues the story about her colleague:

"Now, I will tell you how she found a job. Her best friend found a job as a caregiver in Germany in the same way, three years ago, then he married a German woman, it was a sham marriage ... he got 'papers' (she means a permanent residence permit). In the building where he lived there was a guy who was doing business connecting German families who need someone to look after elderlies and want to avoid to paying 8,5 euros per hour with unemployed women from Serbia ... he is a kind of merchant who trades in women ... maybe it is ugly to say that, but that is how it is. He charges them a commission for each month, he takes the money from their monthly salaries. Since the woman I was replacing was a friend of his neighbour, he took only 100 euros from her, in advance. Neither of us knew German, only English so that's how he found the old lady, he needed someone with whom we could speak English. But she had already collaborated with him before us; six or seven women worked for the granny that she found through him. He is someone who fled Serbia during the 1990s; as a war refugee from Bosnia, he claimed asylum in Germany. Over time he found jobs, met people, made his own social network. He does various jobs ... he doesn't have a profession ... I didn't ask him too much about his jobs. What was important to me was to ask him about my job and conditions. That's how I found out about the many women who are unemployed and work in Germany for him ... of course ... he does everything illegally.

T: How much does he charge women?

I: As I remember, he asks for half of their first salary. Or, 100 euros from a couple of salaries. I think that he charges brokering ... to find you a job, 200 or 300 euros ... sometimes women have to work all week just to pay him off.

T: Do the women know each other?

I: No. No one knew anyone. I only met the woman I replaced when I arrived to Germany. After that, she recommended the young woman who graduated from medical school, so I was replacing her. Then, my replacement was her friend and so on. We all found each other on Facebook.

T: So, five different women circulated in the household over the course of one year, right?

I: Yes ... more precisely, four women per year. After three months, that is it, because you can't endure longer than 12 weeks. In the last three weeks, you feel like you could kill someone, because you are on the edge of your nerves, because you don't have anything of your own, you don't have your own life. It's a like a camp you can't get out, they do not let you do anything, you don't have any privacy, everything bothers them ... you eat potatoes every day, you can't buy and prepare the food you want."

Ivana portrays her recruiter as a "self-made man" who has used his asylum status in order to develop "irregular" business as a "merchant of women" in the black market of German care work and who uses exploitative strategies to make a profit. His social capital comes from the network of affluent German households who are in need of care and from the network of women in Serbia where he is obviously very well positioned thanks to the attractive money that he offers to unemployed women. Later in the interview, Ivana, as a trained psychologist, highlighted a few more aspects of this business. Ivana talked about the woman she was replacing at her first job:

"So, that's how she found a job ... she didn't come to do the job directly from Serbia. First, she came to her friend, who I just mentioned, with the sham marriage ... for a couple of months ... she did not have a job, she didn't have a father or a mother. The easiest way is to recruit people who have problems in the family and do not have a permanent job. She graduated from law school but, since she couldn't find a job in Serbia, she decided to come to Germany. So, she found this job taking care of the old lady but she must have suddenly gone back to Serbia ... her brother had a problem or something, so I had to replace her to keep her job. She was my first contact ... I left for Germany into a relatively safe job and to a person proven to be okay. I mean ... my friend trusted her, so then I decided to trust her too."

The interview excerpt above provides us with two insights. Firstly, Ivana gives her account of how social and emotional vulnerability of persons makes them targets for the exploitative practices of intermediaries. Secondly, she underlines how "trust in a person" generates a greater sense of safety at work. The "chain of trust", or trusting someone because that person trusts we him or her, in this case, serves as a strategy for building working alliances based on reciprocity and trust.

The next type of recruiters are commercial agencies based in Germany who either specialise in giving 24/7 elder care workor who offer workforce and recruitment services in a broad range of sectors. While the one operates within legal and formal German systems of care, the other operate irregularly, without offering care workers contractually stipulated employment. Both type of agencies collaborates with many sub-recruiters, women from ex-Yugoslavian countries who link them with women in search for care work in Germany. Snežana talks about these women in the following manner:

"The agency pays them for finding women. One of them is called Sonja Sabo, she works for the German Pflege agency Fuchs and sends them women from here. We pay them 200 euros for finding us a job. For example, Dana Novaković is one of the recruiters who charges the least. She is the finest and most decent woman among them. The other intermediary ... there was a woman who wanted to work for her, who didn't know German at all but she wanted to go desperately: 'They pay you 150 euros, I will pay you 250, just find me a job. The women are competing for who can offer the most. That woman intermediary raised the fee to 180 for her services. Why not? She was offered a better money."

"Illegalization" of Everyday Life and Work

According to Snežana's experience and the experience of most of the women in my study, the fees paid to job intermediaries have increased dramatically, from 150 to 300 euros, thus generating intense competition between women care workers who compete amongst each other as to who will pay the most to get the job. As we can see from Ivana's case above, however, the fee is sometimes reduced based on friendships between intermediaries and care workers. It is important to note that raising the fees leave out those women who possess language and care skills but cannot pay the fee and gives privilege to those who can pay more. Such practice not only create inequalities among care labourers, but also degrade the quality of care and devalue care work.

In certain cases, the recruitment process occurs in Germany, where women wait to be selected for placement by the agency. The agency provides a package of "services" such as transportation to Germany, accommodation and food during the process of recruitment while women are waiting for a job. This type of recruitment is the most exploatiative one because produces a situation of "involuntary immobility". Waiting for a job tends to be a source of uncertainty and anxiety since the recruitment procedure is entirely non-transparent. Vera Jelić describes her own experience of such a process:

"My first time in Germany I was in Brückenau … close to Frankfurt. I had a very bad experience. They don't care about us, they don't care how it is for us in the family, whether you have enough to eat or not … we have nothing to do with them. They just come and take the money from us … 100 euros. They charged some women 300 euros when they first came. The name of the woman … I am not sure whether she was the owner of that agency or just worked for them … Anja Weitingen – she organized everything. We had accommodation; it was a house. That woman was on the ground floor and we were upstairs, three of us in one room. There was no bathroom, only the toilet – the bathroom was in the basement so, if you wanted to take a shower, you had to go down. We had some food … and as I remember, there were some clothes there. They charge you 300 euros and, once you start working for the family, you give to the woman, Anita, 100 euros from each salary. I also had to pay 120 euros for transport. These are terrible costs. I heard that it was initially a match-making agency, that she had run that business before. Nothing is legal there … it is totally black market, no papers, no contracts, I didn't sign anything. They only took my passport to make a copy and that was it. As for language knowledge … they ask something and then estimate how good or bad your German is. I spent 11 days in that house prior to the first family where I got the job. The other women were coming and going all the time because sometimes the family doesn't accept them, or the woman doesn't know the language or … the elderly person is so sick that they cannot properly take care of him or her."

The second type of recruitment agency can be found in the former Yugoslavian countries that are now EU members. These agencies have mushroomed in Croatia over the last few years as home care agencies have increasingly sought to recruit elderly care workers for Austria and Germany. The nature of the business is not entirely clear and, on several of the websites advertising such services which I visited, the terms and conditions of employment are neither entirely transparent nor legally comprehensive.

The source of information about those who are in need of care comes from medical nurses and doctors in German hospitals. The network of medical and nursing professionals in German hospitals serves as the most reliable and efficient channel for information about potential clients. They usually collaborate with job intermediaries and charge for each recruitment they make. Ana explains her situation:

"Her name was Traudl. She still works at Isar Klinik in Munich. One of my first jobs was via her connections ... not directly. She was supplying Monika, my job intermediary with information ... she always knows exactly who each patient will need to care for them at home. I had her phone number and I called her once when I wanted to leave Frau Müller ... I had enough. Traudl told me that it is not a problem to find me a placement especially because I am in Munich and I speak German fluently. But then ... I changed my mind."

Whilst in the previous case the actors are a German health professionals involved in the care mobility industry and working for Hungarian intermediaries, Snežana reports about nurses from Serbia:

"You know, these women have been working for years, some of them for decades as nurses in Germany. Working as professional Pflege, they visit patients every day in their homes, so they ask who needs care around the clock ... they have the contacts of elderly people who need help and literally sell these contacts to our intermediaries."

Based on the insights into different recruitment strategies that emerged from the interviews it is obvious that the boundaries of the labour mobility industry are porous and constantly growing, forming highly unstable networks comprised of the different actors involved in the mobile and informal transnational market of care. These actors are not just job intermediaries or brokers who connect care giver and care receiver, but an ever-expanding range of individuals who offer various services in the grey economy: drivers, former migrants, current migrants, language teachers, border guards, lodgers, people who are sometimes members of the same family or friends from the same

"Illegalization" of Everyday Life and Work

town, nurses, doctors. Within structural approaches and migration system theory, the "migration industry" is predominantly understood and defined as a *meso structure* operating between the micro and macro levels of large-scale institutional formations. However, this approach fails to sufficiently take into account the wide range of actors external to the job intermediaries and their networks who have an impact on labour mobility processes. The example of the care labour industry shows an interweaving of the informal and formal sector of care across different territories and social contexts. More importantly, the fine distinctions between illegal and legal practices, state and non-state actors, job brokers and state agencies for labour recruitment often become blurred within situations of care labour mobility. The mobility industry for care work which operates in-between Germany and former Yugoslavian countries does not comprise simply job intermediaries as "merchants in the care work force" and agencies operating in the shadow economy of care, but also members of legal state structures such as the German public health sector and public administration organisations in the former Yugoslavian countries. The social networks that women care workers and other actors are part of are also more complex, taking on a variety of different forms such as friendship, kinship, and other relationships on the level of neighbourhoods or towns, all of which constitute a dynamic set of transnational relationships that facilitate, channel, or hinder care labour mobility.

Generally, job intermediaries can be defined as those individuals or organisations who profit from the commodification of care labour mobility process in the grey economy. We should not ignore how the use of the term "profit" with regard to activities such as that of a job intermediary also plays a rhetorical role in discourses surrounding care labour mobility. Intermediaries can be portrayed as "profiteers" that exploit women's vulnerability and desperation. Isidora Bašić describes them as follows:

"T: Did you find this job through a broker?
No, because those brokers are literally human traffickers. They should all be arrested. All of them! I found this job through the previous family I worked for. Granny's daughter had a friend, who recommended me to this family.
But now, I plan to go through a broker, because I don't want to count the days, to calculate where I am going to work and for how long, with whom I will rotate, whether it is convenient for both of us or not … and so on. I will let the broker take care of that. She has a standard price of 50 euros per month, which is okay. I'm even prepared to give her an additional 50 euros if I get a decent job with a good salary. I don't want to think too much about it."

The inconsistency in Isidora's ambiguous statement is the result of a pragmatic approach to the organization of work. In situations where women are working with a trusted and reliable intermediary, there are greater chances that these intermediaries will be characterised as providers of a service. Here, an economic logic of self-interest and a social logic of mutual interest can operate simultaneously in women's attitudes towards intermediaries. In a similar manner, Jasna "defends" the role of job intermediaries:

"I pay to Irena 150 euros for the first two shifts when I start the job, and then 100 euros each month. But look, considering that they stress themselves out over who is the driver, where he drives, who needs a replacement, whether everything is fine or not and things like that, I absolutely wouldn't mind even if she charged 150 euros. It's not a big figure as long as I do not have to worry about anything."

The "Business of Caring"

Most of the conceptualizations of the migration industry elaborated by different authors have two ideas in common: 1) that the migration industry provides migration-specific services to migrants and/or to their employers; and 2) that "migration entrepreneurs" provide these services in pursuit of financial gain. The second, serves to distinguish the migration industry from the assistance that migrants recieve from social networks. Translated into the case of the care labour mobility industry, this would imply that the logic governing the actions of job intermediaries and their relationships with their "customers", women care workers, is qualitatively different from the logic governing mutual aid within women's networks. I would largue that the question of financial gain as a factor motivating job intermediaries does not unequivocally distinguish the logic governing care mobility industry from the logic governing social relations within women care worker's networks. This is not to say that there is no distinction to be made between "for profit" activities and activities of solidarity, only that there may be considerable overlap between these spheres both conceptually and empirically, and that the logic of financial gain and the logic of reciprocal mutual aid may simultaneously govern the same activities in care labour mobility. The case I will describe below, demonstrates relationship between care workers, intermediary, elder person being taken care of, and her family and how interests overlap.

Jasna, a 57-year-old sculptor, introduced in Chapter 5, works as a care giver for a very sick elderly lady in Baden-Württemberg. The old lady suf-

"Illegalization" of Everyday Life and Work

fers from multiple diseases and impaired mobility. Because of the woman's weight, Jasna finds it hard to manually lift and reposition her. Care workers who are not professionals are often exposed to forces that are known to involve risks of back and musculoskeletal injuries. Despite that, Jasna doesn't complain much about her work. As I explained in the previous section, Jasna found this job through Irena, a job broker who is well connected with German families in that region. As Jasna does not speak German, she asked specifically for an elderly person who can communicate in English. Irene connected her with Frau Ursula who had spent a decade of her life in the USA. In this job, Jasna rotates every 6 weeks with 28-year-old Maja from her town. Maja has a two-year-old daughter and an unemployed husband. During the interview, I realized that Jasna and Maja had developed not only a good collegial relationship but also something of a mother-daughter relationship. Jasna spoke of Maja with a protective and caring attitude. In answer to a question regarding the organization of rotational shifts and care work, Jasna recollected an incident that reveals how seemingly commercial relationship between job broker and care workers conceals a set of more complex relationships:

"The incident happened three days after Maja took over her shift. She arrived on Tuesday, and on Friday she called me to say that she couldn't get out of bed and she had to go back home. It seems that, while she was lifting Frau Ursula from the wheelchair, she managed to pinch a nerve between her kidney and her spine. It got twisted in a way that caused inflammation and unbearable pain ... poor child ... since there was no one to look after Ursula, her niece Karin immediately called Irena. She asked if Maja could stay at least a week until they find a replacement, something that is difficult to do quite so quickly."

The biggest risk and danger of performing undeclared care work for women is getting sick at work or suffering injury as the result of lifting heavy patients. Since these women do not possess health insurance to guard against emergencies that would entail hospital admission in Germany, the responsibility for covering these costs is carried by the job broker and care worker. In instances where there are serious health problems, women return to their home country for treatment. In these situations, job intermediaries must react promptly in order to replace the care worker with someone else, sometimes in a matter of hours. This happens either when the elderly person has no family to take over or, what is more often the case, that the family who that do exist cannot perform the task of caring. Through the many interviews which I carried out with women who had experienced or knew people who had experienced this situation, I learned that sometimes the family alone can bridge the temporal gap by hiring a professional caregiver or by re-hiring irregular care workers through their own networks, cancelling the services provided by the job intermediary. For the intermediary, this means losing a client and the chance to make a profit. Jasna describes Irena's behaviour in and attitudes towards such a situation:

"Irena was pissed off. When she heard that Karin had asked for Maja to stay one more week, she asked her: 'Would you sit with a broken leg with Ursula and wait for a replacement to come in a week?' In the meantime, Maja's condition worsened ... she got a fever and painkillers did not work anymore ... On Friday, Maja said to Irena that she could not endure any more. Irena sent the driver to pick her up on Sunday and she was in hospital on the operating table on Monday morning. Horrible! To cut the story short, something was wrong with Maja's kidneys before ... lifting Ursula only triggered that. Maja's doctors said that if she had waited any longer she would have died from sepsis ... that's how serious it was.
T: How did you manage to find a replacement in the end?
J: Oh that ... well, I could not come because I'd used up all of my permitted stay in Germany, so I asked around my friends ... someone I can trust ... who can deal with Ursula. So, my good friend Lena came to replace me, but only for three weeks. I wanted to save Maja's place ... otherwise, you know, Irena would have to find someone else and that is not good for any of us. The other thing, Maja knows how to handle Frau Ursula ... she is not an easy person generally, plus she is old and sick, so not everyone can be with her. This friend of mine who replaced me, Lena, the woman ran away! She couldn't wait until the end of the shift. You see, Ursula often picks a quarrel, she also says awful things ... But Maja knows how to take it. She doesn't argue with Ursula. But she does say to her everything she thinks in a nice way. Unlike me ... (she laughs) I tend to start a fight with her. But Maja is so sweet. I really like her. And I really want to keep this place for her. So, my friend was there three weeks, then, I 'washed' my passport and now I am here for three months, as long as I can, to let Maja recover fully.

Jasna's story about the incident demonstrates how irregular elder care work is fraught with complexities which derive from the following elements: 1) intimate and embodied care work which requires emotional and cognitive investment on the part of care workers; 2) unique tacit knowledge on how to care for elderly people which develops only in collaboration between care workers as the result of a teamwork; 3) the precarious and vulnerable status of care workers. These elements, taken together, induce specific types of relationships between the various actors involved: the job intermediary, the family of the elderly person, the elderly person, and the two care workers. While we might agree that all these relationships are governed by economic logic

"Illegalization" of Everyday Life and Work 315

and profit, they also intersect with feelings of trust, solidarity and reciprocity. Let us examine each actor to see how the social logic of mutual interest and mutual aid works here. We can also examine the meaning of profit in the care labour industry: who profits from whom and in what way?

Job broker Irena profits from the monthly fee that she charges care workers, and she also profits from the families of elderly people who hire her, but these different profits are not mutually exclusive. What connects them is the set of relationships in-between. However, understanding the true meaning of profit here involves identifying the risks to which job intermediaries are exposed. These risks include the loss of particular care workers as "customers", criminal proceedings if the care worker suffers heavy injury or death, and loss of reputation among German families as potential "customers". Irena's social capital and symbolic capital have been built up over time, and the more care workers she recruits who perform their work well, the more satisfied families will refer their friends and relatives to Irena's business. This means, in turn, that Irena profits from the good relationships that the care workers she recruits have built between themselves.

Care workers Jasna and Maja profit economically from Irena's "business networks" in Germany, but they also gain financially directly from Frau Ursula. I found in interview that, especially in situations where the elderly person has family or children, that women are often given extra money for a job well done. Jasna confirms that:

"Frau Ursula can be like this, like that … but she can be also very generous. For example, to me and Maja, to both of us she gave 400 euros and once 200 euros to each of us."

Frau Ursula profits from Jasna's and Maja's dedicated care and loyalty which she seems very much both to appreciate and financially reward, in the knowledge that the risk of losing them would, in turn, affect her own health and wellbeing. During participant observation and interview work, I have noticed that relationships between care workers and elderly people can create a special bond. Caring includes continuous attention and presence which inevitably leads to forming intimate relations that include warm and positive feelings but also anger, despair, fear and shame. As Zelizer (2005: 15) underlines, intimate relations involve different kinds of intimacy that can be physical, emotional and informational. "Informational intimacy" is very important here. Access to information about an elderly's person past, financial status or family secrets creates a connection between care workers and the elderly person that is not easily controlled or governed by commercial logic. The incident I described in Jasna's story is an excellent demonstration of how this connection can develop amongst care workers themselves.

Good relationships at work and a level of collaboration between women care workers are crucial for the performance of work but also for their wellbeing. Physically and psychologically demanding care work requires balanced relationships, understanding, and tolerance between two care workers who rotate in shifts. Trust is not the only element necessary for this arrangement – reliability and a sense of duty and reciprocity must exist for a successful and long-term rotation to function. My interview material suggests that most woman find the ideal type of care work arrangement to be that in which the same two persons continually work in the same family (caring for the same elderly person) for at least a year or more. This means that continuous mobility, arranged by fixed parties with a common (financial) aim, results in better working conditions and working relationships. Overall, women stated that stability, certainty and shared solidarity between care workers reduces stress and the other negative side effects of performing elder care work. The health incident made visible the different interests and potential benefits and risks that parties involved in the "care labour mobility industry" possess or are engaged with. It is in Maja's interest not to lose her job while away, whilst Jasna has an interest in finding a replacement for Maja in order not to lose a "good rotational partner". Jasna evaluates Maja's abilities and personal characteristics in a very concrete manner:

"Maja knows how to handle Frau Ursula … she is not an easy person generally, plus she is old and sick. (…) Not everyone can be with her (…) You see, Ursula often picks a quarrel, she also says awful things … But Maja knows how to take it."

Being a "good rotational partner" thus involves not simply the possession of care skills but relates to the personal characteristics (temperament and personality) of the partner, along with the communicational skills needed for the care of particular elderly individuals with their own specific needs. The mutual dependence of rotational partners arises from the specific nature of labour care mobility: the way in which one person performs care tasks on her shift will affect the care work and working conditions of the person who takes over on the next shift. The compatibility of rotational colleagues' approaches to care work, the organization of work within the household and mutual solidarity are factors that not only make care work mobility easier, but also lay the ground for alliances in negotiations regarding the salary. In the excerpt from Jasna's interview below, we can see how the health incident altered the dynamics of power relationships:

"But in the end … you see … Maja's incident posed a lot of questions about Ursula's condition. A question was raised about why we lift her up and down so often. Well, the truth is that we didn't say how bad her condition is. When Ursula came back from the hospital, we thought that she was going to get better. Instead, she only got worse. We were paid 45 euros per day, but the third category is paid 50 euros per day, and she was in the third category, but we agreed to be paid 45 euros, because we didn't know. But conditions changed. After what happened to Maja, Irena came one day to Frau Ursula's niece Karin and said: 'You know how much the third category costs? So, it is 50 now …'"

In many of the situations I encountered during fieldwork, when the health condition of an elderly person deteriorates, it changes the payment category that is line with the cash-for-care system in Germany. Then, job intermediary should set a new price for care work for the family but not necessarily inform the care workers about this. Since majority of care workers have no knowledge about the cash-for-care allowance in the German system of long-term care insurance, they are unaware of the economic value of elder care work in the formal market economy of care. Often this ignorance is abused by job brokers who profit from it. In this particular case, if Irena had acted guided solely by the motive for profit, she certainly wouldn't have risked letting Jasna find Maja's replacement and, in that way, risking her good reputation in the eyes of German families, neither would she have negotiated their salary in a transparent and fair manner. Considering cases I presented in this subchapter, I come to the conclusion that the "business of care" actually emerges from multiple social relations that are highly personalized and complex in their nature, so that is more fruitful to analyse the organisation of paid care labour as a form of "moral economy" rather than merely economic profit maximisation. Whilst we must concede that all parties share economic interests, the commercial logic of their actions is limited by implicit norms and values which are constantly challenged and negotiated within care arrangement and by various mutually dependant actors.

Constrained Agency

As I pointed out in the opening part of this sub-chapter, if we regard the care mobility industry simply as a business guided by profit, we are at risk of granting no active, participatory role in the mobility process to women care workers themselves. One question which must be raised is in what respect and to what extent the status of women care workers is "agentic" and where their agency lies. In this section I want to provide an account of the ways women can negotiate their financial and working conditions in interaction with various actors in the "care mobility industry". Women care workers are certainly not "free agents", as their options and opportunities are shaped by unequal power relations that emerge from multiple constraints as we saw in Chapter 5. However, in order to avoid labelling women care workers as victims, I use the term "constrained agency" to refer to an agency embedded in the social relations that condition the capacity for "agentic" acting. The narratives expose the strategies, and the information channels women use in order to protect themselves from damaging and unfavourable working conditions and relationships. In what follows I demonstrate how women make use of these channels in their search for mobility options or, as Kaufmann would put it, the "mobility opportunities", and how they negotiate and navigate them in the way that make them far from passive actors. As I showed through the book, women build their *motility* by relying upon the knowledge of the mobility process that has accumulated in their social networks. Throughout that process the actions they take, comprise different forms of agency. I have identified three main strategies of agentic acting: 1) negotiation of the salary; 2) through the sharing and exchanging of information via social media; 3) self-organization of rotational shifts.

Women's decisions to put themselves on the move are based on the level of knowledge about the opportunities for care work available to them. Their knowledge of working conditions, fees payable to job intermediaries, the price of transportation, and salaries are obtained either from their own previous experience or from information passed to them through their social networks. These networks can be found in their immediate surroundings, communities, and neighbourhoods or in virtual networks such as social media. The same tactics are used for acquring knowledge about the nature of the clandestine border-crossing process. This "care labour mobility knowledge" is built up gradually and once accumulated, allows women to negotiate their own terms in relation to jobs and salaries. Ana Wendl, who stopped commuting to Germany with other women once she "emancipated" herself from the network, confirms the pattern:

"I don't know much now because I don't commute anymore with women … I knew much more before because I was travelling with eight women with a mini bus. There

"ILLEGALIZATION" OF EVERYDAY LIFE AND WORK   319

are not always the same women in the bus. You have one group of three women that is fixed group, and the others are Springers (women who jumped in as a replacement). Then you hear that someone died, or one of them gave up on a job, or took another job somewhere else and so on. During the journey, you can hear different stories and experiences.

T: You said some of them give up … Can you ask for another job or family if you are not satisfied?

A: Yes, you can. You can say that the job is not for you and you want something better. You have the right to do that … I mean, you pay them to find you a job and not the other way around. The problem is, you see … when I first left for work, the agency … it's not the agency … but one person … the intermediary … she took 250 euros from me. It should have been 100 euros, that was the rule. Once a family accepts you, and decides that you are staying with them, then you pay the full amount. It was my first job, I didn't know, I was a newcomer … they could have taken half of my salary … I wouldn't have known, because I would have paid any amount of money just to get in, and to get the job. It was my first time, they ripped me off, because you have no clue what the rules are … and you are desperate to get the job. At my first job I got 1200 euros per month … but I paid for the transportation, so it was around 1000, then I had to pay her 250 euros for brokering … I ended up with 850. She robbed me! But I was satisfied, even with that. The next time I didn't want to go below that figure, so I was always negotiating a higher salary. I once had 1700 euros … but that was only once."

In Ana's description we can recognize the exercise of agency in her evaluation of the prices of care labour in the black market of care, an assessment which informs her decision on for how much money she is willing to work for. Ana's introductory comment about her experience in labour care mobility is a good example for how time spent commuting is not simply a "dead time" in which nothing happens besides physical movement through the geographical space. On the contrary, according to my interviewees, the time spent travelling to Germany and back in the minivans and buses – is the time in which the crucial information, experiences, problems and advice related to work are exchanged and discussed. Once women get familiar with these, for example, with which job intermediary offers jobs of poor quality which are underpaid or involve a demanding or difficult elderly person or family, it gives them a firm basis on which they can negotiate with the job intermediary. Such knowledge is a foundation for agency – the ability to evaluate whether they are being paid fairly or being exploited. This ability enables women to select the jobs that increase her financial security and eliminate those where the pay fails to reach the expected level.

However, sometimes women must be resilient and negotiate the price for brokering after a job has been performed under demanding and health-threatening working conditions. Snežana narrates her experience:

"The job was near Frankfurt ... a village with 15 houses, a windmill and some surrounding land ... in the middle of nowhere. The problem is always that you don't know where are you going. This time the woman who sent me there gave me the number for my rotational colleague, who I didn't know. She told me that the house was dirty, there was not much food, there was no place to buy food, but there was a lot of fruit and tea. When I got there, I realized that they don't drink water, only tea and coffee. Something was wrong with the tap water ... it had a strange taste ... I couldn't drink this water and to buy water I needed a car. I found a few bottles in the basement after two weeks. They offered me to a special herb tea which they make to drink, but I couldn't drink that either, it was disgusting. When I came back home, the woman broker who found me the job asked for the fee of 150 euros. I told her: 'Tell me, how much would you pay for not drinking water for three days?' She said: 'Ok, I agree, this was a very difficult job. Give me 100 euros and we are done.'"

In the excerpt, Snežana pinpoints the main cause behind women care workers' vulnerability: "You don't know where you are going." The lack of information about the household, about the health condition of the elderly person in need of care or their personal details, information about the geographical setting where the workplace is situated are all potential dangers which introduce different forms of vulnerability. These forms can range from the abuse of symbolic or physical violence to being "treated like a slave", sometimes not being given enough food to eat, not being given personal space or being denied a decent standard of hygiene. While my material, to a certain extent, shows that women do accept harsh working conditions in order to earn money, closer ethnographic research reveals that women no longer passively accept such working conditions, or the unfair and fraudulent deals offered by job intermediaries.

Over the last few years, I have observed changes in the new emerging markets for live-in care for the elderly through interview work and numerous encounters with care workers. I have realized that space for active resistance and the opportunity to seek the best possible jobs has arisen through a new communicational technology. The element of access to potential mobility or "motility", which I discussed in Chapter 5 should be extended to encompass access to virtual mobility technologies. Modern communication technologies such as the iPhone, smart phones or access to social media have become widely adopted, and this adoption has enabled women care workers to communicate with and instantaneously receive information about jobs and job

"Illegalization" of Everyday Life and Work

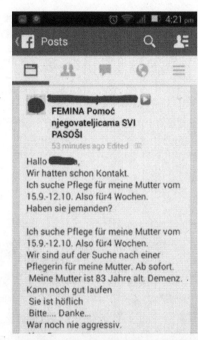

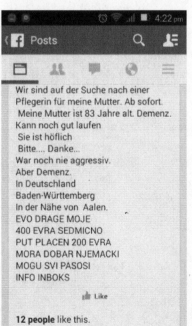

Figure 5: Screenshot of Facebook post of job advertisement, Facebook, November 2018

Hello XY,
We have already been in touch.
I am looking for a care worker for
my mother from 15.09. – 12.10. For
4 weeks.
My mother is 83 years old.
Do you know anyone?
We need someone as soon as possible.
She can still walk. She is polite.
Please ... Thanks ...
She is not aggressive but has dementia.
In Germany.
Baden-Württemberg.

HERE YOU GO MY DARLINGS
400 EUROS PER WEEK
TRANSPORATION COSTS COVERED UP TO 200 EUROS.
GOOD GERMAN IS A "MUST"
ALL PASSPORTS ACCEPTED
INFO IN INBOX

conditions with considerable ease. In this way, job intermediaries no longer remain the unchallenged gatekeepers of the irregular market of elder care and have limited power over "dupe" naive women about the general advantages and disadvantages of live-in care work conditions.

This brings me to the second type of agentic strategy – the distribution of knowledge and experiences regarding care labour mobility through social media. Facebook-mediated communication among care workers who post their experiences in different Facebook groups often leads to discussions regarding the reliability and trustworthiness of job intermediaries, wages, general problems that women face in caring for elderly, experiences in crossing the border and so on. As I explained in methodological Chapter 3, between December 2017 and June 2018 I identified eight Facebook groups set up for the exchange of experiences between care workers. Soon I realized that these groups are administrated mostly by job intermediaries who have been working for some years as care workers themselves. They use the groups to advertise the jobs they are brokering or to advertise jobs from their colleagues. In the screenshot (Figure 5), we can see an advertisement which one of the brokers posted in the group as an original message, allegedly written by a member of a German family who is looking to hire an elder care worker.

Other groups are sometimes administrated by women care workers tehmeselves and are set up both for entertainment and for the exchange of advice regarding jobs and working experiences. These groups are less "market" oriented and seldom advertise jobs. One of these groups, entitled *"Diary of a caregiver"*, encourages women to share stories about their first jobs and the different problems and emotions involved in performing care work. They also, although in a more sophisticated way, inform group members about exploitative practices and unfair brokering. This is a post placed by the administrator of the group (Figure 6).

It is interesting how the administrator of the group makes a powerful moral judgment regarding exploitative practices from a position of authority and respect among care workers. Although there is an unwritten rule that job intermediaries charge care workers a fee after a rotational shift, there are some exceptions where job intermediaries ask women care workers to pay them in advance in order to secure their profit in case women give up on the job in the middle of the shift. For care workers this public announcement is indicative in two respects: firstly, they learn that such practices are not the rule but an exception, so they do not have to accept such terms and conditions; secondly, this is a powerful moral statement that such behavior

"Illegalization" of Everyday Life and Work

Figure 6: Screenshot of Facebook post, complain, December 2018

Good morning, everyone. This morning I was really disappointed by what I heard, and I have to share it with you. This is not a group for gossiping but this is important and concerns you. Whenever I find out something that it is inhuman and unfair, I will announce it here. I was informed from one of you that there is job intermediary who charges women 100 euros and requires payment three months in advance. I am getting sick of such persons and if any person like that is a member of this group, it is better to leave the group now. I don't want this kind of person in the group!

on the part of job intermediaries is not acceptable. As the administrator of the group has a number of years of experience working as a care worker in Germany and Austria, her post can be read as an individual strategy that establishes unwritten rules that promote moral notions of good/bad and just/unjust regard care labour mobility practices and relationships. The deployment of this type of strategy illustrates the point I made at the very start: the "care labour mobility industry" cannot be reduced to a business because all activities both offline and online are laden not only with cultural norms and values, but also with moral dispositions and norms that, in turn, may be compromised, overridden, or reinforced by pressures within the irregular care market.

The previous two examples show that women who have access to the internet and social media can empower themselves with knowledge about jobs, rates of pay, and care work standards, and can discuss them online. Thus, they can communicate about their problems with other women. It is not rare for women to post about their own bad experiences of being underpaid, or not being paid at all, of threats from employers, or of caring for problematic elderly individuals. Some Facebook groups encourage commu-

Figure 7: Screenshot of Facebook post, description of work experience, December 2018

I arrived at a new job on the 13th of October in a village close to Heilbronn. I found the elderly person was suffering from dementia and exhibited aggressive behavior, with no treatment except for medication for high blood pressure and vitamin D supplements. She threw me out of the house several times, threatening me with a big knife. I found this job through the Agency Aura. I left the job on the first of November, after 18 working days. They paid me only 660 euros with an explanation that I didn't work a whole month, but only half a month. As I worked 18 days, I should get 754 euros. The woman who was supposed to replace me came from Romania and she was thrown out of the house just like me. She came back in the same way she arrived in Germany. MY DEAR COLLEAGUES, TRAVELLERS TAKE CARE OF YOURSELF! I will sort this situation out if I can (she was prescribed the therapy Melperon 5 ml, in the morning, but it had no effect. Each penny I earned cost me a life. Especially when I heard how much I was paid for that job ...

"Illegalization" of Everyday Life and Work

nication between care workers and job intermediaries to sustain competition and remove job intermediaries who are "playing unfair" in the market. In the screenshot (Figure 7), one woman writes about a demanding care receiver and about her demand for fair play.

Following the comments and discussions that emerged from this Facebook post, I learned that this case raised questions related to the safety of women taking care of certain categories of elderly people. In the thread of comments, I found that both job intermediaries and recruitment agencies came under scrutiny: should they ever place non-professional care workers in a household with an elderly person who is physically and emotionally demanding? What about those elderly who are cognitively impaired or emotionally unstable? Numerous women working with people with dementia and those with cognitive and behavioral difficulties mentioned verbal abuse or aggressive behavior. In a similar manner to my interviewees, these women had to develop individual coping strategies to deal successfully with such situations, given that in most instances there were no support mechanisms to which they could turn.

Women's access to knowledge about how the irregular care market works create transparency around rates of pay and decent working conditions. For example, over time I have observed how the fee rate for brokering has become more fixed and less arbitrary than at the beginning of my fieldwork when Facebook and Internet were not used as a medium for communication. Fatima confirms this process:

"My job intermediary and I are good friends now. I respect her. I come to Germany, work my shift, 45 days, and when I arrive back home, I transfer 50 euros into her account.
T: Only 50?
A: Yes, she charges 50 euros. If you look at our Facebook group, which I told you about, all those women pay a fee between 50 and 100 euros. Most of the women I know personally, and we all know who works for whom. And we all have a salary of 300 euros per week plus 100 euros for travel expenses. Also, I get 70 euros for food every week. Whether I spend this money or not, is none of their (the family of the elderly person) business. Sometimes I spend everything and sometimes I save 30 or 40 euros and bring the money home."

What Fatima's interview excerpt demonstrates is that online interactions and relationships help to form a community in which the "rules of business" are more visible and build a safer environment in which women care workers can rely on each other and where, to a certain extent, information can circulate. It certainly reduces the risk of exploitation and the uncertainty of unpredictable situations in the process of care labour mobility.

The third type of agentic behavior, as a response to exploitive relationships with job intermediaries, consists of the self-organized systems of rotation, which I tackled in sub-chapter 5.3. There I have underlined how social networks play a crucial role in acquiring mobility potential and in making labour mobility sustainable. But more than that, in analyzing women's narratives I have discovered a pattern – once women gain knowledge of job opportunities and build up firm networks backed up by German employers, labour mobility becomes self-sustaining. Unchaining themselves from the opportunistic and profit-oriented job intermediaries, women hold more freedom in their mobility and lower the costs of organizing work. As Ivana explains:

"The young woman who worked for her (an elderly lady), we all found each other on the Internet, we are all on Facebook … someone knew someone else, so we are all connected through different groups. We each recommended each other to her, and she decided if she wanted that person or not. But that meant that the guy that we pay the fee for brokering, lost a lot of money. He was not pleased with this because he saw the granny as his territory. So, we took over his business … However, when one of us stopped working for her because she was a really hard woman to deal with, other girls lost interest. Then the granny turned back to the guy to get her a new care worker."

The questions around labour recruitment, labour brokerage, and intermediaries bring me back to the problem of how to establish the conceptual boundaries of the migration industry. As it is defined by its principal advocates, the concept of the migration industry presupposes a set of independent "entrepreneurs" who "grease the engines" of migration through their business activities. What kind of care labour mobility industry are we talking about, for example, when Marina (in sub-chapter 5.3) brings in Germany women from her village, thus creating care labour mobility based on solidarity between women care workers which are empowered by the trust of her German employers? Is this "just" the "care labour industry" doing its labour recruitment? My own field research experience suggests that such highly ambiguous "twilight" situations are far from exceptional when it comes to conceptualizing this aspect of the "migration industry". Thus, in my interviews with women care workers I found many situations where women who were friends, cousins, or members of the same community helped each other out

"Illegalization" of Everyday Life and Work   327

without the need for a job intermediary to "recruit" them, just like in Marina's case.

The different strategies that I have discussed above demonstrate how the embeddedness of "care business" in the broader set of social relations, whether virtual or real, allows women to build up a capability for agentic behavior which, in turn, constitutes a kind of social capital that sustains labour mobility free from exploitation and extreme or precarious working and living conditions. However, we must not forget that the extent to which women can exercise their agency is determined by different factors: access to information and knowledge, personal characteristics such as resilience and resourcefulness, their language skills, age, competence with communication technologies, and the resultant extent of their social embeddedness into different networks.

Chapter 7
The Private Household as Microcosm of Social Inequalities

During the interviews and generally, my encounters with women care workers, they often expressed feelings of isolation and loneliness, a being in a situation often compounded by the location in remote rural areas, an isolated working environment with little possibility for social contact outside of the household, and as a consequence of monthly or weekly patterns of shift work, and the demands of 24/7 availability. It is quite understandable that anyone, whether that may be a care worker or someone in other line of work – who finds him/herself in this situation would strive to put efforts into inventing strategies for developing relationships with the individuals who constitute their only company at that particular moment. For this reason, I set out this chapter to investigate the ways in which elder care labor mobility impacts the parties involved in this arrangement and the new forms and qualities of social relationships which arise within it. The term *micro-politics*, suggests that the focus is on the processes through which care workers, care receivers, and the families in their households conceptualize, perceive, negotiate, and manage their relationships. I argue that elder care labour mobility across borders when it is organized rotationally, plays a key role in the development of unique personal commitments and emotional attachments between women care workers and their employers (elderly persons and their families). Moreover, I argue that the relationships created through personal encounters in labour mobility across borders can produce a whole range of different social relations and can thus generate other types of mobility such as tourism or friendship or even lead to permanent economic migration as exemplified in the case of Milica Jeremić in her portrait that follows this chapter introduction.

The majority of women care, workers, I interviewed look after dying people, elderly who are terminally ill, or elderly whose health condition is rapidly deteriorating. The bonds and intimacies developed during the many hours the women spend together with these individuals and their families lead to the formation of emotional attachments, friendships, connect families across the borders and change how people see themselves and others permanently. In this chapter, by providing ethnographic cases and ethnographic examples I want to explore the processes through which these specific relationships are created, thereby contributing to a more nuanced understanding of how intimacy, affection, the monetary value of care work, vulnerability, precariousness, and movements across international borders are interlinked. To begin with, I provide an example of these interconnections with the case of Helena Teleban. I met Helena in Munich in 2016 through Ana Wendl, who was her rotational partner and she recommended her as a potential interview partner. Helena (48-year-old) was looking after an old lady who lived alone in a house in a village near Stuttgart. Helena narrates her situation as follows:

"The village was in the middle of nowhere! A very remote place! When I traveled for the first time, [she laughs] the driver said: 'There is nothing there but the forest. You will have your coffee with wolves and bears.' And, that's how it was. But I felt wonderful there. Oma was a book lover – she knew every book, every movie. Whatever I mentioned to her, she knew it and could discuss it with me. Amazingly, she was 91 years old, and you couldn't see any signs of dementia. But, at some point, Oma's condition started to get worse. At that time only her family was taking care of her. And me. When I left, I said to her: 'Oma, I am coming back in two months.' But she would cry for me every day. Her daughter, Karin, said she asked every day: 'Where is my Lena, where is my Lena.' When I came back after a month and a half, I stayed two months. Shortly before I was going to leave, the doctor said it was over, and that she would not live much longer. Then all the family asked me to stay a bit longer, to be with Oma until her death. Back then, Oma used to ask me when I put her into bed: 'Please, come to me more often to check if I have died ... so that you will know, and can let my family know.' I was sleeping on the sofa next to her bed. Days went by and Oma was still alive. After I had been there almost two and a half months I said to Karin: 'I need to go home. I love Oma very much, but I also have my family. I can't stay. She could live another three months.' Three weeks after I returned to Serbia, Karin called me. She told me that Oma couldn't die, that she was suffering, and that she was calling for me to come so that she could say goodbye to me. They offered to pay for my travel costs. My husband and I sat in the car and, after 10 hours of driving, we arrived in Germany. I will never forget Oma's smile and how she looked at me when she saw us at the door. I will always remember that. She had five children and I don't think that she looked at them like she looked at me. Oma died the next day in the morning, and we slept over at her house. I will never regret taking that trip. Yes, it cost us ... we spent 200 euros, but that's nothing compared to how I felt. Her daughter, of course, offered to cover our travel expenses, but we refused. I wanted to do that for Oma.

As the interview excerpt demonstrates, labour mobility is induced by and induces relationships of care across the borders. In most of the interviews, I conducted, when asked about their jobs, my respondents focussed first and foremost on the micro-level of their relationships with the elderly people they cared for and with other members of the households who were employing them. I found this information valuable source fo analyzing the micro-politics of elder care work in a way that encompasses the intersection of class, ethnicity, nationality, citizenship, and ability because as we shall see throughout the chapter, personal relationships within commodified care reflect inequalities and power asymmetries that are mediated by dimensions such as age, citizenship, education, class, marital status, ethnicity, and race.

The privacy of the households where women care workers perform their work makes the separation of practical and emotional labour, and the distinction between formality and informality is especially ambiguous and problematic. While the relationship between a care worker and her employer/care recipient can be mutually beneficial and positive, these relationships can also be highly complex, unequal, and discriminatory, and they depend on a number of different structural factors which shape and direct individuals' feelings, attitudes, and behaviors.

The live-in elder care arrangements result in informal, sometimes family-like features within care work relationships. This creates challenges for women care workers in defining their position and in ensuring appropriate distance or closeness in the care relationship. The ambiguity of such relationships is mirrored in the fact that women care workers are the perfect example of the intimate and cultural Other in the household of their employer. So, I direct my attention toward the dynamics of closeness and distancing. As my interviewees underline, they are sometimes referred to as "part of the family" by their employers while, at the same time, being excluded from the substance of family life. In the broader literature on domestic and care work, I found that the focus of the inquiry is almost always on the polarized opposition between "being one of the family" or "not being one of the family". However, a neglected topic that hasn't been explained is how these two statuses overlap and alter in specific contexts and cultures. Hence, the questions I pose in my research are: Can women care workers and their (mostly) ethnically homogeneous employers interact harmoniously and understand each other's expectations and ways of communicating? Must we necessarily understand live-in elder care work as detrimental to smooth working relationships? Can actors from diverse cultural and social backgrounds in the household where live-in care work is performed form meaningful and equal relationships? In an unregulated workplace such as the private household, the lack of authority means that women care workers rely on the cooperation of both the elderly person and his/her family. This arrangement can lead to risks in terms of the quality of care but can also have negative impacts on elderly people and women care workers who are left in a slippery situation when encountering each other in the context of an intimate and largely informal relationship. However, this suggests that such relationships are permanently "under construction and reconstruction". The interviews which I analyzed demonstrate that the relationship between individuals changes and evolves as a care worker and care receiver spend time together – it is a relationship "in the making", as Milica puts it. Using the example of seemingly insignificant "cultural norms of treating" Milica shows how mutual understanding is not simply given but is built up over time:

"They are different people. But very positive people. I like that very much. They indeed have a different approach towards some things in life generally, but I have my view as well ... for example ...I say: 'We, in Serbia, when we invite someone to go out to have a coffee, that means we pay for it.' When you say 'let's go out', it is your treat. Do you understand? I don't have a problem with them because they are always taking me somewhere and they always pay. That's okay. But the problem comes when I say: 'I am taking you out for dinner.'
T: Why is that a problem?
M: Oh, they start with 'Please, don't. That is too much money. Don't spend that much'. I get angry. That is not 'too much' for me. When I decide to treat you, nothing is too much for me. But you know, you have to create this kind of relationship with them. When you create that relationship, once you have it, then it is a completely different story.

As I discussed in Chapter 1, the globalization of domestic and care work has attracted increasing academic interest in recent years (Andall 2000; Anderson 2000; Cox 2004; Gamburd 2002; Lutz 2008; Parreñas 2001). This strand of research analyses the phenomenon in the context of local labor markets, emphasizing the vulnerable status of migrant care and domestic workers. In the existing literature, I have identified several common distinctive features of interpretations of working relationships in care and domestic work. However, it seems that these interpretations of working relationships produce homogenization of experiences of women care workers according to a uniform set of features. I will go briefly to some of the prevalent empirical and theoretical examples.

Firstly, migrant workers are often represented as passive victims who stand at the mercy of their employers. With some exceptions, the experiences of domestic and care workers have been described predominantly in negative terms, imbued with the imposition of servitude, racism, exploitation, and asymmetrical power relationships. A central concern in this literature has been the archaic, pre-modern form of labour relations, drawing on empirical evidence collected among domestic workers in Taiwan (Lan 2000), Hong-Kong (Constable 1997), or in Asian or Middle Eastern host countries where an old-fashioned "upstairs, downstairs" distinction embodying models of master-servant segregation often dominates (Ozyegin 2001) as a long-term consequence of colonialism.

For the past two decades there has been a rapid rise in studying domestic work in the United States that has offered valuable insights into everyday experiences that reproduce inequality. Women of color, including immigrants, often have their skills treated as "natural" or "cultural" qualities that construct them as "ideal" nannies, caretakers, or domestic workers and it has been noted how employers frequently express racial preferences for certain racial-ethnic groups based on their "natural" abilities. Analyses of the labour process in such a milieu highlight the types of requests and exchanges that serve to subordinate the worker, establish employer dominance, and maintain racial, gender, and class privilege. Judith Rollins (1985) in her pioneering study of the relationships between "maids and madams" in the suburbs of Boston, observed that white employers played the role of "benevolent mother" as a way of confirming the inferior status of colored workers. Similarly, Pierrette Hondagneu-Sotelo's (2001) interviews of contemporary domestic employers in Los Angeles resulted in even broader findings. She found that although maternalistic acting towards domestic workers is prevalent among wealthy homemaker employers, middle-class double-earner families have neither the time nor the energy to cultivate personal ties with domestic workers. They maintain a distant relationship with part-time housecleaners, or they deploy a kind of "strategic personalism" with live-in nannies in order to ensure the quality of care work.

Further, the research literature on this topic has demonstrated that live-in work involves highly personalized labor relationships, which resemble family relationships characterized by *maternalism* and *familiarism* (Anderson 2000; Constable 1997; Gill 1994; Rollins 1985; Romero 1992). These family-like relationships have been perceived in negative terms as enforcing the worker's dependency on the employer. Rhacel Parreñas summarizes the literature on domestic work, stating that there is a consensus that the perception of domestic workers as "one of the family" enforces, aggravates, and perpetuates unequal relations of power between domestic workers and their employers" (Parrenas 2001: 18). Similarly, Romero argued that defining one's relationship as familial rather than describing it in terms of labor, allows the employer to make requests as a friend or family member, leaving the employee feeling obligated to comply and resulting in an exploitative situation (Romero 1992).

The studies described above very often focus simply on domestic workers understood as a homogenous category that includes nannies, elder care workers, house cleaners, and housekeepers, and disregard aspects and features specific to individual contexts, such as geographical, historical, political, or cultural particularities. With a few exceptions, such as Sabine Hess' work on au-pairs from Eastern European countries in Germany (Hess, Puckhaber 2004) and studies on eldercare workers in Italy (Degiuli 2007; Näre 2009) and domestic workers in Belgium (Safuta 2018), researchers usually do not differentiate between different types of comprehensive category of "intimate labor" (Parreñas, Boris 2010).

Overall, there has been a tendency in the literature to focus on the employer-employee relationship, which is understood as static within a specific time and place. Without a broader empirical time frame, these research accounts fail to grasp the innovative ways in which live-in elder care workers, as a specific group of live-in domestic workers, interact with their hosts on an everyday basis. Considering previous research, this chapter offers an analysis of employer-employee relationships which sets aside the above-mentioned scholarly preconceptions about the nature of these relationships or as Helma Lutz framed "the work of researchers who describe the relationship between employers and domestic employees purely in terms of an exploitative relationship or 'feudalization'" (2011: 16).

My research approach requires looking at this procession not as unidirectional, but as a two-way process of "boundary demarcation" between workers and employers. I argue that these relationships are not, by necessity asymmetrical, but that the form of relationship differs because they arise from different and specific socio-cultural contexts, political geographies, and histories of migration and mobility between two countries. Intimate interactions in my study occur between people who are severely ill, who are dying, or who are in other kinds of vulnerable positions due to their health, age, or gender or because of the socio-economic status of their families and the foreign, strange, and unknown women who take care of them. These interactions happen across national and ethnic divides which, no matter how intimate, emotional, and close the relationship, still involve the drawing of distinctions between "us" and "them". More often, such encounters exacerbate the "process of Otherization" in subtle and sophisticated ways of interaction that do not become obvious without paying close ethnographic attention to the details in particular cases and the comparison between them.

An example from my research illustrates the point above by demonstrating how the closeness and connectedness that care workers and care receivers develop can be a consequence of shared migratory and ethnic history between Germany and former Yugoslavian countries. In 2013, Ana Wendl was caring for a 92-year-old woman in the area around Würzburg. During our first interview, Ana started narrating her experience of spending time with a woman in the last days of her life:

"You know, that granny of mine spoke the Serbian language almost to perfection. She brought that knowledge with her to Germany and she never forgot it.
T: She came to Germany? Where from?
A: From Serbia. Do you know who Volksdeutsche is?
T: Yes. We talked about it.
A: Yes … so, she never forgot the language. In the last days of her life, I listened to her talking quietly during the night, and when she was fully conscious, she even recited some Serbian poems. But she would only speak Serbian when she wanted to. I did not want to force her or initiate a conversation in Serbian. Sometimes she used to say: let us recite something. Several times, she recited some poems, but I couldn't understand very well. And then, all of sudden she started to sing, clearly 'On went marching, on went marching'. She sang the song better than I would:

King Peter's Guard,
On went marching, on went marching King Peter's Guard!
One step follows another,
And I, a hero, follow the banner.
The battle is being fought, fought,
The flag is being waved for the freedom of Serbia!"

Ana Wendl herself is familiar with part of the cultural heritage of the Volksdeutsche or Danubian Swabians, Germans who once populated an area of the Danube basin between Hungary, Croatia and Serbia. Since she had married into a family of Danubian Swabians who didn't leave the northern part of Serbia (Vojvodina) after the Second World War, Ana shared a lot with her "granny". For the readers of this dissertation, I would like to explain some historical context. For the last 800 years, a population of Germans has been living in the former Yugoslavian republics of Croatia and Serbia. They have developed their own distinct culture and dialect. During the Second World War, the Nazi German government founded a military division consisting of ethnic Germans living in the Serbian and Croatian regions of former Yugoslavia. Initially, the Germans were encouraged to volunteer, but as the war turned against Germany, they were conscripted, as occurred in other Eastern European German communities. The division committed several war crimes. At the end of the war, in retribution, Partisans (the Yugoslav National Liberation Army) engaged in the massacre of ethnic Germans, primarily in the Province of Vojvodina, in present-day Serbia. Villages were wiped out, with the inhabitants either killed or forced into concentration camps. As justification for their attempt to eliminate the German minority in Yugoslavia, Partisans applied the principle of collective guilt to the German ethnic group for the atrocities of the Nazi regime. In 1944, all property of ethnic Germans residing in Yugoslavia was confiscated. The majority of Germans living in pre-war Yugoslavia escaped to Austria and Germany in the last days of the war or were subsequently expelled by the Yugoslavian Government. One of these families was the family of the old lady that Ana Wendl was caring for. The old lady remembered her childhood in the Kingdom of Yugoslavia, the state ruled by the Serbian dynasty of Karađorđević, which previously ruled the Kingdom of Serbia under King Peter I from 1903 to 1941. Ana narrates further:

"The granny knew everything. She remembered everything. She said that the Kingdom of Yugoslavia was her Heimat. While she was singing a song, she would tell me the story: 'We had a king, King Peter … Das ist unser König … and his dad was killed …' She said: 'That was my homeland. But I don't hate them, I forgive them. That was the politics of that time … Partisans did what had to be done …' The granny didn't have any resentment or bitterness, you know. She knew some songs that I had never heard of … She also told me that she and her family lived in Crvenka (a town in Vojvodina) until 1944. When the Germans were expelled from Yugoslavia … they came here, to Germany. But they kept a connection to Serbia. There is some kind of association for Volksdeutsche in Vojvodina so they go to visit once, twice a year on organized tours that start from here.

T: Did they know that you are from Vojvodina?

A: Of course, they did. The woman who found me the job, who connected us, she told them. But they didn't know that I am also from a German family. When I came to the family for the first time, the son of granny was curious about my German-surname and German language abilities. Then I explained that my husband is German. That led to a different relationship between us. I don't know … I felt that they respect me … I loved my granny … Her son asked me to read to her in Serbian or talk to her, you know so that she can train her brain. She was a cheerful and good person …

we used to go out and she would sing in the wheelchair ... My granny ..." (Interview log, Munich, 6/6/2016)

The sentiments that Ana expressed in the interview demonstrate the complex nature of relationships between care recipients and care workers, and their ability to go beyond the simple exchange of "care service for cash". The emotions evoked by histories, cultures, heritages, and memories that people share are ingrained into relationships and cannot be separated from elder care work arrangements. In contrast to other studies of care work (for example, Bauer, Österle 2016), I do not consider the life and work of care workers on the move to be detached from their immediate surroundings where they perform their work. I consider them to form a part of mutually constructive relationships with their rotational colleagues, with the elderly persons they care for, with members of the household (husbands and extended family), and with children, neighbors, friends, and so on. I argue that the particular care work live-in arrangements which are the result of monthly alteration between Germany and care workers' homes produce relationships where multi-layered boundaries are established by both parties to include or exclude, the intimate and/or cultural Other. This implies that we need to look at the processes of developing intimacy and closeness, ambivalences, or indifference in a particular context, and a particular household. In previous chapters, I have analyzed interviews that reveal the friendliness, occasional hostility, constant insecurity, and attempts to make sense of relationships that play a role in working "illegally". What does it mean "to belong to the family of a care receiver"? When does a care worker feel like a member of the family and why? I am interested in exploring how proximity and distance interrelate and how they are shaped by the process of "selling" and "othering". As the title of the chapter indicates, my analytic focus is on micro-politics within this micro-cosmos – on the process of establishing, reproducing, and contesting social boundaries between "us" and "them". Hence, the private household both as home and as a working space, becomes a micro-cosmos of in/equalities between parties. Lan (2006) in her work on maids conceptualized two sets of social boundaries:

- Socio-categorical boundaries across differences of class, race, ethnicity, nationality, religion, age, and marital status.
- Socio-spatial boundaries include body proximity and household spatiality and they serve to circumscribe the zone of privacy.

The notion of boundaries and "working of boundaries" (the process in which boundaries are constituted and dismantled) become a fertile thinking tool because of its power to capture fundamental social processes of relationality (Lamont, Molnar 2002). It is particularly vital in the study of the employment of live-in care workers where *boundary-work* doesn't only represent the interactive practice of constituting self and identity but plays an intrinsic role in reproducing and contesting social in/equalities (Lamont 1992: 11). I found this approach in analysis of my ethnographic material useful because it points to what kinds of typification systems, or inferences concerning similarities and differences, groups mobilize to define who they are; how boundaries are shaped by context, and particularly by the cultural repertoires, traditions, and narratives in a specific environment.

In the analysis that follows, I use the lenses of "boundary work" to explore how both care receivers and their families and care workers negotiate the above mentioned two intersecting sets of boundaries. I look at the boundary work consisting of "the strategies, principles, and practices we use to create, maintain, and modify cultural categories" (Nippert-Eng 1995: 7) focusing on ethnographic details in two case studies and on the results of my observation from the field. I pay special analytical attention to the eating and preparation of meals, the utilization of space within the home, and the allowance and delimitation of privacy. All of these involve daily habits, rituals, and practices through which both employers/care receivers, and care workers negotiate class, race, age, gender, ability, and ethnic distinctions and organize the private space, which forms the fabric of everyday life in the household. I found that interpersonal encounters across cultural and national borders sometimes undermine and sometimes enhance the boundaries that divide them. Thus, I find it important to show how boundaries along different divides – cultural, ethnic, generational, etc. – create interactive dynamics, which reproduce, negotiate and contest the social in/equalities, which exist between the t parties in the elder care work arrangements. In my analysis I found three major structural factors which help to explain their distinct preferences toward certain types of boundaries negotiations:

- Class positioning – the disparity or similarity between the employer's class position and the worker's background before taking up an elder care job in Germany.
- The regulatory context of care work, regular (contracted work) and irregular.

The Private Household as Microcosm of Social Inequalities   339

- The balance between elder care work and housework in the job description. In some cases, the scope of care work tasks involves a constant struggle to achieve decent and fair working conditions. Most women do not simply perform tasks directly related to the care of the elderly individual, but also take on domestic tasks, gardening, and the care of other family members and pets. These extra tasks are not required from women care workers, but they can be important in framing the relationship between them and their employers.
- The spatio-temporal composition of the care work setting – the amount of time that care recipient and care worker spend together in the home. This depends on the length of stay in the household (time frame of rotational shifts).

Above listed structural factors interwoven together across a complex map that coordinates a variety of subjective dispositions shape the dynamics of interaction between employers and women care workers which can be recognized in women's narratives. However, as previously stated, these factors cannot be analyzed in isolation from other attributes such as gender and age, among others. Throughout the chapter I strive to better understand and underline not only the functioning of the structural factors themselves, but also how these structural contexts are challenged, negotiated, and altered by care workers, thereby displaying the "transformative power" of care relations in what can be called the "global political economy of care". This wide range of observations, as we shall see in the following sub-chapters, point towards the idea that neither employers nor domestic workers are monolithic groups. They develop different preferences and strategies based on their particular social positions, job descriptions, and employment conditions.

Borrowing a metaphor from Erving Goffman (1959), I describe family life as a "backstage area" that harbors secrets and behaviors which are only accessible to insiders. My analysis follows the ethnomethodologically informed constructionist approach of James Holstein and Jaber Gubrium (1995), who view the family as a "socially constructed, situationally contingent cluster of meanings" (p. 896). Rather than treating the family boundary as a given entity, I explore the interactive construction of private domesticity by studying the dynamics involved in employing "outsiders" in the context of the homely backstage.

In my interviews, I found that "the boundary work" in domestic employment relationships is situated in the domestic micro-politics of food, space, and privacy.

One of the most frequent topics that all women care workers included in their narratives, even without being asked, is food. Dealing with food – its preparation, consumption and the dietary needs of the elderly person – forms a central part of care workers' daily routine. But, more than this, mealtimes provide a routinized setting for sharing information, coordinating activities, and transmitting social norms and cultural values among family members. The preparation of family meals involves the affective work of "constructing the family" based on tacit knowledge about the tastes and nutritional needs of family members (De Vault 1991). The consumption of food in a household also marks out status hierarchies among family members according to age, gender, and economic responsibility. Sometimes food management becomes a crucial mechanism by which employers define the marginal status of care workers in the household. Employers mark family boundaries through the arrangements around eating meals – who is included at the dining table, who sits where who eats before whom – as well as the distribution of food – who gets more food, who gets the better-quality products, who has access to a larger variety of food, and whose tastes or needs are prioritized. In my analysis I focus on the following food-related practices: 1) Consideration of what should be eaten and by whom; 2) food distribution and storage; 3) spatial aspects of food consumption; 4) negotiations around diet that are necessitated by the health condition of the care receiver including special diets e. g. for diabetics.

The use of the household space is another critical practice that delimits and affirms family boundaries; it also symbolizes status distinction among members present in the house. Some of the literature has documented how employers and domestic workers have unequal rights to the use of space (Constable 1997; Rollins 1985). This "spatial inequality" (Parreñas 2001: 165) signifies the lesser social status of the domestic worker compared to their employers. Some of them find themselves subject to food rationing, they are prevented from sitting on the same couch, or they are provided with a separate set of utensils, a separate bathroom, and so on. How do care workers view and perceive the regulation of their bodies in the space or practices of spatial difference in the workplace/household?

Intimacy and privacy, understood as a state of "social inaccessibility" (Zerubavel 1981: 138), can be established through the physical guarding of access but also need to be understood in relation to personal details. This includes two levels:

The Private Household as Microcosm of Social Inequalities   341

- corporeal intimacy – body proximity, touching, shaking hands, bathing, feeding, etc.,
- knowledge about someone's personal life.

Women care workers can easily access the family secrets of their employers and learn about quarrels and family relationships. Employers can either loathe the presence of an outsider in their home or actively disclose personal information to women. Women can perceive their role of confidant either as evidence of personal ties with their employers or as an extra job requirement and emotional burden. Although the protection of privacy concerns both employers and workers, privacy can be a right unequally distributed along class lines. In conditions of irregular employment such as live-in elder care work, negotiating privacy boundaries can be linked to what kind of tasks are performed and to how they are distributed and negotiated within the household.

In the two selected case studies that follow, I will analyze employment relationships grounded in the performances of care workers and their hosts (employers), whether those be linguistic, gestural, spatial, or task-embedded. I analyze how in two radically different structural contexts women care workers and their care receivers and household members negotiate or to work social boundaries: they are either underplayed or highlighted. The questions that guide my analysis is how women care workers perceive and respond to the social distance or closeness between themselves and their employers. They can for example accept ethnic or class divides or challenge them. Both care workers and their employers can perform the underplaying and/or highlighting of social boundaries as two categories of "boundary working". However, these two categories of boundary work, as we shall see, are not mutually exclusive. Rather, they are Weberian ideal-typical polarities along a continuum which varies depending on the class of employers, structure of their household (demography of household), economic status, the time that care worker has spent in the household, biographical characteristics of care workers and care receivers and member of their families involved in the care relationship, etc. Each case study presented in the following sub-chapters 7.2 and 7.3 begins with background information on demography of the household where women perform care work. The protagonist of case studies are Ivana Petrović and Milica Jeremić. Ivana is already introduced in Chapter 5.2 and Milica's portrait will precede these two case studies. The reason why I have chosen these two respondents lies in the contrasting personal backgrounds and structural factors that impel different levels of distancing and personalism as tools of boundary negotiations within the domains of space, food, and privacy.

7.1 Portrait: Milica Jeremić

I got to know Milica Jeremić through a colleague of mine who had taught Milica German a few years ago in Serbia when Milica decided that she wanted to travel to Germany for work. The colleague offered to put the two of us in touch with one other but couldn't offer any guarantee that Milica would agree to talk to me. However, after a few messages and a conversation via Skype, Milica unexpectedly agreed to meet us both in the village in Baden Württenberg where she was working as a caregiver.

(11. 11. 2017 – Baden Württemberg, Fieldwork diary, Interview log)
It is cold and raining. I am on the train to Stuttgart and a colleague of mine is accompanying me on my fieldwork trip. She is about to start her research and, since she has no experience in ethnographic fieldwork, she has asked to join me. I hope that her presence at the interview will make Milica more relaxed and open to talking about her experience. All the trains are delayed, and I am nervously checking my phone to get updates on train departures. To reach the village we need to change several times onto different trains and buses, and the local buses only run once an hour, so I am worried that we will not make it on time. Since Milica plans to meet up with us during her break, it is important for her that we arrive on time.

After five hours of traveling, we arrive in the village on schedule. The meeting point is a local bakery, and Milica arrives ten minutes after us. A member of the family she works for drove her to the meeting, and she says that the house is a few minutes away with a car. She greets Olivera warmly. She assures us that we have enough time because she is taking a free afternoon. Olivera and Milica are reminiscing the days when Milica was attending German classes. The atmosphere is cheerful and relaxing. Milica is very positive and in a good mood. Several times, she underlines that she will help with her story as much as she can which for me as an interviewer is very reliable and reassuring. We order coffees and cakes. It is Sunday, early afternoon and the bakery is very busy. The customers are mainly villagers who are buying cakes and pastries. As different customers come into the bakery, Milica

THE PRIVATE HOUSEHOLD AS MICROCOSM OF SOCIAL INEQUALITIES 343

greets most of them as they pass and they exchange a few words. We begin our conversation with the usual "how are you?" Milica is in the last week of her three-month shift, and she explains:

"The last week always passes quickly for me, it passes like this [she snaps her fingers] ... I know that I am going home: I am packing, I am doing this, I am doing that ... that last week is very busy. There is a lot of work, I have to leave everything clean for my colleague who is coming to replace me – I have to wash everything, tidy up and clean the house ... everything has to be in order ... so I don't have time to think. From morning to almost midnight, I work non-stop ... but I am generally a hard-working woman. I work hard to pass the time, I do not mess around, and this way is much better for me. They keep saying to me (my employers), that you work very hard, you work too much, but I feel better, I feel better mentally. When the day is done I'm tired physically, and that's why, when I lie down in the bed, I fall asleep immediately and do not wake up until the morning ... [she laughs] ... It is also good that something is always happening there, it's never boring. Unlike many of my colleagues who are stuck with a single person all day every day, I have a full house of people, it is a party all day long [she laughs very loudly].
T: What does that mean?
That means – there are four of us in the house, Ursula, the old lady who I'm caring for, her husband Klaus, their younger son, and me ... so, the four of us live together. The other son and the daughter-in-law live a couple of streets away, they come every day. And there's always something ... every day. We have cats ... and there is a garden ... so I get out when the weather's nice of course. I work in the garden ... I keep myself busy and entertained ... I don't want to think negatively. I came here to make money, I have my goal and that's it."

When I ask Milica about her age, she starts to talk about her family and how care mobility practices affect her relationship with her son and her daughter. Her answer is not simply a negative one, and she even describes a positive side to her physical absence from her children and husband:

"I was born in 1979, I am younger than you. I may look a bit older – I gave birth when I was very young, my son is 13 years old, he is growing very fast ... Sometimes when I come back home from Germany I cannot recognize him. My daughter is celebrating her 18th birthday, and I want to buy her a car, to surprise her ... that's why I'm working. She deserves it, she's very good at school, and she works to earn money. She works on Saturdays and Sundays and, during the summer holiday, she worked in the café at the swimming pool from morning to evening. It does not matter, she must work, it's important that she has the working habit and that she wants to work. I want to reward her, and you know ... she is the one who is at home – she looks after her brother, she cooks, she does the laundry, the ironing, all the housework."

In her struggle to manage the family household and care for labour mobility, Milica relies on her daughter. She has developed a special gender-based relationship with her daughter alongside traditional family structures. Her daughter gets compensation, receiving "rewards" for taking over household tasks. Milica's experience of labour mobility alters how gender is ascribed not just in economic terms, but in terms of her self-esteem as a responsible parent and her sense of achievement in her family life:

"They are not bad kids ... I am not saying this because they are mine, but they are both kind and quiet. Well, how long is it going to be like that? I don't know (she laughs). They are not the kind of kids who cause trouble. The friends of my daughter are going out to clubs, drinking alcohol, smoking, and so on – she does none of that!"

Later in the interview, when we talk about her plans and prospects for the future, Milica emphasizes the values that she has inherited from her parents and those which she wants to transmit to her children:

"I raise my children and teach them so that ... you see, I didn't get much from my parents, probably because they didn't have much to give ... but I have always given to my parents. That's how I teach my children. It doesn't matter how someone behaves or whether that person gives you something or not. I am their parent, and they must respect me no matter what. I think that my children will be like that and that I will be able to count on their help when I get old."

It seems that care labour mobility has sharpened her attitudes towards parenthood. Milica compares herself with the other women who she got to know during her journeys to Germany in the context of her care labour mobility, and she again talks about the importance of parental values:

"The women who come to work here, are women in their 60s. Their children sit at home with their asses in the armchair, watching TV, going out, and having fun while their mothers come here to earn their salaries and pensions and to feed their children. I feel sorry for those women. When I was traveling by mini-bus I was listening to their stories ... I got sick. Then, I turned to one of them and said: 'Look, I may be young enough to be your daughter, but I am telling you, you are not normal.' I was brought up by my parents in a patriarchal manner – my father is very strict with me even today. I am very careful what I say in front of him."

In the interview excerpt above Milica implies that her strong character is a consequence of her upbringing and describes her decisive and clear path in life as a parent and care worker. In sub-chapter 5.4 I demonstrated how Milica's attitude towards care work is entrenched in a personal set of beliefs

THE PRIVATE HOUSEHOLD AS MICROCOSM OF SOCIAL INEQUALITIES   345

associated with her identity as an elder care worker – she is hard-working, committed to the person she cares for, aware of the negative side of care work and honest about her position and role in the German household.

During the two interviews I carried out with Milica, she always presented herself as a hard-working working-class woman who is not tied down to one particular place, who has open plans for the future, and who places a strong emphasis on the importance of family happiness and personal fulfillment over and against the maximization of financial income. Milica is a tall woman, energetic, with the hoarse voice of a smoker and a big smile. During our first interview, I couldn't help but notice her big hands with their rough skin and the dark circles under her eyes. Being an observant kind of person, Milica spotted me looking at her hands and started to narrate her life story:

"I had a very bad life ... very bad, it was a disaster ... I went through a lot. Life did not spoil me at all ... not when I was a child, especially not when I was a young girl, not even when I got married and formed my own family ... I can't say which part was the worst. The stairs went lower and lower, until I found myself at the bottom of the well. Then I made a break and said this is enough. I can't continue like this, even if I lose everyone around me. Now I am fine. But you see, my family here, where I work ... they don't know this. They know me as a positive person who is cheerful, untroubled, joyful ... which is how I want them to see me. I don't want people to know I have a problem. And I don't want to talk about that. They do ask sometimes why I am sad, but I don't want to talk about such personal things with them."

Although Milica doesn't reveal the details of the hardships that she faced in her younger days, there is one event in her life that can help to explain who she is today and the life path that she has taken. Milica was born and raised in Croatia until she was 14 years of age, in a village called Borovo on the current border between Croatia and Serbia. At the start of the 1990s, at the beginning of the civil war in the former Yugoslavia, the border zone, and this village, were the site of a military conflict between Serbian para-military forces that led to the massacre and imprisonment of thousands of people both on the Croatian and on the Serbian side. By 1995, most of the ethnic Serbs in the border zone had fled to Serbia and become refugees. Milica and her family escaped the war zone and moved to Novi Sad, the capital of Northern Serbia, in 1993. I cannot say with certainty what Milica might have experienced between 1991 and 1993, but we can guess that during this period military operations in the border area caused thousands of deaths and the complete devastation of towns and villages making everyday life almost impossible. What we do know, however, is that Milica and her family, like many Croatian Serb refugees who were forced to leave Croatia, remained legally Croatian citizens. Today Milica holds two citizenships – Croatian and Serbian. As Croatia became a European Union member state in 2013, Milica has access to regular employment as a caregiver (*Pflegekraft* in German) through a home care recruitment agency. She is not paid by the family or care receiver, but by the agency and she is entitled to social security contributions. This is how Milica explains her working arrangement:

"All women who have Hungarian documents – you know, passports and identity cards, Croatian, Hungarian, or some other EU papers – and who work through an agency must have a job contract. I work regularly. My family [the family where she works] does not want to do it illegally. They do not want problems. Women who work illegally stand in their way. I understand those women … there are a lot of them … I have a lot of friends who do this job without papers or declaring their work but they create problems for themselves. You know why you came, you know you work illegally, you know you can't get a contract … so? But, they are better paid. They keep telling me: 'We would never work for 1000 euros, absolutely not!' Unlike them, I have retirement income, social benefits, and health insurance. After five years of working in Germany, I am entitled to a German pension. I will earn enough and those five years will pass quickly. However, as I told you, I have other plans … nothing is certain until the last moment. I do everything at the last minute. I have a plan for everyone to come here next year in September, October. How that will be, I don't know. I can't say that I will do something, because maybe I won't."

Milica's contract as an elder caregiver defines her duties and job tasks throughout each 24 hours, her breaks during the day, and her entitlement to one free day in each working week:

"My free time is from 13h to 15h every day and I am entitled to one day off per week. But I don't use that day. They told me, if you want, you are free to go.
T: [interrupting] Why not?
What would I do all day? And it's not the whole day, because in the morning I have to prepare granny for the day … and then I have to prepare lunch and then I am free until dinner. Normally, I would have six to seven hours off work and be free to go wherever I want, but I don't need that, I spend this time with them. Every weekend we go somewhere … to the Black Forest for a walk. Klaus (the old man) can't wait for lunchtime. As soon as we are done eating he says: 'Let's go.' I visited so many places with them."

How Milica portrays her relationship with the family she works for, shows exceptional closeness and a level of personal relationship that goes beyond her contract:

THE PRIVATE HOUSEHOLD AS MICROCOSM OF SOCIAL INEQUALITIES 347

"You know, when you get the contract, you can see that it says that you have to do this task or that task and so on. And that's it – most of the women that I know who are contract care workers like me, stick strictly to that piece of paper. Why? If you want to feel good in that family, you simply cannot stick to that document. If you want someone to pay attention to you, to accept you, to make you an equal member of the family you cannot stick to that paper either in life or at work. Well, that's what I think, that's my attitude and I will always be satisfied. I don't want to think, I am not interested in paper. It's just a piece of paper that the agency gave to me, but I live and work in that family. My main obligation is to Ursula (the old lady). I have to cook for her, wash her, iron her clothes, wipe her, tidy up and clean her room – that is my obligation. I also have her husband and their son."

Milica's example demonstrates that, even though her daily tasks are specified by her job contract, in situations where a private home becomes a place of work it can be hard to maintain a sense of distance and not to develop and foster personal relationships. It is interesting to see how Milica constructs and deconstructs social and cultural boundaries between herself and the family and the extent to which these processes are determined by both her work contract and other factors that I analyze meticulously in Chapter 7.2. As mentioned earlier, Milica fled to Serbia during the Yugoslav wars in 1993. Since then she has been living in the town of Novi Sad where she obtained her secondary education, got married, and brought up two children. She never had a vocational job but took up a variety of different positions as a waitress, as a seasonal agricultural laborer, and in sales. She never worked as a caregiver, and before she came to Germany for care work, Milica was working as a cashier in the supermarket for a salary of 200 euros. Like many women with secondary education, she couldn't find a better-paid job, and the income she had was not enough to keep her household economy alive.

"At some point I had enough and decided to quit my job ... suddenly ... just so ... without thinking at all ... one day I said: 'I am not working tomorrow ... I'm quitting.'"

With the help of her brother's wife, who at the time also worked as a care worker in Germany, Milica found her route into care labour mobility.

"When I left for Germany for the first time, I did not know the German language, everything was new to me. But I wanted it. I wanted to try, at any cost ... if it is bad – good! I'll go back ... that's not a problem."

The excerpt above shows that, like most of the women care workers I have interviewed, Milica's aspirations and motivation for care labour mobility are a combination of the opportunity to overcome financial difficulties and the prospect of adventure or "trying something out". The usual associations of "trying something out" when understood as putting minimal investment into something that may or may not work, however, contrast with the actual investment of time and the money that is needed to start to travel to Germany as a care worker. As someone with little knowledge of German, Milica had to attend language school and take private German lessons before searching for a job. Her job search itself was carried out through friends and relatives. And, in the end, she found the job which she described above through a woman who worked as a sub-recruiter for a German agency that recruits care and domestic workers from Eastern Europe. She has been working in that position caring for an elderly lady with Alzheimer's disease for the last two years:

"I came to this family only as a replacement. I should have changed family after three weeks. But then Klaus and his sons said that they would like me to stay as a contracted worker for a longer time if I wanted to. That's how it was."

When I asked Milica how she decided to come to Germany, she described herself as someone without a need to be rooted in one place:

"Well you know, me and my husband function alone. He has his dad and I have my dad ... but his family is a disaster. We have been together for the last 15 years. For a while, we lived with his parents. Then, they threw us out on the street, and we have been alone since that day. We don't get any help, either from my side of the family or from his. We don't own the house, we are renting an apartment and we are tenants ... the rent must be paid every month. But, that's not a problem for me. I always say that I do not need to own a house, to have a home. My home is where I am. Right now, my home is here (in Germany). When I say to my husband and children that I am going to Germany, I always say 'I am going to my second home'. Because the house here is also my home.
My husband and I always make decisions together and that's it. He would now like him to come here too, even though I am not sure about that because our life [in Serbia] differs from the life here in Germany. It's all nice, you can earn more here ... yes ... but, in a way, I want my children to have a better future, but I don't want this kind of life for them. I want them to live like me, not to suffer, but to live. There is no such thing here.
T: What is that thing that you miss here?
What do they have here? They go to school after they finish school, they start to work ... and work and work. There is no friendship like we have in Serbia ... and friendship means a lot to me. I have many friends. I have people who love me and that's the most important thing to me. The most important thing is that you have

someone who loves and respects you wherever you are and that is why money is not crucial in my life at all. It is important, but it is not crucial. I came here for the money. When I look back, I think I made a lot of money. Where is that money now? Gone. It's just a paper. Today you have it, tomorrow it is gone."

Milica's sense of not being anchored in one place, which may have arisen out of her experience as a refugee, stands in contrast to her idealization of a "sedentary life" in her home country, which centers around the values and norms that stem from a dynamic social and family life, family commitment and "location-specific values", all of which she misses in Germany. Factors such as good earning opportunities and her combination of care labour mobility with life in her home country cut down on the extra expenses of a second household in Germany. This cost-saving constellation is one of the main motives that keep Milica commuting back and forth:

"What I am telling everyone is that, when someone comes to live in Germany to work and pays the rent, she … or he cannot earn as much money as we do like this moving back and forth. We earn a lot more like this. I know that I wouldn't have the money I earn now if my family came here too. Because I would automatically have to pay for the apartment, all kinds of bills, buy food, and so on … of course, my husband would earn money as well … that's okay. But that's not it! It would not be like this … when I go home, the money I earned here in Germany, I spend it … yes, I do but I enjoy it. To live in Germany with that amount of money – I wouldn't enjoy that, for sure. I know that.
T: Because the living costs would be higher, right?
No, no, it's not that. For example, now I am going back home, and I will be at home with my kids for six weeks. I will enjoy every moment I am given with them. Christmas is coming, there are birthday parties to go to, then we will go to Kopaonik [a ski resort in Serbia] to ski, we go here, we go there … What do I have here? I would have a vacation once, maybe twice, a year, 20 days. I may have the same money, but I wouldn't have any friends. I've got some friends here as well but that's not it. I always say, people here are cold-hearted … I don't know how to explain that. That's not what I want, although, it's not only up to me to decide. We may all be here next year."

Milica's preference for circular mobility between Germany and Serbia has both cultural and social dimensions to it, as the excerpts above make clear. The impossibility of relocating the center of her life to Germany enhances her care labour mobility. The constraining factors which Milica describes concerning migration into Germany have been formed throughout her life and are assessed in relation to imagined alternatives. Economic calculations as well as her negative perceptions of the German "way of life" further strengthen her mobility preferences. However, when I bring up the topic of the future, Milica offers a much less clear-cut decision about migration:

"T: How long do you think you will do this job?
M: I don't know how long. They [the family she works for] want me to stay here as long as Ursula is alive. Well, tomorrow, Klaus will need someone to take care of him … so, they would like me to be there.
T: And would you like to?
V: Well I don't know what I would like. I don't know at the moment what I want. I would like this and that. I've talked to them before. They told me that if I wanted to come here to live with my family, they would help me. Well, then I said that I wanted it, and then came a period when I didn't want it, and then again came a period when I wanted it, and so on.
T: And what do the children say?
V: My son would move to Germany immediately. My daughter would like to finish her last year in high school here in Serbia, and then she would like to go to university in Germany. We'll see …"

Today Milica Jeremic lives with her family in Heilbronn. She has two part-time jobs. Her husband attends German language school and works part time and her son goes to school whilst her daughter is studying at university. Frau Ursula died in January 2019, but her husband, Klaus, is still alive. The two families formed a very strong bond and visit each other regularly. After Frau Ursula's death, Milica worked as a caregiver in two families and, in the summer of 2020, she finally moved to Germany with her family.

7.2 Underplaying Social Boundaries. *"Du bist mein Goldstück!" – "Well, I Am."*

The household setting: A village in Baden Wurttemberg; a family house with a large garden
The length of time Milica had worked for the family at the time of the interview: 2 years
Members of the household:
Ursula (the elderly woman who Milica cares for, age 78)
Klaus (Ursula's husband, age 83)
Stefan, their youngest son (age 40, single, employed in an auto-industry Mercedes Benz)

THE PRIVATE HOUSEHOLD AS MICROCOSM OF SOCIAL INEQUALITIES 351

Two cats
In the other house, in the same village live:
Martin, the oldest son
Conny, Martin's wife
Their three children

As can be seen from her portrait that opens this chapter, Milica is well integrated into the family, primarily as a result of her work caring for Ursula, who suffers from Alzheimer's disease. In the previous chapters, I demonstrated how Milica has become invested in the care relationship because of the physical and emotional strains of the care process. Here, Milica describes the family knowledgeably, and in her own words:

"Grandpa Klaus worked for 'Mercedes-Benz' for 35 years. He has been retired for almost thirty years now. Klaus is 83 years old. But he looks like a young guy … let me show you the pictures [Milica searches for the photos on her phone; there are a lot of pictures]. Ursula is 78 years old and she was a housewife. She has no pension, she has never worked … nothing. Klaus worked in the Mercedes engine production facility … you know, on the engine itself. He explained to me in detail what exactly he was working on … something about fuel cells … I forgot because I am not interested in it. Every morning he tells me stories from the factory, but I just pretend I am listening [she laughs].
Granny Ursula can't feed herself. She can't drink without assistance. She wears diapers 24 hours a day. She can't do anything, she doesn't know how to hold a spoon. Sometimes she can hold the spoon, but she can't bring it to her mouth. She speaks indistinctly, we can't make out what she is saying. She doesn't know how to say when she is hungry, she doesn't know how to say when she is thirsty. Sometimes she recognizes us, sometimes she doesn't. Often, she just stares in front of her. Sometimes she talks to dead people …

Alongside her care work, Milica cleans, washes, cooks and takes care of the rest of the family, including their two cats. She sees her role as someone who is an equal member of the family but who has specifically defined tasks. Her job, and the regulatory context of that job, becomes a context for the construction and deconstruction of family boundaries as Milica and the rest of the family negotiate different issues that arise out of their working relationship:

"I know what my tasks in the household are. They live a completely different life from me. They get up in the morning and they don't care whether, for instance, this glass is over here or over there, or whether it's in the sink or it's been washed. When I come out of that kitchen, I leave the kitchen as clean as if no one's ever been in it. Of course, there are dirty plates, glasses, pans. I go to the kitchen three times a day and clean everything. What happens in the meantime, that's not my problem. I do my job, they can see it and that's that."

Although Milica's job contract as a "care assistant" (Germ. *Pflegeaushilfe*) specifies tasks that she has to carry out, relating to the elderly lady's hygiene and nutrition, Milica also does the laundry, cooks, gardens, feeds the cats, and so on. However, from the following excerpt, we can see that Milica defines the labor relationship and the labour contract in her way:

"My opinion is … you know … you get the contract, and the contract states you must do this, you must do that – that's it. All the women I know stick strictly to this contract. Why do they do that? If you want to feel good in the family, to have someone to pay attention to you, to accept you, to be an equal member of the family, you cannot stick to that piece of paper – either in life or at work. That's how I think, and I will always be fine. Do you know why? Because I am not interested in the paper. The contract is just a piece of paper given to me by an agency. I live and work in this family! That's something different."

This illustrates not just that being a live-in care worker in the big family as Milica frames it, cannot be based on a common labour contract with a set timetable and clearly defined and separate roles. In answer to my question about the workload in the household Milica explained in a very direct way what it means to "not to stick to the contract":

"Naturally, I do everything! In the house, I've got a sick, immobile old woman and two men. What else should I do? I wash, I clean, I iron, and I do the garden. Yes … because that is life. For example, I never go to Stefan's room. It is private. He cleans his room. But I wash his bedding, you know, his sheets and bed covers … because I don't know how not to do it. If I wash my bedding, grandpa's bedding, and grandma's bedding, how can I say, 'Hey Stefan, you wash yours separately'? That's impossible. But I don't have to do it. They could hire a cleaning lady, to help out but Katarina [her rotational colleague] and I would never agree to that. They discussed that with us, hiring a third woman who would come in from time to time to help. Katarina and I agreed – NO! A third woman is out of the question. Katarina and I are a really good team. We met at work; we didn't know each other before. We exchange information, solve problems together and have full confidence in each other."

It is clear that there is a blurred line between the tasks that Milica does for the old lady and those that she carries out for other members of the household, and that boundaries between the private and the professional are a matter of negotiation which form part of a moral contract. However, Milica stressed

The Private Household as Microcosm of Social Inequalities   353

several times that the family helps her a lot and that even tasks related to her care work are shared with Frau Ursula's sons.

"I cook for the four of us – grandma, grandpa, and the son who lives with them. When Martin and Conny come at the weekend I cook something they like, to indulge them. Then, the next weekend, they invite us. They say: 'Milice, don't cook next weekend. You come to us. We will make a grill.' Or, if I am tired, not in the mood for cooking, the youngest son brings Döner, and then we have that for lunch or dinner. It depends on the day ..."

Milica continues her narrative, stressing how the "extra" tasks she does do not remain unrewarded and unappreciated by the family:

"Well, yes ... all the things I do, like cooking, like warming the meal up when Stefan comes back from work ... I don't have to do any of that. But I do it out of goodwill. The truth is, we are very well rewarded for that, both Katarina and I. We really get a lot of gifts from all of them ... Stefan [the youngest son] brings us flowers and chocolates and other stuff. For example, I am a smoker. Grandfather buys me cigarettes. Since I came to this family, I have been smoking cigarettes that cost 7 Euros a packet. If I bought them myself, it would be too much for me. I have everything I need here. More than that. To be honest, I can't complain. When I go home, I always get a gift from the family. I know when it's Easter, when it's Christmas when it's my birthday. Although I've been to Serbia for my birthday every year, I always get a greetings card and money. I get Weihnachtsgeld from Klaus separately from the others. Grandpa adores me, he says: 'You are our Schatzi. You are my everything in the world.'"

It is evident, from the excerpt above, that Milica's labour relationship with the family is characterized by a strong degree of personalization. She works as if the house is hers, and she receives both responsibility and gratitude from the family. While this description of her "contract" is based on notions of gratitude, shared responsibilities, a sense of duty, and reciprocity, Milica frames her work for the family as altruistic, without any ambition to simply "take the money". Even in labour relationships like this one, with their resemblance to family relationships, negotiations over the salary and working conditions are inevitable.

When Milica came to the family as a care worker, she was employed through a placement agency operating in Germany with a sub-intermediary from Serbia. However, Milica wasn't satisfied with their new payment policy. Signing a contract with an agency gave Milica a certain level of protection when it comes to working rights, social benefits, and a pension, but being tied to the agency put her in a legally precarious position because it wasn't easy to leave the contract. She explained this situation in very emphatic terms:

"They started to cause trouble with payments … Because you know, when we go home, we are always paid in advance – a day or two before we leave, they transfer money to our account. However, they introduced a new rule that they would pay us on the 5th day after the beginning of the month. And I go home earlier. So, how can I have my money? I don't want that. I protested, but the agency said that the boss had made the decision. I said to them: 'That's the boss's problem, not mine.' They asked whether I wanted to stay with them or not. I replied that I didn't know if I would stay or not, but I didn't want to work under such conditions. The agency threatened me with court action and blocked my account. I said: 'Do what you think you have to do. I know my rights and my obligations.' I was so upset, Tanja, I was shouting, my hands were shaking. After the phone call with the agency I had to feed Ursula and I couldn't do it."

Milica's conflict with the agency resulted in a crisis in the household where she worked. Since Milica couldn't change the contractual conditions, she was ready to terminate the contract with the agency and leave the family. When I asked her whether she wasn't afraid of losing a job in a family where she felt good, suddenly Milica started drawing boundaries between economic and moral contract:

T: It seems that they are good employers, aren't they? It would be tough to lose that job, right?
M: Yes, but I would not work for other people. I have no fear. If I am not satisfied with something, I say goodbye. The biggest problem with our women is that they have a great desire to work, to earn money, on the one hand, and on the other hand, they have fear, at the same time. I think that when you come to work here – you must not DO anything! Why? There is no 'have to do' …
T: Well, those who work here without a contract, they have to be careful not to get fired?
M: Correct. But if the job is bad, you have nothing to fear … there are all the elderly people you could want. I had so many offers … you wouldn't believe it, even for 1700 euros."

Milica can negotiate because she is aware that there is a shortage of care workers in the care labour market in Germany. She doesn't face financial pressure because she knows she can find a similar or a better job. The second reason is that Milica has the self-confidence in her care performance as she has been loyal and hard working for the last two years, taking good care of the old lady. When the family realized that Milica would leave if they did not come to another agreement, she initiated negotiations over contract condi-

THE PRIVATE HOUSEHOLD AS MICROCOSM OF SOCIAL INEQUALITIES

tions with the family by using the possibility of a better wage as bargaining leverage. This is how Milica described the process:

"I told them: the first condition is that I do not want to stay longer than two months at a time. That was always a problem (…) You know, we were very angry because they asked us to rotate rigidly every three months. Since they cover our travel costs, rotating more frequently would mean that Grandpa would have to pay more for travel, and he said he doesn't have that money. Then we offered to pay for these extra trips with our own money. They didn't accept that either. Then, I was tough and asked to go home every two months. The second condition is that I will not work for 1000 euros. Then Martin asked me: 'How much do you want to work for?' I said from 1200–1300 euros per month, minimum. I didn't want to go below that figure. The third condition is that, when I say that something is a problem, it is a problem. You know what your rights and obligations are, and so do I. You can't treat me as you want. I want my salary on time. Right? Right.

They said: 'All right, we will tell you tomorrow what we decide.' I said to them that they had 13 days to decide what they want. The next day Martin came to me and said: 'We will make a contract with you without the agency. You will have a salary of 1200 euros, netto. You will have everything paid for like it's been up to now. Just give us a few days to make inquiries about the contract.' I said okay and it was like he said."

Milica can afford to risk the consequences of open confrontation because she is "not afraid to lose the job". In the excerpt below she is resorting to the principle of equality and mutuality – "if you say things to me, I will say them back":

"I didn't want to work for that money anymore. And I got it. Yes … I did. But … you see … if you keep your head down and do not fight for yourself no one will look at you. They would never look at me if I kept quiet. I believe that, do you understand? I do not let them do whatever they want with me … whatever they say to me, I say back to them. I always say that I only want what is mine. I don't need what's theirs. I can always say goodbye! If you can find someone better than me, then go on, and good luck with that! They had Polish women; they had Romanians, and they created chaos, they stole from them. Conny told me that, after the Polish woman left, she had to scrub the kitchen, the bathroom, and take the garbage out because she didn't do anything. She would just sit down from morning until noon doing her nails and putting make-up on. And now after what they experienced with me … this older son, Martin, he says you are my 'Goldstück', my piece of gold. Well, I am. They respect us and they show that."

Milica's description of her working relationship demonstrates that her work is rewarded and appreciated. Through the course of the interview, Milica referred to the best working relationships as those that "feel like being a part of the family". While much of my research findings have demonstrated that "familiarise" in the working relationship is simply a strategy used by employers to demand extra work or increase the workload, in Milica's case we find no evidence for that. Her story about negotiating working conditions demonstrates that Milica openly establishes boundaries between professional and private, and between distancing and closeness in the context of labor regulations. She challenges her status by switching from a "moral contract" embedded in the dense social and generational relations of the family, to a "rational, monetary contract" where she demonstrates the agency necessary to negotiate her position, deploying a firm knowledge of the market of commodified care in Germany and the level of market demand as well as rates of pay. The fact that she "knows her worth", which she confirms when being compared "piece of gold" allows us to depict Milica as a person with dignity and self-respect who can constantly navigate unwritten rules that are under constant negotiation.

It is important to point out that Germany's "person-related services" market (*personenbezogene Dienstleistungen* in German) is differently structured and regulated from those of post-colonial countries such as France, the United Kingdom, the US and Asian and Middle Eastern countries, which have long traditions of service and servitude and where most of the research on domestic and care work has been conducted. Power relations in Germany are more complex, and it would be wrong, therefore, to apply the concept of "instrumental personalism" as a strategy for ensuring a good quality of care, or to look at the personalism of employers necessarily as manipulation of family ideologies for the extraction of extra (unpaid) labour. Instead, we need to examine carefully how, and for what reasons, care workers describe a working relationship as good. When Milica talks about familiarity, emotions, and being a kin-like member of the household, that does not mean that her statement is not authentic. If we, as researchers, position ourselves as omnipotent observers who can detect the "true condition" of women as oppressed and exploited, then we are at risk of overlooking the ways in which women are often aware of analogizing them as daughters or sisters. Also, if we overlook their capability for using this analogy as simply a rhetorical means deployed by employers to maximize the quality or quantity of labour, we will brush off cases where strong sentiments of mutual affection, really can develop in care work. Consider the following situation, when Milica found herself in personal emotional hardship because of a sick parent whom she couldn't help because she was in Germany:

THE PRIVATE HOUSEHOLD AS MICROCOSM OF SOCIAL INEQUALITIES   357

"Soon after I arrived here for the first time, my dad had a stroke … I couldn't do anything. I cried so much. I couldn't concentrate on my job … I could hardly do anything for the granny. I called Martin and Conny to come to help me with granny … although I know that she is my responsibility, and I would never ask for them to come. They have a life of their own. It was me that said that I will call them only if I really need them … if there is a problem I cannot solve. But they always say: 'If you need something, we will always come.' So, when that happened with my dad, they drove me 150 km from here to see my friends, to have someone to talk to in my mother tongue. They are really … I cannot explain that … they are like my second family. No, they ARE my second family. I know that I am not alone, I have them."

Situations like this show that Milica's closeness to the family is not something artificial or acted but, rather, that it has been brought about by human and caring gestures from her employers at the moment when she needed support. While it has been argued, in the majority of studies on domestic work, that power inequalities make domestic workers more dependent on employers, when it comes to elder care work, care receivers and their families also invest themselves into treating care workers "as one of the family". More specifically, Parreñas has shown that female care workers can manipulate the attachment that develops from the closeness between domestic workers and employers just as much as their employers. Researchers often forget that employers can also become attached to domestic workers. As the excerpt below shows, personalization of the labour relationship can also be generated through the "attachment" of family members to the person being cared for:

"For example, when someone from the family, their sons, or Conny wants to tell me something, show me how to do something, or correct me, Klaus starts shouting: 'Please, leave her alone.' I am as his child. He cries every time I go to Serbia. It is a tragedy. Three days before leaving, every morning at breakfast he cries: 'What am I going to do without you now? Do you know how long three months is? What am I going to do?' Then I comfort him saying: 'Grandpa, now we will rotate more quickly, every two months.' But for him, that is stressful. He cries for Katarina (the colleague Milica rotates with) just as much. He is like that, they are all like that. We may have been lucky because you know, they're very emotional. They are not that cold and distanced like Germans."

The excerpt above demonstrates how Milica finds emotionality and affection towards her to be an exception from the common image of Germany as a cold-hearted and aloof nation that stems from cultural and ethnic stereotypes. She has been "adopted" by her employers as their "fictive kin", a term which refers to "those who provide care like family and do what family does and are given the labor of kin with its attendant affection, rights, and obligations" (Karner 1998: 70). However, her status, as she narrates in the interview excerpt below, is not peripheral. This becomes obvious during family celebrations and in the social organization of space during festive meals:

"This was when I came here for the first time ... now I can't remember exactly when that was ... but it was some celebration ... someone's birthday or something. There was a table in the dining room which wasn't that big ... a few people could sit down, but the house was packed. Many people came. I was in the kitchen, preparing the food for serving and Martin was with me helping. I told him: 'Would you please go and sit with Ursula and feed her some cake ... I don't want to make a crowd over there, okay?' You know, I was thinking that there was no need for me to be there ... I didn't know anyone and my German was awful at that time. I was talking normally with the family because I wasn't ashamed if I made mistake. But with other people, I didn't feel comfortable. As I said that he closed the kitchen doors, turned to me, and said: 'You said that this once, but never again. You are an equal member of the family here as we all are. You have your place at the table and please don't shy away from us.'"

In most cases, women care workers do not experience spatial segregation like other domestic workers do, because the nature of their care tasks requires physical presence. In households without a spatial deficit and where the family lives with an elderly person, women can sometimes be allowed to use only the space where the elderly person resides. In some cases, like in Isidora's case, which I discussed in the previous chapter, the elderly person and care worker can use a whole floor for themselves, while the rest of the family lives separately in the rest of the house. This arrangement allows more freedom for the care worker and privacy for the family. In Milica's case, the whole space of the household is available to her. There are no social boundaries put up on the side of employers, nor does Milica seek to establish any, as she prefers to socialize with the rest of the family:

"I have my room in the house. I have my TV. But I spend the least time in my room. I don't like being alone. My room is on the ground floor, I just sleep there. From morning until midnight, I am upstairs with the family. When I put the granny to bed, then I take a shower, put my pyjamas on and watch a movie with them upstairs. Or, we go out, or have dinner together and so on. If I had to be the only person in a house with an elderly person, I would probably die."

Milica's integration into the family is shown by her participation in family celebrations, visits to the cemetery, religious holidays, family outings, small trips, etc. The main reason that she has become respected and accepted by the family is Milica's attitudes towards cultural differences. She is highly flex-

THE PRIVATE HOUSEHOLD AS MICROCOSM OF SOCIAL INEQUALITIES   359

ible and shows her ability to adapt to the family's needs, habits, and everyday way of life. The significance of national-ethnic distinctions can be seen in the consumption and preparation of food. One of the biggest constraints that hinders a good relationship between women care workers and their employers is a lack of interest in the preparation of traditional German food and associated customs. Milica's example demonstrates the opposite. Making a comparison with her rotational colleague, Milica asserts:

"You see Tanja, they are used to eating their food. They have eaten it all their life. And, you see, my colleague, for example, doesn't want to cook German dishes. She does not want to learn how to cook them, nothing. From the start she was straight with them: 'I am a fifty-something-year-old woman and I simply do not want to learn how to cook now at this age. I will cook what I know and in the way, I know how.' This was not a big issue for Ursula, because she doesn't notice what she eats. For Klaus and Stefan, it is different because they are healthy ... so I said I wanted to learn how to cook.
T: How did you learn?
M: They all taught me, but mostly, Stefan. He would say 'take this, take that, cook this long, put that inside' and so on. I make Schwäbische potato salad better than them ... as if I had been born here [she laughs].

Cultural values and beliefs have a pivotal role in the employment dynamics and boundary work within the household. In situations where women care workers and employers (elderly individuals and their families) do not share the same cultural outlook there can be difficulties in forming a closer personal connection. In the narrative below, Milica describes how a culture of "gift-giving" and attitudes towards money serves to establish an interactive dynamic between aspects of distancing and personalization:

"Grandpa Klaus told me once ... we were discussing ... I don't remember what exactly, but he went: 'You have little money. You have to be careful with money. You have to save, you have children.' We were in the bakery, all together and I bought Brezel for myself and all of them. I can't buy for just myself and not for them. That's crazy, I would never do that. So, I paid for everyone ... and he immediately goes: 'How much was that? Let me give you the money.' He wanted to pay for it. I say: 'It costs nothing, Klaus. Put the money away!' I was thinking ... get lost, you and your money! I have my own money! He sees it differently. I understand that. He wants to pay me back ... but they are used to receiving gifts from me. That's normal to me. When I go shopping if I see something that, for example, Stefan would like ... or I am going to buy this for Conny for Christmas, I will buy this for Martin. It is completely normal to give gifts. I live with them! Then they say: 'You shouldn't spend that much on us, you have to save the money.' And I reply to them: 'You are original Schwaben. You always save the money, you will take the money to the grave ...

People, what are you doing? However, I have the impression that they have changed because of me ..."'"

In a very subtle way, Milica makes a distinction between her collective culture of sharing and gift-giving and more-individualistic German attitudes towards money through a process of cultural Othering. Here we can see how Milica's value judgment is tightly linked to cultural stereotyping of Germans as cheap, stingy money savers. In Milica's narrative, attitudes towards money show how distance and closeness interact. While "gift-giving" demonstrates Milica's way of expressing personal and affectionate relationships with the family, at the same time she highlights their equal status by strategically insisting on paying for Brezel in the bakery. Through insisting on paying, Milica contests the asymmetry of power relations and the protective behavior exhibited by family members who, in expressing their concern regarding Milica's mastery of her finances, position themselves as moral guardians, with Milica as their inferior protégé.

The question of paternalism and maternalism in domestic employment sometimes arises in the literature. For instance, Hondagneu-Sotelo (2007: 184) describes how acting as a personal benefactor to a migrant domestic worker can allow (mostly female) employers to experience themselves as "generous, altruistic, and kind" and to receive "personal recognition and appreciation" (Hondagneu-Sotelo 2007: 187). As Rollins (1985) documented, "benevolent maternalism" can be illustrated through the example of "gift-giving" – where employers give away second-hand or discarded items, especially old clothes, as "gifts" to domestic workers. However, my material indicates that the practice of "gift-giving" does not necessarily signify control, but instead can demonstrate gratitude and respect on the part of employers, which, in turn, can result in better relationships and greater benefits for women care workers, for their families and the elderly person themselves.

The situation that Milica describes in the excerpt below demonstrates the negotiation of the boundary's privacy (on both sides) concerning money and spending:

"Conny asked me why I work so hard. It was not clear to her why, for example, I work both here and at home. Because I can. I can always go back to the company where I worked before and work part-time. For example, for three months I work for them and then two months at home. I arranged it like that. I kept my status in my previous company because I was a very good worker and I earned that trust. But they are so curious about what I am doing with all this money that I earn. Because you know, they are puzzled that I cannot live on just the salary I earn here when

The Private Household as Microcosm of Social Inequalities   361

before I could live on 200 euros per month. Well, I say: 'Conny, I spend more now because there are other desires and goals in life. I don't know how to describe this … but I want to live! I am alive!' Then she tried to calculate how much I earn and how much my husband earns … I don't like that! I don't like that she interferes with my finances. It's mine! And I decide about that. But she apologized to me at the end. She realized that she hurt me … that's because we talk about everything openly."

Conny's curiosity regarding Milica's expenditures is not understood simply as interfering in her private life, rather well-intentioned practices and concerns regarding finances conceal broader issues of control. In refusing to talk about money, Milica chooses to confront Conny's judgment of her lifestyle and intrusion into her privacy to preserve her dignity and self-identity. Maintaining a sense of distance from the family when it comes to her private life seems to work differently for her and her employers. Another aspect of boundary work that raises tensions is the issue of family secrets. At the beginning of our interview, when I asked Milica how big the family is and whether the son who lives separately with his wife has children, she answered at great length, presenting her knowledge about the personal lives of each member of the family. In answering at length, Milica displays her close relationship with the family:

Well … they do have children, but the family will not have offspring.
T: What do you mean by that?
I mean, Martin is not the biological father of their kids. His wife, Conny, married him 19 years ago. However, she had three children from a previous marriage. I asked him … it's not a problem for me to ask … 'Do you mind not having your own children?' He replied that that was not a problem for him at all. He knew that she couldn't have more children. And that's it … he made his peace. He says: 'I have three children. They are my children too.' They were small when she married him. It is interesting … he is not the biological son of his father, Klaus. Martin is the son of Ursula's first marriage. And this son who lives with them, he is their biological son. I didn't know all this at the beginning. I found it out a year ago. But now … now I know everything. I know everything about their life. Their younger son, who lives here with us … he is somehow different … something is wrong there … I think that comes from his parents and upbringing … but I wouldn't go into intimate details. I know a lot. Klaus told me everything. Who is going to inherit what, what he gave to whom, is the size of his pension, and so on. He always mentions when he gets the Weihnachtsgeld from Mercedes."

Although Milica's relationship with Klaus is close and open, the rest of the family members confide their secrets and personal information selectively, while requesting from Milica details of her financial affairs. She finds it de-

362 PERIPHERAL LABOUR MOBILITIES

grading and offending when the family shows openly that some information is out of her reach:

"But you know, I was open with them – I don't like secrets. I can't stand it when someone is hiding something in front of me. I can't stand it when someone lies. I said to them: 'If you have something to say which is not for my ears, then please say it when I leave the room or ask me to leave. Don't whisper at the table while I'm sitting there.'"

Milica describes her reaction to a situation when Conny talked about how much they pay for different insurance policies by whispering to make sure that Milica couldn't hear:

"I told her: 'Conny, feel free to speak out loud. You are not paying it out of my pocket. Pay 300 or 3 million euros – it's irrelevant to me. It's none of my business. I am not interested in anything that is not related to me.'"

When I asked Milica whether she thinks that they do not want to be open with their finances because they think she might make some calculations regarding her salary she said:

"It is definitely like that. I looked into their eyes, saying 'how much does your family spend per month?'. They said they spend 500 euros on food and basic things. Then, I continued to ask how much they pay for different kinds of insurance, for health insurance, car insurance, and so on. I asked them 'how much do you earn at the end of the month? You do know how much I earn, right? You don't feel comfortable talking about that, right? Well, I am sorry, but for me, it is uncomfortable as well. You would rather not talk about it … I work here for peanuts … Germans would never work for this money. That's why you brought us here – there you go.' I always say to them what I think. I have never remained quiet.

It seems that the negotiation of privacy is intertwined with struggles over personal and intimate details on the one hand, and, as the excerpt above describes, over fair working conditions on the other. Generally, we can conclude that Milica constructs and deconstructs social boundaries to highlight her equal relationship with her employers by confronting them regarding her salary and contract conditions, drawing boundaries to preserve her dignity and pride. In conclusion, I do not claim that Milica's affectionate and close relationship with the family is entirely based on equal power relations – it is not. But we know that power relations exist even within biological families and real kin relationships. Although we cannot overlook the importance of monetary exchange, we should be aware that care relationships involve complex forms of exchange – not only money but also mutual affection and love. On the other hand, it allows us to better see and understand Milica's agency and inventiveness in resisting the power inequalities inherent in paid reproductive labour.

7.3 Highlighting Social Boundaries. *"Don't Touch Me, Your Hands Are Dirty."*

Household setting: Baden Württemberg; family house
The length of time Ivana worked for the family: one year and a half in rotations of two-three months
Members of the household:
Elizabeth von XY: age 91, blind; a widow
Elizabeth's daughters:
Isabella has three children: a widow
Antonia has one (nonmarital) daughter

In the previous case, I demonstrated how the micro-politics of the household is characterized by the downplay of social distance and power asymmetries. This is mirrored in sitting at the table with the family while having meals, joining family outings, welcoming them into the living room to watch television together with the family, seek conversations about Milica's background and family life. In contrast to this, Ivana's case falls into the category of boundary work conducted by upper-class employers who highlight the hierarchical differences between themselves and Ivana. With an analysis of Ivana's narratives, I want to show how the boundaries are negotiated in domestic politics of food, privacy, and spatial and temporal aspects of Ivana's work and life in the household and Ivana's attempts to make these boundaries permeable and construct alternative ones. Secondly, I aim to describe the situations where the employer determines to what extent to include or exclude Ivana and when the hierarchical differences are highlighted or downplayed between two parties.

Ivana's labour relationship with her employers is specific and unique in my research sample for several reasons. Firstly, her working language is English which is very unusual among care receivers, as the majority of elderly people that I encountered through the research process do not speak any other language than German. Secondly, the family where Ivana worked is a German nobility family whose family members hold the rank of Count (Germ. Graf) or Countess (Germ. Gräfin), but they are not wealthy. The family has a long history of hiring domestic workers and has thus embodied class "habitus" (Bourdieu 1977), such as carrying more condescending verbal expressions and distant body language toward the domestic workers. The household is placed in a modern spacious house that allows a sufficient physical space, as well as social distance, to exist between Ivana and employers. The third distinctive characteristic of Ivana's job is a care task. The elderly woman, Elizabeth von XY is a blind woman in her nineties who was searching for the person who will be her assistant but also a domestic servant:

"I had to clean the house … including certain parts of the garden … cook, tidy up, to take care of things and her. I washed, ironed. But I had at least, I had some freedom to organize myself. For example, when I am going to wash or iron. I went to the store but only to do the shopping for myself or some small things for the household. Her daughter Antonia was doing weekly grocery shopping."

Ivana was required to be "always at the service". That means that Ivana's role in the household falls somewhere between an old lady's carer and housemaid.

Elizabeth is a moveable woman, of generally good health who was mostly dependent on assistance with personal hygiene and eating. During our interview, Ivana underlines several times how the recent sight loss affected Elizabeth's emotional state and her changed perceptions of self in relation to the world around her, as becoming dependant and thus vulnerable.

"You need to know that she lost her sight relatively late in her life. She drove a car until she was 89. When I came for the first time, she was crying for days … She cried because she went blind at her age."

The old lady's psychological state and specific set of physical and emotional needs have had a significant impact on the "boundary demarcations" in the household and on establishing relations that, in this case, are characterized by processes of cultural and intimate Othering. The complexity of Ivana's relationship with members of the household as a result of emotional dynamics between members of the family and their personal lives that greatly affected Ivana's working life. She describes them as follows:

"Granny has two daughters. The older one, Isabella, was coming once a month or every two weeks, every three weeks. She lived somewhere between France and Switzerland. She traveled to see her mother and usually stayed on Friday, Saturday and Sunday. When I arrived at the family those three days were the worst for me. Because that woman is even worse than Elizabeth. If it would be her way, we wouldn't be allowed to breathe the same air as them. Her English was very bad so I could barely communicate with her. The woman was pure evil. The younger daughter, Antonia, lives with Elizabeth. I could talk to her. She insisted on giving us breaks, helping with some things. She didn't interfere much in our work in the first year, at least not in mine. She helped us with the recipes since granny insisted on us cook only German cuisine. She helped us with the food in general. When I first came, she told me where what was, for example, here is the main street, here is the supermarket, here is this, there is that. So, some things were ok … far from being good, but I could talk to her during that first year. In the second year, the roles were reversed. The younger daughter, Antonia, was overwhelmed by taking care of her mother because it affected her relationship with her partner in their apartment. She moved in with granny because she couldn't have travelled from Wiesbaden every day. As time went by, she was getting more and more nervous. So, I was to be blamed for everything: for her messy life, for granny, for everything. Surprisingly, Isabella, the older one, who lives far away, started to be good to me … Atypically for the Germans, they had very close relationships in the family. There was always someone to visit granny: grandchildren, relatives, and friends. The granny used to gather them to hear what is happening in their lives. Antonia has a nonmarital daughter. Isabella has three children. Her husband has died. For every Easter and Christmas, the whole family was there."

Distinctive features of Ivana's narrative about her experience as a care worker is her biographical characteristics. I have already introduced Ivana in the Chapter 5.1. As a student of psychology in her last year of studies and the youngest interviewee in my research, Ivana's accounts of her experience differ from other women care workers. While most of the women, when voiced their difficult experiences as abusive behaviors, disrespect, and exploitative practices they usually explained them as a display of care receivers' health condition (Alzheimer's disease), generational differences or families' insensitiveness, small-mindedness or cruelty, but never as expressions of social inequalities. Demonstrations of classism or racism and labour exploitation are seen as character flaws of individual employers, sometimes as national or ethnic traits, but never as manifestations of intersectional systems of domination and social inequalities. Through her narrative, Ivana highlights undeniably racist comments and describes the emotional, cultural, and linguistic barriers that she was facing. Being asked about her overall experience at the beginning of the interview, Ivana focused on discriminatory attitudes, particularly racism underlining the typical "master-servant" relationship:

The point is how long you can endure. The first time I endured 10 weeks and I could hardly wait to get back home.
T: Why?

I: Because the granny is a Nazi. She was born in 1923, as Countess from the surroundings of Frankfurt. She is one of 200 that are still alive. Born as the last child from a very rich Frankfurt family, she didn't have to do much in her life. She married a count and became a countess and received a title that gave her a right to mistreat everyone around her. Unlike in England, in Germany, anyone who was born into a noble family can be a count or something like that. She has always had people who worked for her: cooked, washed, cleaned … She had, for example, a Spanish gardener and his wife who worked for her for 20 years. Nowadays she has, besides me, a tenant, a guy from Ukraine. She rents him a small apartment, like a studio, in the house but very cheap … in return, he does the work around and in the house like repairing the roof, mowing the grass, chopping the wood, throwing out the garbage cans … stuff like that. By the way, there are those handbells for servants … all over the house … she used to ring women who worked for her before. She rang them for service … the cook, the maid to bring coffee. She doesn't do that today. Today she just shouts at me. That is how she calls me when she needs me. She can be very loud when she wants.

Also, she does not like to be watched. I shouldn't look at her. She hates her neighbors. She requires everyone to address her as Countess … if someone on the street addresses her without a title … God forbid … then she corrects them. People who are not close to her and address her by her name, she lectures them about the title and so on … I used to excuse her by saying: 'Don't listen to her, she is old.' She used to blame me for the neighbors not wanting to talk to her."

As Ivana didn't have any knowledge of the German language, in her search for the job she was looking for an elderly person to take care of who can speak English. However, the preferences of her employer were somewhat different. Asking her how she communicated with the person who is blind without being able to speak German, Ivana provided a response that reveals how the care labour relationship incorporates a power dynamic based on, not only her employer's class status, but also racial superiority and white supremacy:

"We communicated in … well, not so perfect English. She spoke English perfectly, let's say, 10 years ago. But, in the meantime, she forgot a lot of words. The main problem was that she didn't want to speak English all the time. She wanted to teach us German because that was convenient for her and for meeting her needs.
T: Wasn't her criteria for choosing girls to have German spoken knowledge?
The main criteria, as I heard from the person who found us a job is – to be a woman. No, I am sorry … first was – to be white. That I am white; that I am a woman and that I can communicate with her. Plus, I had to be someone she can trust, someone knows me and can vouch for me. So, we made up the story that the girl I was replacing … that we know each other for a long time since we live in the same city."

The Private Household as Microcosm of Social Inequalities 367

Many studies have been already detected that negative stereotypes of foreign workers have been identified as contributing to racism and discrimination (Anderson 2007). This finding is echoed in my research, only in the case of Ivana. Here it is quite obvious how Ivana's employer, the old lady she cares for, constructs racial stereotypes of carers based on their nationality and indicates a preference for nationalities that are assumed to have, for example, acceptable levels of hygiene, reliability, submissive temperaments and so on. Ivana continues her narration by revealing how Elizabeth's racial preferences reflect the spatial, social, corporeal, and emotional segregation:

"The granny was only interested in whether I could help her with bathing, applying milk to her body after bath, to not being ashamed of me and that I am white. At the time when I was working there, the hourly wage was 8.5 euros … which was prescribed by the law. But … still … she could have found a bunch of women who would agree to work for that money: refugees, Turkish women, women from South America, etc. … but she says: 'No, no, no, no … I am looking for a white one.' According to her, we are reliable, because of the color of our skin!"

This statement provides a valuable insight into how the color of the skin plays a vital role in the process of constructing intimate and cultural Other in commodified care labour and the development of care relationships between two parties. The racial preferences for "a white woman from Europe" are based on their natural abilities for care, reliability, and trustworthiness. Although Ivana had previous experience in assisting persons with visual impairments and the knowledge of how to guide such persons while walking, in this case, she faced challenges in performing her tasks. The excerpt below illustrates how Ivana perceives and recognizes the racial superiority that is exercised through bodily distancing and physical boundaries:

"She didn't use to go for a walk when she had eyesight. Only when she lost it, she insisted to do on walks every day. I don't know how much, you know, about blind people, but blind people are mostly dependent on others. They are those who follow. I had blind people in the family, so I learned everything about blind people's needs. The granny was such a difficult character that she was the one who wanted to lead, and I was the one who should follow her. I couldn't hold her hand, because she kept her hands in her pockets. The interesting thing about being her guide was that when I first met her, I wanted to give her a hand, to shake hands because we just met, she said: 'Don't touch me, your hands are dirty.' You know, like she is an Aryan race. 'If you want to guide me, you have to grab my forearm.' I did not dare to grab her by the arm but by the forearm and that's how we walked from point A to point B in the house."

Ivana's interpretation of Elizabeth's behaviors as "malignant racism" is as we can see grounded in "racial hygiene" that produces and maintain the social hierarchy. During this part of the interview, Ivana talks with great anger. She rightly pointed to the contradiction of racial stratification by bodily interactions is demonstrated in the rituals before sleep:

"I was allowed to take her hand only in the morning and in the evening when we say Good morning and Good night. When she is in bed, just before sleep, she used to give me her hand ... to shake it ... I don't know what that exactly meant ... but I didn't want to do that. Well, all of sudden my hand is not dirty, right? I would assume that's how she asked for my forgiveness for those little nasty things she did during the day. At the end she used to say: 'Gute Nacht, schlafen Sie gut.' Yeah ... right. I don't need your Gute Nacht. That's what I was thinking. So, that was the only moment when I was allowed to touch her hand. During the walks, I can touch her hand when she wears gloves. She doesn't mind someone touching the food she eats ... well, she used to do that because all her life she had cooks and people who worked for her. According to her, in this world this is the order: God comes first, then Germans, then English people, then Europeans, and at the end everyone else."

If we look at Ivana's narratives below, we can see that like in the colonial homes and households of 19th and the beginning of the 20th Century in Victorian England, class boundaries are produced through the spatial segregation that displays a transparent hierarchy. In Ivana's case, the substantial status difference that exists between her and the household is mirrored in the deployment of the space in the house aimed to affirm family boundaries and to symbolize a status distinction among members present in the house. The spatial arrangement in the house embodies a typical example of "master-servant" segregation: separate entrances, separate toilets, separate living space far from the eyes of the employer to prevent as Ivana puts it "contaminating the household". In the interview excerpt below Ivana describes not only the spatial separation to prevent permeability of class boundaries but also spatial and temporal control of Ivana's existence. By controlling Ivana's movements through the space and making her every move accountable, employers make sure that they are in control over the workload and working hours. Ivana expresses her experience in an emotionally intense way and remembers it as highly psychologically strenuous and abusive:

"Tanja, the worst thing was a psychological mistreatment: the lunch is not well cooked, the living room is not ventilated, she did not sleep well ... whenever she feels some change in her eyesight ... sometimes she can see blurred, sometimes cannot see at all – than everything is my fault. It is my fault because I can see, because I am young, and because I work there. It is my fault if I go out if I spend

The Private Household as Microcosm of Social Inequalities   369

money that I earned. I am guilty when I cannot immediately find something that she mislaid in some of the closets who knows how long time ago. So, the harassment was psychological … don't do this, don't do that … if she calls me and I don't answer right away, I do not appear instantly in front of her, she screams asking where I am, what I am doing. I used to take a break during the day only when she doesn't see what I'm doing. For example, I go to the kitchen and make a noise with pots and dishes to make a sound like I am busy doing something. Sometimes I find something to sew. But literally, she was constantly asking where I was and what I was doing, at every moment. If she could see, I would probably work 16 hours per day without breaks. It happened very rarely that I had time to read something or to sort out my things. In case I have no special task, she would immediately find me one to do. For example, some corner in some wardrobe needs to be cleaned or so. I must be used every second … and whether I slept, or I didn't, whether I ate well, or I was hungry – she didn't care about that. At some point, she wanted to set up a baby alarm so that she could ring me at any time during the night if she wants to eat. Then I was sleeping in the basement. But the basement was turned into a normal living space. The first year was great because I had my room and my peace there. Then, one night I realized that she is roaming around. She got lost. She left her room and didn't know how to come back. After she did this several times I had to move upstairs to the room next to her … where was a huge pendulum wall clock. I haven't gotten used to the sound so I had to wait until midnight for the clock stops. I couldn't have slept normally."

Being treated as an object and "possession", Frau Elizabeth manipulates Ivana into accepting as "natural" the employer's dominance navigating her closeness to and distance. However, as the "intimate stranger" in the house Ivana is aware of the paradox of closeness and distance at the same time:

"But you see, instead of having one girl for the day, one for the night … they only hire one who must do everything. On the other hand, she wanted us as far away from her as possible, to do not contaminate her, or endanger her living space. We were allowed to use her floor only for food. Unfortunately, we had to use her bathroom … that was very difficult for me. That toilet was a guest toilet. When I put her to bed, I can go to the toilet, and the next time only in the morning. If I use the toilet during the night and she hears me, she would ask me to come to her … she would make up something. Nevertheless, I managed somehow … I was sneaking around, walking on my toes … like a thief … so that she would not hear me. I was trying to close the toilet door as quietly as I could … so that she and her daughter would not hear when I came out."

In the interpretation of Ivana's story, we must not neglect the context where social boundaries are negotiated. It is obvious from Ivana's story that changes in the structure of the household and Elizabeth's health deterioration enforced the permeability of household physical boundaries. Elizabeth's sight loss and frequent movements during the night moved Ivana from class segregated spaces such as the basement to the same floor where Elizabeth sleeps. This movement from downstairs to upstairs doesn't weaken the status distinction. However, as spatial and physical boundaries become more porous, they also induce the shaping of new interactive dynamics between Ivana and members of the household as well as Ivana's attentive behavior and creativity in micro-movements through the house.

As previously mentioned, the consumption of food, management of food, and food preparation were markers of status hierarchies and the preserver of household domination. Ivana experienced an employer's boundary work primarily in food management where food for Ivana and the rest of the family is spatially separated:

"Her younger daughter was very direct and strict with me – 'this food is for my mother, not for you'. I said: 'Good.' There were two refrigerators one bigger and one smaller. The smaller one was mine. For example, I was buying eggs that were not with a 'bio' label, and those 'bio' were especially for her. The daughter said that the eggs from the farm were especially for her mother as well as fruit. I was not allowed to eat them. So, there were these little things."

The hierarchical distribution of food was displayed not only by the rules of what should be eaten and by whom as the excerpt above demonstrate, but also by the limitation in terms of variety and the amount of food that was available to Ivana. Ivana's meal arrangement is organized as she narrates:

"I had breakfast and dinner separately from them. Every week they were giving me 10 euros – That was for breakfast and some evening meals. By the way, if Elizabeth would needed something from the store, I should buy it for her with my own money and they would refund it afterwa. I had to keep all bills. For lunch, I had what I cooked for them."

The family boundaries were produced also through the prioritization of taste. As Ivana had no autonomy to cook the kinds of food she likes, she must follow Elizabeth's preferences:

"Elizabeth also insisted that I eat what I cook for her. Therefore, I could not have chosen the food. Even if I do not like it, I had to eat it. I never liked it. It was German cuisine is awful, disgusting … completely tasteless!
T: Really? How come?
Well, unsalted. She insisted on eating only vegetables, cooked in 1001 different ways and I have never cooked any or did not know any of those things how to cook. I did not even know what they looked like. For example, they like cucumber and they like

THE PRIVATE HOUSEHOLD AS MICROCOSM OF SOCIAL INEQUALITIES 371

to cook it and eat it, and I could not do that. Then béchamel sauce or something had to be made for every food. It was cooked vegetables. She does not eat olive oil. She only eats butter. Very German tasteless food. The hardest part was figuring out the German recipes."

In comparison to the other women I interviewed, the reason why Ivana struggled with German cuisine is as she said, was a total absence of knowledge of German meals and dishes. The reason for this is of cultural and regional nature. As someone who came from the Southern Serbia where culinary tradition is characterized by a strong influence from Byzantine (Greek), Mediterranean, and Ottoman (Turkish) cuisines. The women who are from Northern Serbia, province of Vojvodina, close to the Hungarian border as a territory that was a part of the Austro-Hungarian Empire had already a knowledge of German cuisine as they, most likely, cooked it all their lives. By contrast to them, for Ivana as a young woman, with not so much experience in cooking, without knowledge of the German language, the task of making meals that are entirely unknown to her, on an everyday basis – must have caused a lot of stress and required a lot of efforts and energy, along wit with other tasks in the household.

While in Milica's case we could observe a strong personal relationship with a family and permeability of household boundaries, the distinctive characteristic of Ivana's case is "depersonalization". Depersonalization of the labour relationship was the creation of distance by the employer as we could see from Ivana's narratives, spatial but also symbolic. The symbolic ones consist of denial of rights to free time, personal zone, communication with the outer world, and neglect of Ivana's social and emotional needs. Being dependent on an employer for work and accommodation amplified the vulnerability of a live-in care worker. The boundaries between work and leisure were not always clearly defined, with free time and private space often being transgressed. As a thirty-something young woman, Ivana expected that she could sometimes go out or visit her friends. In the interview excerpt below she describes isolation due to the reduction of social contact:

"I was not allowed to go out. I could go out to take a stroll or so. I did not have any free time except when granny's daughter intervened. She always has insisted that we should have breaks during the day. After granny goes to bed, which was quite early, I had an hour or two to check my email, chat with the family, surf on Internet, to read a book. I was too tired to go anywhere. After 16 hours of work, you are destroyed. My friends did not live far away, only two S-Bahn stations away. I could go … but then, I was thinking about how to come back. I am usually done with granny by 20.30. Then, I need to walk 20 minutes from the house to the station. That means that I have one hour and a half to spend with friends. I must be back by 23h. Therefore, I went out once or twice and even that was a problem for granny. Each of us, who worked for her, was isolated during the three months. We must have reduced all contact with our families and friends."

Access to the internet and communication was also one of the "depersonalization" strategies for maintaining the boundaries between Ivana's privacy and work life in the household. The limitation of Ivana's private time and the private zone was an excuse for exploitative emphasis on "efficiency":

"I was in touch with family and friends only via the Internet. But only when granny's daughter turns on Wi-Fi – which was always except on evenings when I was free! She said that she cannot sleep with the Wi-Fi because of the radiation that wireless device produces … you know … that is a health hazard. As they never gave me the password, I could not access the internet. I depended on them whether they would let me apologize to my family or not. I think that the Internet is a basic right. I should have fought for that. You see, their logic was if I do not have access to the Internet, I would be more focused on my work.
    In addition, I expected to be free for Christmas. Because the girl who was before me had a sister near Frankfurt and they let her go to relatives for Christmas. She had breaks and free time and everything … and I started to wonder why I do not have and realized that they forbid everything so that you must fight … than they give you a bit … and then again continue as before."

The way in which Ivana expressed the consequence of "boundary work" of her employers, captures the whole labour relationship which in her case involved a great loss of personhood and intensified forms of humiliation for Ivana:

"The hardest thing for me was to figure out what Elizabeth likes, how she likes it, what she does not like, how I should position myself, to what extent I should lose my personality so that I would literally be a shadow that follows her because she demands it. I was not there to think. I was not allowed to think. You know … that suppression of who I am and what do I feel – was the hardest to get used to."

Ivana's employers use a variety of means to draw boundaries between her and them. One way is "objectification" and the other is "strategic depersonalization". Strategic depersonalism is an absence of emotional involvement and keeping a social and spatial distance between Ivana and the employer. In this case, I identified three means of distancing: overt showing of distrust, employer's separation of family backstage and frontstage, and minimizing Ivana's intervention in the employer's private lives. From the previous

THE PRIVATE HOUSEHOLD AS MICROCOSM OF SOCIAL INEQUALITIES 373

interviews, I can conclude that the more mutual trust in the relationship, the closer women care workers and the employer are to the familiarisation end of the spectrum; the less mutual trust, the closer they are to depersonalized work relations. However, these types of relationships are not mutually exclusive. They were often used interchangeably by women care workers when working for different employers, in households with different structures and intensities of interaction. Ivana falls in the category of absolute distrust by her employers. The fears of theft and stealing make Ivana's hosts attentive to her movements through the house. Ivana provides below examples of their fear of family valuables and money being stolen:

"Whenever I returned from shopping, I had to submit a paper bill together with a change. She was not strict with cents but she was controlling only the coins of one or two Euros. Whatever she needed, I was buying with my money, and then she refunds it to me. However, I do never have the money in advance.

The first time I came to the family, I remember, I had to count every day if there were enough spoons, enough forks, enough knives because granny thought that one of us would steal her silver cutlery. I have silver cutlery at home. I come from such a family … Sometimes, long time ago; my family was one of the wealthiest families in the town. At some point, I told them something like 'People I don't need that junk. I will not steal anything. I have that at home'.

The second time, they were cleaning some silver and gold cutlery, dishes and plates, and some of the family jewellery … antique stuff … as I said that's the junk for me … anyway … they were counting the pieces. I was standing in the middle of the room because it was time to feed Elizabeth, it was her lunchtime. So I asked them should I bring lunch as I usually did. They turned to me saying: 'Why are you here? Go, have a break. We will feed our mother.' They did not want me there because they feared I was going to steal some of their rings, earrings … and these were supposed to be very expensive and valuable. Later on, I was asked to polish and clean the silver. After my job is done, I had to leave the room … no, first I had to wait for Isabella or Antonia to come, to count everything, and then I could leave. They were paranoid. They don't get that I don't care about their silver or gold. They asked me if I knew how to clean and polish silver and I said to them: 'I have that at home. I have been doing that for years.' I am used to rich houses and wealthy people. Some of my relatives even today have 'treasures', antiquities, and so on. Only I was surprised when I came to his or her house … I expected much more from someone who holds such a title …"

Besides distrust, the excerpt above reflects an unusual attempt from Ivana's side to challenge the class superiority of her employer by claiming the status of similarity in wealth and family valuables. The fear of theft was not the only cause of the "boundary work" of her employers. Equally, the fear of Ivana's emotional or even sexual transgression of family boundaries induced spatial demarcation. The interview excerpt below demonstrates how the intimate presence of Ivana was excluded from the front regions of family life. The homely frontstage and backstage were kept separated to maintain the class distinction but also Ivana's status as intimate Other:

"It took seven days for Elizabeth to tell me that her granddaughter was illegitimate and that her boyfriend was from Ethiopia. When she talks about her daughters and grandchildren, she also talks about their partners, children. But she never mentioned that boyfriend. No one has a problem with him except Elizabeth. Once they had a family gathering and I was there helping with serving food and drinks. But before guests arrived, Elizabeth instructed me whispering: 'Be nice and when guests come don't be surprised – Mia's boyfriend is black. Don't stare at him.' Awful! It turned out that the person was nice, speaks English, plays football, has many interests … I enjoyed talking to him on various topics. Well, until they told me to leave. I am convinced that they thought I was flirting with him."

The last depersonalization strategy from the employer's side was the minimization of the time-consuming burden of personal interactions. Keeping emotional and personal distance by showing no interest in her personality Ivana narrates as follows:

"The problem was that Elizabeth was spending most of the time with me. She was 'sentenced' to life in my company. She talked a lot. Almost the same stories every day. If I would start to talk about something, for example, something that I am interested in, or my view on something, opinion and alike … she refused to listen. Especially if that is something that she disagrees with … which was all the time. Sometimes, but that's was rare, when she is bored or needs to fill her time somehow, then she asks something about my family, my hometown, my country. Since she was musical, she even expressed a wish to hear our traditional music. But she never really insisted on me playing music for her. During my stay there, an awful thing happened … my friend, 26 years old died from cancer. I was devastated. I explained to them what happened, that I am in emotional distress, and that I cannot work. I just wanted everyone to leave me alone. When Elizabeth heard about this, she started to cry … I am not sure if she was genuine, but I could say that she was quite shaken. After that, she asked a bit more about my family. What she did not want to listen is about the war in the former Yugoslavia, the dissolution of Yugoslavia, the NATO bombing of Serbia in 1999, and so on. She does not have a clue about that. Though, she did know that Yugoslavia split apart and she only knew that because of the refugees and asylum seekers who came to Germany. Among others is the guy who found a job … who works for her. Also, there are a lot of her girlfriends who hire cleaning ladies and care workers from the former Yugoslavia. In short, she is not interested in anything, which is not in her interest."

Conclusions

Mobility and inequality have been the focus of mobility studies across the disciplines for the last two decades. Mobility as an imperative of modernity has been foregrounded as a reducer of inequality and inducer of social mobility. In the grand narratives of modernity, globalization, hypermobility, transnationalism, and the flux and fluidity of societies, mobility has gained an overly positive value – the more an individual is mobile, the more possibilities are available to them. An emphasis has been placed on understanding mobilities both as a result of and contributing factor to social inequality (Onmacht, Maxim, Bergman 2009), especially by urban sociologists. The quantitative and qualitative research that emerged in the field of transport and urban studies strived to explain how social exclusion and access to mobility are interwoven, particularly in Western European societies, for instance in Switzerland, Germany, or the United Kingdom. Studies such as Manderscheid and Bergman's (2008) have investigated the connection between Swiss citizens' access to public transport infrastructure and social differentials in acquiring professional opportunities. Labour mobility or "mobile work" (Kesselring, Vogl 2008, 2010) in Germany has been investigated by a wide range of studies on corporate mobility, business travel and mobile work which theorize mobile work and business travel as signifiers for social change in the organization of work based on empirical research conducted among mobile workers in the IT, mechanical and chemical industries.

In this day and age, the increasing pluralization of labour mobilities – often characterized by differentiation and social inequality – creates polarized mobile subjects that range from the wealthy educated bankers and managers, who move between global financial centres, to the poor rail commuters that pack the trains in India, and from Romanian circular labour mobility in the agricultural sector to the elder care workers who are the subjects of this book. Only recently has research on "mobile labour" (Bastos, Novoa, Salazar 2021) become linked to the reproduction of ideologies associated with segregation, discrimination and hierarchization through the various axis of difference such as race, gender, age. When compared to a time in which slave ships traversed the oceans or a colonial plantation economy, the contemporary world does not seem to differ as much as one might hope. We are living in a world where movement flows are becoming increasingly intense as a result of financial crises, environmental disasters, the intensification of border violence, military interventions, and global neoliberal capitalism. These have pushed many people into often involuntary cross-border labour mobility and some of them into occupations that endanger their health and even sometimes lives. These "peripheral labour mobilities", as I have called them, include truck drivers, care workers, mobile sex workers, cabaret dancers, circus performers, construction workers, mobile labourers in the Arctic petroleum industry, maritime labour workers, and many others whose geographic movements are inseparable from the performance of the work which is both cause and consequence of their mobility. Their mobile work lives deserve our undivided ethnographic attention.

This book is written to add valuable ethnographic insight into the lives of short-term mobile care workers who share a destiny with the other contemporary mobilities described above. The paradoxical nature of elder care labour mobility arises from the demand of elder care workers, as rich Western ageing societies face a crisis in long term care. On the other hand, elder care workers are caught up in restrictive labour and border regulations that prevent them from continuous mobility. Through the three empirical chapters in this volume, I have described and analysed the movements of care workers which range from travel between cities to regional travel, travel across state borders, mobilities in villages, micro-movements in households and movement through the virtual spaces of the internet. This book offers an in-depth investigation into the everyday experiences of elder care workers in care labour mobility that encompasses mentioned multiple scales of movements – topic that have been underexplored so far.

Notwithstanding the evidence of care work as a form of mobility-related exploitation, I believe that this book provides a balanced understanding of how such work mobility is bound to specific space-time rhythms of movements that require specific knowledge, creativity and resourcefulness on the part of women care workers Exploring the spatial and experiential dimensions of commuting rhythms in care labour mobility, I suggest that commuting can alternatively be conceived as a mobile practice that offers a rich variety of social situations and interactions. In what follows, I will highlight the main results and insights of my research and their potential to improve or alter existing concepts and theoretical perspectives in field of labour, mobility and inequality.

Motility for Care Labour Mobility

Applying an ethnographic and anthropological approach to Vincent Kaufmann's sociological concept of motility (Kaufmann 2014) I have modified the concept through a focus on the way socially, geographically, and politically contextualised interaction between immobility and mobility play out in producing and reproducing labour mobility inequalities in the case of cross-border elder care work. This fundamental interaction, previously framed as the concept of "im/mobility", draws our attention not only to the socio-cultural complexity of movement for labour but also to limitations, "stuckness" and entrapment within these mobilities. Therefore, the crucial questions that this book has set out to answer using the dense ethnographic material provided in the three empirical chapters can be summarized as follows: Who and what moves women for elder care work in Germany? What are the factors that not only encourage mobility, but also potentially block mobility, or make it impossible? How do these shape the working lives of mobile care labourers and how do they shape the nature and quality of care work they provide? To answer these questions, I have analysed an interplay between three constitutive elements of motility in the sense of Kaufmann: access, competence and the appropriation of options and skills in elder care labour mobility.

An analysis of the process of acquiring labour mobility and building of potential for that mobility, has shown that spatialized cross-border inequalities are tightly linked to other types of unequal social relations in terms of gender, citizenship, nationality ethnicity and race. My ethnographic evidence demonstrates that the capacity to move for care, to make journeys across borders is conditioned by rotatonal pattern of care labour mobility and myriad of actors and networks. In these, skills and knowledge, such as the ability to navigate the travel routes, language and care work skills, as well as the access to transportation are elements of "mobility capital". They induce variations in mobility experiences in relation to the geopolitical constraints that are created by the spatial dynamic of networks, communication, and modes of transportation. The networks, play a pivotal role in strategies and negotiations surrounding the limited access to the "care labour industry" as a dominant model of informal "care business", and regional disparities in the permeability of border crossings and border regimes.

Regional differences in access to border-crossing and travel are evident in the case of three different border zones in the non-EU member states examined: Northern Serbia, Central Serbia, and Bosnia and Herzegovina. Territorial and political constraints such as border regimes, job recruitment schemes and practices of control at border checkpoints demand both a knowledge of how to permeate the borders and experience of travel, since these play important roles both in the freedom of women to organize their journeys and in reducing the potential risks that they encounter in doing so.

For example, my interviews reveal that accessibility to labour mobility for women from Northern Serbia radically differs from that of their colleagues from the South as a result of a history of dynamic migration across Hungarian, Austrian and German borders. The Serbo-Hungarian border, at the southern edge of European external border has one of the busiest exit points, where the "business of bordering" has mushroomed in the last decades due to the refugee crisis. These geopolitical conditions have created a highly commercialized and commodified irregular care labour market, with private business in transportation that direct and limit potential for movement, mobility choices, mobility freedom and access to safe journeys and fair working conditions for women care workers.

In contrast to the northern region, Eastern Serbia is a region populated with "Gastarbeiter", who have worked as "guests" in Germany. This was a historically important economic phenomenon in the former Federal Socialist Republic of Yugoslavia and had a major social and economic impact on the area. The organization of care labour mobility has taken shape around historical dis/continuities in labour migration over the last six decades. Here, the social ties with those who still work in Germany represent an alternative source of information about potential employers in Germany for women care workers. Accessibility to care work and mobility is thus based on the possession of "movement capital" – privileged access to information that circulates among inner circles. This access is influenced on the one hand, by the level of trust which has been established between German families and women care workers and, on the other, by patterns of solidarity and reciprocity among women.

Making and sustaining labour mobility heavily depends on the formation of social networks – either on a local or community level, online on social media such as Facebook, or simply through friendship, family or ethnic networks. Lack of knowledge, isolation from social networks, unreliable job intermediaries and employers, and limited support networks can frequently push women into having to agree to unwanted working conditions. In this respect, the self-organized system of rotation has an important role in freeing women from agencies and intermediaries as well as from risky and exploitative working arrangements. The more women rely on one another and form their own networks, the less they become exposed and vulnerable to sexual harassment and abuse, excessive working hours for no additional payment and poor living conditions.

Labour mobility is enacted once women obtain access to information about how to get a job, how to develop mobility potential and how to sustain labour mobility. Once stabilised, these elements form *the motility for labour movement*. Access to social media offers access to information shared by the members of particular Facebook groups created especially for this purpose, as well as assistance in the form of advice on certain problems related to care or to border crossing practices and job advertisements. Gaining access to more information about the potential job requires becoming involved in a complex interaction between different actors, such as friends and acquaintances, job intermediaries (brokers), drivers, etc. Familiarity and closeness to job intermediaries, results in more predictable working conditions (payment, workload, etc.), security, and access to privileged information (e. g. about new and better jobs). However, access is unequally distributed and depends on demographic and social factors such as age, stage in life, educational attainment, previous work experience, computer literacy, and knowledge and possession of IT technologies. These shape access to information and to social networks. Just as importantly, travelling experience and transportation competencies in Western Europe often hinder women's decisions in relation to autonomous and independent travelling. Coming from areas that are remote and disadvantaged in terms of transport, or a lack of finances to engage in such travelling inhibits women's potential for putting themselves on the move.

The interview analysis revealed three types of social relations that serve as ingredients in producing a rotation system 1) strong ties with a job intermediary; 2) strong ties with the German family that offers employment; 3) strong ties on the level of the community such as those found in the villages of Eastern Serbia where women operate their rotation systems. These relationships prove to be vital in enabling the sustainability and certainty of labour mobility, ultimately turning into "mobility capital".

Overall, my findings demonstrate that the development of the potential for mobility is not determined only by unalterable and fixed macro factors such as border regimes, the possession of an EU passport or labour laws. Instead, it also relies on personal traits, personal individual social and cultural capital (knowledge, specific skills, personal connections, and experience in care work), solidarity, trust and the free circulation of information within women's networks.

Structure/Agency Dilemma: Contesting Victim Narratives

Theories of the commodification of care, often grounded in neo-Marxist theories, have had a prominent role in explaining the mechanisms supporting economic inequalities between the global North and the global South. They have drawn unquestionable portrayals of women care workers as victims of oppression and hardship who must migrate to ensure the economic survival of their families. Women are depicted highly vulnerable, on the losing side of the coin, dragged into a world of precarious, exploitative work responding to the demands of migration and welfare regimes. Whilst this holds a partial truth, as vividly described in the narratives of my interviewees, it requires the approach that moves beyond the binaries of agency and victimhood and beyond homogenised social constructs of women. My approach to the notion of elder care work which focuses on personhood, identity-building, daily care labour processes, skills, and motivations, has led to an emphasis on the subjectification of care workers – on their position as a subject tied to structural necessities, yet still owning personal agency. Adressing the relation between structure and agency, has brought to the fore several striking findings.

Much of the work on migration, gender and commodification of care over the last two decades has reinforced the assumption that labour mobility can be reduced to a focus on escaping from poverty and hardship expressed in materialistic terms. The ethnographic portraits and interviews that I accumulated during participant observation reveal that the majority of women elder care workers who decide to put themselves on the move do not live in severe poverty and hardship. Many of them own houses and land or drive

CONCLUSIONS

381

a car, and a few of them run a family business or have a permanent job in the public sector along with commuting to Germany for care work. Some of them even live in bigger houses than their hosts (German families). Political and economic macro factors contributed to their inability to sustain desired living standards, achieve retirement, or simply to avoid precarious living caused by long-term unemployment and the never-ending cycle of bank loans. I have discovered that the development of motivations and experiences during the period of mobility exposes other hidden motives and aspirations besides those income-induced. Hence, I have paid attention to motives, aspirations and the decision to commute for care work to Germany as imaginative, emotional and mutable in relation to plans, ideas and goals but also to matters of agentive will, cognition and emotion. I looked at the temporal distribution of motivation and aspiration during labour mobility that resulted in evidence that does not relate only to present-oriented economic calculative decisions. My findings suggest that, aside from financially pressured situations, women's aspirations are driven by specific economic goals often combined with an aspiration for independence, adventure, for gaining cultural and symbolic capital by being abroad that promise to realize their personal projects filled with hopes and dreams. As such, aspirations and motivations for mobility involve a range of feelings such as anger, bitterness, curiosity, hope, excitement, avoidance, and fear, and emerge with present material circumstances.

By insisting on researching and analysing the experiences of women care workers purely from an economic perspective we inevitably divide the scholarship into binary perspectives of empowerment, viewing migration and mobility as an opportunity to escape oppressive marriages or gain economic independence by becoming a self-sufficient earner. Predefined categories and concepts such as "status paradox" or "contradictory social mobility" which highlight processes of downgrading by taking low-skilled and stigmatized jobs cannot be generalized and applied in every context and, more importantly, are not corroborated by my findings. I apply a perspective that facilitates a layered and heterogeneous approach to studying the ambivalent and multifaceted processes and situations in which women are becoming empowered and/or disempowered, and which are tightly related to the interaction between citizenship, gender, age and nationality that permeates the process of labour mobility.

Within a complex network of care, the labour industry consists of varieties of interconnected actors, and women are far from being passive participants. On the contrary, women care workers are active constructors of the mobility worlds which they both inhabit and navigate. To avoid labelling women care workers as victims, I coin the term "constrained agency" to refer to the discovery of agency embedded in the social relations that condition the capacity for "agentic" acting. Narratives make visible the strategies and channels that women use to protect themselves from damaging and dangerous working conditions and relationships. These are used in searching for mobility options or, as Kaufmann would put it, "mobility opportunities", and how to negotiate and permeate the obstacles they face.

The vulnerability which comes from crossing the border several times per year as illegalized labourers, uncertainty whilst travelling, arriving at unknown people's homes and residing in these homes for care work requires the ability to strategize their movements. In elder care labour mobility, women's commuting back and forth is linked to the mode of job recruitment, their access to the border crossing and their empowerment through the trust of their employers. All three factors intersect in one location: in their access to and embeddedness in social networks. As one of the cases in Chapter 5 showed, a self-organized system of rotational journeys plays an important role in freeing women from fraudulent agencies and money-grabbing job intermediaries. An additional advantage of self-organization is that women retain a certain amount of agency and can open new pathways and new routes. On the one hand, such a system requires mutual trust between women whilst, on the other, it introduces other risks such as potential competition and conflict between care workers. The knowledge of the mobility process is based upon experience of actual movement and accumulation of contacts that together helps them to negotiate the value of their work. I have identified three different forms exercising agency: 1) in the negotiation of the salary; 2) through the sharing and exchanging of information via social media; 3) in the self-organization of rotational shifts.

Rather than strengthening existing arguments surrounding injustices, irrationalities and violence of border regimes and repressive border controls of labour mobility, in this book I highlighted productive nature of such controls – women's agency in resisting borders, their inventiveness and resourcefulness they use in the conflicts and negotiations in circumvention of border regimes, as these present the acquisition of motility or the potential for mobility. Strategies for crossing the border, and knowledge of how to cross or avoid being stuck on it, include, for example, passport washing, having a second passport, paying the penalty for overstaying, or bribery and corruption.

Although rarely discussed in the literature on mobility studies and transportation, commuting and commuter are often dystopian, passive, and boring (Edensor 2011: 189), and the time spent commuting is a "dead time" in which nothing happens besides physical movement through a geographical space. In contrast to this, the journeys that care workers take, offer a good example of how the time spent travelling to Germany and back in minivans and buses is used for discussion and the exchange of crucial information, experiences, problems and advice. Once women become familiar with this information, for example, which job intermediary offers jobs of poor quality which are underpaid or involve a demanding or difficult elderly person or family, it gives them a firm basis upon which they can negotiate with the job intermediary. Such knowledge is a foundation for their agency – the ability to evaluate whether they are being paid fairly or being exploited. This ability enables women to select the jobs that increase their financial security and eliminate those where the payment fails to reach the expected level.

The strategies I mentioned previously mirror how the embeddedness of "care business" in the broader set of social relations, whether virtual or real, allows women to build up a capability for agentic behaviour which, in turn, constitutes a kind of social capital that sustains labour mobility free from exploitation and extreme or precarious working and living conditions. However, we must not forget that the extent to which women can exercise their agency is determined by different factors: access to information and knowledge, personal characteristics such as resilience or resourcefulness, language skills, age, and competence with communication technologies.

Moving and Caring across the Borders – Lessons from "the Periphery"

In the literature on migration and domestic and care work, which I discussed extensively in Chapter 1, gendered scholarly knowledge on domestic and care migration has often fallen into the trap of methodological sexism, being overly focused on the feminine caring subject. Inspired by neo-Marxism, theoretical concepts of "care drain" and "global care chains" have reduced migrant care work to a commodified extension of "motherly love". A vast scholarly literature that adopt this perspective, neglects the involvement of men in reproductive labour, failing to consider other forms of caregiving, such as care for elderly and/or disabled persons, the process of acquiring specific knowledge and achieving specific goals related to care work and care relationship or the development of new skills that can be learned or improved within mobility and migration contexts. I have underlined several times throughout the book that researching care work from this theoretical position pre-defines "care" as an attribute attached to a specific category of gender, and that care, nurture, and love are qualities tied to the biological female body and migrant care workers as "transnational mothers" who end up in low-skilled and underpaid jobs in domestic niches in Western affluent households. Thus, women care workers are portrayed in terms of their social remit rather than as bearers of knowledge.

The findings from my studies do not corroborate previous assumptions and conceptions. To start with, the most striking result that emerges from my material is that women who start to commute to Germany to perform elder care work are in their 50s or 60s with grown children and without caring responsibilities. During interviews, unless I specifically asked, they did not speak about issues related to transnational motherhood such as suffering because of physical absence, "motherly" love that is outsourced to another family, or emotional deprivation because of the separation of the family. When they did, they usually spoke of the feeling of "missing the family", which includes friends, relatives, and other persons close to them. The second piece of empirical evidence relates to the presence of men. The majority of interviewed women who live with their partners/husbands are supported in their care labour mobility projects either in terms of care for the family and children or through emotional and psychological support. The case of Isidora Basic (Chapter 6), although an exception in my empirical evidence, demonstrates that even men such as her husband can follow a woman and join her in performing elder care work abroad. Being asked about how they perceive and experience care work across the borders, women's narratives mainly revolve around the interpretation and evaluation of their skills and knowledge and how they act in the process of caring for them. Attitudes towards care work are generally expressed in relation to evaluation of the working conditions in the household where they take care of the elderly, their relationship with the care-receiver and his/her family, their own physical and mental preparedness and the reaction to the care work they perform.

None of the women I interviewed possess any professional or semi-professional knowledge of caring for the elderly, apart from their experience of unpaid care work within their own families. The cultural conceptualizations of care work as a gender-related role that I find in the narratives are a consequence of "double socialization" as a figure of the "working mother" in socialist Yugoslavia. However, one piece of evidence that proves how cultural ideals commonly assigned to the concept of care as gendered unpaid labour have been always taken for granted, is the frequency with which women express their appreciation and gratitude for care work and the sense of achievement, fulfilment, purpose and pride which it offers them.

Women's cognitive and emotional reactions to unprecedented working conditions and to the caring tasks they narrated while I was interviewing and spending time with them, demonstrate the complexity of elder care work across the borders. I found that informal elder care work comprises a range of skills and knowledge including knowledge of the German language, cooking skills, and caring skills (maintaining the personal hygiene of the person, using equipment for lifting, transferring and repositioning immobile elderly, etc.). In addition to this, in the narratives, I have identified the themes of "a feeling for work" and "artistry and improvisation" as components of the "tacit knowledge" that arises while performing care work in labour mobility. The process of learning how to care for the elder person and job execution are closely intertwined. The knowledge is built up over time through personal connections with a care receiver, his/her family, rotational colleagues, and the job intermediary. The specific knowledge that emerges from rotational mobility arrangements is emotional labour as a form of tacit knowledge that can be achieved only from deep interpersonal interactions in the work of caregiving, and in the complex deployment of emotional self-management. "Knowing how to care" has a personal dimension which is developed through a relationship possessing a "family-like" intimate quality. My empirical evidence suggests that women are developing and learning how to achieve flexibility in relation to changing schedules, and situations because the care needs of the care recipient continuously evolve, making care approach modifications necessary.

However, it appears that care work performance depends not just on women's physical and mental preparedness. The way in which women cope with the new, unknown, and demanding tasks of caring for sick elderly persons depends mainly on the quality of information about the them that they get from that person's family, from the job intermediary who found them a job or from the colleague they rotate with. Most women find the ideal type of care work arrangement to involve the same two persons continually work in the same family (caring for the same elderly person) for at least a year or more. This means that continuous rotational mobility, arranged by fixed parties, results in better working conditions and working relationships. Overall, women stated that stability, certainty, and shared solidarity between care workers reduces stress and other negative side effects of performing care work in an irregular market.

The "business of care" comprises a whole range of actors and as well as multiple social relations that are highly personalized and complex. As I described in Chapter 5, although all parties involved in business share economic interests, the logic of their actions is led by moral norms and values that are both implicit and constantly changing and challenged in the context of various households. In my interviews about attitudes to care and care work mobility, care was regarded as a genuine, mindful, and compassionate activity that goes beyond its economic value. Therefore, care work is thought of and understood as a value morally loaded and entrenched into the cultural norms of the persons who perform work. As a result, it is crucial and more fruitful to analyse the organisation of paid care labour as a form of "moral economy" rather than simply in terms of economic profit maximisation or as a good that circulates between the Global South and Global North and the centre and the periphery.

Taken together, my evidence led to the conclusion that irregular elder care work is fraught with complexities that derive from the following elements: 1) intimate and embodied care work which requires emotional and cognitive investment on the part of care workers; 2) unique tacit knowledge on how to care for elderly people which develops only in collaboration between care workers as the result of teamwork; 3) the precarious and vulnerable status of care workers. These elements, create specific types of relationships between the various actors involved: the job intermediary, the family of the elderly person, the elderly person, and the two care workers. While we might agree that all these relationships are governed by economic logic and profit, they also intersect with feelings of trust, solidarity and reciprocity.

Even though elder care workers are subject to multidimensional insecurity and precariousness (physical, emotional, financial, mental) in the care labour industry, we must not neglect the knowledge and skills they use in negotiating the spatiality and temporality of borders and border regimes. The women care workers from my study are integrated into multiple social and economic systems within the "migration institution". The two-passport strategy facilitated by dual citizenship is a perfect example of how the changing historical dynamics of borders result in creative responses which utilise "bordering knowledge" for the gaining of "mobility capital". This demonstrates that elder care cross-border mobility is produced by and produces spatial inequalities that are the result of uneven access to the ability to exercise the right to a certain citizenship, for example. In addition, mobility inequalities are intensified by the possession (or the lack) of the appropriate travel documents, linguistic competence and by differing levels of access to the "migration institutions" that permit border crossings.

Phenomenology of Illegality

In calling for the investigation of "peripheral labour mobilities", their practices and experiences through the lens of subjectivity, I have demonstrated how theories and conceptions that see migration and mobility as derivative or dependent variables of "objective" factors such as wage differentials or "structural" forces, such as the expansion of capitalism and neoliberal economies, are misleading in explaining human movements. Whilst macro-factors such as the dissolution of Yugoslavia, the post-socialist economic transition, and neoliberal reform are important in inducing eldercare labour mobility, they do not account for the desires, aspirations, or deceptions that inform and drive care mobility, as my ethnographic evidence has shown. I have highlighted the subjective dimension of care work mobility using the concept of "subjectivity", which oscillates between an understanding of the subject as subjected by power and a view of the subject as imbued with the power to transcend the processes of subjection that have shaped it. This recognition of subjectivity avoids the voluntaristic and individualistic undertones that haunt the notion of agency. More precisely, it avoids the framing of care labour workers as atomized individual rational-choice actors confronting external structures.

The lens of subjectivity brings out the materiality of the processes of illegalization which make these people intelligible as "illegal workers" or "guest workers" and so forth. Using a phenomenological ethnographic approach, I investigated how different social and legal contexts function to effectively "illegalize" women care workers whilst regarding "illegalization" as a process that shapes subjective lived experiences of illegality, a "mode of being-in-the-world", in relation to its experiential, sensory and embodied aspects.

As my empirical findings have demonstrated, "being illegalized" is a social process involving the legal production of a person's illegality not only through the migration and mobility regimes but through the acts of nonstate agents such as drivers, job intermediaries, family members or the elderly person and their family, as well as other actors involved in care labour mobility industry. This adds insight to the discussion of the re-politization of the private sphere and the invisibility of irregular "intimate labour". I demonstrated in sub-chapter 6.3 how the space of the home can become a space of phenomenological unsafety leading to unprecedented forms of "illegalization" and criminalization amongst other concerns. The ethnographic cases I provide show how well-being and level of dependency do not depend on the spatial organization of work (live-in or live-out), but on the relationship between care worker and employer where "illegalization" often leads to the formation of adverse psychological conditions, thereby making women care workers vulnerable and exploitable as cheap labourers.

Thus, the results of my ethnographic and phenomenological approach offer insights into two important issues. First, neither the research literature nor the academic and public discourses which claim that "living-out" arrangements enable greater independence for care workers find any proof in my empirical evidence. The same goes for related claims connected to freedom of movement, the possibility of emotional distancing, and opportunities for the negotiation of working and living conditions. Secondly, my research reveals how women's self-imposed feeling of being illegal create a specific psychological dynamic in the household, resulting in tensions and conflicts that expose women care workers to extreme physical and emotional vulnerability. The level of trust established between women and their employers is a crucial element in women's experiences of "illegality". Furthermore, the women subject themselves to different procedures and forms of governance and surveillance by adopting "self-disciplinary practices" because of persistent feelings of uneasiness and watchfulness. Not only do legal procedures and practices "illegalize" women, but they also create forms of subjectification in the Foucauldian sense, as women constantly develop and employ their own strategies for not being endangered or detected in this regime of governance and surveillance.

In seeking to undermine dominant border regimes and exploitative labour arrangements in the interest of migrant domestic and care workers, scholarly discussions have given way to broader ideological debates on their agency. The labour rights and human rights of domestic and care workers are often advocated by researchers who, in turn, have tended to explain these workers' lives with respect to social, economic, legal and political determinants in relation to the commodification of care in global capitalism. Yet, "illegality" as a constitutive element of irregular care work and understood as an everyday somatic experience remains understudied in the critical literature on gender, migration and reproductive work. This lacuna is what philosopher Miranda Fricker (2007) refers to as a "hermeneutical injustice", which occurs "when a gap in collective interpretive resources puts someone at an unfair disadvantage when it comes to making sense of their social experiences." I showed how this gap can be filled when we turn our analytical attention to the embodied and experiential consequences of being illegal – the sensory and bodily vigilance and somatic modes of attention enacted by women care workers.

The Micro-Politics of Elder Care Work

In contributing to the literature on the globalization of domestic and care work and focusing on the micro-politics in the privacy of the household, I have attempted to avoid several common understandings of working relationships in the care and domestic sector. The interpretation of working relationships and working identities often suffers from their framing in static terms, fixed within a specific time and place and described predominantly in negative ways, imbued with the imposition of servitude, racism, exploitation, and asymmetrical power relationships. Such interpretations inspired by feminist and poverty approaches have undoubtedly made important contributions to the study of care and migration. However, we must set aside preconceptions about nature relationships such as "strategical personalism" and "benevolent maternalism" rooted in theories of exploitation to make a space for the innovative ways in which live-in elder care workers, as a specific group of live-in domestic workers, interact with their hosts on an everyday basis in a specific time and space.

In this book, I argue that the relationships created through personal encounters in care labour mobility across borders can produce a whole range of different social relations. In addition, such established relationships give impetus for a wide range of new movements of care workers whether that be tourism, permanent migration, or the movements of a family member.

Drawing attention to the processes through which care workers, care receivers, and families conceptualize, perceive, negotiate, and manage their relationships, I have set out to explore the relationship between care workers and their employers (elderlies and their families) where multi-layered boundaries are established by both parties to include or exclude the intimate and/or cultural Other. Due to the temporalities of rotational care labour mobility, such processes inevitably include different stages of developing intimacy and closeness, ambivalences, or indifferences and of establishing, reproducing, and contesting social boundaries between "Us" and "Them". I have shown how boundaries along different divides – cultural, ethnic, generational, etc. – create interactive dynamics which reproduce, negotiate and contest the social in/equalities which exist between the parties in the care work arrangements. I found three major structural factors which help to explain their distinct preferences toward certain types of boundaries negotiations: class positioning, the regulatory context of work (declared or undeclared work) and the spatio-temporal composition of the care work setting.

Based on two ethnographic case studies, I have identified two categories relating to the "work of social boundaries". The first one is to be found in middle-class households where the relationship between the care worker and the family is characterized by a strong degree of personalization. The second is placed in upper-class family where the process of highlighting social boundaries – depersonalization takes place. What the comparison of these two cases show is how geographical proximity and political, cultural, economic exchange and shared histories between countries or regions influence the dynamic, quality, and type of relationship alongside dimensions such as age, citizenship, education, class, marital status, ethnicity, and race. To avoid any overgeneralization, the researcher must understand these relationships as part of specific social and cultural contexts. Both care workers and their employers can perform the underplaying and/or highlighting of social boundaries since these two categories of boundary work are not mutually exclusive, nor polarized forms of boundary work. They must be seen in a continuum where variations in the social class of employers, the demographics of the household where care work is performed, economic and social status, the time that a cares worker has spent in the household, the biographical characteristics of care workers, care receivers and members of their families involved in the care relationship, and the health status of the elderly person, etc. – serve to create processes of closeness and distancing.

The contribution of this book cannot be complete without referring to the originality of the methodological approach and framework. To answer the crucial research question of "how motility for care labour mobility is built", I had to "get moving" together with my respondents and to observe labour mobility processes and mobility flows from the inside. These two actions, both features of my own "research condition", resulted in the scattered field sites where chance/opportunity, choice, and external constraints determining my own mobility became salient factors in how my field was built, what kind of methods I used and what kind of data I obtained.

As labour mobility is above all a movement, it implies a continual change of natural and social contexts – both for the researcher and for the research participants. Hence, "mobility" represents an integral and specific part of my fieldwork. The dialectic dynamics of researcher mobility and the mobility of research participants are scarcely addressed in the literature. Because of this, I want to highlight four main methodological approaches that emerged from my research practice and which I find to be vital in the ethnography of "care labour mobilities": an ethnography of movement, a multi-dimensional understanding of the field (particularly the link between temporal and spatial dimensions), expanded ethnography (polymorphous engagements with participants, online and offline locations), and limited participant observation.

Doing ethnographic research on im/mobility for care labour poses specific challenges and difficulties that have constitutive power within what I call an "ethnography of movement". Travelling with women care workers between different places allowed me to access different phases in the formation and reconfiguration of their plans for mobility, routes, and interruptions. Working within labour mobility flows enabled me to document the ephemeral moments of contact between care workers on the move and state actors such as border police, customs officers, and bus drivers, providing me with crucial ethnographic evidence for the "phenomenology of illegality". Here, the role played by the mobility of the researcher is essential for a full understanding of im/mobility processes. Thus, "ethnography of movement" encompasses the following actions on the part of the researcher: a) being immobile and observing and interviewing those who are mobile b) being mobile and observing those who are immobile; c) being mobile and observing those who are in movement. These methodological tactics are crucial for understanding the tension between travelling and being temporarily immobilized. In rotational care labour mobility, one person is always on the move and the other stays put. Alterations to these dynamics shape labour mobility processes and the way mobility is built. It is not a question of opposing these "moments" to one another, but of understanding the relations that unite them as two aspects of the same process.

Care labour mobility also demands a multi-dimensional approach to fieldwork, its temporal and spatial aspects. Understanding fieldwork as a temporalized entity shows how fieldwork experience is structurally limited in time and resources and how these are affected by particular structural factors. Consequently, fieldwork itself entails rhythms, and it is marked by temporal ruptures such as waiting, repetition, and delays. My academic im/mobilities, the biographical temporal cycles of my respondents, the temporalities of border regimes and the spatio-temporal configuration of informal care work (waiting periods whilst preparing and searching for a job, getting the job and the structure of time within a period of working) all served to shape and re-shape my field sites. External factors that limited my mobility re-shaped my fieldwork turning it into an online process supplemented by polymorphous engagements in the form of a Messenger log diary, Skype interviews, and social media contents (Facebook). The constraints that are typical of research on short-term labour mobility, such as scattered field sites and encounters that arrive in dribs and drabs, have been surpassed through the use of social media as an ethnographic field. This switch to the online world allowed for multiple presences and a multiplicity of roles and identities, providing a multi-textured arena for the experiences of care workers. My research confirmed that offline (face-to-face relationships) and the online world are interwoven since online is part of offline contexts where social relations (for instance, between job intermediaries and care workers and between care workers themselves) are formed and re-enforced. As I have shown, elder care workers manage online relationships with their employers and their colleagues, which are simultaneously mediated offline. This calls for ethnographic practice mediated by social media as a type of "expanded ethnography" which supplements the real interactions that come from real ethnographic fieldwork locations and fieldwork encounters.

Taken together, the people I met, the encounters I made, the situations I witnessed, and the conversations I heard and observed in various spaces from buses and trains to the houses where women perform their work, have produced descriptions and narratives that otherwise would have passed unnoticed, undocumented and undescribed. This work has brought to the light the life stories and experiences of mobile labour subjects that would otherwise never have reached a broader public or academic audience. This book goes beyond its scientific contribution to studies of labour, mobility, and care – it contributes to the societal memory of those who are not among us anymore and those who are ageing for generations yet to come. Looking at the future, I hope that the women you get to know in this book will one day be care receivers in someone else's research, since it is uncertain who is going to take care of them in their old age and the majority of them do not have retirement plans or the certainty of long-term care. Or is it wrong to hope for this?

List of Maps

Map 1: Picturing the break-up of Yugoslavia. Source: https://reportingbalkans.com/the-bbc-break-up-of-yugoslavia-timeline

Map 2: The map of the Former Yugoslavia countries, with bullet-marked areas where care workers come from. Google Maps, from https://www.google.de/maps/place/Bosnia+and+Herzegovina/@45.6165104,15.0134669,6.99z/data=!4m5!3m4!1s0x134ba215c737a9d7:0x6df7e20343b7e90c!8m2!3d43.915886!4d17.679076?hl=en

Map 3: Map of the former Yugoslavia countries and their neighbouring countries in relation to the EU. Source: https://www.oscebih.org (accessed December 2019)

Map 4: Map of Germany, with marked areas where my respondents are employed. OpenStreetMap, from https://www.openstreetmap.org/search?query=Germany#map=6/51.842/11.689

Map 5: The border-crossing point along the Serbo-Hungarian border shows Ana's route. Google Maps, from https://www.google.de/maps/search/border+crossing/@46.1596475,18.8622232,8z/data=!3m1!4b1?hl=en

Map 6: The route from Eastern Serbia to Germany. Google Maps, from https://www.google.com/maps/@46.6884269,15.6601279,5.98z

Map 7: The route from Bosnian towns through Croatia and Slovenia. Source: Google Maps, from https://www.google.com/maps/place/Bosnia+and+Herzegovina/@45.2676988,15.7527862,6.99z/data=!4m5!3m4!1s0x134ba215c737a9d7:0x6df7e20343b7e90c!8m2!3d43.915886!4d17.679076

List of Figures

Figure 1: Female unemployment 1991–2019 in Serbia, from https://tradingecono mics.com/serbia/unemployment-female-percent-of-female-labor-force-wb-data. html (accessed 1. December 2019)

Figure 2: Screenshot of the Facebook post, an advertisement for minibus transporta-tion services that display destinations and the price list. Facebook, January 2019. (The link is withheld to protect the privacy of the respondent)

Figure 3: Screenshot of the Facebook post. Facebook, January 2019

Figure 4: Letter of gratitude. Smartphone screenshot of the private photo. Courtesy of F. J.

Figure 5: Screenshot of the Facebook post of the job advertisement. Facebook, No-vember 2018

Figure 6: Screenshot of the Facebook post. Facebook, December 2018

Figure 7: Screenshot of Facebook post. Facebook, December 2018

Note about the anonymity of Facebook screenshots

My respondents are assured prior to Facebook data collection, that their material (screenshots of their status updates, their comments, images) would remain con-fidential and would be used for academic purposes solely. Facebook images shown in the book are not referenced to protect the privacy and preserve the anonymity of my respondents and the anonymity of other Facebook users. According to Facebook Pages Terms: "If you collect content and information directly from users, you will make it clear that you (and not Facebook) are collecting it, and you will provide notice about and obtain user consent for your use of the content and information that you collect, Regardless of how you obtain content and information from users, you are responsible for securing all necessary permissions to reuse their content and information." (https://www.facebook.com/policies_center/pages_groups_events/, accessed 20 June 2020)

Literature

Adey, P. (2006): If Mobility Is Everything then It Is Nothing: Towards a Relational Politics of (Im)Mobilities. *Mobilities* 1 (1), 75–94.

Adler, Patricia A./Adler, Peter (1987): *Membership Roles in Field Research*. Newbury Park: Sage.

Ahmed, S. (2020): Women Left Behind: Migration, Agency, and the Pakistani Woman. *Gender & Society* 34 (4), 597–619.

Ally, S. (2005): Caring about Care Workers. Organizing in the Female Shadow of Globalization. *Labour, Capital and Society* 38 (1/2), 185–207.

Ally, S. (2009): *From Servants to Workers: South African Domestic Workers and the Democratic State*. Ithaca, NY: Cornell University Press.

Amelina, Anna (2017): *Transnationalizing Inequalities in Europe: Sociocultural Boundaries, Assemblages and Regimes of Intersection*. New York: Routledge.

Amit, Vered (2002): An Anthropology without Community? The Trouble with Community. Anthropological Reflections on Movement, Identity and Collectivity (eds. Vered Amit, Nigel Rapport). London: Pluto Press, 13–65.

Andal, Jacqueline (2013): Gendered Mobilities and Work in Europe: An Introduction. *Journal of Ethnic and Migration Studies* 30 (4).

Anderson, Bridgit, (2000): *Doing the Dirty Work? The Global politics of Domestic Labour*. Zed Books.

Anderson, Bridgit (2007): A Very Private Business: Exploring the Demand for Migrant Domestic Workers. *European Journal of Women's Studies* 14 (3), 247–264.

Anderson, Bridgit (2009): What's in a Name? Immigration Controls and Subjectivities: The Case of Au Pairs and Domestic Worker Visa Holders in the UK. *Subjectivity* 29, 407–424.

Anderson, Bridgit (2019): New Directions in Migration Studies: Towards Methodological De-Nationalism. *Comparative Migration Studies* 7, Article no. 36.

Anderson, B./Ruhs, M. (2010): *Who Needs Migrant Workers? Labour Shortages, Immigration, and Public Policy*. Oxford: Oxford University Press.

Andersson, R. (2014): *Illegality, Inc.: Clandestine Migration and the Business of Bordering Europe*. Oakland, CA: University of California Press.

Andresen, Sünne/Dölling, Irene (2005): Umbau des Geschlechter-Wissens von ReformakteurInnen durch Gender Mainstreaming? In: Ute Behning/Birgit Sauer

(Hrsg.), Was bewirkt Gender Mainstreaming? Evaluierung durch Policy Analysen. Frankfurt am Main, New York: Campus Verlag, 171–187.

Andrijasevic, R. (2010): *Migration, Agency and Citizenship in Sex Trafficking*. London: Palgrave.

Anthias, Floya (2001): The Concept of "Social Division" and Theorising Social Stratification: Looking at Ethnicity and Class. *Sociology* 35 (4), 835–854.

Anthias, Floya/Lazaridis, Gabriella (2000): Gender and Migration in Southern Europe: Women on the Move. Oxford: Berg.

Anthias, Floya/Morokvasic-Müller, Mirjana/Kontos, Maria (2012): *Paradoxes in Integration: Female Migration in Europe*. Springer-Verlag.

Apitzcs, Ursula (2010): Care and Migration. Die Ent-Sorgung menschlicher Reproduktionsarbeit entlang von Geschlechter- und Armutsgrenzen (Hg. mit Schmidbauer, Marianne). Opladen: Budrich-Verlag.

Apitzcs, Ursula (2010): Care and Reproduction (mit Schmidbauer, Marianne) In: Apitzsch/Schmidbauer (Hg.): *Care and Migration*. Opladen: Budrich Verlag, 11–22.

Apitzcs, Ursula (2010): Care, Migration and the Gender Order. Apitzsch/Schmidbauer (Hg.): *Care and Migration*. Opladen: Budrich Verlag, 113–125.

Apitzsch, Ursula/Irini, Siouti (2007): *Biographical Analysis as an Interdisciplinary Research Perspective in the Field of Migration Studies*. The York University Papers in Integrative Research Methods, Research Integration.

Appadurai, A. (1996): *Modernity at Large: Cultural Dimensions of Globalization*. Minneapolis: Press.

Arber, S./Ginn, J. (1990): The Meaning of Informal Care: Gender and the Contribution of Elderly People. *Ageing and Society* 10 (4), 429–454.

Archambault, Caroline (2010): Women Left Behind? Migration, Spousal Separation, and the Autonomy of Rural Women in Ugweno, Tanzania. *Signs* 35 (4), 919–942.

Bakan, A./Stasiulis, D. (1997): *Not One of the Family: Foreign Domestic Workers in Canada*. Toronto, ON: University of Toronto Press.

Baker, S. (2013): Conceptualising the Use of Facebook in Ethnographic Research: As Tool, as Data and as Context. *Ethnography and Education* 8 (2), 131–145.

Baldassar, L./Baldock, C./Wilding, R. (2007): *Families Caring Across Borders*, New York: Palgrave McMillan.

Baldassar, L./Merla, L. (2014): *Transnational Families, Migration and the Circulation of Care: Understanding Mobility and Absence in Family Life*. Abingdon: Routledge.

Balibar, Etienne (2004): *We, the People of Europe? Reflections on Transnational Citizenship*. Princeton, NJ: Princeton University Press.

Basch, L. G./Glick Schiller, N./Szanton Blanc, C. (1994): *Nations Unbound: Transnational Projects, Postcolonial Predicaments, and Deterritorialized Nation-States*. Langhorne: Gordon and Breach.

Basu, A./Grewal, I./Kaplan, C./Malkki, L. (2001): Editorial. *Signs: Journal of Women in Culture and Society* 26, 943–48.

Bauer, G./Österle, A. (2016): Mid and Later Life Care Work Migration: Patterns of Re-Organising Informal Care Obligations in Central and Eastern Europe. *Journal of Aging Studies* 37 (2), 81–93.

Bauman, Z. (1998): *Globalization. The Human Consequences.* Cambridge: Polity Press.

Bauman, Z. (2000): *Liquid Modernity.* Cambridge: Polity Press.

Bauman, Z. (2002): *Society Under Siege.* Cambridge: Polity Press.

Bauman, Z. (2007): *Liquid Times: Living in an Age of Uncertainty.* Cambridge: Polity Press.

Beck, U. (2000): The Cosmopolitan Perspective: Sociology of the Second Age of Modernity. *British Journal of Sociology* 51 (1), 79–105.

Beck, U. (2002): The Cosmopolitan Society and Its Enemies. *Theory, Culture and Society* 19 (1/2).

Beck, U./Bonss, W./Lau, C. (2003): The Theory of Reflexive Modernization: Problematic, Hypotheses and Research Programme. *Theory, Culture & Society* 20 (2), 1–33.

Becker, Karina (2016): Live-in and Burn-out? Migrantische Pflegekräfte in deutschen Haushalten. *Arbeit. Zeitschrift für Arbeitsforschung, Arbeitsgestaltung und Arbeitspolitik* 25 (1–2), 21–46.

Becker-Schmidt, Regina (1987): Die doppelte Vergesellschaftung – die doppelte Unterdrückung: Besonderheiten der Frauenforschung in den Sozialwissenschaften. Unterkirchen, Lilo/Wagner, Ines (Hg.): *Die andere Hälfte der Gesellschaft*. Österreichischer Soziologentag. Wien, 10–25.

Becker-Schmidt, Regina (1992): Geschlechterverhältnisse und Herrschaftszusammenhänge. C. Kuhlke/H. K. Degetoff/ U. Ramming (Hg.): *Wider das Schlichte Vergessen*. Orlanda: Campani editor Sigma, 216–236.

Beckmann, J. (2000): Auto Mobilization as Mobility Paradigm – Reflections on Car Drivers and Their Spatial Temporalities *Dansk Sociologi* [Danish Sociology] 1, 11, Årg. København.

Beckmann, J. (2001): Risky Mobility – the Filtering of Automobility's Unintended Consequences. København: Sociologisk Institut, Københavns Universitet.

Bélanger, Danièle/Silvey, Rachel (2019): An Im/mobility Turn: Power Geometries of Care and Migration. *Journal of Ethnic and Migration Studies* 46 (16), 3423–3440.

Bell, Martin/Ward, Gary (2000): Comparing Permanent Migration with Temporary Mobility. *Tourism Geographies* 2 (1), 97–107.

Beneito-Montagut, R. (2011): Ethnography Goes Online: Towards a User-Centered Methodology to Research Interpersonal Communication on the Internet. *Qualitative Research* 11 (6), 716–735.

Benhabib, Sheyla/Resnik, Judith (2009): *Migrations and Mobilities: Citizenship, Borders, and Gender,* edited by S. Benhabib and J. Resnik. New York: New York University Press.

Benson, M./O'Reilly, K. (2009): Migration and the Search for a Better Way of Life: A Critical Exploration of Lifestyle Migration. *The Sociological Review* 57 (4), 608–625.

Bergmann, S./Sager, T. (2008): *The Ethics of Mobilities: Rethinking Place, Exclusion, Freedom and Environment.* Routledge.

Bernard, H. Russell (1994): *Research Methods in Anthropology: Qualitative and Quantitative Approaches.* Walnut Creek, CA: AltaMira Press.

Black, R./Collyer, M. (2014): "Trapped" Populations: Limits on Mobility at Times of Crisis. S. F. Martin/S. Weerasinghe/A. Taylor (eds.): Humanitarian Crises and Migration: Causes, Consequences and Responses. Abingdon: Routledge, 287–305.

Blagojević, Marina (2009): *Knowledge Production at the Semiperiphery – A Gender Perspective.* Belgrade: Institut za kriminološka i sociološka istraživanja.

Bloch, A./Chimienti, M. (2011): Irregular Migration in a Globalizing World. *Journal for Ethnic and Racial Studies* 34, 1271–1285.

Boccagni, P. (2017): Aspirations and the Subjective Future of Migration: Comparing Views and Desires of the "Time ahead" through the Narratives of Immigrant Domestic Workers. *Comparative Migration Studies* 5 (4), 1–18.

Bojadžijev, Manuela/Karakayali, Serhat (2007): Autonomie der Migration: 10 Thesen zu einer Methode. *TurbulenteRänder: Neue Perspektiven auf Migration an den Grenzen Europas*, ed. Forschungsgruppe TRANSIT MIGRATION. Bielefeld: Transcript, 203–209.

Bonss, W./Kesselring S. (2001): Mobilität am Übergang von der Ersten zur Zweiten Moderne. U. Beck/W. Bonss/C. Lau (eds.): *Reflexive Modernisierung Überlegungen zur Transformation der industriellen Moderne* [Reflexive modernization: considering the transformation of the industrial modernity]. Frankfurt: Suhrkamp, 177–190.

Bonss, W./Kesselring S./Weiss, A. (2004): Society on the Move: Mobilitätspioniere in der Zweiten Moderne [Society on the move: mobility pioneers in an age of second modernity]. *Entgrenzung und Entscheidung: Perspektiven reflexiver Modernisierung [Shifting boundaries and decision: perspectives of the theory of reflexive modernization]*, eds. U. Beck, C. Lau. Frankfurt: Suhrkamp, 258–280.

Bourdieu, P. (1977): *Outline of a Theory of Practice.* Cambridge: Cambridge University Press.

Bourdieu, Pierre (1986): The Forms of Capital. *Handbook of Theory and Research for the Sociology of Education*, edited by John G. Richardson. Westport, Connecticut: Greenwood Press, Inc., 241–258.

Bourdieu, P. (1997): *Forms of Capital Education: Culture, Economy, Society*, ed. by A. H. Halsey. Oxford University Press.

LITERATURE 401

Bourdieu, P. (1998): *La pre "carite" est aujourd'hui partout*. Paris: Liber-Raisons d'agir, 95–101.

Bourdieu, P. (2003): Participant Objectivation: The Huxley Medal Lecture. *Journal of the Royal Anthropological Institute* 9 (2), 281–294.

Bourdieu, P./Wacquant, L. (1992): *An Invitation to Reflexive Sociology*. Cambridge: Polity Press.

Brennan, Denise (2004): *What's Love Got to Do With It? Transnational Desires and Sex Tourism in the Dominican Republic*. Durham, NC, London: Duke University Press.

Brewer, John, (2000): *Ethnography*. Buckingham: Open UP.

Brubaker R. (1999): The Manichean Myth: Rethinking the Distinction Between "Civic" and "Ethnic" Nationalism. *Nation and National Identity: The European Experience in Perspective*, edited by H. P. Kriesi. Chur, Zürich: Verlag Ruegger, 55–73.

Bryceson, Deborah/Fahy, Vuorela Ulla (2002): *Transnational Family: New European Frontiers and Global Networks*. Bloomsbury Academic.

Burawoy, M. (1979): *Manufacturing Consent: Changes in the Labor Process Under Monopoly Capitalism*. Chicago: University of Chicago Press.

Burawoy, M. (1998): The Extended Case Method. *Sociological Theory* 16 (1), 4–33.

Burawoy, M. (2000): *Global Ethnography: Forces, Connections, and Imaginations in Postmodern a World*. Berkeley: University of California Press.

Carling, J. R. (2002): Migration in the Age of Involuntary Immobility: Theoretical Reflections and Cape Verdean Experiences. *Journal of Ethnic and Migration Studies* 28 (1), 5–42.

Carling, Jørgen/Kerilyn, Schewel (2018): Revisiting Aspiration and Ability in International Migration. *Journal of Ethnic and Migration Studies* 44 (6), 945–963.

Castles, S./de Haas, H./Miller, M. (2013): *The Age of Migration. International Population Movements in the Modern World*. London: Palgrave Macmillan.

Castles, Stephen/Miller, Mark J. (1993): *The Age of Migration*. London: Palgrave.

Catarino, C./Morokvasic, M. (2005): Femmes, genre, migration et mobilités. *Revue européenne des migrations internationales* 21, 1–1.

Chamberlayne, P./King, A. (2000): *Cultures of Care. Biographies of Carers in Britain and the Two Germanies*. Bristol: Policy Press.

Chappell, N. L. (1992): *Social Support and Aging*. Toronto: Butterworths.

Clifford, James (1997): *Routes: Travel and Translation in the Late Twentieth Century* Cambridge, MA: Harvard University Press.

Collier, Jane Fishburne/Junko Yanagisako, Sylvia (1987): *Gender and Kinship: Essays toward a Unified Analysis*. Stanford University Press.

Collins P. H. (1986): Learning from the Outsider within: The Sociological Significance of Black Feminist Thought. *Social Problems* 33 (6), S14–S32.

Constable, N. (1997): *Maid to Order in Hong Kong: Stories of Filipina Workers*. Ithaca: Cornell University Press.

Constable, N. (2002): Filipina Workers in Hong Kong Homes. *Global Woman*, edited by B. Ehrenreich, A. Hochschild. London, Granta Books, 115–140.

Cox, R. (2004): *The Servant Problem. Domestic Employment in a Global Economy.* London: I. B. Tauris.

Cox, R. (2012): Gendered Work and Migration Regimes. *Transnational Migration, Gender and Rights*, edited by R. Sollund. Bingley, UK: Emerald, 33–52.

Cox, R. (2015): *Sisters or Servants? Au Pairs' Lives in Global Context.* Basingstoke: Palgrave Macmillan.

Cresswell, T. (2006): *On the Move: Mobility in the Modern Western World.* New York.

Cyrus, N. (2008): Being Illegal in Europe: Strategies and Policies for Fairer Treatment of Migrant Domestic Workers. Helma Lutz (ed.): *Migration and Domestic Work. A European Perspective on a Global Theme.* Aldershot: Ashgate.

Cyrus, N. (2008): Managing a Mobile Life: Changing Attitudes among Illegally Employed Polish Household Workers in Berlin. Sigrid Metz-Göckel/Mirjana Morokvasic/A. Senganata (eds.): *Migration and Mobility in an Enlarged Europe. A Gender Perspective.* Leverkusen: Budrich.

Dalsgaard, Steffen (2013): The Field as a Temporal Entity and the Challenges of the Contemporary Social Anthropology. *Anthropologie Sociale* 21 (2), 213–225.

Dalsgaard, S./Nielsen M. (2013): Introduction: Time and the Field. *Social Analysis* 57 (1), 1–19.

Dannecker, Petra (2005): Transnational Migration and the Transformation of Gender Relations: The Case of Bangladeshi Labour Migrants. *Current Sociology* 53 (4), 655–647.

Davies, C. A. (1999): *Reflexive Ethnography: A Guide to Researching Selves and Others.* New York: Routledge.

De Genova, N. (2002): Migrant "Illegality" and Deportability in Everyday Life. *Annual Review of Anthropology*, 419–447.

De Haas, H. (2010): The Internal Dynamics of Migration Processes: A Theoretical Inquiry. *Journal of Ethnic and Migration Studies* 36 (10), 1587–1617.

De Haas, H. (2010): Migration and Development: A Theoretical Perspective. *International International Migration Review* 44 (1), 227–264.

De Munck, Victor C./Sobo, Elisa J. (1998): *Using Methods in the Field: A Practical Introduction and Casebook.* Walnut Creek, CA: AltaMira Press.

De Regt, M. (2009): Preferences and Prejudices: Employers' Views on Domestic Workers in the Republic of Yemen. *Signs* 34, 559–581.

De Soto, H. (1989): *The Other Path.* New York: Basic Books.

De Vault, Marjorie (1991): *Feeding the Family: The Social Organization of Caring as Gendered Work.* Chicago: The University of Chicago Press.

De Walt, Kathleen M./De Walt, Billie R. (2002): Participant Observation: A Guide for Fieldworkers. Walnut Creek, CA: AltaMira Press.

Degiuli, F. (2016): *Caring for a Living: Migrant Women, Aging Citizens, and Italian Families.* Oxford: Oxford University Press.

LITERATURE

403

Diner, H. R. (1983): *Erin's Daughters in America: Irish Immigrant Women in the Nineteenth Century.* Baltimore, Md: Johns Hopkins Press.

Dirlik, Arif (1996): The Global in the Local. *Global/Local: Cultural Production and the Transnational Imaginary,* edited by R. Wilson and W. Dissanayake. Durham, NC: Duke University Press, 21–45.

Dölling, Irene (2005): „Geschlechter-Wissen" – ein nützlicher Begriff für die "verstehende" Analyse von Vergeschlechtlichungsprozessen? *Zeitschrift für Frauenforschungund Geschlechterstudien* 23 (1+2), 44–62.

Donato, Katherine/Gabaccia, Donna (2015): *Gender and International Migration: From the Slavery Era to the Global Age.* New York: Russell Sage Foundation.

Dörre, K. (2006): Prekäre Arbeit. Unsichere Beschäftigungsverhältnisse und ihre sozialen Folgen. *Arbeit* 15 (3), 181–193. doi: https://doi.org/10.1515/arbeit-2006 -0305.

Dumitru, Speranta (2014): From "Brain Drain" to "Care Drain": Women's Labor Migration and Methodological Sexism, *Women's Studies International Forum.*

Durkheim, E. (1982): *The Rules of Sociological Method.* New York: Free Press.

Eade, J./Drinkwater, S./Garapich, M. P. (2007): *Class and Ethnicity: Polish Migrant Workers.* London: Full Research Report, Swindon: ESRC.

Edensor, T. (2010): Commuter: Mobility, Rhythm and Commuting. *Geographies of Mobilities: Practices, Spaces, Subjects,* edited by Tim Cresswell and Peter Merriman. Ashgate.

Edward, Said (1978): *Orientalism.* New York: Pantheon.

Ehrenreich, B./Hochschild, A. R. (2002): *Global Woman: Nannies, Maids and Sex Workers in the New Economy.* London: Granta.

Elliot, Norum/Salazar N. B. (2017): *Methodologies of Mobility. Ethnography and Experiment.* Berghahn Books.

Elliott, A./Urry, J. (2010): *Mobile Lives.* New York, London: Routledge.

Ellis, C./Bochner, A. P. (2000): Autoethnography, Personal Narrative, Reflexivity: Researcher as Subject. *Handbook of Qualitative Research.* Thousand Oaks, CA: Sage, 733–768.

England, Kim (1994): Getting Personal: Reflexivity, Positionality, and Feminist Research. *The Professional Geographer* 46 (1), 80–91.

England, Kim (2017): Home, Domestic Work and the State. *Critical Social Policy* 37, 367–385.

England, Paula (2005): Emerging Theories of Care Work. *Annual Review Sociology* 31, 381–399.

Faist, T. (2012): Toward a Transnational Methodology: Methods to Address Methodological Nationalism, Essentialism, and Positionality. *Revue Européenne des Migrations Internationales* 28 (1), 51–70.

Faist, Thomas (2013): The Mobility Turn: A New Paradigm for the Social Sciences? *Ethnic and Racial Studies* 36 (11), 1637–1646.

Ferreira, V./Tavares, T./Portugal, S. (1998): *Shifting Bonds, Shifting Bounds: Women, Mobility and Citizenship in Europe.* Oeiras: Celta Editora.

Fetterman, D. M. (1998): *Ethnography: Step by Step*. Thousand Oaks, Calif.: Sage.

Fine, Michael (2007): *A Caring Society? Care and the Dilemmas of Human Services in the Twenty-First Century*. Basingstoke: Palgrave Macmillan.

Fine, Michael (2015): Cultures of Care. *Routledge Handbook of Cultural Gerontology*, edited by J. Twigg and W. Martin. Routledge: Abingdon UK, 269–276.

Flamm Michael/Kaufmann, Vincent (2006): Operationalising the Concept of Motility: A Qualitative Study. *Journal Mobilities* 1 (2).

Folbre, N. (2001): *The Invisible Heart: Economics and Family Values*. New York: New Press.

Frändberg, L. (2008): Paths in Transnational Time-Space: Representing Mobility Biographies of Young Swedes. *Geografiska Annaler* 90B (1), 17–28.

Fricker, Miranda (2007): *Epistemic Injustice: Power and the Ethics of Knowing*. Oxford: Oxford University Press.

Gabaccia, Donna (1996): Women of the Mass Migrations: From Minority to Majority, 1820–1930. *European Migrant. Global and Local Perspectives*, edited by Hoerder, Dirk and Moch, Leslie P. Boston: Northeastern University Press, 90–11.

Gallo, E./Scrinzi, F. (2016): *Migration, Masculinities and Reproductive Labour: Men of the Home*. (Migration, Diasporas and Citizenship). Basingstoke, Hampshire: Palgrave Macmillan.

Gamburd, M. R. (2000): *The Kitchen Spoon's Handle: Transnationalism and Sri Lanka's Migrant Housemaids*. Ithaca, NY: Cornell University Press.

Gardner, K. (1995): *Global Migrants, Local Lives: Travel and Transformation in Rural Bangladesh*. Oxford: Oxford University Press.

Geissler, Brigitte (2006): Haushalts-Dienstleistungen als informelle Erwerbsarbeit: neue Ungleichheit oderAusdifferenzierung des Arbeitsmarktes? *Arbeit* 15 (3), 194–205.

Gherardi, Laura (2011): Human Costs of Mobility: On Management in Multinational Companies. *The Politics of Proximity. Mobility and Immobility in Practice* edited by Giuseppina Pellegrino. Ashgate.

Gibson-Graham, J. K. (1996): *The End of Capitalism (As We Knew It): A Feminist Critique of Political Economy*. Minneapolis: University of Minnesota Press.

Giddens, A. (1982): *Profiles and Critiques in Social Theory*. Berkeley, CA.

Giddens, A. (1991): *Modernity and Self-Identity*. Cambridge: Polity Press.

Giddens, A. (1994): Living in a Post-Traditional Society. *Reflexive Modernization: Politics, Tradition and Aesthetics in the Modern Social Order*, edited by B. Beck, A. Giddens and S. Lash. Cambridge: Polity.

Gill, Lesley (1994): *Precarious Dependencies: Gender, Class, and Domestic Service in Bolivia*. New York: Columbia University Press.

Glenn, Evelyn Nakano (2002): *Unequal Freedom: How Race and Gender Shaped American Citizenship and Labor*. Cambridge, Mass.: Harvard University Press.

Glick Schiller, N./Basch, L./Szanton-Blanc, C. (1992): Transnationalism: A new Analytic Framework for Understanding Migration. N. Glick Schiller/L. Basch/ C. Szanton-Blanc (eds.): *Towards a Transnational Perspective on Migration: Race,*

Class, Ethnicity and Nationalism Reconsidered. (Annals of the New York Academy of Sciences, Vol. 645), 1–25.

Glick Schiller, N./Salazar, N. B. (2013): Regimes of Mobility Across the Globe. *Journal of Ethnic and Migration Studies* 39 (2): 183–200.

Goffman, Erving (1959): The Presentation of Self in Everyday Life. Doubleday: Anchor Books.

Gold, Raymond L. (1958): Roles in Sociological Field Observations. *Social Forces*, 36, 217–223.

Górny, Stola (2001): Akumulacja i wykorzystanie migracyjnego kapitału społecznego [Accumulation and use of migrant social capital]. E. Jaźwinska/M. Okólski (eds.): Ludzie na Huśtawce. Migracje między Peryferiami Polski a Zachodem [People on a swing: Migration between peripheries of Poland and the West]. Warsaw: Wydawnictwo Naukowe Scholar.

Goss, Jon/Lindquist, Bruce (1995): Conceptualizing International Labor Migration: A Structuration Perspective. *The International Migration Review* 29 (2), 317–351.

Götz, Irene (2010): Ethnografien der Nähe – Anmerkungen zum methodologischen Potenzial neuerer arbeitsethnografischer Forschungen der Europäischen Ethnologie. *Arbeits-und Industriesoziologische Studien* 3 (1), 101–117.

Götz, Irene (2016): Mobility and Immobility: Background of the Project. Miriam Gutekunst/Andreas Hackl/Sabina Leoncini/Julia Sophia Schwarz/Irene Götz (eds.): *Bounded Mobilities. Ethnographic Perspectives on Social Hierarchies and Global Inequalitites.* Bielefeld: Transcript.

Götz, Irene (2019): *Kein Ruhestand: Wie Frauen mit Altersartmut umgehen.* Verlag Antje Kunstmann.

Götz, Irene/Lemberger, Barbara (2009): Prekär arbeiten, prekär leben: Einige Überlegungen zur Einführung. *Prekär arbeiten, prekär leben. Kulturwissenschaftliche Perspektiven auf ein gesellschaftliches Phänomen.* Frankfurt/New York: Campus Verlag, 7–30.

Graham, H. (1983): Caring: a Labour of Love. *A Labour of Love: Women, Work and Caring,* edited by J. Finch and D. Groves. London: Routledge and Kegan Paul.

Granovetter, M. (1973): The Strength of Weak Ties. *American Journal of Sociology* 78 (6), 1360–1380.

Grassmuck, S./Pessar, P. (1991): *Between Two Islands: Dominican International Migration.* Berkeley: California University Press.

Grosz, Elizabeth (1992): Bodies-Cities. *Sexuality and Space,* edited by Beatriz Colomina. New York: Princeton Architectural, 241–253.

Gubrium, J. F. (1975): *Living and Dying in Murray Manor.* New York: St Martins.

Gurak, D. T./Cace F. (1992): Migration Networks and the Shaping of Migration Systems. *International Migration Systems,* edited by M. M. Kritz et al. Oxford: Oxford University Press.

Gutiérrez Rodríguez, Encarnación (2007): The "Hidden Side" of the New Economy: On Transnational Migration, Domestic Work, and Unprecedented Intimacy. *Frontiers: A Journal of Women Studies* 28 (3), 60–83.

Gutierrez Rodriguez, Encarnacion (2010): *Migration, Domestic Work and Affect: A Decolonial Approach on Value and the Feminization of Labor*. London: Routledge.

Haidinger, Bettina (2008): Contingencies Among Households: Gendered Division of Labour and Transnational Household Organization – The Case of Ukrainians in Austria. *Migration and Domestic Work: A European Perspective on a Global Theme*, edited by Helma Lutz. Ashgate Publishing Limited.

Hall, C. M./Williams, A. M. (2002): *Tourism and Migration: New Relationships Between Production and Consumption*. Boston: Kluwer.

Hammersley, M./Atkinson, P. (1995): *Ethnography: Principles in Practice*. Second ed. London: Routledge.

Hann, C./Humphrey, C./Verdery, K. (2002): Postsocialism as a Topic of Anthropological Investigation. *Postsocialism: Ideals, Ideologies, and Practices in Eurasia*. 1–28.

Hannam, K./Sheller, M./Urry, J. (2006): Mobilities, Immobilities and Moorings. *Mobilities* 1, 1–22.

Hannerz, U. (2003): Several Sites in One. Thomas Hylland Eriksen (ed.): Globalisation: Studies in Anthropology, trans. Daniel Winfree Papuga. London: Pluto Press, 18–38.

Hansen, Karen T. (1986): Household Work as a Man's Job: Sex and Gender in Domestic Service in Zambia. *Anthropology Today* 2 (3), 18–23.

Hampton, K./Wellman, B. (2003): Neighboring in Netville: How the Internet Supports Community and Social Capital in a Wired Suburb. *City & Community*, 2 (4), 277–311.

Haraway, D. (1989): *Primate Visions: Gender, Race, and Nature in the World of Modern Science*. New York: Routledge.

Harding, Sandra (1987): Is There a Feminist Method? *Feminism and Methodology. Social Science Issues*, ed. S. Harding. Bloomington: Indiana University Press, 1–14.

Hardt, M./Negri, A. (2009): *Commonwealth*. Cambridge, MA: Harvard University Press.

Harvey, David (1989): *The Condition of Postmodernity. An Enquiry into the Origins of Cultural Change*. London: Blackwell.

Harvey, David (2006): *Spaces of Global Capitalism*. London: Verso.

Harzig, Christiane (1997): Creating a Community: German-American Women in Chicago. *Peasant Maids – City Women: From the European Countryside to Urban America*. Ithaca, N.Y.: Cornell University Press, 185–222.

Haubner, Tine (2014): Osteuropäische Care Workers im Licht der neueren sozialwissenschaftlichen Forschung und Theoriebildung. *Zeitschrift für Gerontologie und Ethik* 2, 9–27.

Hedican, E. J. (2001): *Up in Nipigon Country: Anthropology as a Personal Experience*. Halifax, Canada: Fernwood.

Herrera, G. (2013): *"Lejos de tus pupilas", Familia transnacionales, cuidados y desigualdad social en*. Quito, Ecuador: FLACSO.

LITERATURE

Hess, Sabine (2005): Feminized Transnational Spaces – Or Interplay of Gender and Nation. *Anthropological Yearbook of European Cultures* 14, 227–246.

Hess, Sabine (2005): *Globalisierte Hausarbeit: Au-pair als Migrationsstrategie von Frauen aus Osteuropa*. Wiesbaden: VS Verlag für Sozialwissenschaften.

Hess, Sabine (2017): Border Crossing as Act of Resistance: The Autonomy of Migration as Theoretical Intervention into Border Studies. M. Butler/P. Mecheril/ L. Brenningmeyer (eds.): *Resistance: Subjects, Representations, Contexts*. Transcript Verlag.

Hess, Sabine/Kasparek, Bernd/Kron, Stefanie/Rodatz, Mathias/Schwertl, Maria/ Sontowski, Simon (2017): *Der lange Sommer der Migration: Grenzregime III*. Berlin: Assoziation A.

Hess, S./Puckhaber, A. (2004): "Big Sisters" are Better Domestic Servants?! Comments on the Booming au Pair Business. *Feminist Review* 77 (1), 65–78.

Heyl Sherman, Barbara (2001): Ethnographic Interviewing. *Handbook of Ethnography*, edited by Paul Atkinson, Amanda Coffey, Sara Delamont, John Lofland, Lyn Lofland. Sage Publications Ltd.

Hine, Christine (2000): *Virtual Ethnography*. London, Thousand Oaks, Calif.: Sage.

Hochschild, A. (1983): *The Managed Heart: Commercialization of Human Feeling*. Berkeley: University California Press.

Hochschild, A. R. (2000): Love and Gold". *Global Woman: Nannies, Maids, and Sex Workers in the New Economy*, edited by B. Ehrenreich and A. R. Hochschild. New York: Holt.

Hochschild, A. R. (2001): Global Care Chains and Emotional Surplus. *On the Edge. Living with Global Capitalism*, edited by W. Hutton and A. Giddens. London.

Holstein, James A./Gubrium, Jaber F. (1995): Deprivatization and the Construction of Domestic Life. *Journal of Marriage and the Family* 57, 894–908.

Hondagneu-Sotelo, P. (1994): *Gendered Transitions: Mexican Experiences of Immigration*. University of California Press.

Hondagneu-Sotelo, Pierrette (2000): Feminism and Migration Scholarship. *The Annals of the American Academy of Political and Social Science*, special issue on "The Social Sciences: A Feminist View", guest editor Christine Williams, vol. 571, 107–120.

Hondagneu-Sotelo, P. (2007): *Doméstica: Immigrant Workers Cleaning and Caring in the Shadows of Affluence*. Berkeley: University of California Press.

Hondagneu-Sotelo, Pierrette/Avila, Ernestine (1997): I am here, but I am there: The meaning of Latina Transnational Motherood. *Gender and Society* 11 (5).

Horst, H./Miller, D. (2012): *Digital Anthropology*. London: Bloomsbury.

Hosltein, James A./Gubrium, Jaber F. (1995): *The Active Interview*. Thousand Oaks, CA: Sage.

Hrzenjak, Majda (2014): Globalizacija skrbstvenega dela in polozaj primorksih skrbstvenih delavki. *Dve domovini, International Migration Review* 40 (1), 64–81.

Hugo, G. (1996): Environmental Concerns and International Migration. *International Migration Review* 30 (1), 105–131.

Inowlocki, Lena/Lutz, Helma (2000): Hard Labour. The Biographical Work of a Turkish Migrant Woman in Germany. *Special Issue of the European Journal of Women's Studies* 7 (2), 289–308.

Isaksen, Lise Widding (2010): *Global Care Work. Gender and Migration in Nordic Societies*. Lund, Sweden: Nordic Academic Press.

Jervis, L. L. (2001): The Pollution of Incontinence and the Dirty Work of Caregiving in a U. S. Nursing Home. *Medical Anthropology Quarterly* 15 (1), 84–99.

Kaneff, D. (2002): The Shame and Pride of Market Activity: Morality, Identity and Trading in Post-Socialist Rural Bulgaria. *Markets and Moralities*, edited by C. Humphrey and R. Mandel. Oxford: Berg, 33–52.

Karacan, E. (2020): Coping with Vulnerabilities in Old Age and Retirement: Cross-Border Mobility, Family Relations and Social Networks of German Retirees in Alanya. *Journal of Intergenerational Relationships*.

Karakayali, Juliana (2009): *Transnationale care workers in Haushalten Pflegebedürftiger: Biographische Interviews mit Migrantinnen aus Osteuropa*. Frankfurt am Main: VS Verlag.

Karakayalı, Serhat/Tsianos, Vassilis (2015): Movements that Matter. Eine Einleitung. *Turbulente Ränder: Neue Perspektiven auf Migration an den Grenzen Europas* (2. Auflage), edited by TRANSIT MIGRATION Forschungsgruppe. Bielefeld: transcript Verlag, 7–22.

Karner, Tracy (1998): Professional Caring: Homecare Workers as Fictive Kin. *Journal of Aging Studies* 12, 69–82.

Kaufmann, Vincent (2002): *Re-thinking Mobility*. Ashgate.

Kaufmann, Vincent (2011): *Re-thinking the City*. EPFL Press.

Kaufmann, Vincent (2014): Mobility as a Tool for Sociology. *Sociologica*

Kaufmann, V./Bergman, Manfred Max/Joye, Dominique (2004): Motility: Mobility as Capital. *International Journal of Urban and Regional Research* 28 (4).

Kellerman, Aharon (2006): *Personal Mobilities*. London, New York: Routledge.

Kellerman, Aharon (2012): Potential Mobilities. *Mobilities* 7 (1), 171–183.

Kesselring, S. (2006): Pioneering Mobilities: New Patterns of Movement and Motility in a Mobile World. *Environment and Planning* 38, 269–279.

Kesselring, S./Vogl, G. (2008): Networks, Scapes and Flows – Mobility Pioneers between First and Second Modernity. *Tracing Mobilities: Towards a Cosmopolitan Perspective*, edited by W. Canzler, V. Kaufmann and S. Kesselring. Farnham and Burlington: Ashgate, 163–180.

Kilkey, Majella (2010): Men and Domestic Labor: A Missing Link in the Global Care Chain. *Men and Masculinities* 13 (1), 126–149.

Kilkey, M./Perrons, D./Plomien, A. (2013): *Gender, migration and domestic work: Masculinities, male labour and fathering in the UK and USA*. Springer.

King, R./Ruiz-Gelices, E. (2003): International Student Migration and the European Year Abroad: Effects on European Identity and Subsequent Migration Behaviour. *International Journal of Population Geography* 9 (3), 229–252.

Kofman, Eleonore (1999): Female "Birds of Passage a Decade Later: Gender and Immigration in the Eurpean Union. *International Migration Review* 33 (2).

Kofman, Eleonore (2004): Family-Related Migration: A Critical Review of European Studies. *Journal of Ethnic and Migration Studies* 30 (2), 243–262.

Kofman, Eleonore/Phizacklea, Annie/Raghuram, Parvati/Sales, Rosemary (eds.) (2000): *Gender and International Migration in Europe.* London: Routledge.

Koh, S. Y./Wissink, B. (2018): Enabling, Structuring and Creating Elite Transnational Lifestyles: Intermediaries of the Super-Rich and the Elite Mobilities Industry. *Journal of Ethnic and Migration Studies* 44 (4), 592–609.

Kontos, Maria (2013): Negotiating Social Citizenship Rights of Migrant Domestic Workers: The Right to Family Reunification and Family Life in Policies and Debates. *Journal of Ethnic and Migration Studies* 39 (3), 409–424.

Koser, Khalid/Lutz, Helma (eds.) (1998): *The New Migration in Europe: Social Constructions and Social Realities.* London: Macmillan Press.

Kosnick, Kira (2010): Sexuality and Migration Studies. The Invisible, the Oxymoronic and Heteronormative Othering. Helma Lutz/Maria Teresa Herrera Vivar/Linda Supik (ed.): *Framing Intersectionality. Debates on a Multi-faceted Concept in Gender Studies.* Farnham: Ashgate, 121–135.

Krzyżowski, L. (2013): *Polscy migranci i ich starzejący się rodzice. Transnarodowy system opieki międzygeneracyjnej.* Warszawa: Wydawnictwo Naukowe Scholar.

Lamont, Michèle (1992): *Money, Morals, and Manners: The Culture of the French and the American Upper-Middle Class.* United Kingdom: University of Chicago Press.

Lamont, Michèle/Molnár, Virág (2002): The Study of Boundaries Across the Social Sciences. *Annual Review of Sociology* 28, 167–195.

Lan, Pen Chia, (2006): *Global Cindarellas: Migrant Domestics and Newly Rich Employers.* Duke University Press.

Lapadat, J. C./Lindsay, A. C. (1999): Transcription in Research and Practice: From Guide to Research Methods. London: Sage, 111–131.

Leivestad, H. H. (2016): Motility. *The Keywords of Mobility: Critical Engagements,* edited by Noel B. Salazar and Kiran Jayaram. Oxford: Berghahn.

Leon, M. (2014): *The Transformation of Care in European Societies.* Basingstoke: Palgrave Macmillan.

Levitt, Peggy (2001): *The Transnational Villagers,* Berkeley: University of California Press.

Levitt, P./Khagram, S. (2007): *The Transnational Studies Reader: Intersections and Innovations.* London: Routledge.

Levitt, P./Lamba-Nieves, D. (2010): Social Remittances Revisited. *Journal of Ethnic and Migration Studies* 37, 1–22.

Lewis, J. (2001): The Decline of the Male Breadwinner Model: Implications for Work and Care. *Social Politics* 8 (2), 152–69.

Lewis, O. (1954): *Five Families.* New York: Basic Books, Inc.

Libin, A./Libin, E. (2005): Cyber-Anthropology: A New Study on Human and Technological Co-Evolution. *Studies in Health Technology and Informatics* 118, 146.

Lim, A. (2016): Transnational Organising and Feminist Politics of Difference and Solidarity. *Asian Studies Review* 40, 70–88.

Lindquist, J. A. (2009): *The Anxieties of Mobility: Migration and Tourism in the Indonesian Borderland.* Honolulu: University of Hawaii Press.

Lindquist, J. (2010a): Labour Recruitment, Circuits of Capital and Gendered Mobility: Reconceptualizing the Indonesian Migration Industry. *Pacifica Affairs* 83 (1), 115–132.

Lindquist, J. (2010b): Images and Evidence: Human Trafficking, Auditing, and the Production of Illicit Markets in Southeast Asia and Beyond. *Public Culture* 22 (2), 223–236.

Lindquist, J./Xiang, B./Yeoh, B. (2012): Opening the Black Box of Migration, Brokers, the Organization of Transnational Mobility and the Changing Political Economy in Asia. *Pacific Affairs* 85 (1), 7–19.

Loncar, Sanja (2013): Etnografije hrvatskih migrantica u Minhenu: važnost razvijanja društvenih mreža novih osobnih znanja i vještina. *Hrvatska svakodnevica: etnografije vremena i prostora*, Jasna Čapo and Valentina Gulin Zrnić (red.). Zagreb: Institut za folkloristiku.

Lubkemann, S. C. (2008): Involuntary Immobility: On a Theoretical Invisibility in Forced Migration Studies. *Journal of Refugee Studies* 21 (4), 454–475.

Lutz, Helma (1997): The Limits of European-ness. Immigrant Women in Fortress Europe. *Feminist Review* 57 (3), 112–139.

Lutz, Helma (2008): *Migration and Domestic Work. A European Perspective on a Global Theme.* Aldershot: Ashgate.

Lutz, Helma (2010): Gender in Migratory Process. *Journal of Ethnic and Migration Studies* 36 (10), 1647–1663.

Lutz, Helma (2011): *The New Maids: Transnational Women and the Care Economy.* London: Zed Books.

Lutz, Helma (2017): Care as a Fictitious Commodity: Reflections on the Intersections of Migration, Gender and Care Regimes. *Migration Studies.*

Lutz, Helma/Palenga-Möllenbeck, Eva (2010): Care Work Migration in Germany: Semi-Compliance and Complicity. Majella Kilkey u. a. (Hg.): *Domestic and Care Work at the Intersection of Welfare, Gender and Migration Regimes: Some European Experiences.* (Special Issue for the Journal Social Policy and Society 9, 3). Cambridge University Press.

Lutz, Helma/Palenga-Möllenbeck, Ewa (2015): Care-Arbeit, Gender und Migration: Überlegungen zu einer Theorie transnationaler Migration im Haushaltssektor in Europa. Uta Meier-Gräwe (Hrsg.): *Die Arbeit des Alltags. Gesellschaftliche Organisation und Umverteilung.* Wiesbaden Springer, 181–200 (Wiederabdruck) (zus. mit Ewa Palenga-Möllenbeck).

LITERATURE

Macbeth, D. (2001): On "Reflexivity" in Qualitative Research: Two Readings and a Third. *Qualitative Inquiry* 7 (1), 35–68.

Madianou, M./Miller, D. (2013): Polymedia: Towards a New Theory of Digital Media in Interpersonal Communication. *International Journal of Cultural Studies* 16 (2), 169–187.

Mahler, S. J./Pessar, P. (2001): Gendered Geographies of Power: Analyzing Gender Across Transnational Spaces. *Identities: Global Studies in Culture and Power.*

Mahler, S. J./Pessar, P. (2006): Gender Matters: Ethnographers Bring Gender from the Periphery toward the Core of Migration Studies. *International Migration Review* 40 (1) (Gender and Migration Revisited, Center for Migration Studies, New York).

Mai, N. (2013): Embodied Cosmopolitanisms: The Subjective Mobility of Migrants Working in the Global Sex Industry. *Gender, Place and Culture* 20, 107–124.

Malkki, L. H. (1992): National Geographic: The Rooting of Peoples and the Territorialization of National Identity among Scholars and Refugees. *Cultural Anthropology* 7 (1), 24–44.

Manalansan, Martin (2006): Queer Intersections: Sexuality and Gender in Migration Studies. *IMR* 40 (1), 224–249.

Manderscheid, K./Bergman, M. M. (2008): Spatial Patterns and Social Inequality in Switzerland: Modern or Postmodern? *The Social Fabric of the Networked City*, edited by G. Pflieger, L. Pattaroni, C. Jemelin, V. Kaufmann. London: EPFL Press, 41–65.

Maranto, G./Barton, M. (2010): Paradox and Promise: My Space, Facebook, and the Sociopolitics of Social Networking in the Writing Classroom. *Computers and Composition* 27, 36–47.

Marcus, G. (1998): *Ethnography Through Thick and Thin.* Princeton: Princeton University Press.

Marcus, G. E./Fischer, M. J. (1986): *Anthropology as Cultural Critique: An Experimental Moment in the Human Sciences.* University of Chicago Press.

Massey, Doreen (1993): Power-Geometry and a Progressive Sense of Place. *Mapping the Futures*, edited by J. Bird et. al. London: Routledge, 56–69.

Massey, Douglas/Garcia Espana, Felipe (1987): The Social Processes of International Migration. *Science* 237.

Massey, S. Douglas/Arango, Joaquin/Hugo, Graeme/Kouaouci, Ali/Pellegrino, Adela/Taylor, J. Edward (1993): Theories of International Migration: A Review and Appraisal, *Population and Development Review.*

Massey, G./Hahn, K./Sekulic, D. (1995): Women, Men, and the "Second Shift" in Socialist Yugoslavia. *Gender and Society* 9 (3), 359–379.

Mauthner, Natasha S./Doucet, A. (2003): Reflexive Accounts and Accounts of Reflexivity Inqualitative Data Analysis. *Sociology* 37 (3), 413–431.

Mavrinac, Duga (2015): "A LABOUR OF LOVE?" Informal Eldercare Work and Domestic Space in Contemporary Croatia. *Etnološka tribina* 38, Vol. 45, 86–96.

May, R. A. B. (2014): When the Methodological Shoe Is on the Other Foot: African American Interviewer and White Interviewees. *Qualitative Sociology* 37, 117–136.

Merry, S. E. (2000): Crossing Boundaries: Methodological Challenges for Ethnography in the Twent First Century. *Political and Legal Anthropology Review* 23 (2), 127–134.

Merton, Robert K. (1972): Insiders and Outsiders: A Chapter in the Sociology of Knowledge. *American Journal of Sociology* 78, 9–47.

Metz-Göckel, Sigrid/Morokvasic, Mirjana/Senganata, A. (2008): *Migration and mobility in an enlarged Europe. A gender perspective.* Leverkusen: Budrich.

Michel, S./Peng, I. (2012): All in the Family? Migrants, Nationhood, and Care Regimes in Asia and North America. *Journal of European Social Policy* 22 (4), 406–418.

Mikuš, M. (2019): Contesting Household Debt in Croatia: The Double Movement of Financialization and the Fetishism of Money in Eastern European Peripheries. *Dialect Anthropol* 43, 295–315.

Miller, Daniel (2001): *Tales from Facebook.* Cambridge, UK: Polity Press.

Milosavljević, Ljubica/Antonijević, Dragana (2015): Nursing Homes as the Perspective and Reality of Guest Workers in Old Age. *Etnoantropološki problemi* 10 (2), 333–355.

Moch Page, Leslie (2003): *Moving Europeans: Migration in Western Europe since 1650.* Indiana University Press.

Mol, Annemarie/Law, John (1994): Regions, Networks and Fluids: Anaemia and Social Topology. *Social Studies of Science* 24, 641–671.

Momsen, J. (1999): Maids on the Move. *Gender, Migration and Domestic Service*, edited by J. Momsen. London: Routledge.

Moore, Henrietta L. (1994): *A Passion for Difference.* Cambridge: Polity Press.

Morokvasic, M. (1984): Birds of Passage Are also Women. *International Migration Review* 18.

Morokvasic, M. (1994): Wanderungsraum Europa. Menschen und Grenzen in Bewegung (L'Europe comme espace migratoire: les hommes et les frontières en mouvement) (dir. avec H. Rudolph). Berlin : Sigma.

Morokvasic, M. (1996): *Migrants. Les nouvelles mobilités en Europe* (avec H. Rudolph). Paris: L'Harmattan.

Morokvasic, Mirjana (2004): Settled in Mobility: Engendering Post-Wall Migration in Europe. *Feminist Review* 77 (1), 7–25.

Morokvasic, M. (2006): *Crossing Borders and Shifting Boundaries of Belonging in Post-Wall Europe. A Gender Lens.* (English version of text published in Ariane Berthoin Antal and Sigrid Quack (eds.): Grenzüberschreitungen – Grenzziehungen. Implikationen für Innovation und Identität. Berlin: Sigma.)

Morokvasic, M. (2010): Feminizacija migracija? *Stanovnistvo* 2, Beograd.

Moya, Jose C. (2007): Domestic Service in a Global Perspective: Gender, Migration, and Ethnic Niches. *Journal of Ethnic and Migration Studies* 33 (4), 559–579.

LITERATURE 413

Murphy, Elizabeth/ Dingwall, Robert (2001): The Ethics of Ethnography. *Handbook of Ethnography*, edited by Paul Atkinson, Amanda Coffey, Sara Delamont, John Lofland, Lyn Lofland. Sage Publications Ltd.

Näre, Lena (2009): The Making of "Proper" Homes – Everyday Practices of Migrant Domestic Work in Naples. *Modern Italy* 14 (1), 1–17.

Näre, Lena (2010): Sri Lankan Men Working as Cleaners and Carers: Negotiating Masculinity in Naples. *Men and Masculinities* 13 (1), 65–86.

Näre, L. (2011): The Informal Economy of Paid Domestic Work – The Case of Ukrainian and Polish Migrants in Naples. *Foggy Social Structures: Irregular Migration and Informal Economy in Western Europe*, edited by M. Bommes and G. Sciortino. Amsterdam: Amsterdam University Press, 67–87.

Näre, Lena (2014): Agency as Capabilities: Ukrainian Women's Narratives of Social Change and Mobility. *Women's Studies International Forum*.

Nieswand, Boris (2011): *Theorising Transnational Migration: The Status Paradox of Migration*. New York: Routledge.

Nieswand, Boris/Drotbohm, Heike (2014*): Kultur, Gesellschaft, Migration: Die reflexive Wende in der Migrationsforschung.*

Nippert-Eng, Christena (1995): *Home and Work: Negotiating Boundaries through Everyday Life*. Chicago: University of Chicago Press.

Nowicka, M. (2007): Mobile Locations: Construction of Home in a Group of Mobile Transnational Professionals. *Global Networks* 7 (1), 69–86.

Nyíri, Pál (2010): *Mobility and Cultural Authority in Contemporary China*. Seattle: University of Washington Press.

Ohnmacht, Timo/Maksim, Hanja/Bergman, M. M. (2009): *Mobilities and Inequality*. Farnham, England: Ashgate Pub. Co.

Okely, Judith (1992): Anthropology and Autobiography: Participatory Experience and Embodied Knowledge. *Anthropology and Autobiography: Gender Implications in Fieldwork and Texts*, edited by Judith Okely and Helen Callaway. London: Routledge.

Okely, Judith, (2012): *Anthropological Practice: Fieldwork and the Ethnographic Method*. London: Bloomsbury.

Ong, Aihwa (1999): *Flexible Citizenship: The Cultural Logics of Transnationality*. Duke University Press.

Osella, Filippo/Osella, Caroline (2000): *Social Mobility in Kerala: Modernity and Identity in Conflict*. London: Pluto.

Oso, Laura/Catarino, Christine (2013): From Sex to Gender: The Feminisation of Migration and Labour-Market Insertion in Spain and Portugal. *Journal of Ethnic and Migration Studies* 39 (4), 625–647.

Oso Casas, L./Garson, J. P. (2005): *Migrant Women and the Labour Market: Diversity and Challenges*. OECD and European Commission Seminar, Brussels, 26–27 September.

Ozyegin, Gul (1996): Verwandtschaftsnetzwerke, Patronage und Klassenschuld. Das Verhältnis von Hausangestellten und ihren Arbeitgeberinnen in der Türkei. *Frauen in der Einen Welt* 7 (2), 9–27.

Ozyegin, Gul (2000): *Untidy Gender: Domestic Service in Turkey.* Philadelphia: Temple University Press.

Pajnik, M. (2008): *Prostitution and Human Trafficking: Gender, Labor and Migration Aspects.* Ljubljana: Mirovni inštitut (Peace Institute).

Palenga Möllenbeck, Ewa (2011): Care, Gender and Migration: Towards a Theory of Transnational Domestic Work Migration in Europe. Martha Worsching (ed.): *Crises and the Gendered Division of Labour in Europe Today.* (Special Issue of the Journal of Contemporary European Studies, 19, 3), 349–364 (with Helma Lutz), http://www.tandfonline.com/doi/abs/10.1080/14782804.2011.610605.

Palenga Möllenbeck, Ewa (2013): New Maids – New Butlers? Polish Domestic Workers in Germany and Commodification of Social Reproductive Work. Brigitte Aulenbacher/Cecilia Innreiter-Moser (ed.): *Making the Difference – Critical Perspectives on the Configuration of Work, Diversity and Inequalities.* (Special issue of Equality, Diversity and Inclusion: An international Journal, 32, 6), 557–574.

Palenga Möllenbeck, Ewa (2014): Care-Migrantinnen im geteilten Europa – Verbindungen und Widersprüche in einem transnationalen Raum. In: Brigitte Aulenbacher/Birgit Riegraf/Hildegard Theobald (Hg.): *Care im Spiegel der soziologischen Diskussion.* (Sonderheft der Sozialen Welt 20), 217–231 (mit Helma Lutz).

Palmer, P. (1989): *Domesticity and Dirt: Housewives and Domestic Servants in the United States, 1920–1945.* Philadelphia: Temple University Press.

Papadopoulos, D./Stephenson, N./Tsianos, V. (2008): *Escape Routes: Control and Subversion in the Twenty-First Century.* Pluto Press.

Papastergiadis, Nikos (2000): *The Turbulence of Migration. Globalisation, Deterritorialization and Hybridity.* Cambridge: Polity.

Parreñas, R. S. (2001): *Servants of Globalization: Women, Migration and Domestic Work.* Stanford University Press.

Parreñas, R. S. (2005): *Children of Global Migration: Transnational Families and Gendered Woes.* Stanford University Press.

Parreñas, R. S. (2009): Inserting Feminism in Transnational Migration Studies. *Migrationonline,* URL: http://migrationonline.cz/en/inserting-feminism-in-transnational-migration-studies.

Parreñas, Rhacel Salazar/Boris, Eileen (2010): *Intimate Labors: Cultures, Technologies, and the Politics of Care.* Redwood City: Stanford University Press.

Passerini, L./Lyon, D./Cappussoti, E./Laliotou, I. (2007): *Women from East to West: Gender Mobility and Belonging in Contemporary Europe.* New York, Oxford: Berghahn Books.

Pessar, Patricia (1999): Engendering Migration Studies: The Case of New Immigrants in the United States. *American Behavioral Scientist* 42 (4), 577–600.

Pessar, P./Mahler, S. J. (2006): Gender Matters: Ethnographers Bring Gender from the Periphery toward the Core of Migration Studies. *International Migration Re-*

view 40 (1) (Gender and Migration Revisited, Center for Migration Studies, New York).

Petzen, J. (2005): Wer liegt oben? Türkische und deutsche Maskulinitäten in der schwulen Szene. IFADE (ed.) *Insider–Outsider: Bilder, ethnisierte Räume und Partizipation im Migrationsprozess*. Bielefeld: Transcript Verlag, 161–181.

Pfau-Effinger, B. (2005): Culture and Welfare State Policies: Reflections on a Complex Interrelation. *Journal of Social Policy* 34 (1), 3–20.

Phizacklea, Annie (1998): Migration and Gobalization: A Feminist Perspective. *The New Migration Europe: Social Constructions and Social Realities*, edited by Khalid Koser and Helma Lutz. London: Macmillan Press.

Phizacklea, Annie (2003): Transnationalism, Gender and Global Workers. *Crossing Borders and Shifting Boundaries, Vol. 1: Gender on the Move,* edited by Mirjana Morokvasic-Müller, Emut Erel and Kyoko Shinozaki. Opladen: Leske + Budrich, 79–100.

Pink, S. (2016): *Digital Ethnography: Principles and Practice*. London: Sage.

Piper, N. (2006): Migrant Worker Activism in Singapore and Malaysia. *Asian and Pacific Migration Journal* 15, 359–380.

Polanyi, M. (1983): *The Tacit Dimension*. Gloucester, Mass.: Peter Smith.

Portes, Alejandro/Guarnizo, Luis E./Landolt, Patricia (1999): The Study of Transnationalism: Pitfalls and Promise of an Emergent Research Field. *Ethnic and Racial Studies* 22 (2), 217–237.

Portes, A./Walton, J. (1981): Labour, Class and the International System. New York: Academic Press.

Portes, A./Walton, J. (1981): Labor, Class and the International System, coll. "Studies in Social Discontinuity". New York: Academic Press.

Portes, Alexander (2003): Conclusion: Theoretical Convergences and Empirical Evidence in the Study of Immigrant Transnationalism. *International Migration Review* 37, 847–892.

Postill, J. (2010): *Localizing the Internet*. Oxford: Berghahn.

Pratt, G. (2012): *Families Apart: Migrant Mothers and the Conflicts of Labor and Love*. Minneapolis: University of Minnesota Press.

Predraza, Silvia (1991): Women and Migration: The Social Consequences of Gender. *Annual Review of Sociology* 17.

Pries, Ludger (1998): Transnationale Soziale Räume. Ulrich Beck (Hrsg.): *Perspektiven der Weltgesellschaft*. Frankfurt/Main: Suhrkamp, 55–86.

Pries, Ludger (2001): Disruption of Social and Geographic Space: Mexican-US Migration and the Emergence of Transnational Social Spaces. *International Sociology* 16 (1), 51–70.

Puri, A. (2009): Webnography: Its Evolution and Implications for Market Research. *International Journal of Market Research* 51 (2), 273–275.

Radcliffe, S. (1990): Ethnicity, Patriarchy and Incorporation into the Nation: Female Migrants as Domestic Servants in Peru. *Environment and Planning D: Society and Space* 8, 379–93.

Ranis, G./Fei, J. C. H. (1961): A Theory of Economic Development. *American Economic Review* 51: 533–565.

Rao Mehta, Sandhya (2017): Contesting Victim Narratives: Indian Women Domestic Workers in Oman. *Migration and Development* 6 (3), 395–411.

Ray, R./Qayum, S. (2009): *Cultures of Servitude: Modernity, Domesticity, and Class in India.* Stanford: Stanford University Press.

Redlová, P. (2013): Employment of Filipinas as Nannies in the Context of Post-Socialist Czech Republic. *Lidé města/Urban People* 15 (2), 185–215.

Reed-Danahay, D. (1997): *Auto/ethnography: Rewriting the Self and the Social.* Oxford, UK: Berg.

Rerrich, Maria (1997): *Frauenarbeit in der Familie zwischen Lohn und Liebe – Überlegungen zur Repolitisierung des Privaten,* Vortrag anlässlich der Verleihung des Helge-Pross-Preises der Universität GH Siegen.

Rerrich, Maria (2002): Bodenpersonal im Globalisierungsgeschehen: „Illegale" Migrantinnen als Beschäftigte in deutschen Haushalten. *Mittelweg 36.*

Rickly, J./Hannam, K./Mostafanezhad, M. (2017): *Tourism and Leisure Mobilities.* London: Routledge.

Rigo, E. (2005): Citizenship at Europe's Borders: Some Reflections on the Post-Colonial Condition of Europe in the Context of EU Enlargement. *Citizenship Studies* 9 (1), 3–22.

Rivoal, Isabelle/Salazar, Noel B. (2013): Contemporary Ethnographic Practice and the Value of Serendipity. *Social Anthropology, "Young Scholar's Forum: Contemporary Ethnographic Practice and the Value of Serendipity"* 21 (2), 178–185.

Robertson, R. (1995): Glocalization: Time-Space and Homogeneity-Heterogeneity. M. Featherstone/S. Lash/R. Robertson (eds.): *Global Modernities.* London: Sage, 25–44.

Roig, Emilia (2014): Care Crisis: Racialised Women at the Crossroads of Migration, Labour Market and Family Policies, Migrationspolitishes Portal, Heimatkunde, Heinrich Boell Stiftung, E-Paper, URL: http://heimatkunde.boell.de/2014/03/27/care-crisis-racialised-women-crossroads-migration-labour-market-and-family-policies.

Rollins, Judith (1985): *Between Women: Domestics and Their Employers.* Philadelphia: Temple University Press.

Romero, M. (1992): *Maids in the U.S.A.* New York/London: Routledge.

Rummery, K./Fine, M. (2012): Care: A Critical Review of Theory, Policy and Practice. *Social Policy & Administration* 46 (3), 321–343.

Safuta, Anna (2018): Fifty Shades of White: Eastern Europeans' "Peripheral Whiteness" in the Context of Domestic Services Provided by Migrant Women. *Tijdschrift voor Genderstudies* 21 (3), 217–231.

Salazar, N. B. (2011a): The Power of the Imagination in Transnational Mobilities. *Identities: Global Studies in Culture and Power* 18 (6), 576–598.

Salazar, Noel B./Smart, A. (2011): Anthropological Takes on (Im)Mobility. *Identities* 18 (6).

LITERATURE 417

Salih, Rubi (2003): *Gender in Transnationalism: Home, Longing and Belonging among Moroccan Migrant Women*. London: Routledge.

Salt, J./Stein, J. (1997): Migration as a Business: The Case of Trafficking. *International Migration* 35 (4), 467–494.

Samarasinghe, V. (1998): The Feminization of Foreign Currency Earnings: Women's Labor in Sri Lanka. *The Journal of Developing Areas* 32 (Spring), 303–326.

Sanjek, Roger/Shellee, Colen (1990): *At Work in Homes: Household Workers in World Perspective*. (American Ethnological Society Monograph Series, no. 3.) Washington, DC: American Anthropological Association.

Sarti, R. (2002): *Europe at Home: Family and Material Culture, 1500–1800*. New Haven, London: Yale University Press.

Sarti, R. (2008): The Globalisation of Domestic Service: An Historical Perspective. *Migration and domestic work: A European perspective on a global theme*, 77–98.

Sassen, Saskia (1998): *Globalization and Its Discontents: Essays on the New Mobility of People and Money*. New York: New Press.

Sassen, Saskia (2000): Women's Burden: Counter-Geographies of Globalization and the Feminization of Survival. *Journal of International Affairs* 53 (2).

Sassen, Saskia (2003): The Feminisation of Survival: Alternative Global Circuits. *Crossing Borders and Shifting Boundaries, Vol. I: On the Move*, edited by M. Morokvasic-Müller, U. Erel, K. Shinozaki. Opladen: Leske + Budrich.

Sassen, Saskia (2003): Global Cities and Survival Circuits. Barbara Ehrenreich/Arlie Russell Hochschild (eds.): *Global Woman: Nannies, Maids and Sex Workers in the New Economy*. London: Granta Books.

Scârneci-Domnişoru, Florentina (2013): Narrative Technique of Interviewing. *Bulletin of the Transilvania, University of Braşov, Series VII: Social Sciences*, Vol. 6 (55) No. 1.

Scheel, Stephan (2013): Studying Embodied Encounters: Autonomy of Migration beyond Its Romanticization. *Postcolonial Studies* 16 (3), 279–288.

Scheibelhofer, Elisabeth (2010): Gendered Differences in Emigration and Mobility Perspectives among European Researchers Working Abroad. *Migration Letters, Transnational Press London, UK*, vol. 7 (1), 33–41.

Schensul, Stephen L./Schensul, Jean J./LeCompte, Margaret D. (1999): *Essential Ethnographic Methods: Observations, Interviews, and Questionnaires*. Walnut Creek, CA: AltaMira Press.

Schewel, Kerilyn (2019): Understanding Immobility: Moving Beyond the Mobility Bias in Migration Studies. *International Migration Review* 54 (2), 328–355.

Schilliger, Sarah (2015): „Wir sind doch keine Sklavinnen!" – (Selbst-)Organisierung von polnischen Care-Arbeiterinnen in der Schweiz. *Zeitschrift Luxemburg*, URL: http://www.zeitschrift-luxemburg.de/wir-sind-doch-keine-sklavinnen.

Schneider, David Murray (1984): *A Critique of the Study of Kinship*. University of Michigan Press.

Schultz, S. (2006): Dissolving Boundaries and Affective Labor: On the Disappearance of Reproductive Labour and Feminist Critique in Empire. *Capitalism Nature Socialism* 17 (1), 77–82.

Schwenken, Helen (2011a): An ILO Convention for Domestic Workers: Contextualizing the Debate. Conversations section of the *International Feminist Journal of Politics* 13 (3) (mit Elisabeth Prügl).

Schwenken, Helen (2011b): *Domestic Workers Count: Global Data on an often Invisible Sector.* Kassel: Kassel University Press (Hg. mit Lisa-Marie Heimeshoff).

Schwenken, H. (2016): The Emergence of an Impossible Movement: Domestic Workers Organize Globally. D. Gosewinkel/D. Rucht (eds.): Transnational Struggles for Recognition. New York, NY: Berghan Books, 205–228.

Schwenken, Helen/Eberhardt, Pia (2008): Gender Knowledge in Economic Migration Theories and in Migration Practices. *GARNET Working paper* no. 58/80. Warwick: University of Warwick, Centre for the Study of Globalization and Regionalisation.

Sciortino, Giuseppe (2004): Between Phantoms and Necessary Evils. Some Critical Points in the Study of Irregular Migration to Western Europe. *IMIS-Beiträge. Migration and the Regulation of Social Integration* 24, 17–43.

Scrinzi, F./Sarti, R. (2010): Introduction to the Special Issue: Men in a Woman's Job: Male Domestic Workers, International Migration and the Globalization of Care. *Men and Masculinities* 13 (1), 4–15.

Shamir, Ronen (2005): Without Borders? Notes on Globalization as a Mobility Regime. *Sociological Theory* 23: 197–217.

Sheller, M. (2013): Sociology After the Mobilities. *The Routledge Handbook of Mobilities.* Routledge.

Sheller, M. (2018): *Mobility Justice: The Politics of Movement in an Age of Extremes.* Verso Books.

Sheller, M./Urry, J. (2004): *Tourism Mobilities: Places to Play, Places in Play.* London: Routledge.

Sheller, M./Urry, J. (2006): The New Mobilities Paradigm. *Environment and Planning D* 38 (2).

Shinozaki, Kyoko (2003): Geschlechterverhältnisse in der transnationalen Elternschaft: Das Beispiel philippinischer HausarbeiterInnen in Deutschland. *Beiträge zur feministischen Theorie und Praxis* 62, 67–85.

Shinozaki, Kyoko (2015): *Migrant Citizenship from Below: Family, Domestic Work and Social Activism in Irregular Migration.* New York: Palgrave Mac.

Silvey, R. (2004): Power, Difference, and Mobility: Feminist Advances in Migration Studies. *Progress in Human Geography* 28 (4), 490–506.

Silvey, R. (2004a): Transnational Migration and the Gender Politics of Scale. *Singapore Journal of Tropical Geography* 25, 141–155.

Silvey, R. (2004b): Transnational Domestication: State Power and Indonesian Migrant Women in Saudi Arabia. *Political Geography* 23, 245–264.

Silvey, R. (2006): Geographies of Gender and Migration: Spatializing Social Difference. *International Migration Review* 40.

Smart, Alan (1993): Gifts, Bribes, and Guanxi: A Reconsideration of Bourdieu's Social Capital. *Cultural Anthropology* 8 (3), 388–408.

Smith, Adrian/Stenning, Alison (2006): Beyond Household Economies: Articulations and Spaces of Economic Practice in Post-Socialism. *Progress in Human Geography* 30 (2), 190–213.

Smith, M. P./Guarnizo, L. (1998): *Transnationalism from Below*. New Brunswick: Transaction.

Smith, N. (1992): Contours of a Spatialized Politics: Homeless Vehicles and the Production of Geographical Scale. *Social Text* 33, 55–81.

Spaan, E. (1999): *Labour Circulation and Socioeconomic Transformation. The Case of East Java, Indonesia.* The Hague: Netherlands Interdisciplinary Demographic Institute.

Stacey, Judith (1988): Can there Be a Feminist Ethnography. *Women's Studies International Forum* 11 (1), 21–27.

Standing, G. (2011): *The Precariat: The New Dangerous Class*. London: Bloomsbury Academic.

Stanley, L./Wise, S. (1993): *Breaking Out Again: Feminist Ontology and Epistemology*. London, New York: Routledge.

Strathern, Marilyn (1992): After Nature: English Kinship in the Late Twentieth Century. Vol. 1989. Cambridge University Press.

Strüver, A. (2013): Ich war lange illegal hier, aber jetzt hat mich die Grenze übertreten. *Geographica Helvetica* 68, 191–200.

Szőke, Alexandra (2006): New Forms of Mobility among Western European Retirees: German Migrants in South-Western Hungary. Alice Szczepaniková/Marek Čaněk/Jan Grill (eds.): *Migration Processes in Central and Eastern Europe: Unpacking the Diversity.* Prague : Multicultural Center.

Taylor, T. L./Pearce, C./Nardi, B./Boellstorff, T. (2012): *Ethnography and Virtual Worlds: A Handbook of Method.* Princeton University Press.

Theobald, H. (2009): Pflegepolitiken, Fürsorgearrangements und Migration in Europa. C. Larsen/A. Joostand/S. Heid: *Illegale Beschäftigung in Europa. Die Situation in Privathaushalten älterer Personen.* München: Hampp, 28–39.

Thrift, N. (1996): *Spatial Formations*. London: Sage.

Tomlinson, John (1999): *Globalization and Culture*. Oxford: University Press.

Triandafyllidou, A. (2013): *Circular Migration Between Europe and Its Neighbourhood: Choice or Necessity?* Oxford: Oxford University Press.

Triandafyllidou, A. (2016): *Irregular Migrant Domestic Workers in Europe: Who Cares?* New York, London: Routledge.

Trouillot, M. R. (2001): The Anthropology of the State in the Age of Globalization: Close Encounters of a Deceptive Kind. *Current Anthropology* 42 (1), 101–128.

Tsing, A. (1993): *In the Realm of the Diamond Queen: Marginality in an Out-of-the-Way Place.* Princeton: Princeton University Press.

Tsing, A. (2000): The Global Situation. *Cultural anthropology* 15 (3), 327–360.

Tsing, A. (2005): *Friction: An Ethnography of Global Connection*. Princeton: Princeton University.

Turner, B. S. (2007): The Enclave Society: Towards a Sociology of Immobility. *European Journal of Social Theory* 10 (2), 287–303.

Twigg, J. (2000): *Bathing: the Body in Community Care*. London: Routledge.

Urry, J. (2000): *Sociology Beyond Societies: Mobilities for the Twenty-First Century*. London.

Urry, John (2007): *Mobilities*. Cambridge: Polity Press.

Uteng, T. P./Cresswell, T. (2008): *Gendered Mobilities*. Farnham, Burlington, VT: Ashgate.

Van Maanen, J. (2011): *Tales of the Field: On Writing Ethnography*. Chicago, IL: University of Chicago Press.

Van Walsum, S. (2011): Regulating Migrant Domestic Work in the Netherlands: Opportunities and Pitfalls. *Canadian Journal of Women and the Law/Revue Femmes et Droit* 23, 141–165.

Vertovec, S. (2004): Cheap Calls: The Social Glue of Migrant Transnationalism. *Global Networks* 4 (2), 219–224.

Vertovec, S. (2007): Is Circular Migration the Way Forward in Global Policy? *Around the Globe* 3 (2), 38.

Vertovec, S./Cohen, R. (2002): *Conceiving Cosmopolitanism: Theory, Context and Practice*. New York: Oxford University Press.

Vianello, F. A. (2008): Migrando sole. Pratiche femminili di mobilità transnazionale tra Ucraina e Italia. [Migrating alone. Female practices of transnational mobility between Ukraine and Italy]. Padova: Università di Padova.

Vianello, F. A. (2014): Ukrainian Migrant Workers in Italy: Coping with and Reacting to Downward Mobility. *Central Eastern European Migration Review* 3, 85–98.

Višić, Tanja/Poleti, Dunja (2018): Gender and Migration Re-Visited: Production of Knowledge and Feminism (in) between Semi-Periphery and the Core. *Journal Sociologija* 60 (1), URL: http://www.sociologija.org/books/.

Voss, G./Pongratz, H. J. (1998): Der Arbeitskraftunternehmer. Eine neue Form der Ware Arbeitskraft? [Entrepreneurs of the self-employed: a new model of the workforce as a commodity]. *Kölner Zeitschrift für Soziologie und Sozialpsychologie* 50, 131–158.

Walters, W. (2002): Mapping Schengenland: Denaturalizing the Border. *Environment and Planning D: Society and Space* 20 (5), 561–580.

Wetterer, A. (2008): Geschlechterwissen & soziale Praxis: Grundzüge einer wissenssoziologischen Typologie des Geschlechterwissens. [Gender knowledge & social practice: Main features of a typology of gender knowledge from the perspective of a sociology of knowledge]. *Geschlechterwissen und soziale Praxis. Theoretische Zugänge – empirische Erträge*, ed. ibid. Königstein, 39–63.

Wickramasekara, P. (2011): Circular Migration: A Triple Win or a Dead End? *International Labour Organisation*. Geneva.

Williams, F. (2012): Converging Variations in Migrant Care Work in Europe. *Journal of European Social Policy* 22, 363–376.

Williams, F./Gavanas, A. (2008): The Intersection of Child Care Regimes and Migration Regimes: A Three-Country Study. H. Lutz (ed.): *Migration and Domestic Work: A European Perspective on a Global Theme.* London: Routledge.

Wilson, S. M./Peterson, L. C. (2002): The Anthropology of Online Communities. *Annual Review of Anthropology* 31, 449–467.

Wimmer, A./Glick Schiller, N. (2002): Methodological Nationalism and Beyond: Nation-State Building, Migration and the Social Sciences. *Global Networks* 2, 301–334.

Winker, G. (2015): *Care Revolution.* Transcript-Verlag.

Withaeckx, S./Schrooten, M./Geldof, D. (2015): Living across Borders: The Everyday Experiences of Moroccan and Brazilian Transmigrants in Belgium. *Crossings: Journal of Migration & Culture* 6 (1), 23–40.

Wolkowitz, C. (2006): *Bodies at Work.* London: Sage.

Wulff, Helen (2002): Yo-yo Fieldwork: Mobility and Time in a Multi-Local Study of Dance in Ireland. *Anthropological Journal on European Culture* 11, 117–136.

Xiang, B./Lindquist, J. (2014): Migration Infrastructure. *International Migration Review* 48 (S1), S122–S148.

Yeates, Nicola (2004): Global Care Chains. Critical Reflections and Lines of Enquiry. *International Feminist Journal of Politics* 6 (3), 369–391.

Yeates, Nicola (2009): Production for Export: The Role of the State in the Development and Operation of Global Care Chains. *Population, Space and Place* 15 (2).

Yeoh, B./Huang, S. (2010): Foreign Domestic Workers and Home-Based Care for the Elderly in Singapore. *Journal of Aging & Social Policy* 22, 69–88.

Zelizer, Viviana A. (2009): *The Purchase of Intimacy.* Course Book ed. Princeton University Press.

Zelizer, Viviana A. (2013): *Economic Lives: How Culture Shapes the Economy.* Princeton, NJ: Princeton University Press.

Zempi, I./ Awan, I. (2017): Doing "Dangerous" Autoethnography on Islamophobic Victimization. *Ethnography* 18 (3), 367–386.

Zerubavel, Eviatar (1981): Hidden Rhythms: Schedules and Calendars in Social Life. Chicago: University of Chicago Press.